PRESERVING

PICKLING, FERMENTING, FREEZING, DRYING, CURING AND CANNING

An Hachette UK Company
www.hachette.co.uk

First published in Great Britain in 2013 by Kyle Books,
an imprint of Octopus Books Ltd
Carmelite House
50 Victoria Embankment
London EC4Y 0DZ
www.octopusbooks.co.uk

This edition published in 2024

This material was previously published as *The Gentle Art of Preserving*

Distributed in the US by
Hachette Book Group
1290 Avenue of the Americas
4th and 5th Floors
New York, NY 10104

Distributed in Canada by
Canadian Manda Group
664 Annette St.
Toronto, Ontario, Canada M6S 2C8

ISBN: 978 1 8041 9240 5

A CIP catalogue record for this title is available from the British Library

Printed and bound in the UK

10 9 8 7 6 5 4 3 2 1

Publisher: Lucy Pessell
Designer: Isobel Platt
Editor: Feyi Oyesanya
Assistant Editor: Samina Rahman
Illustrations: Isobel Platt
Illustration (page 71): Esther Coombs
Production Controller: Sarah Parry

This FSC® label means that materials used for
the product have been responsibly sourced.

MIX
Paper | Supporting
responsible forestry
FSC® C104740

PRESERVING

PICKLING, FERMENTING, FREEZING, DRYING, CURING AND CANNING

Katie Caldesi & Giancarlo Caldesi

KYLE
BOOKS

To our children, Giorgio and Flavio. Thank you for joining us on the journey to learn the art of preserving; from eating hot-smoked fish on Scottish shores, making chutney in Sri Lanka, picking endless berries in summer and making sausage chains in winter.

CONTENTS

INTRODUCTION

It was never my intention to produce a bible on the subject of preserving – as there are so many wonderful, detailed books on different aspects of preserving already out there. Rather I wanted to produce something personal and celebratory, full of simple techniques that hopefully every family can draw some inspiration from – even if it is just one aspect of conserving food. I promise that once you give some of the ideas a go, you will begin to rethink your whole attitude to cooking, eating and shopping. We did.

Curing, smoking, freezing, pickling, bottling, fermenting, drying, ... These time-honoured skills for preserving food have never been so topical. More and more we are growing uneasy with our throwaway and fast-living society and becoming actively concerned about food costs and waste, air miles and additives, and looking for ways to become more self-sufficient. Sometimes the way forward is to look back, and so we have spent years delving into long cherished traditions of home-conserving foods, converting our old Wendy house and barbecue into smokeries, turning an old refrigerator into a curing chamber for hanging bacon and sausages, packing the freezer with homemade sauces; festooning the kitchen with bunches of drying herbs and covering every surface with jars of chutneys and bottles of fruit and scrumptious hedgerow booze. It has been a journey into sometimes familiar territory – for example, making use of the freezer and microwave in entirely different ways – and sometimes unknown territory, in terms of curing and smoking – but everyone in the family has made a contribution – and it has changed all of our lives.

Also to be considered is the current discussion of the microbiome. Fermented foods as we now know are brilliant for keeping our friendly gut bugs happy. A healthy microbiome can help maintain a healthy body.

Both I and my husband Giancarlo thought we were pretty good at valuing and preserving food. Giancarlo grew up in a family in Tuscany which never, ever, wasted food and yet there was no refrigerator in the house. They kept their own pig and butchered it each November, and every part of the animal would be used – some for eating fresh, the rest for curing as ham or salami. And in every appropriate season there would be food – from tomatoes to porcini – that could be conserved for the rest of the year. I grew up in an English seaside town, watching my mother make chutneys, jams and marmalades throughout the year and helping my father pack apples and potatoes into boxes to store in winter. And our whole family have always enjoyed foraging. But during these last few years, I realize I had only scratched the surface of the enormous world of preserving. Even Giancarlo has admitted that there are so many more fascinating things to discover about self-sufficiency than he ever dreamt of. In the course of writing this book, we have worked alongside expert artisans, collected long-standing family recipes and techniques from friends and tapped into diverse preserving traditions from Thailand and Italy to France, Sri Lanka, Japan, Sweden and America.

There is something about preserving, I have discovered, which forges a link with other people – perhaps it is the sense that we have been doing these things throughout the history of mankind, so wisdom is handed down and passed on. Around the world, groups of friends and family come together to preserve their fresh produce – whether in Korea to make kimchi, in Sri Lanka to salt and dry fish or in Italy to make the annual tomato passata. It is quite special to spend time chatting and chopping, spreading the workload and sharing the rewards. I had friends around for a 'marmalade morning' and we had great fun. The oranges were cut up in no time, we were able to have three preserving pans on the go at once, and now we all have jars of marmalade that taste better than anything you could buy. Next up a piccalilli party, sharing our gluts of vegetables or supermarket special offers! I often give courses at our cookery school, showing people how to cook quick, but tasty and nutritious, meals. However, now I also encourage people to sometimes allow themselves a few hours to slow down, unwind and enjoy some simple aspect of preserving food – and, of course, the two often go hand in hand: what you preserve today makes for a quick meal tomorrow.

Though I never really considered myself wasteful, writing this book has made us, as a family, much more conscious of all the things we could do to be more food-thrifty. There are appalling statistics from Wrap, the government-backed Waste and Resources Action Programme, which flag up the fact that as a nation we throw away around one-third of the food we buy (much of which ends up in landfill, producing the greenhouse gas methane). This is largely because we don't plan our shopping trips, or end up leaving food at the back of refrigerator until it has passed its sell-by date. Our grandparents' generation knew how to budget and eke out food, and that is what working on this book has taught me too.

These two years have changed my attitude so much that I can't bear to throw anything away. Offcuts of carrot, parsley and celery leaves are in bags in my freezer for making into stock, along with prawn shells, vacuum-bagged so that they stack neatly. Potato peelings get turned into crisps, squeezed lemons are stored in the freezer for adding to the bathtub at the end of the day.

After writing this book, I have also become more aware of gluts of seasonal fruits and vegetables – from courgettes to strawberries – that can be snapped up for preserves. And our two boys now know all the best local lanes for blackberries, wild pears, little apples, herbs, elderberries, rowans, rosehips, sloes and nettles, depending on the season. Even if there is not much to be had on one trip, we pick what we can find – for example, blackberries – and put them in the freezer until eventually there is enough for a pie and some bottles of fruit liqueur. Even Giancarlo, who was raised on bottles and jars of homemade tomato passata, preserved vegetables and home-cured salami, has found himself experimenting with very English chutneys and Thai curry pastes to make the best use of the basketfuls of seasonal fruit and vegetables we have picked.

Without these trustworthy preservation techniques our population could not have survived. However, over the generations, people have also conserved food not just out of necessity, but also for pure pleasure – as a way of evoking the joys of summer on a drizzly winter day, or to rekindle autumnal pleasures long after the hedgerows are bare – and that is what our whole family has found so enjoyable. And there really is added satisfaction when you are savouring and relishing food that you have produced yourself, since you understand in a completely different way the time and care that goes into such processes.

It was never our intention to produce a bible on the subject – as there are so many wonderful, detailed books on different aspects of preserving already out there. Rather we wanted to produce something personal and celebratory, full of simple techniques that hopefully every family can draw some inspiration from – even if it is just one aspect of conserving food. We promise that once you give some of the ideas a go, you will begin to rethink your whole attitude to cooking, eating and shopping.

As I have mentioned, one of the joys of curing, bottling, freezing and generally stockpiling food is that you can make your life easier and create a meal in a hurry, without compromising what you are feeding the family. And if friends or family turn up unexpectedly, no panic, you can feed them without even having to go to the shops. Imagine a cocktail before dinner made with your own cordials; homemade vegetable crisps to nibble; a quick lunch of home-cured fish or salami; supper of pasta with the bottled tomato sauce that you made in the summer; little tubs of spicy sauces, frozen and ready to go for a speedy curry; or a dessert made with preserved plums bottled when the trees were laden.

All this might seem like a lot of work, but I have found that once you change your mindset and begin to take a different approach to food, you can happily build preserving food into a busy lifestyle.

* GENERAL ADVICE AND INSTRUCTIONS

TRUSTING YOUR INSTINCTS

Preserving is a science, but it is not an exact science, and there is no foolproof way of preserving in the home environment. However, what I have discovered on this journey is to learn to trust my instincts – the more I pickle, cure, air-dry and smoke, the more I understand how to spot problems and adapt, and also to accept the occasional failure.

Our grandparents knew how to judge for themselves whether a food was spoiled, whereas in our supermarket-dominated world, governed by use-by and sell-by dates, it is easy to abandon the fundamental sensual skills of looking and smelling. But once you enter the world of preserving, it is important to re-hone your senses, as well as to understand and feel comfortable with what you are doing.

FOOD SAFETY

All around us in the air, on the surface of our food, on our equipment and ourselves are micro-organisms such as yeasts, moulds and bacteria. Some of these are good and we encourage them to grow in our food, such as *Lactobacillus* in yogurt and the typical green mould in cheese. However, some are positively harmful, such as *Clostridium botulinum*, and the rest are just downright unpleasant. This is why we have to be as clean as possible and take every care that we do not encourage unwanted micro-organisms also known as 'spoilers'.

Washing, blanching and peeling fruit can help remove spoilers. Heat-processing jars of food, if done correctly, destroys the spoilers that would naturally cause food to decay. This also creates a vacuum in the jar by driving the air out of it. When the jars cool after heating, this vacuum sucks the lid on tight and prevents other spoilers getting in.

THE FOUR SPOILERS

ENZYMES

Enzymes are in all living things, be they plants or animals. Their activity can cause food to change colour, flavour and texture. They are discouraged by blanching and inhibited by cooking or processing at approx. 140°C (275°F).

MOULDS AND YEASTS

Moulds and yeasts are fungi; they are usually visible as fur, patches or specks on the food. Mould thrives in acidic conditions – hence why you sometimes see white fur appear on old tomato sauce or green patches on yogurt. Yeasts cause food to ferment, which might be positively encouraged in the fermenting chapter, but is usually discouraged. Acid environments create a hostile atmosphere for most bacteria, but they offer no protection against moulds or yeast.

BACTERIA

Yes, I know it is an ugly word and no one wants to think about it when making beautiful jars of peaches suspended in a rich cinnamon syrup, but some moulds and yeasts are good and are actively encouraged when you want to ferment something. Once you understand about bacteria, you can begin to discern when to encourage and when to avoid them. Bacteria are not as easily destroyed as moulds and yeast. Salmonella is destroyed when foods are held at 60°C (140°F) for a specific time, depending on their acidity level. *Staphylococcus aureus* or 'staph' is destroyed at 115°C (240°F) when held for a specific time. Botulism, caused by *Clostridium botulinum*, is destroyed by boiling, but the spores that cause it are not. They are anaerobic, meaning they do not need air to survive. They need to be heated to 115°C (240°F) for a period of time to destroy them. Since water boils at 100°C (212°F) at sea level (and at a lower temperature in areas over 1,000ft), you can see that processing food in boiling water isn't going to do the job of destroying them. Temperatures such as this can only be achieved in a pressure canner due to the pressurized steam. *Clostridium botulinum* spores flourish in low-acid environments; this means they at home in a jar of food such as canned vegetables or meat sauce.

USE YOUR EYES, NOSE AND TASTE

If you see mould, be bold and discard your pot of preserves. Although many of us have scraped mould off jam before and lived to tell the tale, the mycotoxins from mould can go deep into the jam. The same goes if you smell the product and it has an unpleasant or 'off' smell. If it fizzes when you unscrew the lid, but looks and smells normal, throw it away.

QUALITY OF INGREDIENTS

Fresh, undamaged produce is key to a good preserve. If it is not in tip-top condition when it is preserved, it will not be good when you come to eat it.

* STERILIZING JARS AND LIDS

Make sure all jars and bottles are in pristine condition. Scrape off old labels with a knife under hot water and finish with a metal scourer to get off any glue.

To sterilize jars in the oven the temperature we recommend is 140°C/ 275°F/gas 1 for a minimum of 20 minutes. Dishwashers don't generally heat to adequate temperatures to sterilize jars –

most cycles are 50°C (122°F) or 60°C (140°F) – however they are useful for washing them. We recommend that you sterilize bottles and jars in an oven, microwave or waterbath instead.

STERILIZING IN THE OVEN

This is our preferred method for sterilizing jars. Give them a good wash with hot soapy water, followed by a very good rinse to get rid of any odours. Put them upside down into the oven at 140°C/275°F/gas 1 for a minimum of 20 minutes. Store in a warm oven until they are ready to be filled. They will dry as they sterilize.

STERILIZING IN THE MICROWAVE

Fill up to four jars with water so they are quarter full. Heat on high until the water boils. Remove wearing oven gloves and tip out the water. Turn the jars over to dry on a clean rack. Fill while still warm.

STERILIZING IN A WATERBATH

Wash the jars in hot soapy water and rinse very well. Put them upright onto a rack in a stockpot, pressure cooker or canner without the lid. Fill the jars and pot with warm water to cover the jars by 3cm (1¼in). Bring the water to the boil and continue to boil for 10 minutes; reduce the heat and keep the jars in the hot water until you are ready to fill them.

STERILIZING LIDS

Either use new clean lids or immerse old ones in boiling hot water in a large saucepan for 10 minutes. Remove them from the water and drain, inside facing downwards, on a clean rack. Make sure they are dry before fastening them onto the jars. NOTE: Preserves made with vinegar should be sealed with vinegar-proofed lids – i.e. ones that are plastic-coated.

VINEGAR

Vinegar is highly acidic and most harmful to bacteria, which cannot survive in acid environments. Even 1 teaspoon of standard strength vinegar (6 per cent) in a 250ml (9fl oz) glass of water will create too much acidity for most bacteria to survive. Vinegar can be measured by the percentage of acetic acid in it and this varies according to what it is made from – rice vinegar being the mildest, followed by beer and cider, with wine and distilled vinegar being the strongest. Usually the acetic acid percentage in vinegar is written on the bottle.

The sophisticated Babylonians in 4,000 BC used vinegar from fermented raisin and date wines to preserve vegetables and meats. They even flavoured the vinegar with spices and herbs just as we do today. The Romans too enjoyed a dressing made from honey and vinegar, and drank it with water in a drink called posca, while the ancient Chinese created vinegar from fermented plums and a dark, complex vinegar from rice and wheat.

Recent studies have shown that although vinegar is high in acid and does not support the growth of *Clostridium botulinum* bacteria it could support the growth of *Escherichia coli bacteria*. To avoid this use dried spices and herbs or cook anything fresh that you add to vinegar to boiling point, including herbs, fruit and flavourings.

This chapter concentrates on chutneys, pickles and sauces that are made with vinegar, as well as vegetables that are preserved in vinegar to make them crisp and sour.

WHICH VINEGAR?

Always use reasonable quality vinegar for preserving with an acetic acid content of at least 5 per cent. Most chutney recipes call for malt vinegar, but it is possible to use spirit, cider or wine vinegar for certain recipes, depending on the flavour and colour wanted in the finished product. If you don't like a sharp acidic flavour to a recipe, you can always add a little sugar; it will balance the flavour but it won't take away the acidity required to make the product safe.

HERB-FLAVOURED VINEGAR

Herbs such as tarragon completely change mediocre white wine vinegar into a savoury, mouthwatering potion, which is wonderful in sauces such as hollandaise, dressings and creamy sauces that need some acidity to cut through the fat. Store in bottles with corks or plastic lids. Swing-top bottles with rubber seals are ideal.

METHOD For best results, pick the herbs first thing in the morning when their essential oils are at their height. Four sprigs about the length of your hand are enough to flavour a 500ml (18fl oz) bottle of white wine vinegar. Shake and wash the herbs to make sure that there are no insects clinging to them. Put the sprigs and the vinegar into a saucepan and bring to the boil for 2 minutes. Pull the sprigs out of the vinegar with tongs and put into a warm, sterilized bottle, pour over the vinegar and close the lid. Store in a cool, dark place for 3–4 weeks, then strain the vinegar through a sieve lined with muslin to remove the herbs and pour it back into the bottle. Keep in a cool, dark place or the refrigerator and use within 3 months.

VARIATION

Heat a mixture of rosemary, sage and thyme leaves in white wine vinegar. Use in salad dressings with extra virgin olive oil, drizzle over sautéed courgettes or add to sauces.

USES My friend Karin Piper makes a delicious chicken recipe with tarragon vinegar: brown the chicken pieces in a large frying pan and set aside; sauté some finely chopped onion, pour in a splash of tarragon vinegar and reduce so the onion takes on the flavour; add a good splash of white wine or vermouth and reduce a little, then add a little stock; return the chicken to the pan to cook gently for 15–20 minutes; finish with a dash of cream and some freshly chopped tarragon and cook gently for another couple of minutes or until the chicken is cooked through.

SHALLOT VINEGAR

This has bite and sweetness without the overpowering odour of raw onion.

METHOD Finely chop 1 shallot or ½ banana shallot and mix it with 300ml (½ pint) red wine vinegar. Bring to the boil in a saucepan and then remove from the heat. Leave it to infuse for 2 hours, then strain, discarding the onion. Store the vinegar in a sealed bottle in the refrigerator and use within a month.

USES Shallot vinegar makes a wonderful vinaigrette mixed with extra virgin olive oil and mustard for use in salads. Alternatively, serve it on its own as a traditional dressing for oysters.

FRUIT VINEGARS

Historically fruit vinegars were used not only for cooking but also as drinks diluted with water. Fruit vinegars are easy to produce and make a great addition to sauces, gravy and salad dressings. Use anywhere you might use balsamic vinegar.

Raspberry and blackberry vinegar are our favourites as we enjoy berry picking in the summer. To use, simply pour them directly over salad or mix them with an equal quantity of extra virgin olive oil and a pinch of salt and freshly ground black pepper.

BLACKBERRY VINEGAR

MAKES 1 BOTTLE (APPROX. 750ML/ 1¼ PINTS)

- 750g (1lb 10oz) blackberries, stalks and leaves removed
- 500–600ml (18–20fl oz) cider vinegar, white wine vinegar or red wine vinegar
- up to 200g (7oz) golden caster sugar, to taste

> Put the blackberries in a non-reactive bowl and crush them gently with a potato masher. Pour 500ml (18fl oz) vinegar over the fruit, making sure it covers them, adding more if not. Cover the dish with a plate or a lid and set aside to infuse for 3–5 days (or longer, if you wish, to impart a stronger bramble flavour).
> Strain the blackberries through a jelly bag or a sieve lined with two layers of muslin; this is best done overnight. Measure the strained juice and calculate the quantity of sugar needed, allowing 30–50g (1–1¾oz) sugar per 100ml (3½fl oz) juice, according to taste. Pour the juice (and any additional spices and flavourings) into a heavy-based saucepan and set over a medium heat. Bring to a simmer for 2

minutes, then reduce the heat and add the sugar, stirring to dissolve. Skim off any scum that forms on the surface. Taste and adjust the sugar as necessary. Remove from the heat and pour into a warm, sterilized bottle. Leave to cool and store in a cool, dark place or the refrigerator for up to a year.

VARIATIONS

You can use strawberries or raspberries in place of the blackberries; just make sure you adjust the quantity of sugar to taste. Ripe figs also work well if cut into quarters first. Fig vinegar is good sweetened with maple syrup instead of sugar.

For spiced fruit vinegar, add a few spices with the crushed fruit at the beginning. We love raspberry vinegar infused with a sprig of rosemary and 1 teaspoon of crushed pink peppercorns. To give the blackberry vinegar a kick, try adding 1 teaspoon of allspice berries and a few black peppercorns.

ELDERFLOWER VINEGAR

On a dry and sunny spring day take yourself on a foraging trip to pick young heads of elderflowers. Try to pick the flowers early on a sunny morning when their essential oils are at their best. This delicate, flowery vinegar is ideal for salads, hollandaise sauce or for Pickled elderberries (see page 14).

MAKES 2.5 LITRES (4½ PINTS)

- 2.5 litres (4½ pints) English cider vinegar
- 20–30 elderflower heads

> Pour a little vinegar out of the container to use another day or pour all the vinegar into a non-reactive container with a lid.
> Check for any insects in the flower heads, but do not be tempted to wash them

>>>

or they will spoil. Using scissors, trim the flowers from the stems into a funnel so that they fall into the vinegar. Put the lid on the container and leave in a cool, dark place for up to 3 weeks.

> Taste the vinegar and if you are happy that the flavour is strong enough, strain it through muslin to get rid of the flowers. If the flavour is weak, add some more flowers and repeat as above. Pour the vinegar into a saucepan and bring to the boil. Let it bubble for 5 minutes, then remove from the heat. Allow to cool. The vinegar can then be left in the container or bottled and labelled. It will keep in a cool, dark place for up to a year.

PICKLED ELDERBERRIES

I was first shown these by the North London Urban Harvest group on a foraging trip. These tiny, poky little berries are somewhere between a caper and a green peppercorn. They make a great spicy sauce or add a little kick to salads and pasta dishes.

MAKES 500ML (18FL OZ)

- 2–3 handfuls of green elderberries
- 2 teaspoons fine sea salt
- approx. 300ml (½ pint) Elderflower Vinegar (see pages 13–14)

> Pick the elderberries while still green. Use a fork to strip the berries, scatter over the salt and stir through. Leave in a cool, dark place, covered, overnight.
> The following day, rinse the salt off the berries and dry them on kitchen paper. Put the berries into a sterilized jar and top up with the vinegar to the top of the jar. Close the lid – remember to use a rubber seal or a vinegar-proof lid. Store in a cool, dark place and use after a month and for up to a year.

PONTACK SAUCE

This old English sauce made with elderberries is named after Monsieur Pontack, who owned the famous Pontack's Head Tavern in Lombard Street, London, in the 17th century.

Pontack sauce is said to improve with age, rather like a vintage red wine. Our version changed in the bottle and is still improving after a year – see how long you can wait before you sample yours! Serve drizzled over steak that has been cut into strips straight after cooking or stir into a gravy or hearty casserole.

MAKES 400ML (14FL OZ)

- 500g (1lb 2oz) elderberries
- 500ml (18fl oz) cider vinegar
- 50g (1¾oz) golden caster sugar
- 1 red onion, finely chopped
- 10g (¼oz) bruised fresh ginger (gently squeezed with your fist)
- 1 tablespoon black peppercorns
- 6 allspice berries, lightly crushed in a pestle and mortar
- 6 cloves
- fine salt and freshly ground black pepper

> Use a fork to strip the berries off the stalks. (Don't wear your best white clothes, the juice stains horribly.) Put all the ingredients into a casserole, stir through and cover. Cook in a low oven (approx. 100°C/225°F/gas ¼) for 4 hours, stirring occasionally. Strain the vinegar through a piece of muslin over a sieve into a saucepan, pushing down on the fruit to release as much juice as possible. Bring to the boil for 5 minutes and adjust the seasoning if necessary. Pour the sauce into a sterilized jug and pour into a sterilized bottle. Seal. Keep for several years in a cool, dark place. Wait at least 3 months before tasting.

SPICED VINEGAR

Spiced vinegar is used as a base in many of the chutney recipes in this book. According to my sister Louise and our friend Penny Wragg, in order to make the very best spiced vinegar you should put your spices into bottles of cold vinegar a year before you need them. Apparently if you shake the bottles from time to time you will encourage the flavour of the spices to really penetrate the vinegar. I am hopelessly impatient, but I am going to try this in future as the ingredients are not expensive and once made the vinegar can be left in the garage and forgotten about for a year.

Of course, not everyone will have the foresight to make their spiced vinegar a year in advance, so here is a shortcut that involves heating the ingredients to speed up the process.

QUICK SPICED VINEGAR

This is my speedy version for people who need their spiced vinegar in a hurry.

MAKES 1 LITRE (1¾ PINTS)

- 1 litre (1¾ pints) vinegar of your choice (make sure it is at least 5 per cent acetic acid)
- 6cm (2½in) cinnamon stick
- 1 teaspoon cloves
- ½ teaspoon mace (optional)
- pinch of cayenne pepper
- 2 teaspoons allspice
- 1 teaspoon black peppercorns
- 1 teaspoon mustard seeds
- 2–3 bay leaves

> Put the vinegar and spices in a saucepan, cover with a lid and bring to just below boiling point – do not allow it to bubble. Remove from the heat and set aside for a minimum of 2 hours (preferably overnight). The longer you leave it, the better the flavour. Strain the vinegar through a sieve lined with muslin and bottle once cold if not using immediately. Store in a cool, dark place for up to a year.

LOUISE'S PICKLED EGGS

My sister Louise remembers pickling eggs with our grandmother in her cramped little kitchen. She would traditionally make the eggs in autumn to give as Christmas presents later in the year. Our grandmother used malt vinegar, but any vinegar is fine. My sister always uses Spiced vinegar (see left), which imparts a lovely flavour to the finished dish. Homemade pickled eggs are so much nicer than the commercially made versions you can buy. We eat them with slices of cold ham, pâté, cheese or curries.

MAKES 2 X 500G (1LB 2OZ) KILNER JARS

- 14 fresh organic eggs
- 1 litre (1¾ pints) Spiced or Quick Spiced Vinegar (see left) or white wine vinegar and the chilli below
- 1 teaspoon salt
- 2 teaspoons roughly crushed black peppercorns
- 2 small pieces of dried chilli (optional)

> Hard-boil the eggs for approx. 10 minutes. Put the cooked eggs under cold water to cool and give each one a quick tap to break the shells (this should stop the blue ring appearing around the outside of the yolk). Peel off the shells. Put the eggs into your Kilner jars and top up with the cold vinegar, salt, peppercorns and chilli, if using, making sure they are completely submerged. Seal with non-reactive lids and store in a cool, dark place. Leave for 1 month before opening and consume within 6 months. Once opened, store in the refrigerator and eat within a week.

For a really pretty version of pickled eggs, add 250ml (9fl oz) pasteurized beetroot juice to the pan with the vinegar.

* PICKLED VEGETABLES

Most recipes require you to soak your vegetables in brine or layer them up with dry salt before immersing them in vinegar. This preliminary process removes excess moisture in the veggies, improves their texture and helps destroy bacteria. As a general rule, brining is used for vegetables such as onions to soften them, while dry salt is used for brassicas such as cabbage to keep them crisp. After brining or salting you must rinse your veggies in clean, cold water and drain them thoroughly before packing them into jars and covering with vinegar.

For best results, always pickle fresh vegetables or fruit as soon as possible after harvesting and never be tempted to use bruised produce. Make sure your vegetables are totally immersed in the vinegar solution at all times to stop them from becoming contaminated. I always allow 2.5cm (1in) headroom above the vegetables to leave plenty of space for the vinegar. Don't be tempted to squash the vegetables down inside the jar or they will bruise and the vinegar won't be able to reach all the surfaces.

As a general rule, use cold vinegar for making crisp pickles and warm vinegar for soft pickles, so that it lightly cooks the food before it cools. Always use non-reactive (vinegar-proof) lids.

Pickled onions remind me of the Sunday evenings of my childhood. After a big roast lunch and a walk along the blustery seafront of Eastbourne we would settle down for a simple supper in front of the telly consisting of Cheddar cheese, bread, butter and my mum's homemade pickled onions – heaven!

MAKES 2 X 500G (1LB 2OZ) KILNER JARS AND 1 X 250G (9OZ) JAR

- 1 litre (1¾ pints) medium brine (see page 74)
- 1kg (2lb 4oz) small pickling onions, unpeeled
- 100g (3½oz) golden caster sugar (optional)
- 600–800ml (20fl oz–1⅓ pints) cold Quick Spiced Vinegar (see page 15), to cover the onions

> Make up the brine and set aside to cool. Meanwhile peel the onions. The easiest way to do this is to cut off the tops and roots (just the very tips and ends to keep them intact and so not to waste too much of the onion) and plunge them into a bowl of boiling water. Set aside for 1 minute, then drain and plunge into cold water. You should now be able to peel off the skins easily along with any tough leathery layers.

> Put the onions into a mixing bowl and cover them with the cold brine, weighing them down with a plate so that they are fully submerged. Set aside for 12 hours in a cold place. Meanwhile, dissolve the sugar (if using) in the vinegar and set aside to cool.

> Drain the onions and pat dry on kitchen paper. Pack the onions into sterilized jars and cover with the cold, spiced vinegar, making sure they are totally submerged.

Put on the non-reactive lids tightly and store in a cold, dark place for up to a year. However, you can start eating them after a month.

VARIATION

To make the jars look pretty and add a little more spice, put a couple of bay leaves, a few black peppercorns and either a dried red chilli or 1 teaspoon of mustard seeds into each jar.

PICKLED RED CABBAGE

This is great with roast pork belly, cold turkey or ham or as part of a stir-fry. My favourite way to eat pickled cabbage is slightly warm with homemade British or Italian sausages (see pages 91–3).

You can vary the texture of the finished cabbage by pickling it in hot or cold vinegar (see below). Use hot vinegar for a softer texture or cold vinegar if you like a bit of crunch.

MAKES APPROX. 1KG (2LB 4OZ)
- 1 small red cabbage, shredded
- 3 tablespoons fine salt
- 700ml–1 litre (1¼–1¾ pints) Quick Spiced Vinegar (see page 15)
- 1 teaspoon cumin seeds
- 10 black peppercorns, lightly crushed

> Mix the shredded cabbage with the salt in a non-metallic bowl. Weigh it down with a plate and set aside overnight.
> Meanwhile, put the vinegar and spices in a saucepan and heat to boiling point; remove from the heat and set aside to infuse. Depending on whether you like your cabbage soft or crunchy, you can either use the vinegar straight away or leave it to cool. Drain through a sieve, reserving the spices.

> Squeeze out the cabbage and give it a good rinse in cold water, discarding any juice from the bowl. Drain it well and tip onto kitchen paper to dry. Pack the cabbage into sterilized jars, sprinkling it with the reserved seeds and peppercorns. Pour in the vinegar to cover the cabbage completely and then poke it several times with a clean chopstick or wooden skewer to release any air bubbles. Seal with non-reactive lids. Store in a cool, dark place. It should be ready to enjoy after a week but will keep for up to 3 months. Once opened, store in the refrigerator and eat within 2 weeks.

SWEDISH PICKLED CUCUMBERS

My Swedish friend Pernilla gave this recipe to me. Her sister-in-law, Lotta Gustafsson, loves to grow her own vegetables and forage for herbs. Each time Pernilla goes home to Sweden she comes back laden with jars of pickled vegetables.

MAKES APPROX. 1KG (2LB 4OZ)
- approx. 800g (1lb 12oz) small cucumbers
- 1 tablespoon fine sea salt
- a handful of dill
- 2 tablespoons white mustard seeds
- 100g (3½oz) caster sugar
- 500ml (18fl oz) distilled white vinegar

> Wash the cucumbers, removing any blossom from the ends. Dry on kitchen paper and cut into 5mm (¼in) slices. Put them into a non-metallic bowl and use your hands to mix them with the salt. Cover with a saucer and leave in the refrigerator or a cold room overnight.
> The following day, rinse the cucumbers really well in cold water and pat dry with kitchen paper. Layer them up with the dill, mustard seeds and sugar in a clean

>>>

non-metallic bowl. Pour the vinegar over the top and set aside to steep for a further 24 hours, stirring occasionally with a wooden spoon to encourage the sugar to dissolve so it comes into contact with all of the cucumber slices.

> The following day, put the cucumbers into sterilized jars and top them up with the vinegar. Seal with vinegar-proof lids and store in a cool, dark place for up to 6 months. You can start eating them within a week.

GARLIC RELISH

This recipe is from our friend Kam Degun. It was her mother's recipe and she serves the relish with samosas, spring rolls and lentil curry. She kindly gave us a jar and we loved it. We discovered it goes really well with many European foods – try it spread thinly on hot sourdough toast, mixed into mashed potatoes, stirred into hot, steamed green beans or added to stir-fries and marinades (see Dragon Chicken, pages 30–1). Use it wherever you see garlic being used: a teaspoon is equal to one garlic clove.

MAKES 250G (9OZ)

- 4 whole heads of garlic
- 125ml (4fl oz) extra virgin olive oil
- 1 tablespoon cider vinegar
- 1 tablespoon lemon juice
- ½ teaspoon chilli powder or paprika
- 1 level teaspoon golden caster sugar
- good pinch of salt

> Peel the garlic cloves and grind them to a coarse or smooth paste in a pestle and mortar or using a stick blender. Stir in the olive oil, vinegar, lemon juice, chilli powder (or paprika), sugar and salt. Scoop into a cold, sterilized jar with a lid and store in the refrigerator. Consume within a month.

MALAYSIAN PICKLED VEGETABLES

This is our friend and chef Caroline Mili Artiss' recipe. She serves the pickled vegetables up at parties as a pre-dinner nibble or as an accompaniment to curries. They also work really well on a board of charcuterie and cheeses.

MAKES APPROX. 2KG (4LB 8OZ)

- 1kg (2lb 4oz) mixed vegetables, such as cauliflower, carrots, red pepper, baby onions, green beans, celery, cucumber (discard the soft middle and seeds)
- 100g (3½oz) fine sea salt

FOR THE DRESSING

- 1 tablespoon oil
- 1 tablespoon mustard seeds
- 1 heaped teaspoon ground turmeric
- 1 heaped teaspoon chilli powder
- 3 garlic cloves, finely sliced
- 2.5cm (1in) piece of fresh ginger, finely sliced
- 1 litre (1¾ pints) distilled white vinegar
- 600g (1lb 5oz) caster sugar
- 1 heaped teaspoon salt

> Chop the vegetables into bite-sized pieces – batons, wedges or florets, the choice is yours. Put them into a large plastic or glass bowl and scatter the fine sea salt over the top. Toss carefully with your hands to coat the vegetables evenly in the salt. Place a plate on top so it rests directly on the vegetables and weigh it down with something heavy. Set the bowl aside for approx. 8 hours in a cool place. A garage is ideal, just make sure it doesn't attract pests or flies.

> Meanwhile, make the dressing. Heat the oil in a large saucepan and add the mustard seeds. Once they start to pop, add the turmeric and chilli powder, garlic and ginger and let them cook for 1 minute.

Pour in the vinegar and stir in the sugar and salt. Bring slowly to the boil, stirring to dissolve the sugar, and then reduce to a simmer for 3 minutes. Set aside to cool. (At this stage you can store the dressing in a sterilized bottle in the refrigerator for up to 1 month.)

> Tip the vegetables into a colander and rinse really well with plenty of cold water. Put them into a bowl of clean, cold water and leave them to soak for a few minutes before rinsing again. Repeat this process to get rid of the salt. Taste the vegetables to make sure they are not too salty and rinse again if necessary. Drain really well and pat dry on kitchen paper.

> Put the vegetables in a glass or ceramic bowl, pour over the dressing and set aside to marinate in the refrigerator for approx. 1 hour.

> Serve the vegetables straight away or pack them into sterilized glass jars and seal with sterilized non-reactive lids – just make sure the vegetables are fully submerged in the dressing or they will spoil. Store in a cool, dark cupboard for up to 6 months. Once opened, the jars should be kept in the refrigerator and eaten within a month.

PICKLED GRAPES

This is based on a recipe by Patrick Eude, Le Havre, from the fascinating book Preserving Food Without Freezing or Canning. Pickled grapes are really unusual; they have an initial acidity followed by an intense sweetness as you eat them. We have increased the sugar content from the original recipe to tone down the mouth-puckering vinegar shock and to allow for my sweet tooth. We serve pickled grapes alongside pâté or rillettes to counteract the richness or with cold meats.

MAKES 1 X 500G (1LB 2OZ) KILNER JAR

- 650g (1lb 7oz) mixed seedless white and red grapes in bunches
- 300ml (½ pint) white wine vinegar
- 250g (9oz) golden caster sugar
- 6 white peppercorns
- 4 cloves
- 2 sprigs of tarragon

> Wash the grapes while still on the bunch and snip them off individually with scissors, keeping a very short stalk. Put the vinegar and sugar in a large saucepan, add the peppercorns and cloves, and bring to the boil to dissolve the sugar. Reduce the heat to a very gentle simmer and add the grapes and tarragon. Simmer very gently for 3 minutes, then remove the grapes with a slotted spoon into a sterilized jar. Allow the vinegar mixture to cool to room temperature before pouring it over the grapes. Tuck the tarragon sprigs and spices in amongst the grapes and ensure that the grapes are pushed down under the level of the vinegar. Seal with non-reactive lids and store in a cool, dark place for up to a year. Leave for 3 months before opening.

VARIATION

Use gooseberries or cherries in season in place of the grapes.

PICKLED NECTARINES

These have a delightful flavour – sweet fruit with the sourness of vinegar and a hint of spice. A bit like Marmite, they might not be everyone's cup of tea, but we love them with cold smoked ham or roast duck. The recipe also works with peaches or pears.

MAKES 1 X 1KG (2LB 4OZ) KILNER JAR

- 10 just ripe but firm nectarines (approx. 850g/1lb 14oz)

>>>

- 200ml (7fl oz) water
- 500ml (18fl oz) white wine vinegar or cider vinegar
- 6cm (2½in) cinnamon stick
- 1 teaspoon allspice berries
- 5 cloves
- 5cm (2in) piece of fresh ginger, peeled and cut into matchsticks
- 1 teaspoon freshly ground black peppercorns
- 400g (14oz) golden caster sugar

> Peel the nectarines, cut into quarters and remove the stones. Put the remaining ingredients into a large saucepan and bring to the boil. Add the nectarine quarters and poach them very gently until just tender, approx. 6–8 minutes. Remove the fruit with a slotted spoon and pack into a warm, sterilized jar. Return the poaching liquor to the heat and boil up vigorously for 5 minutes to reduce a little. Pour over the nectarines, including the spices, making sure they are totally submerged, and seal immediately with a non-reactive lid. Store in a cool, dark place for up to a year. Allow at least 6 months before opening.

PICKLED CHILLIES

Mexican pickled chillies, also known as chiles en escabeche, are a spicy addition to fajitas, enchiladas, cheeses, or cut small to pep up a salad. Often this recipe is made with jalapeños but any chillies such as habaneros, long Hungarian chillies or the common green and red chillies are fine to use; they all have their individual strengths of heat.

MAKES 1KG (2LB 4OZ)

- 500g (1lb 2oz) chillies
- 3 carrots, peeled and cut into batons
- 3 onions, peeled and cut into eighths
- 3 tablespoons extra virgin olive oil
- 6 garlic cloves, peeled
- 1 teaspoon oregano
- 2 bay leaves
- 2 teaspoons marjoram
- 10 black peppercorns, lightly crushed
- 3 tablespoons granulated cane sugar
- 2 teaspoons salt
- 500ml (18fl oz) cider vinegar, plus a little extra for topping up the jars
- 250ml (9fl oz) water

> Wash all the vegetables. Leave the stems intact but cut a cross in the tip of each chilli to allow the vinegar to penetrate. Add the oil to a saucepan over a medium heat and fry the chillies, carrots, onions and garlic for 10 minutes, turning the vegetables frequently to avoid burning. Add the herbs, peppercorns, sugar and salt and stir through. Pour in the vinegar and water and bring to the boil. Reduce the heat to a simmer and cook for a further 10 minutes. Bottle hot into sterilized jars, topping up with extra vinegar if necessary to make sure that all the vegetables are covered. Seal and allow to cool. Store in the refrigerator for up to 2 months or waterbath for 15 minutes following the hot-pack method on page 253.

PICKLED WALNUTS

Our good friends Dee and Barrie at Chalfont Chillies gave me this recipe. Apparently their local vicar asked them to make some for him and they were so popular they have continued making them. Eat pickled walnuts with cheese or ham to make a more interesting ploughman's lunch. Barrie's favourite way to eat them is in the charmingly named dish of beef collops.

MAKES APPROX. 4 X 350G (12OZ) JARS

- 6 tablespoons fine sea salt, for the brine
- 4.6 litres (6 pints) water
- 900g (2lb) green walnuts, in their husks
- 2 tablespoons black peppercorns
- 1 tablespoon allspice berries
- 2 teaspoons cloves
- 1 teaspoon yellow mustard seeds
- 2 garlic cloves, sliced
- 4 thin slices of fresh ginger
- 1.8 litres (3 pints) malt vinegar
- 450g (1lb) light soft brown sugar

> **DAY ONE** First make the brine. Heat 1.2 litres (2 pints) of water with 2 tablespoons of sea salt in a saucepan over a medium heat, stirring to dissolve; pour into a glass or plastic bowl and set aside to cool to room temperature.
> Wearing rubber gloves, top and tail the walnuts, pierce each one several times with a large needle and drop them into the brine. Set aside for 3 days, covered loosely, at room temperature.
> **DAY FOUR** Make up a fresh solution of brine: dissolve 2 tablespoons of sea salt in 1.2 litres (2 pints) of boiling water and set aside to cool. Drain the walnuts, discarding the old brine, and transfer them to the new brine. Set aside for a further 3 days.
> **DAY SEVEN** Make up a fresh solution of brine: dissolve 2 tablespoons of sea salt in 1.2 litres (2 pints) of boiling water and set aside to cool. Drain the walnuts, discarding the old brine, and transfer them to the new brine. Set aside for a further 3 days.
> **DAY TEN** Drain the walnuts one final time and spread them out on a tray lined with newspaper to dry. In fine weather you can place the walnuts outside to dry, protected with a net, or you can put them inside on a sunny windowsill. Set aside for 2–3 days, turning occasionally, until they blacken.

> **DAYS 12–13** Lightly crush the spices in a pestle and mortar to bruise them slightly. Wrap them in a piece of muslin, putting in the garlic and ginger as well, and tie with a knot. Heat the vinegar and sugar with the spice bag in a large saucepan to dissolve the sugar. Bring to the boil and then reduce to a simmer for 15 minutes. Set aside to cool before removing the spices.
> Pack the walnuts into dry, sterilized jars, cover with the vinegar and seal immediately. Store for 8–12 weeks before using. Pickled walnuts will keep for a year. Refrigerate after opening and use within 2 months.

HORSERADISH SAUCE

Horseradish grows easily in the UK and it is often a problem to get rid of in gardens. We stumbled across a patch near where we live and occasionally go and dig a root up. The white root buries itself deep in the ground and can be hard to dig up, but even a little piece goes a long way.

To preserve fresh horseradish for a few weeks in the refrigerator, finely grate it and spoon into a small jar or container adding enough white wine vinegar to cover. When grating horseradish, do it at arm's length and don't take a big sniff of the root as it is really powerful stuff. Wash your hands well afterwards and avoid touching your eyes.

SERVES 4

- 2 heaped tablespoons finely grated fresh horseradish
- 2–3 teaspoons white wine vinegar
- 1–2 teaspoons lemon juice, to taste
- 1–2 teaspoons golden caster sugar, to taste
- good pinch of salt
- 2–3 tablespoons crème fraîche (see page 180) or double cream

> Mix all the ingredients together to taste. Store in the refrigerator for up to 3 days in a sealed jar or plastic container. This is not just to be eaten with roast beef – try it stirred into buttery mashed potato, with steak or with the Peppered Mackerel (see page 138).

CHRAYNE

This was introduced to us by a group of lovely women from the Cooking Lunch Girls, a group of foodie Jewish women from North London. We taught them about Italian food and in return they took us on a tour of the Golders Green delicatessens and introduced us to the tastiest versions of typical Jewish dishes. I relished the soft just-baked challah bread, tangy cream cheese, subtle smoked salmon, pickled gherkins, slivers of pastrami and salt beef, but I had never seen chrayne before and just loved it.

This pickle combines the strong flavour of horseradish with the sweetness of beetroot. Horseradish grows in wild abundance where we live, so occasionally we take a trowel and go and dig some up. It always needs a good wash afterwards and you must take care when grating it as it can sting your eyes and take your breath away. This is why I make a little of this at a time. Chrayne is lovely on toasted bagels or rye bread with cream cheese, or with Salt Beef (see pages 101–2). Beetroot takes a long time to roast in the oven (up to 2 hours to become tender), but the end result is sweeter tasting than boiled beetroot. Feel free to experiment with the quantities, according to taste, and don't worry about exact measurements.

MAKES APPROX. 300G (10½OZ)

- 275–300g (9¾–10½oz) boiled or roasted beetroot (approx. 4 medium beetroots) – I wrap them in foil and roast them in a hot oven until tender
- 2–3 heaped tablespoons grated horseradish
- 4–6 teaspoons white wine vinegar
- 4 teaspoons lemon juice
- 4–6 teaspoons caster sugar
- fine sea salt

> Put all the ingredients in a food processor (or use a stick blender) and purée to a smooth paste. Adjust the seasoning to taste with salt and sugar. Store in a covered container in the refrigerator for up to a month.

JAPANESE PICKLED GINGER

Pickled ginger is usually served with sushi and is called *gari*. Try to find fresh young ginger (*shin shoga*) for this – look out for the yellow-skinned tender ones with a tinge of pink at the end of the roots. If you use old root ginger it might not turn pink naturally. Sometimes colouring is added to alter the appearance, however I think that is a shame. For best results use a mandolin to cut the ginger into transparent slices. This is also lovely with steamed or grilled fish for a simple supper or shredded or tossed into stir-fries and salads. Try it in the marinade for Beef Jerky (see pages 114–15) in place of raw ginger and marinate beef or fish in it before grilling.

MAKES 1KG (2LB 4OZ)

- 800g (1lb 12oz) young fresh ginger
- 2 teaspoons sea salt
- 720ml (1¼ pints) rice vinegar
- 225g (8oz) golden caster sugar

> Cut the woody ends off the ginger roots and scrape off the skin using a teaspoon. Slice the ginger really thinly using a

mandolin or a very sharp knife and mix with the salt in a bowl. Set aside for 1 hour at room temperature, covered with a cloth.

> Remove the ginger from the bowl, dry the slices with kitchen paper and transfer them to a sterilized jar. Put the rice vinegar and sugar in a saucepan and bring to the boil to dissolve the sugar. Pour the hot liquid over the ginger slices in the jar and set aside to cool, loosely covered with a piece of muslin to allow the heat to escape but nothing to fall in. The ginger will turn light pink as it cools. Put a non-reactive lid on the jar and store in the refrigerator for up to 3 weeks.

* PICKLED FISH

MARINATED ANCHOVIES

These remind me of being on holiday by the sea in Italy. The sun shines, the white wine is crisp and cold and a little dish of silver vinegary fish is presented before the meal to eat with bread. Heaven. However, marinated anchovies still taste good in a cloudy, cold climate (so I tell myself). In fact, our son Giorgio gobbles them up even before I have a chance to lay them on a plate.

Marinated anchovies look really pretty dressed with parsley and red onion, and make great antipasti. Fresh small sprats can also be used if you can't find anchovies.

MAKES 500G (1LB 2OZ)/SERVES 8–10

- 400g (15oz) fresh anchovies, filleted
- 200–300ml (7fl oz–½ pint) white wine vinegar
- 100–150ml (3½–5fl oz) extra virgin olive oil

TO SERVE

- 1 red onion, cut into thin strips
- a small handful of fresh parsley, roughly chopped
- extra virgin olive oil, for drizzling
- salt and freshly ground black pepper

> Place the anchovy fillets side by side on a non-metallic tray and pour over enough white wine vinegar to cover them completely. Set aside in the refrigerator to marinate (preferably overnight) or until the flesh turns white.
> Drain the anchovies, discarding the vinegar, and pat dry on kitchen paper. Lay them side by side in a plastic container and pour over enough oil to cover them completely. Put the lid on and transfer the container to the refrigerator, where the anchovies will keep for up to 3 weeks.
> To serve, remove the anchovies from the oil and lay on a plate. Rinse the onion strips in water to soften the flavour and scatter them over the fish with the parsley. Drizzle with olive oil and season with salt and pepper.

VARIATION

This dish can also be made with the Salted Anchovies on pages 78–9 – just make sure you give them a good rinse under cold water and pat dry before use, and avoid adding any extra salt later.

SCANDINAVIAN PICKLED HERRINGS

'Silver darlings', as herrings were once known, have brought wealth, health and prosperity to the shores of the UK from the Middle Ages right up until the present day. In Scotland, in particular, towns grew on their herring trade and railway lines were extended to places like Wick, Ullapool and Mallaig to allow for their transportation south.

The Scandinavians and Dutch, too, ate and sold herrings in massive quantities, fishing for them in the Baltic Sea from the 10th century onwards. It is said that Amsterdam was built on the bones of herrings and historian Jules Michelet referred to it as the place where 'herring fishers transmuted their stinking cargo into gold'.

Herrings are pelagic, meaning they are continually on the move, similar to sardines and mackerel. And like them they are oily fish rich in omega 3, so they are really good for you. Herrings don't keep for long in their fresh form, which is why they are often preserved by being smoked, when they become known as kippers, or pickled and stored in jars as they are in this recipe.

Herrings continued in popularity right up until the mid-20th century, so much so that they were overfished and stocks became dangerously low. However, we are now seeing quantities return to levels that are sustainable and for now, at least, we can enjoy them guilt-free. This Swedish recipe was given to me by Lotta Gustafsson. Pickled herrings are delicious served plain with toasted rye or pumpernickel bread, or hot boiled potatoes and hard-boiled eggs, or you can chop them up and serve them with the Dill, Mustard and Honey Sauce on page 80.

SERVES 4 AS A MAIN COURSE
(OR 8 AS A STARTER)
- 500ml (18fl oz) distilled white vinegar
- 2.5 litres (4½ pints) water
- 150g (5½oz) fine sea salt
- 1 heaped tablespoon sugar
- 2.5kg (5lb 8oz) herrings, filleted
- 1 small white onion, finely sliced into rings (optional)
- Dill, Mustard and Honey Sauce (see page 80), to serve (optional)
- 2 tablespoons crème fraîche (see page 180, optional)

> Pour the vinegar and water into a large shallow dish, such as one you would use for lasagne, and stir in the salt and sugar to make a brine. Lay the fish and the onion rings (if using) in the liquid, making sure they are totally submerged. Cover the dish with a plate and set aside to marinate in the refrigerator for 24 hours.

> Drain the herrings and onions and either serve them plain or chop into bite-sized pieces and mix with the dill sauce, adding the crème fraîche. If you want to preserve them for longer, mix with the dill sauce (omitting the crème fraîche) and pack into sealed jars. Like this, they will keep in the refrigerator for up to 4 weeks.

SWEET MARINATED MACKEREL
WITH BABY LEEKS

This recipe is from Anton Edelmann, who was head chef at the Savoy for 21 years. This is one of his mother's recipes. She used to make this dish using trout or herring when he was a child growing up in a small village in Bavaria, West Germany. We thought it was quite easy to make and really delicious.

SERVES 4
- 2 small carrots, peeled and cut into thin slices
- a bunch of baby leeks, trimmed with leaves removed but kept whole
- 2 shallots, finely sliced
- 5 tablespoons extra virgin olive oil
- 250ml (9fl oz) water
- 90g golden caster sugar
- 200ml (7fl oz) cider vinegar
- a sprig of thyme
- 4 juniper berries
- 1 bay leaf
- 4 medium mackerel, filleted
- fine sea salt and freshly ground black pepper
- 1 teaspoon ground coriander

- 50g (1¾oz) '00' or plain flour
- 1 tablespoon sultanas, soaked in water for 30 minutes
- a small handful of chives, finely chopped

> Blanch the carrots in boiling water for 3 minutes and the leeks for 2 minutes. Drain, refresh under cold running water and drain again once cold; set aside. Fry the shallots in 2 tablespoons of the olive oil over a low heat until softened but still pale. Meanwhile, place the water, sugar, vinegar, thyme, juniper berries and bay leaf in a saucepan and boil for 5 minutes; remove from the heat. Season the mackerel fillets with salt, pepper and the coriander and toss in the flour. Shake well to get rid of the excess.

> Heat the remaining 3 tablespoons of olive oil in a non-stick frying pan. Add the mackerel fillets, skin-side down first, and fry until golden brown and just cooked through. Drain on kitchen paper. Combine the shallots, carrots, leeks and sultanas in a large dish and top with the fish. Strain the hot vinegar over the top, so the fillets are completely submerged, and then set aside to cool. Once cold, cover with a plate and transfer to the refrigerator to marinate overnight. It will keep for 3 days.

> Serve at room temperature: spoon the leeks onto a plate, top with the mackerel fillets and garnish with the carrots, sultanas, shallots and chives. Accompany with brown toast.

* CHUTNEY

Chutney, which derives from the Hindi word *chatni*, was traditionally used to describe the range of relishes that were brought back to Europe during the colonial era. The brand Major Grey was famous for its mango chutney during this time. Today chutneys take on various forms and the term is used to describe both a simple mixture of fresh ingredients to be eaten on the day, as well as slow-cooked fruit or vegetables sweetened with honey or sugar and preserved with vinegar.

CHUTNEY-MAKING TIPS
EQUIPMENT

- When some metals are combined with the acids in vinegar, fruit juices and wine they can form an unpleasant taste. It is better to use glass, plastic or stainless-steel pans, bowls and utensils for chutney-making.
- Use vinegar-proofed lids, which are usually plastic coated; never be tempted to reuse old lids if they are damaged or rusty.
- Preserving or Maslin pans are wider at the top than the bottom to allow steam to escape from a large surface area, hastening the cooking of your chutney. They also have a heavy base so that your preserves don't burn easily.
- It is a good idea to keep one large wooden spoon for chutney-making and another one for jam-making, so the flavours cannot be confused. My favourite spoon is one with a hook on it that stops it falling into the pan.

INGREDIENTS

- Make sure vegetables and fruit are in perfect condition; if possible use them as soon as possible after harvesting.

- Cut vegetables and fruit into similar-sized pieces so they have the same cooking time.
- To peel ginger, scrape the skin off with a teaspoon.
- Always use whole herbs and spices rather than ground ones; powdered spices tend to make the chutney go cloudy; whole spices are easy to pick out if necessary.
- Spice bags can be bought online or from kitchen shops and are really useful and can be reused. To make your own, wrap your spices in a circle of muslin and tie with string.

BOTTLING

- Chutney is ready for bottling when it reaches the 'trail stage'. To test, draw a wooden spoon across the mixture in the pan and see if it leaves a furrow or trail; it should last for a few seconds before refilling with syrupy juices.
- Bottle chutney straight away after it reaches the trail stage. Ladle through a jam funnel or pour from a sterilized jug into sterilized jars and seal straight away with vinegar-proofed sterilized lids.
- Use sterilized jars and lids for chutney, always pouring hot chutney into a hot jar. For tips on sterilizing jars and bottles, see page 10.
- When packing your chutney into the jar, make sure the fruit and vegetables are fully submerged in the sauce and not exposed to the air to prevent spoiling.
- Fill the jars to 5mm (¼in) from the top, which might seem quite high but the chutney will shrink.
- Label all pickles and chutneys as soon as they are cool in the jars; you really won't remember what they are a few months later!

TASTING

- Remember that flavours tend to mellow over time, so don't judge an acidic-tasting pickle straight after cooking. As I have learned from experience, flavours really change in the jars. For best results, store them for at least 3 months before tasting.

STORING

- Store chutneys and pickles in a cool, dark place.

MRS WISHDISH'S PLUM AND GINGER CHUTNEY

This recipe is adapted from Delia Smith's Spiced Plum Chutney in her *Complete Illustrated Cookery Course*. I noticed when making this with our friend, Mrs Wishdish, that her recipe book is marked with lots of ticks made with a pencil so that she knows she has added that ingredient. Good idea, I thought. She and I decided to add a little heat in the form of red chilli and some fresh ginger. We made this recipe together when the plums were ripe and falling from the trees in summer.

MAKES APPROX. 3 LITRES (5¼ PINTS)

- 1.5kg (3lb 5oz) firm, ripe plums
- 500g (1lb 2oz) apples (cooking apples are ideal but you can make the weight up with some of each)
- 3 large brown onions
- 1.3 litres (2¼ pints) malt vinegar
- 450g (1lb) dark brown sugar
- 450g (1lb) demerara sugar
- 350g (12oz) sultanas
- 4 fat garlic cloves, grated
- 75g (2½oz) fresh ginger, peeled and cut into short matchsticks
- 1 red chilli, finely chopped
- 2 heaped tablespoons salt

FOR THE SPICE BAG
- 25g (1oz) allspice berries
- 2 teaspoons cloves
- 2 x 6cm (2½in) cinnamon sticks

> Cut the plums into quarters, remove the stones and discard. Core the apples and cut into small pieces, leaving the skin on, either using a sharp knife or in a food processor. Peel and chop the onions in the same way. Put the plums, apples and onions in a large, heavy-based saucepan along with the remaining ingredients (except the spices in the spice bag). Put the loose spices into a small spice bag or wrap in a piece of muslin and tie with string. Fasten the spice bag onto the handle of the pan, letting it fall inside. Bring everything to the boil, stirring to dissolve the sugar, and simmer for 2–3 hours, stirring frequently to prevent sticking. When the chutney reaches the trail stage (see page 26), pour into warm, sterilized jars and seal straight away. Store in a cool, dark place and allow at least 3 months before tasting. Unopened, the chutney will keep for a year. Once opened, store in the refrigerator and consume within a month.

TOMATO KASUNDI

This spicy Indian chutney also works as a quick sauce. My favourite way to serve it is heated with halved boiled eggs, dollops of Greek yogurt and a generous scattering of coriander. It is so tasty and pretty, I'm going to make three times the amount next time tomatoes are in season.

MAKES APPROX. 6 X 340ML (12FL OZ) JARS
- 3kg (6lb 8oz) ripe tomatoes
- 2 tablespoons black mustard seeds
- 2 tablespoons cumin seeds
- 200g (7oz) fresh ginger, peeled
- 100g (3½oz) garlic, peeled
- 2–3 red chillies, depending on the heat you prefer
- 1 tablespoon ground turmeric
- 600ml (20fl oz) malt vinegar
- 4 tablespoons extra virgin olive oil
- 1 tablespoon salt
- 500g (1lb 2oz) light soft brown sugar

> First, prepare the tomatoes. Make a cross in the bottom of each tomato and remove the green core. Plunge into boiling water for 30 seconds–1 minute, remove with a slotted spoon and plunge immediately into very cold water. Peel off the skins, cut each tomato in half, scoop out the seeds and set aside.

> Toast the mustard and cumin seeds in a dry pan for 3–4 minutes until they start to pop and release their aroma. Tip them into a mortar and pestle and grind to a rough powder. Place the ginger, garlic and chillies in a food processor and blend to a coarse purée. Add the spices to the food processor along with approx. 200ml (7fl oz) of the vinegar and blend again.

> Heat the oil in a heavy-based pan, scoop in the paste and fry for a few minutes to release the fragrance. Add the remaining vinegar with the salt and sugar, followed by the tomatoes. Bring to the boil, stirring to dissolve the sugar, and then reduce the heat and simmer for approx. 2 hours, stirring occasionally to prevent it sticking on the bottom. The chutney is ready when it reaches the trail stage (see page 26). Taste and adjust the salt and chilli as necessary before bottling into warm, sterilized jars. Seal with vinegar-proofed plastic-lined lids, label and store in a cool, dark place for up to a year. Eat with curries, cheese or heat up and use as a sauce.

GREEN TOMATO CHUTNEY

No matter what we do, we always seem to suffer with gluts of green tomatoes that simply refuse to be moved by the sun's rays to change their hue. I have tried frying them, inspired by the famous film's title, putting them into ratatouille or making them into soup – but their sharp and acidic personality seems to overpower everything else. At last, good news, I have tamed them by tempering them with spices and sweetness. This delicious, sweet and tangy chutney pairs with a wide variety of foods – from curries and cold meats to hot sausages or cheese. Our friend Vivien Lloyd adds bananas to her green tomato chutney for sweetness.

MAKES 2.5 LITRES (4½ PINTS)

- 1.5kg (3lb 5oz) green tomatoes, skinned and roughly chopped into 1cm (½in) dice
- 600g (1lb 5oz) onions, roughly chopped into 1cm (½in) dice
- 500g (1lb 2oz) cooking or eating apples, cores removed and cut into small pieces, leaving the skins on (it will be sweeter with the latter)
- 3 bananas, diced into 1cm (½in) cubes (optional)
- 1.4 litres (2½ pints) distilled white vinegar
- 1 tablespoon salt
- 500g (1lb 2oz) demerara sugar
- 300g (10½oz) granulated sugar
- 1 red chilli, finely chopped
- 3 fat garlic cloves, finely chopped
- 1 tablespoon ground ginger
- 100g (3½oz) stem ginger, chopped into little cubes (see page 63)

FOR THE SPICE BAG

- 3 star anise
- 10 cardamom pods, husks removed and seeds lightly crushed
- 1 teaspoon cloves
- 1 tablespoon allspice berries

> Put the spices into a spice bag or wrap them in a piece of muslin and fasten with string. Tie the bag onto the handle of a preserving pan, allowing the bag to hang inside. Put the remaining ingredients into the pan and bring to the boil, stirring to dissolve the sugar. Reduce the heat to a simmer and continue to cook for approx. 2–2½ hours until the chutney reaches the trail stage (see page 26). Bottle into warm, sterilized jars and put on the lids straight away. Store in a cool, dark place and allow at least 3 months before tasting. Unopened, the chutney will keep for a year. Once opened, keep in the refrigerator and consume within a month.

MANGO CHUTNEY

We eat a lot of mango chutney in our house and we are quite fussy about the brands we buy. We love it to be mild and sweet, but packed with flavour and spices, so it took a lot of trial runs before we were happy with this homemade version. Now we make it in big batches so there is always plenty for all of us to enjoy. We enjoy it served with curry and sometimes with cheese, however my elderly father liked it with almost everything, including eggs, soup, fish pie and even Giancarlo's pasta with *ragù* – to his horror!

MAKES APPROX. 1.5KG (3LB 5OZ)

- 6 firm but ripe mangoes (approx. 2.6kg/5lb 11oz in weight)
- 1 onion, finely chopped
- 600ml (20fl oz) white wine vinegar
- 50g (1¾oz) fresh ginger, peeled and finely chopped
- 1 small dried chilli, crushed
- 6 garlic cloves, finely chopped
- 1 teaspoon cloves
- 1 teaspoon cumin seeds

- 8 cardamom pods
- 1 tablespoon coriander seeds
- good pinch of fenugreek seeds
- 600g (1lb 5oz) light soft brown sugar
- 1 teaspoon salt, to taste
- 3 teaspoons nigella seeds (optional)

> Peel the mangoes with a potato peeler and slice the flesh from the stone into approx. 2cm (¾in) pieces. Put the mango, onion, vinegar, ginger, chilli and garlic in a large, heavy-based saucepan and cook over a low heat for approx. 10 minutes.
> Meanwhile, toast the spices (not including the nigella seeds) in a dry pan until they release their aroma. Tip them immediately onto a plate to cool (don't leave them in the pan or they will carry on cooking).
> Once cold, grind the spices in a pestle and mortar or spice grinder to a coarse powder; remove the cardamom husks after they have released their seeds. Add the spices to the pan along with the sugar and salt. Bring to the boil, stirring to dissolve the sugar, and then reduce the heat and simmer gently for 2–3 hours or until the chutney reaches the trail stage (see page 26). Stir in the nigella seeds. Spoon into warm, sterilized jars and put on the lids straight away. Store in a cool, dark place and allow 3 months before tasting. Unopened, the chutney will keep for a year. Once opened, store in the refrigerator and consume within a month.

DEBI'S TOMATO, CHILLI AND GINGER JAM

A regular customer at Caldesi in Campagna, our restaurant in Bray, Debi Peppin told us about a chilli jam she had bought at a farmers' market and loved. She was never able to find the stallholder again, so she ended up developing her own recipe. Debi serves the jam with grilled halloumi, on a cheese board, with cold meat or with fried chicken. She gave us the recipe and it is so good we now keep a jar permanently in our refrigerator. Every time I serve it people ask me for the recipe, so here it is.

MAKES APPROX. 600ML (20FL OZ)

- 450g (1lb) caster sugar
- 8 tablespoons water
- 16 medium tomatoes
- 8 tablespoons white wine vinegar
- 4 medium red chillies, deseeded and chopped
- 50g (1¾oz) fresh ginger, peeled and finely chopped
- 2 teaspoons fine sea salt

> Dissolve the sugar in the water over a medium heat in a large, heavy-based saucepan. Meanwhile, prepare the tomatoes. Make a cross in each one at either end. Drop them into boiling water for 1 minute, or until the skins start to split, and then remove them with a slotted spoon and peel. Discard the green cores and dice the flesh into 1cm (½in) cubes. Remove most of the seeds, but don't worry about some of them being included.
> Add the tomatoes to the sugar syrup in the pan, pour in the vinegar and add the chillies and ginger. Season with salt and pepper. Bring to the boil, stirring, and then reduce the heat and simmer for 30–45 minutes or until the jam reaches the trail stage (see page 26). Spoon into warm, sterilized jars and seal straight away. Put on the lids and store in a cool, dark place for up to a year. Once opened, keep in the refrigerator.

DAWID'S SWEET CHILLI JAM

Dawid Bakowski was the patisserie chef at our restaurant, Caldesi in Campagna. He is a real stickler for detail and loves to do things properly – including cutting the chillies for this recipe by hand, which not only takes time but must also sting your hands and eyes. However, he likes the fact that all the little pieces of chilli end up almost the same size, which you could never achieve in a food processor. If you do follow his method, make sure you wear protective gloves.

Note: Do taste the chillies first to gauge their strength, as it is impossible to tell the difference between a blow-your-socks-off chilli and a mild, sweet and cuddly one just by looking at them. This recipe is meant to be hot, so adjust your chillies accordingly by adding some dried chilli flakes if they are particularly mild in flavour.

MAKES APPROX. 1.1 LITRES

- 650g long medium-hot red chillies
- 1 litre malt vinegar
- 1 tablespoon finely grated fresh ginger
- 2 tablespoons tomato purée
- 1.2kg soft light brown sugar

> Remove the stalks and tips of the chillies. To deseed them, roll them between your palms with the tips facing down. Chop the chillies by hand or, if Dawid isn't looking, put them into a food processor and blitz until finely chopped. Place the chopped chillies in a heavy-based saucepan with the remaining ingredients and set over a medium heat, stirring to dissolve the sugar. Simmer for 2–3 hours, stirring occasionally to stop everything sticking, or until the trail stage is reached (see page 34). Spoon into warm, sterilised jars and seal straight away. Store in a cool, dark place for up to a year. Once opened, keep in the fridge.

DRAGON CHICKEN

This is our younger son Flavio's recipe for his favourite way of cooking spicy chicken. It is one of my favourites too, as it is so easy – in fact, every member of my family likes it. We serve it with a simple vegetable stir-fry and noodles. When I asked Flavio why it should be called Dragon Chicken, he told me to say: 'Enjoy it or a dragon will come and get you!' You can't argue with that.

SERVES 6

- 600g (1lb 5oz) lean chicken (preferably a mixture of thigh and breast meat), cut into bite-sized pieces
- 1 garlic clove, finely chopped or 1 heaped teaspoon Garlic Relish (see page 18)
- 4 tablespoons extra virgin olive oil
- 1 teaspoon pink or black peppercorns, crushed
- 1 heaped tablespoon Dawid's Sweet Chilli Jam (see page 30)

> Put all the ingredients in a bowl and mix together thoroughly. Cover the bowl with a plate and set aside to marinate in the refrigerator for up to 1 hour (preferably overnight).
> To cook the chicken pieces, either tip them into a non-stick frying pan with a little oil or thread them onto skewers and cook under a hot grill for approx. 15 minutes until cooked through and golden.

PAPA'S BANANA AND DATE CHUTNEY

'Soft and sweet and easy to eat': this was my 88-year old father's mantra. He could eat oodles of this chutney on almost anything. We find the mellowness of the fruit marries beautifully with hot curries. This is a great way to use up black-spotted bananas that are on the turn.

MAKES APPROX. 1–1.25KG (2LB 4OZ– 2LB 12 OZ)

- 250g (9oz) cooking apples, peeled and roughly chopped
- 200g (7oz) white or brown onions, roughly chopped
- 225ml (8fl oz) malt vinegar
- 8 ripe bananas (approx. 750g/1lb 10oz), peeled and roughly chopped
- 100g (3½oz) stem ginger, finely chopped
- 200g (7oz) dark soft brown sugar
- 250g (9oz) pitted dates, roughly chopped
- 1 teaspoon fine sea salt
- 100ml (3½fl oz) water

FOR THE SPICE BAG

- 4 allspice berries
- 1 small cinnamon stick
- 4 cloves
- 2 pieces of orange peel

> Put the apples and onions in a large, heavy-based saucepan, pour in the vinegar and cook over a low–medium heat until soft, approx. 20 minutes. Stir in the remaining ingredients and bring to the boil, stirring to dissolve the sugar. Reduce the heat to a simmer and bubble away gently for 1–2 hours or until the chutney reaches the trail stage (see page 26). Spoon into warm, sterilized jars and put on the lids straight away. Store in a cool, dark place for up to a year. Once opened, keep in the refrigerator and consume within a month.

APPLE AND GINGER CHUTNEY

A great way to use up windfall. Eating apples are fine to use and will give a sweeter result.

MAKES APPROX. 2KG (4LB 8OZ)

- 1kg (2lb 4oz) cooking or eating apples
- 340g (11¾oz) onions
- 25g (1oz) garlic cloves
- 100g (3½oz) sultanas
- 100g (3½oz) fresh ginger
- 10g (¼oz) salt
- 750ml (1⅓ pints) cider vinegar
- 675g (1lb 8oz) dark soft brown sugar

FOR THE PICKLING SPICE

- 4 teaspoons coriander seeds
- 1 teaspoon mustard seeds
- 1 teaspoon fennel seeds or aniseed
- 6 cloves
- 2 teaspoons black peppercorns
- 2 teaspoons cumin seeds

> Peel, core and chop the apples, cutting away any bruised areas. Peel the onions and garlic and chop finely. Mince or chop the sultanas. Peel and grate the ginger. Put the pickling spices into a piece of muslin. Tie the muslin up and add it to a large un-lidded preserving pan with the chopped apples, onion, garlic, ginger, salt and sultanas. Pour in the cider vinegar.
> Bring the pan slowly to the boil, reduce the heat and simmer gently until the contents of the pan are pulpy and soft, stirring occasionally. Add the sugar and dissolve it carefully. Continue to cook gently until you reach the trail stage (see page 26). This will take 1½–2 hours. Stir frequently to prevent the chutney sticking to the bottom of the pan.
> Remove the pan from the heat, and ladle the chutney into a glass or plastic jug. Pour the chutney into hot, sterilized jars and seal straight away. Store in a cupboard for 2–3 months before opening and consume within a year. Once opened keep in the refrigerator.

SPICED RED ONION MARMALADE

This Anglo-Sri-Lankan recipe is based on the flavours of British red onion marmalade and *Sini Sambal*, a spicy condiment eaten with Sri Lankan hoppers and curry. It is also a good sweet partner to sharp Cheddar and goat's cheese. I also use it to enrich gravies. The Sri Lankans use tamarind paste but we found that chopped prunes added the same rich body and tang.

To limit unnecessary crying, you can use a food processor for speed to chop up the onions, but remember to open the doors. While the chutney was cooking, our house filled with the smell of spices, and the end product was well worth a few tears.

MAKES APPROX. 2KG (4LB 8OZ)

- 6 tablespoons extra virgin olive oil
- 2kg (4lb 8oz) red onions, thinly sliced
- 200g (7oz) prunes, diced into 1cm (½in) cubes
- 300ml (½ pint) balsamic vinegar
- 400ml (14fl oz) water
- 4 level teaspoons fine sea salt
- 250g (9oz) dark muscovado sugar
- 1–2 dried red chillies, to taste
- 6cm (2½in) cinnamon stick

> Heat the oil in a large preserving pan and gently cook the onions over a low heat until soft and translucent, approx. 1½ hours, partially covered. Stir them frequently to stop them burning or sticking to the bottom. You can add a little more oil to prevent them burning, but the key to successful onion marmalade is slow cooking to maximize the sweetness of the onions.

> Add the remaining ingredients and bring to the boil, stirring to dissolve the sugar. As soon as it comes to the boil, reduce the heat to a simmer and bubble very gently for 30–45 minutes or until the chutney reaches the trail stage (see page 26). Taste for seasoning; remember the vinegar taste will subside with time. Spoon into warm, sterilized jars and put on the lids immediately. Store in a cool dark place for up to a year; taste after at least 3 months. Once opened, store in the refrigerator and consume within 1 month.

PICCALILLI

Piccalilli, or 'Paco-Lilla' or Indian Pickle as it was also known, can be traced back to a cookery book by Mrs Raffald published in 1772. It is based on a traditional Indian pickle and the name could be a mixture of 'pickle' and 'chilli'.

This is a great way to use up surplus vegetables, which are kept crisp in the sauce rather than being cooked until soft. Mrs Raffald recommends: 'You may put in fresh pickles, as things come into season, and keep them covered with vinegar.' However, I think it is safer to make it in one go – although her method does demonstrate you can happily alter the ingredients to suit whatever is in season.

MAKES APPROX. 1.5KG (3LB 5OZ)

- 1kg (2lb 4oz) mixed vegetables, such as cauliflower, green beans, cucumber, courgettes, silverskin onions, peppers, carrots
- 50g (1¾oz) fine sea salt
- 600ml (20fl oz) white wine vinegar
- 300g (10½oz) golden caster sugar
- 30g (1oz) cornflour
- 30g (1oz) ground turmeric
- 25g (1oz) English mustard powder
- 1 teaspoon ground coriander
- 10g (¼oz) ground ginger

> Peel the vegetables and chop them into even bite-sized pieces. Imagine eating the finished pickle in a sandwich and you will gauge the size of each piece correctly. Layer up the vegetables in a plastic or glass bowl, sprinkling each layer with salt. Using your hands, mix everything together to ensure the vegetables are evenly covered, and then cover the bowl with a tea towel. Set aside in a cool place overnight.

> The following day, wash the vegetables under plenty of cold running water and set aside to drain. Meanwhile, pour the vinegar into a large saucepan, add the sugar and stir over a medium heat until dissolved. Combine the cornflour with the spices in a small bowl, pour in a ladleful of the hot vinegar and mix to a smooth paste. Scoop the paste into the saucepan and whisk thoroughly to remove any lumps. Bring to the boil, stirring, and then reduce the heat. Simmer for approx. 8 minutes, stirring frequently. Remove the pan from the heat and carefully fold in the drained vegetables so they are evenly coated in the sauce. Spoon into warm, sterilized jars, topping up with the hot sauce so the vegetables are completely submerged. Put on the lids straight away. Store in a cool, dark place for up to a year. Taste after at least 6 weeks. Once opened, keep in the refrigerator and consume within a month.

SALLY DAVIDSON'S RATHER SPECIAL LEMON CHUTNEY

Sally makes chutney for her local farmers' market in Ruislip, Middlesex. I love her produce and asked her for this lovely lemon chutney recipe. It is great with fish such as salmon or trout, but also with chicken curry. I warned you at the beginning of this section not to judge your chutney until it has had time to mature, and this is especially true with this one. The lemons really mellow after a couple of months, so be patient and wait for at least 3 months before tasting.

MAKES 1.4KG (3LB 3OZ)

- 4 large organic, unwaxed lemons
- 225g (8oz) onions
- 25g (1oz) fine sea salt
- 550ml (19fl oz) cider vinegar
- 100g (3½oz) sultanas
- 25g (1oz) mustard seeds or roughly crushed coriander seeds
- 1 teaspoon cayenne pepper
- 1 heaped teaspoon finely chopped red chilli
- 450g (1lb) demerara sugar

> Wipe the lemons with a damp cloth but don't wash them. Chop finely, skins and all, removing the pips as you see them. Peel and finely chop the onions. Combine the lemons and onions in a plastic or glass bowl, sprinkle with the salt and set aside in the refrigerator overnight.

> The following day, tip the contents of the bowl into a preserving pan and cook over a medium heat for 15–20 minutes until the onions are soft but the lemons still have a little bite to them. (If the pan starts to dry out, add a little water if necessary.) Add the remaining ingredients and simmer for 1 hour, stirring occasionally, until the chutney reaches the trail stage (see page 26). Spoon the hot chutney into warm, sterilized jars and seal straight away. Store in a cool, dark place for 6–9 months. Refrigerate once opened and consume within a month.

SWEETCORN RELISH

As a child I used to love sweetcorn in sandwiches with Cheddar cheese and sliced tomatoes. Now we eat it with homemade beef burgers or sausages. The sweetness is great with grilled meat, chicken or vegetables. We grow corn in our garden at home and I can't believe how different and sweet it tastes when it is cooked straight from the plant.

NOTE: This is another relish that really mellows with time. After 3 months in the jar the sweetness of the corn will really come through.

MAKES 1.75KG (4LB)

- 6 cobs of corn
- 2 teaspoons mustard seeds
- 2 teaspoons cumin seeds
- 1 dried red chilli
- 1 teaspoon allspice berries
- 4 ripe but firm, medium tomatoes, diced into 1cm (½in) cubes
- 1 green pepper, diced into 1cm (½in) cubes
- 1 red pepper, diced into 1cm (½in) cubes
- 1 onion, finely chopped
- 2 garlic cloves, finely chopped
- 1 cooking apple, cored and diced into 1cm (½in) cubes
- 400ml (14fl oz) distilled white vinegar
- 200g (7oz) golden caster sugar
- approx. 1 teaspoon fine sea salt, to taste

> Boil the cobs in plenty of salted water for 8–10 minutes or until just tender. Remove from the pan and set aside to cool.
> Meanwhile, toast the mustard and cumin seeds in a dry frying pan for 2 minutes until they pop and release their aroma. Tip into a pestle and mortar or spice grinder and grind them with the dried chilli and allspice berries to a fine powder.

> Remove the kernels from the corn with a sharp knife by cutting downwards onto a board. Scoop them into a large, heavy-based saucepan and add the remaining ingredients. Bring to the boil, stirring to dissolve the sugar, and then reduce the heat. Simmer for approx. 1 hour until the relish reaches the trail stage (see page 26). Bottle immediately into warm, sterilized jars and put on the lids. The relish will keep for up to a year in a cool, dark place. Wait at least 3 months before trying it and store in the refrigerator once opened.

* MISCELLANEOUS

CHINESE PLUM SAUCE

This is my take on the classic Chinese sauce. According to my Chinese friends, I will never make it like they do in China because British plums are completely different. However, we love to make this sauce with a mixture of Victoria plums and the little wild ones that grow near our home. We cooked our version in the oven because we wanted to concentrate the flavour of the plums without burning them. Any slight caramelization adds to the flavour.

MAKES 2 X 340G (11¾OZ) JARS

- 500g (1lb 2oz) ripe plums of your choice
- 200g (7oz) dark soft brown sugar
- 2 tablespoons grated fresh ginger
- ½ dried red chilli
- 1 teaspoon fine sea salt
- 1 fat garlic clove, finely grated
- 1 small onion, finely chopped
- 2 star anise
- 1 small cinnamon stick
- 2 tablespoons dark soy sauce
- 2 tablespoons rice wine or red wine vinegar

> Preheat the oven to 180°C/350°F/gas 4. Wash and quarter the plums, discarding the stones. Put them in an ovenproof dish and bake in the oven for 45 minutes. (If you prefer, you can do this on the hob in a heavy-based saucepan over a low heat. However, keep an eye on them in case they catch, in which case add a few tablespoons water.)

> Pass the roasted plums through a sieve to remove the skins. Put the plum purée into a preserving pan with the remaining ingredients and bring to the boil, stirring to dissolve the sugar. Reduce the heat to a simmer and cook very slowly for 1 hour, stirring frequently, until it reaches the trail stage (see page 26). Spoon into warm, sterilized jars and seal. Store in a cool dark place for up to a year. Wait at least 4 months before tasting and store in the refrigerator once opened.

MUSHROOM KETCHUP

This curious condiment has been in use in the UK for centuries. It can be added to recipes almost anywhere you see soy or Worcestershire sauce mentioned. It works a little like a liquid flavour enhancer, offering a kick of umami where it is needed such as in gravies, stir-fries, beef stews or simply drizzled over grilled steak or lamb. The choice of flavourings is up to you – I sometimes include a touch of lemon zest or a little grated ginger for a bit of punch, and it is equally delicious. For a really intense mushroom flavour, use your own home-dried mushrooms (see page 107), preferably porcini.

MAKE APPROX. 150ML (¼ PINT)

- 1.25kg (2lb 12oz) fresh, flavourful mushrooms, such as portobello or chestnut
- 1 tablespoon fine sea salt
- 15g (½oz/2 large handfuls) dried porcini and/or chestnut mushrooms
- 200ml (7fl oz) cold water
- 1 white or brown onion, finely chopped
- 250ml (9fl oz) malt or cider vinegar
- a small sprig of rosemary
- 5cm (2in) cinnamon stick
- 5 cloves
- 5 allspice berries

> Do not wash the fresh mushrooms but wipe them clean, and then roughly chop into 2cm (¾in) pieces. Put them in a plastic, glass or stainless-steel bowl and sprinkle over the salt, tossing it through with your hands. Cover with a small plate and set aside in a cool place for 24 hours. Meanwhile, place the dried mushrooms in a bowl with the water and set aside to rehydrate in a cool place overnight, covered.

> The following day, place all the mushrooms, along with their juices, in a heavy-based saucepan. Add the remaining ingredients and bring to the boil, stirring. Reduce the heat and simmer over a low heat for 30 minutes, covered. Remove from the heat and set aside to cool overnight, covered with a tea towel.

> The following day, strain the mushroom mixture through a sieve lined with muslin into a clean saucepan. Squeeze out as much of the liquid as you can from the muslin. Place the saucepan over a medium heat and allow the liquid to reduce by one-third. Taste and adjust the seasoning if necessary. Pour into warm, sterilized bottles. If you are going to keep the ketchup for longer that 2 months, you should waterbath the bottle for 10 minutes at this stage (see pages 206–7). Alternatively, store in the refrigerator and consume within 2 months.

TOMATO KETCHUP

The word catsup comes from the Chinese *ke-tsiap*, a term used to describe a brine leftover from pickling fish. In Europe, catsup has been made for centuries using the leftover vinegary brine from pickled walnuts and mushrooms. However, it was the Americans who first added tomatoes to their catsup and a man called Joshua Davenport from Massachusetts who became the first person to add sugar. He bravely added two cups of sugar to a gallon of tomato stock and half a pint of flavoured vinegar and began to sell it. Now ketchup is a worldwide phenomenon.

We love making our own ketchup at home, and enjoy playing with the sweetness and spices. Do use the best-flavoured tomatoes you can find, as this will affect the final flavour. I often end up using a mixture of cherry and large tomatoes, with any bruised parts cut away.

MAKES APPROX. 500G (1LB 2OZ)

- 2kg (4lb 8oz) ripe but not soft tomatoes, cut in half if large
- 500g (1lb 2oz) white or brown onions, roughly chopped
- 2 celery sticks
- 40g (1½oz) fresh ginger, peeled and grated
- 4 garlic cloves, peeled
- 2 teaspoons fine sea salt, or to taste
- 100g (3½oz) golden caster or granulated sugar
- 50ml (2fl oz) cider or red wine vinegar

FOR THE SPICE BAG

- 1 teaspoon cloves
- 1 teaspoon allspice berries
- 5cm (2in) cinnamon stick
- 6 cardamom pods

> Put the tomatoes in a food processor with the onions, celery, ginger and garlic. Pulse until roughly chopped – you may have to work in batches – or chop by hand with a knife. Scoop the contents into a large preserving pan, add the salt and bring to the boil.

> Meanwhile, put the spices into a spice bag (see page 26) and give them a bash with a rolling pin to lightly crush them. Add the spice bag to the simmering tomatoes. As soon as the tomato mixture starts to bubble, reduce the heat and simmer gently for 1–1½ hours, stirring frequently, or until the vegetables are soft.

> Pass the softened tomato mixture through a food mill or sieve to get rid of the tomato skins, seeds and cores; discard. Pour the strained juice back into the preserving pan, stir in the sugar and vinegar and return to the heat. Bring to the boil, stirring to dissolve the sugar, and then reduce the heat to very low and let the ketchup bubble away gently for approx. 1 hour, stirring frequently so it doesn't catch on the bottom of the pan. The sauce should reduce in this time by approx. half to leave a bright red, thick velvety sauce. Taste and add more salt or sugar if you feel it needs it. Pour into warm, sterilized bottles and seal immediately. (If you want to keep the ketchup longer than 3 months, it is safest to waterbath the warm bottles for 10 minutes at this stage, see pages 206–7.) Alternatively, store in a dark, cool place for up to 3 months. Once open, store in the refrigerator and consume within a month.

SUGAR

Afternoon tea may be more of a chic treat these days than a regular meal for most families, but that hasn't stemmed our love of jams, particularly homemade. And breakfast just isn't right without marmalade – I have even got Giancarlo eating it on toast before he goes to work after years of skipping the first meal of the day. And, of course, there are so many other things you can do with fruit and sugar, from making cordials and syrups to sauces. Our favourite quick dessert is homemade Greek-style yogurt layered up with raspberry sauce and sliced bananas: simple and utterly delicious.

According to Sue Shephard's brilliant and fascinating book, *Pickled, Potted and Canned*: 'the earliest kind of jam-making dates back to pre-Roman times when fruit pulp was mixed with honey and spices and dried in the sun'. The Greeks followed suit in the first century AD by stuffing peeled quinces into jars filled with honey. After a year they became soft and the resulting treat was known as *melomeli*. Many centuries later this transformed into *marmelada*, a quince preserve made by the Portuguese with sugar and flavoured with rosewater. In the 16th century, wooden boxes of *marmelada* were transported to England where the locals reproduced the idea, using other fruits such as damsons, plums and pears. Eventually, oranges became the main fruit of choice, and the name of the preserve became marmalade.

It wasn't until the 17th and 18th centuries that people started to make preserves on a larger scale, as sugar became available and affordable to a wide population.

* JAM

The word 'jam' appeared in a cookbook by Mrs Eales in 1718 in which she described apricot, raspberry and cherry jams. *The Oxford English Dictionary* suggests that the word may have come from the process of jamming – i.e. bruising or crushing fruit. It also suggests that it may have derived from the French *j'aime*, meaning 'I love', which is what might have been said about this delicious substance! At some point in Britain, the division was made between preserves made with citrus (marmalade) and other fruit/sugar concoctions (jam) – whereas the rest of continental Europe tend to retain one term for all sweet preserves, for example *mermelada* in Spain, confiture in France and *marmellata* in Italy.

In 1929 the Agriculture and Food Research Centre produced a book called *Home Preservation of Fruit and Vegetables*. This was based on a study of sugar-based preserves conducted by a research centre in Bristol. The book is currently out of print (the 14th edition was printed in 1989), although it can be found in second-hand bookshops and online, however it is still regarded as a bible of preserving fruit and vegetables today. It was the AFRC that came up with the 60/40 per cent ratio of sugar to fruit that is necessary to keep jam out of the refrigerator. Today, by law, 'jams' must contain 60 per cent sugar (including natural fruit sugars of up to 5 per cent) although this should be about to change to 50 per cent sugar to allow makers of lower sugar jams to call their product a 'jam' instead of a 'spread'.

HOW JAM WORKS

The idea of jam-making is to stop the natural decay of fruit due to micro-organisms, so that you can enjoy it for months ahead. To find out more about the science behind the process and how to avoid problems, please read the information below.

Here is the process in a nutshell:
First, you cook the fruit. During this time, moisture is evaporated away in the perfumed clouds of steam that are produced, concentrating sugar levels. The high concentration of sugar that results, along with the acid from the fruit, creates an environment that is inhospitable to bacteria. Next, the jam is boiled, destroying any micro-organisms. Finally, it is bottled in sterilized airtight jars; the vacuum prevents the regrowth of bacteria and yeasts.

CALCULATING THE RATIO OF FRUIT TO SUGAR

Experimenting or playing with fruit and sugar is fun, simple and jolly tasty. If you take fruit and start mixing it little by little with sugar, you will go through many stages and create many delicious combinations – from simple sweetened fruit to fruit coulis and low-sugar jams. However, until you reach a ratio of 60 per cent sugar to 40 per cent fruit, the sugar is simply acting as a sweetener and flavour enhancer, not a preservative. Since bacteria find it hard to flourish in an environment that is this high in sugar and acid, preserves made with at least 60 per cent sugar can be bottled and left out of the refrigerator. Typically jams are made with equal or near equal quantities of sugar and fruit; after boiling the sugar levels increase as the moisture is evaporated off so that they end up closer to 60 per cent. This includes an amount of fructose, the natural sugar from the fruit.

LOW-SUGAR JAMS

Of course, if you want to increase the ratio of fruit to sugar that is fine, it's just that you will have to store your produce in the refrigerator. This applies to low-sugar jams, which should either be made in small batches and kept in the refrigerator or freezer, or heat-treated after bottling (see page 43) to extend their shelf-life. For further low-sugar recipes, see www.thegoodkitchentable.com.

TIPS ON JAM-MAKING

Once you start making preserves, it is more than likely that you will find yourself hooked. Of course, most of us make jam for our own enjoyment and we are not too fussed about winning competitions, but if you want to take your jam-making to the next level here are some tips from jam-making expert Vivien Lloyd, who teaches jam judges what to look out for when judging for the Women's Institute:

1) CHOOSE A GOOD RECIPE. According to Vivien Lloyd, many beginners win prizes with a good recipe while many experienced jam-makers fail to succeed with a bad one.

2) COOKING THE FRUIT. This should be done over a gentle heat to drive off water before adding the sugar. Cooking times vary between 10 minutes for raspberries to up to 2 hours for oranges.

3) ACHIEVING A GOOD SET. The point at which you add the sugar to form a gel is key in jam-making. For best results, the sugar should be added after the fruit has been cooked thoroughly to avoid toughening it. Keep the heat low to begin with, stirring to dissolve the sugar. Only once the sugar has completely dissolved should you increase the heat to a rolling boil. As a rule of thumb, boil the fruit and sugar together for as little time as possible to discourage any caramelization of the sugar that could darken the jam – Vivien suggests 5–7 minutes. Obviously large quantities will take longer to reach setting point, however Vivien suggests making jam in small batches so you reach setting point more quickly, in a matter of minutes, rather than more slowly. Jams that are brought to setting point quickly usually result in a better flavour and colour. Jams that are boiled for over 10 minutes will generally be darker as the sugar will start to caramelize.

JAM JARS AND LIDS

Most of the time it is fine to reuse old jam jars as long as they are washed thoroughly and sterilized before use (see page 10). Providing the lids are in perfect condition, all you need to do is sterilize them first by boiling them for 10 minutes. If your lids are rusty or you have lost them, you can always seal your jars with cellophane lids. If using cellophane lids, make sure you cover the surface of the jam first with wax paper, wax-side down. To create a good seal, wet one side of the cellophane only and put it on top of the jar, wet-side up. Secure tightly with elastic bands or ribbon.

The only time I wouldn't recommend recycling jam jars is if you are planning to waterbath your produce after bottling to extend its shelf-life, since most jam jars don't have thick enough glass to withstand the vigours of heat-processing. If you want to waterbath, buy Kilner jars (or similar brands) that come with two-part lids with a separate metal disc that you replace each time. This is held in place with a screw band that is fitted after the disc has formed a good seal. For more information on waterbathing, see pages 206–7.

PERFECT PRODUCE

As with all forms of preservation, choose fruit and vegetables in tip-top condition, as bruised and insect-damaged foods are more likely to harbour spoilers. For best results, choose ripe (but not overripe) fruit, since unripe fruit will affect the sugar levels of your finished product. Ideally fruit should be processed as quickly as possible after picking.

ACIDITY

Acid helps bring out the pectin in fruits, which is needed to achieve a good set. Most fruits are naturally high in acid, however those that are not can be helped along by adding lemon juice or citric acid. Recipes for strawberry preserve, for example, always contain added lemon juice because strawberries are low in acid. In order to extract as much pectin as possible, make sure you add the lemon juice or acid at the start of the recipe while the fruit is cooking, before you put in the sugar. This should speed up the setting process, meaning the jam sets as quickly as possible, so that you avoid the caramelization and subsequent darkening of the sugar that occurs with excessive boiling. As a rule of thumb, allow 3 per cent lemon juice to your weight of low-acid fruit.

PECTIN

Pectin is needed to make jam, jellies and marmalade set. It occurs naturally in fruit and is released during cooking. Pectin levels are high in underripe fruit as well as specific types, such as apple, citrus fruit, quince and damsons, which are all quite sour to the taste, as they are all high in acid too. These fruits have no problem setting and are therefore good to mix with low-pectin or low-acid fruits or they can be made into stock to add to your jam at a later stage.

We discovered in Pam Corbin's book, *Preserves*, that there is less pectin in the pips of fruit than in the pith and peel. Many recipes tell you to collect the pips

of the fruit when making marmalade to put into a bag and boil up with the fruit, while Pam suggests you discard them. We put this to the test and couldn't see any difference between the batch of marmalade with pips in and the one without. However the choice is yours.

THE PECTIN TEST

To determine the amount of pectin in your fruit, remove 1 teaspoon of the cooked juice only (with no seeds or fruit pieces) from the simmered fruit and put into a small jar or ramekin. Add 1 tablespoon of methylated spirits and swirl them both together.

If the mixture comes together into a jellified lump, the juice is high in pectin; if it forms small clumps, the juice has medium levels of pectin; if it forms tiny lumps or no lumps at all, your fruit is low in pectin.

MAKING YOUR OWN PECTIN STOCK

Homemade pectin stock is very easy to make and useful for adding to low-pectin fruits such as strawberries, pineapple and passion fruit. It is made from the juice extracted from high-pectin fruits such as apples, crab apples, gooseberries and redcurrants. You can use commercial liquid pectin instead, but we prefer not to because it contains sulphur dioxide.

HIGH   *******
HIGH–MEDIUM *****
MEDIUM   ***
LOW   *

FRUIT	PECTIN	ACID
Apples (cooking)	*******	*******
Apples (dessert)	***	*
Apricots	***	*
Blackberries (early)	***	*
Blackberries (late)	*	*
Blackcurrants	*******	*******
Cherries (dessert)	*	*
Cherries (sour)	***	*******
Cherries (sweet)	*	*
Citrus fruits	*****	*****
Crab apples	*******	*******
Cranberries (ripe)	*******	***
Currants (red, black and white)	*******	*******
Damsons	*******	*******
Elderberries	*	*
Figs	*	*
Gooseberries	*******	*******
Grapes (unripe)	***	***
Greengages	***	***
Loganberries	***	*******
Nectarines	*	*
Peaches	*	*
Pears	*	*
Plums (sweet)	***	***
Plums (sour)	*******	*******
Quince	*******	*
Raspberries (ripe)	***	***
Raspberries (unripe)	***	*
Rhubarb	*	*
Sloes	***	*******
Strawberries	*	*

HOMEMADE PECTIN STOCK

This is made in the same way as fruit jelly and strained afterwards to obtain a stock. Apples and crab apples make a slightly murky stock. Redcurrants leave a clear stock. To calculate the amount needed, allow 150ml (¼ pint) pectin stock for every 500g (1lb 2oz) low-pectin fruit.

- 1kg (2lb 4oz) of each the following or a mixture of cooking or crab apples, gooseberries and redcurrants
- 1–1.5 litres (1¾–2½ pints) water (enough to cover the fruit)

> Chop the fruit into bite-sized pieces (including the peel and core, but discarding the stems). Put in a saucepan and cover with the water. Put a lid on the pan and bring to the boil, then simmer until the fruit is really soft and pulpy, up to 1 hour.

> Transfer the pulp to a jelly bag and set aside to hang for at least 5 hours (preferably overnight), covering with a tea towel to keep out fruit flies. The following day, measure out the clear juice (your pectin stock) and use straight away, or freeze in small amounts, allowing 100ml (3½fl oz) pectin stock per 500g (1lb 2oz) low-pectin fruit used in the recipe.

SUGAR

We prefer our cooking to be as natural as possible, therefore we use pure sugar and fruit in most of the recipes. We prefer to use granulated cane sugar for jam-making.

Preserving sugars, in our opinion, are an unnecessary expense and our recipes are not designed to use them. Jam sugar has added pectin, which gives the jam an uncharacteristically bright colour and also changes the flavour – the resulting jam often doesn't have a cooked fruit flavour. Do use it, but be aware that it can make the jam too firm in consistency and it does leave an aftertaste.

Often the sugar is warmed beforehand in an oven: this is useful because it means the sugar will dissolve more quickly and come to boil rapidly. It is vital that the sugar is completely dissolved before you bring your jam to the boil or it could crystallize.

SETTING POINTS

Three things are needed to achieve a good set: pectin, sugar and acid. Setting point is reached after the rolling boil stage – this is when the heat is high and the bubbles are foamy, plentiful and cover the surface. If you put a spoon through the surface, the bubbles don't stop.

When checking for a set, always remove the jam from the heat as those vital few minutes may result in overcooked jam. If necessary, you can always put the jam back on the heat again if you are not there yet. You can repeat this process until you are confident you have reached setting point.

Never continue with the rolling boil for more than 15 minutes – if you reach 10 minutes and you haven't achieved a set, there is probably something wrong with your ingredients. Overboiling ruins the fresh flavour of most jams and also caramelizes the sugar, resulting in a darker jam with a bitter taste. A runny jam can always be used as a sauce for ice cream or yogurt.

TESTING FOR A SET

There are three ways of checking for a set: the flake test, the cold saucer test and the temperature test. In my opinion, the latter is the least reliable method, although it is helpful as a guide alongside the other methods.

THE FLAKE TEST I tend to use this method. Dip a wooden spoon into the jam and then hold it above the surface. Twist it three times and watch the drops. Do they fall frequently as individual drops or do they slowly come together into one large, long drip? If the latter is the case, your jam will set.

THE COLD SAUCER TEST Put a saucer or small plate into the freezer until chilled. When you feel you are close to setting point, drip a few drops of jam onto the cold saucer. Return it to the freezer and wait a couple of minutes. Remove the plate from the freezer and push your finger across the surface. If wrinkles form, your jam has reached setting point.

THE TEMPERATURE TEST Take the temperature of your jam using a digital thermometer. Supposedly, if it reads 104.5°C (220°F) your jam will set, however I have read this temperature in the past in a very liquid-looking jam and found that it didn't set. Saying that, it certainly shouldn't be lower than this temperature, so use this method as a guide only and double-check using the flake or cold saucer method.

WHEN TO BOTTLE AND WHEN TO WATERBATH?

Waterbathing is a form of heat-processing that is carried out after bottling to extend the shelf-life of certain preserves, especially ones that are low in sugar (see page 39). If you follow the 60/40 rule (that is, 60 per cent sugar to 40 per cent fruit), there is no need to waterbath jam after bottling. The only time you need to waterbath is if you reduce the quantity of sugar to under 60 per cent and plan to store your produce outside of the refrigerator.

BOTTLING

Have your jars, lids and jam funnel sterilized and hot before you start to make jam (see page 10). When setting point is reached (see above) it is time to bottle your jam.

> Have a ladle in the jam for the last few minutes so that it sterilizes in the jam. Some jams need to be left to settle before bottling – if this is the case, we have stated it in the recipe.
> Remove any scum before bottling. I find the best method is to allow the jam to settle in the pan for 5 minutes to form a skin, and then simply scrape it back with a sterilized spoon and discard.
> Remove the jam from the heat and take out your first warmed jar, put the funnel into the jar and ladle out the jam into the jar. Some people prefer to use a jug for this, in which case you need to sterilize that in the oven too and hold it firmly with a cloth. Fill to the neck of the jar and put on the lid tightly.
> Leave the jars to cool. Check the seals are depressed and tighten the lids if necessary.

JAM-MAKING EQUIPMENT

I always find that jam-making is much more fun if I have the right tools. All of the following can be bought from cook shops or online (see page 242–3):

PRESERVING OR MASLIN PAN – this is essential for preserving because it has a heavy base that protects the jam from burning. A lid is a good idea to bring the fruit up to the boil quickly (although this should be removed once the jam comes to the boil).

LONG WOODEN SPOON – keep a long wooden spoon specially for jam-making and a separate one for chutneys and pickles. My favourite spoon has a hook halfway down the handle to stop it falling into the pan.

JAM FUNNEL – this avoids lots of mess, enabling you to fill your jars quickly without the jam going everywhere.

SUGAR THERMOMETER – this has a higher range than most thermometers, enabling you to check the temperature of your jam as setting point is reached.

LADLE – this is useful for spooning your jam into the jars.

WIDE, SILICONE-TIPPED TONGS – for gripping the jars from the oven.

MAGNETIC PRONG – to pick up lids.

WOODEN STICK – for prodding fruit into jars and releasing air bubbles.

HEATPROOF GLOVE (OR WELL-FITTING OVEN GLOVE) – to manoeuvre hot jars, funnels and lids into position.

JAM-MAKING TIPS

Fruit – pick fruit when the weather is dry; avoid using wet fruit or you will dilute your jam.

Mrs Wishdish (see page 27) **warms lemons** in the microwave for 1 minute on high to make them juicier and easier to squeeze.

Heat the fruit first before adding the sugar (unless it has been pre-mixed with the sugar the night before). The less you heat the sugar, the less likely you are to get caramelization – when the sugar darkens in colour.

When the **colour** of your bubbling jam darkens, it indicates the sugar is starting to caramelize.

Add alcohol later to a jam or marmalade so that you do not get rid of the flavour and alcohol.

Remove the scum at the end by pushing it to one side and discarding it; there is no need to use butter to disperse it.

Put newspaper down when decanting the jam from pan to pot to absorb sticky splashes.

Use a jam funnel to avoid wastage.

Keep jam in a cool, dark cupboard for up to a year unless we have specified otherwise in the recipe.

STRAWBERRY AND WHITE PEACH JAM

White peaches come into season at the same time as strawberries. Both flavours shine through equally in this jam, which is lovely on fresh scones with cream. As both fruits are low in pectin it is necessary to add pectin stock to achieve a good set. Ideally the pectin stock should be made of redcurrants as it will be clear and pink in colour. Apple pectin stock will cloud the preserve but taste just as good.

MAKES APPROX. 1.25KG (2LB 12OZ)

- 900g (2lb) granulated cane sugar
- 500g (1lb 2oz) strawberries, hulled and halved if small, or quartered if large
- 500g (1lb 2oz) white peaches or nectarines, peeled, stoned and cut into pieces the same size as the strawberries
- 300ml (½ pint) pectin stock (see page 42)
- juice of 2 lemons

> Preheat the oven to 140°C/275°F/ gas 1. Line a roasting tray with baking parchment, pour in the sugar and put into the oven to warm for 20 minutes. Put the fruit in a large preserving pan with the pectin stock and lemon juice. Simmer the mixture over a low-medium heat to soften the fruit, approx. 15 minutes. Pour in the sugar and stir until dissolved. Increase the heat and bring to a rolling boil. Boil hard until setting point is reached (see pages 42–3). Bottle into warm, sterilized jars (see page 43) and keep in a cool, dark place for up to a year.

VARIATIONS

STRAWBERRY AND RED PLUM JAM

Hard red plums have good acidity and pectin levels, so they help the strawberries to set and mean that you won't need the pectin stock.

MAKES APPROX. 700G (1LB 9OZ)

- 500g (1lb 2oz) strawberries, hulled and halved if small, or quartered if large
- 400g (14oz) golden caster sugar
- 6 small, round, hard red plums, quartered and stoned
- juice of 1 lemon

> Follow the method for the Strawberry and White Peach Jam (see left), swapping the white peaches for plums.

STRAWBERRY, RED PLUM AND LIME JAM

Make as for Strawberry and Red Plum Jam (above), omitting the lemon juice and replacing it with the juice of 2 limes and the zest of 1 lime.

RASPBERRY AND VANILLA JAM

This recipe is from Vivien Lloyd, a cookery writer and WI judge who also teaches the judges. Giancarlo and I were lucky enough to be taught by her and loved this classic recipe with Vivien's addition of vanilla. She uses ndali vanilla, which comes from Uganda and is organic and ethically farmed. The pods are fat and oily and full of seeds, hence the amazing flavour. When we make this jam the house fills with the wonderful aroma of comfort food and summer scents. Vivien prefers to use the later voluptuous autumn raspberries, which are packed with flavour. If using frozen fruit, add 10 per cent more fruit. Raspberries are medium-pectin and therefore do not need lemon juice, however it is a good idea to do a pectin test

to make sure (see page 40). If the pectin is weak, you can add a little pectin stock to compensate (see page 42).

MAKES APPROX. 1.4KG (3LB 3OZ)

- 1kg (2lb 4oz) raspberries
- 1 vanilla pod or 1 teaspoon organic vanilla powder or extract
- 1kg (2lb 4oz) granulated cane sugar

> Put the raspberries in a large, heavy-based saucepan. Split the vanilla pod, scrape out all of the seeds and add them to the pan. Cut the pod into four and add to the pan (or add the vanilla powder or extract). Simmer the fruit and vanilla gently for approx. 10 minutes. Meanwhile, warm the sugar in an oven at 140°C/275°F/gas 1.
> If using a vanilla pod, remove the pieces from the pan. Add the warmed sugar to the pan and stir until it has dissolved. Bring the jam to a rolling boil and boil hard until setting point is reached (see pages 42–3).
> Start testing for a set after 4 minutes using the flake, cold saucer or thermometer test (see pages 42–3). As soon as setting point is reached, remove the pan from the heat and leave it to stand for a few minutes. Push any scum from the surface of the pan to the side and remove it with a metal spoon.
> Gently stir the jam and pour it into warm, sterilized jars, up to the brim. Seal the jars immediately either with new twist-top lids or waxed discs and cellophane covers secured with rubber bands. Store in a cool, dark place for up to a year.

RHUBARB AND GINGER JAM

This jam is often made with stem ginger, however we have used grated fresh ginger to give a pleasant kick of heat.

MAKES APPROX. 500G (1LB 2OZ)

- 450g (1lb) rhubarb, roughly chopped into 2cm (¾in) lengths
- 1 heaped tablespoon finely grated fresh ginger
- 350g (12oz) granulated cane sugar
- juice of 1 lemon

> Follow the instructions for Strawberry and White Peach Jam (see page 44), including the ginger with the macerated fruit.

HEDGEROW JAM

A walk in the country is never the same once you start picking wild berries. The finished product is different every time we make hedgerow jam, but that is part of the fun. As long as you include one-third apples in your mix you will have enough pectin for a set. Bump up your load of wild berries with bought berries such as redcurrants and raspberries. The spices make this great on toast or with goat's cheese, lamb and game.

MAKES 900G (2LB)

- 350g (12oz) apples, peeled, cored and roughly chopped
- 650g (1lb 7oz) hedgerow fruit, such as haws, hips, blackberries, elderberries
- 500ml (18fl oz) water
- 700g (1lb 9oz) granulated cane sugar
- 1 heaped teaspoon black peppercorns, lightly crushed
- 1 heaped teaspoon juniper berries, lightly crushed
- 200ml (7fl oz) red wine

> Put the apples, haws and hips into a large, heavy-based saucepan and pour over the water. (If you don't want blackberry pips in your finished jam, you can put in the blackberries now too.) Bring to the boil and simmer until the fruit is tender, approx. 10–20 minutes. Pass through a food mill or sieve to remove the skins and large pips. Put the strained fruit back into the pan along with the rest of the fruit. Add the sugar and stir over a low heat to dissolve. Put the peppercorns and juniper berries into a spice bag, fasten with string and drop into the pan, securing it to the handle. Add the wine and bring to the boil. Boil hard until setting point is reached (see pages 42–3). Bottle into warm, sterilized jars (see page 43). Store in a cool, dark place for up to a year.

ITALIAN DAMSON OR PLUM JAM

Stefano Borella is the head teacher at our cookery school, La Cucina Caldesi. His grandmother lived on a farm in the hills near Parma, northern Italy. Every year she and the family collected *susine*, a type of small, dark red plum to make *marmellata di susine*, a treacly black jam. She would cook the jam for ages, ignoring any worries about caramelization of the sugar, as that was the way she liked it. Giancarlo's family in Tuscany did the same and the result was eaten in a jam tart or on bread. There is a bittersweet quality to this jam that we love.

MAKES APPROX. 1.5KG (3LB 5OZ)

- 1.75kg (4lb) damsons or plums
- 1kg (2lb 4oz) granulated cane sugar

> Wash and pick over the plums and put them into a pan with the sugar. Put over a medium heat and stir until the water comes out of the fruit. Reduce the heat

to a mere simmer and continue to cook, stirring occasionally, for 2 hours. Scoop out the stones with a slotted spoon when they pop up to the surface. Keep cooking until the jam is thick, dark and firm, by which time it should set easily when you test it (see pages 42–3). If you want a smooth finish, put the jam through a food mill before bottling into warm, sterilized jars (see page 43). Store in a cool, dark place for up to a year.

CLAUDIA'S TOMATO AND APPLE JAM

This is a Portuguese recipe from Claudia Moreira. Sometimes orange peel is included as a flavouring, however Claudia and her partner Gregorio prefer it plain to enjoy with Brie or Robiola.

MAKES APPROX. 750ML–1 LITRE (1⅓–1¾ PINTS)

- 1kg (2lb 4oz) round, ripe, flavourful tomatoes
- 2 cooking apples, peeled, cored and roughly chopped
- 750g (1lb 10oz) golden caster sugar

> First, prepare the tomatoes. Make a cross in the bottom of each one and remove the stalk from the other end. Plunge into boiling water for 20–30 seconds, remove with a slotted spoon and immerse immediately into cold water. Peel off the skins, cut each tomato into quarters and scoop out the seeds with a teaspoon or knife.
> Put the tomatoes and apples into a blender and whizz until smooth. Transfer the mixture into a large, heavy-based saucepan and bring to the boil. Simmer until the mixture has reduced by one-third, approx. 45 minutes depending on

the water content of the fruit. Add the sugar, stir over a low heat to dissolve and bring to a rolling boil. Cook until setting point is reached (see pages 42–3). Bottle into warm, sterilized jars (see page 43) and keep in a cool, dark place for up to a year.

LIVIA'S OVEN-BAKED QUINCE JAM

I adore the floral perfume of quinces and this baked jam really concentrates their flavour. It is normally cooked to a soft set and used as a jam for bread or for filling jam tarts. Our friend Livia Cecuzzi runs a smallholding in Tuscany and makes this jam every year. Nello, her husband, uses a wood-burning oven for cooking and often makes the jam in it. He likes the fact that when it is cooked in the oven Livia doesn't ask him to stir it constantly, which he ends up having to do if she makes it on the hob. It won't catch on the bottom if it is made in the oven, but it may get a little discoloured on the top if you don't stir it occasionally.

MAKES APPROX. 1KG (2LB 4OZ)

- 2 lemons
- 1.2kg (1lb 10oz) quinces
- 1 litre (1¾ pints) water
- 800g (1lb 12oz) caster sugar
- 500ml (18fl oz) white wine

> Cut the lemons in half and squeeze out the juice; set the juice aside for later. Peel the quinces and cut them into quarters. Remove the cores with a sharp knife and cut the flesh into small pieces, approx. 2cm (¾in) in size. To stop the pieces discolouring, place them in a bowl of cold water with the lemon halves.
> HOB METHOD Drain the quinces, discarding the lemon halves and water. Put them in a large, heavy-based saucepan with 1 litre (1¾ pints) fresh water, the reserved lemon

>>>

juice and the rest of the ingredients. Bring to the boil, reduce the heat to medium and cook for 1 hour, stirring every now and again, until the fruit is really tender. Remove the pan from the heat and set aside to cool slightly before puréeing with a stick blender (being careful not to splash yourself). Return the pan to the heat and simmer until setting point is reached (see pages 42–3), approx. 30 minutes. Bottle into warm, sterilized jars (see page 43). Store in a cool, dark place for up to a year.

> OVEN METHOD Preheat the oven to 200°C/400°F/gas 6. Drain the quinces, discarding the lemon halves and water. Place them in a large, ovenproof dish with 1 litre (1¾ pints) fresh water, the reserved lemon juice and the rest of the ingredients. Bake in the oven for 1 hour, stirring occasionally to stop the fruit from sticking. Remove the quinces from the oven and purée to a smooth paste in a food processor or with a stick blender. Return to the oven or tip the mixture into a saucepan and cook until setting point is reached (see pages 42–3). Bottle and keep as above.

GREENGAGE AND VANILLA JAM

As the greengage season is fairly short, I make the most of them by preserving their wonderful flavour and colour in jam.

MAKES APPROX. 1.5KG (3LB 5OZ)

- 1kg (2lb 4oz) golden caster sugar
- 1kg (2lb 4oz) ripe (but not soft) greengages
- 100ml (3½fl oz) water
- juice of 1 lemon
- ½ organic vanilla pod or a few drops of vanilla extract

> Preheat the oven to 140°C/275°F/gas 1. Line a roasting tray with baking parchment, pour in the sugar and put into the oven to warm for 20 minutes.

> Meanwhile, halve the greengages, discard the stones, and put into a preserving pan with the water, lemon juice and vanilla. Bring to the boil, stirring, and then reduce the heat to a simmer. Simmer until the fruit is tender and soft, approx. 10–15 minutes. Pour in the warmed sugar and stir over a low heat to dissolve. Bring the jam to a rolling boil and boil hard until setting point is reached (see pages 42–3). Leave to stand for 5 minutes, and then scrape off the scum with a sterile spoon and remove the vanilla pod. Bottle into warm, sterilized jars (see page 43). Store in a cool, dark place for up to a year.

PINEAPPLE AND PASSION FRUIT JAM

This rich, bright yellow jam was shown to us in Sri Lanka during our visit there. Mrs Wimalarathne, an energetic teacher in her late seventies, worked furiously to show me how to make this delicious, exotic jam. It is not only glorious on scones, but also it is wonderful scooped onto meringues with soft whipped cream for a quick dessert. Pineapple and passion fruit have very little pectin in them, so it is necessary to add some here. We have given the quantities for homemade pectin stock, however you could use liquid or powdered pectin and follow the manufacturer's instructions instead.

MAKES 1.5 LITRES (2¾ PINTS)

- 2 medium pineapples
- 6 passion fruit
- approx. 1–1.25kg (2lb 4oz–2lb 12oz) granulated cane sugar
- juice of 1 lemon

- approx. 300–400ml (½ pint–14fl oz) pectin stock (see page 42)

> Peel the pineapples and cut out any 'eyes' so there are no dark areas. Discard the hard cores and chop the flesh into approx. 1cm (½in) cubes. This can be done in a food processor. Scoop out the flesh and seeds from the passion fruit and put with the chopped pineapple in a bowl. Weigh the fruit to calculate the correct amount of sugar, allowing equal quantities of sugar to fruit. Also calculate the amount of pectin stock, allowing 150ml (¼ pint) pectin stock per 500ml (18fl oz) pulp.

> Put the sugar in an ovenproof dish and warm in a low oven (140°C/275°F/gas 1) while you cook the fruit.

> Put the fruit in a large preserving pan with the lemon juice and pectin stock. Cook over a medium heat for approx. 15–20 minutes until the fruit is just soft. Add the warmed sugar, stirring until it dissolves. Bring the mixture to a rolling boil and boil hard until setting point is reached, approx. 10–15 minutes (see pages 42–3). Bottle into warm, sterilized jars (see page 43). Store in a cool, dark place and use within a year.

* CONSERVES

A conserve has whole or large pieces of fruit suspended in a thick syrup. Unlike most jams,

conserves should be allowed to rest and settle for up to 10 minutes before bottling; this ensures an even dispersion of fruit in the jar. Usually when making a conserve, the fruit is layered with the sugar and lemon juice in a bowl and left to macerate in the refrigerator overnight. This helps to firm up the fruit and draws out some of the liquid and pectin. However, with strawberries I don't find the sugary juices helpful, so I leave out that stage. Any alcohol should be added after boiling and before bottling.

STRAWBERRY CONSERVE

Small whole strawberries picked during summer burst in your mouth when you eat them. Strawberries are low in pectin, so this is a tricky preserve to set. We have added homemade pectin stock to counteract this.

MAKES APPROX. 1.5KG (3LB 5OZ)

- 1kg (2lb 4oz) granulated cane sugar
- 1kg (2lb 4oz) strawberries, stalks removed
- 300ml (½ pint) pectin stock (see page 42)
- juice of ½ lemon

> Preheat the oven to 140°C/275°F/gas 1. Line a roasting tray with baking parchment, pour in the sugar and put into the oven to warm for 20 minutes.

> If the strawberries are large, cut them in half, otherwise leave them whole.

> Put the fruit, pectin stock and lemon juice into a preserving pan and slowly bring to the boil. Cook until just tender. Reduce the heat and add the warmed sugar. Stir to dissolve. Bring to a rolling boil and cook until setting point is reached (see pages 42–3). Remove from the heat and allow the jam to settle for 10 minutes before bottling into warm, sterilized jars (see page 43). Store in a cool, dark place for up to a year.

APRICOT CONSERVE

This reminds me of my favourite French jam. I like this jam to be soft set with large pieces of fruit; ideal for eating with warm croissants and huge cups of café au lait. Peeling away the skins is a sticky job so do omit this stage if you don't mind leaving them on.

MAKES APPROX. 850G (1LB 14OZ)

- 1kg (2lb 4oz) apricots
- 1kg (2lb 4oz) granulated cane sugar
- juice of 1 lemon

> Cut the fruit into quarters and put the stones to one side. Layer the apricots with the sugar and lemon juice in a bowl, cover with a plate and set aside to macerate in the refrigerator for 2 hours.
> Meanwhile, crack the stones inside a folded tea towel using a meat mallet or small saucepan. This will release the almondy kernels inside. Gather them into a muslin bag and put this with the apricots. Discard the shells.
> Tip the macerated fruit mixture into a large preserving pan, along with the muslin bag. Cook over a medium heat until the sugar dissolves, stirring frequently but gently so as not to break up the fruit. Once the sugar has dissolved completely, bring the conserve to boil. Remove from the heat and leave to cool. Pour through a sieve, reserving the liquor for later.
> Peel the skins off the apricots. Tip the fruit and liquor back into the pan and boil hard until setting point is reached (see pages 42–3). Discard the muslin bag and allow the conserve to settle for 10 minutes before bottling into warm, sterilized jars (see page 43). Store in a cool, dark place for up to a year.

DELUXE APRICOT AND ALMOND CONSERVE

To make a deluxe version, add 75g (2½oz) shelled almonds to the pan and 75ml (2½fl oz) brandy after setting point is reached. Stir through to disperse.

FIG AND MUSCAT CONSERVE

This conserve is perfect for eating with cheese or cold ham. It also makes a great canapé, generously spread onto hot toast and topped with soft goat's cheese.

MAKES APPROX. 1.2KG (2LB 10OZ)

- 1kg (2lb 4oz) figs, peeled and quartered, stems removed
- 650g (1lb 7oz) golden granulated or caster sugar
- 4 cloves
- 5cm (2in) cinnamon stick
- sprig of thyme
- 300ml (½ pint) pectin stock (see page 42)
- 375ml (13fl oz) sweet wine, such as muscat, Sauternes or port
- 100g (3½oz) toasted walnuts (optional)

> Put the figs and sugar in a bowl, cover with a plate and set aside to macerate in the refrigerator for a minimum of 5 hours (preferably overnight). Meanwhile, put the cloves, cinnamon and thyme together in a muslin bag.
> Tip the macerated fruit mixture into a large preserving pan, put in the spice bag and the pectin stock and stir over a medium heat until the sugar dissolves. Add the wine and bring to a rolling boil and boil hard until setting point is reached (see pages 42–3). Discard the muslin bag and stir in the walnuts, if using. Remove from the heat and allow the conserve to settle for 10 minutes before bottling into warm, sterilized jars (see page 43). Store in a cool, dark place for up to a year.

MARMALADE

There are two methods for making marmalade – the first involves cooking the whole fruits in water first and then cutting up the tender flesh to cook with sugar and the second involves slicing the raw fruit and cooking it with sugar in a similar way to jam. Both methods work well, however we find the first method results in a softer texture and a better set as the longer cooking time releases more pectin and acid. We love to make marmalade with Seville oranges. Their joyous fragrance is like no other fruit and the bittersweet flesh means they make perfectly balanced marmalade. Besides, the smell of sweet oranges cooking in midwinter cheers up a cold household no end. We like to look for organic fruit.

MRS BUN'S MARMALADE

Our friend Paul Wilson makes his own sourdough and we are frequently swapping tips. On one of our visits to see his bread he gave us some to try with his homemade marmalade. It was divine and so, of course, we asked him to show us how he made it. This marmalade is one he has been making for years and it was shown to him by his grandmother, affectionately known as Mrs Bun.

Like Mrs Bun, we prefer thick-cut marmalade, so to make this version we cut diagonally across each quarter of skin to give long lengths of peel. However, if you prefer, you can cut the peel into very small pieces. Paul got us to pick out the pips – Giancarlo preferred to use the point of the knife to do this and I preferred to use my fingers. Giancarlo didn't agree and proceeded to tell me his way of doing it, so we said we would race the next orange. Paul said this was just what he didn't want... competitive Seville orange-cutting! He said this was why

he preferred to make marmalade alone! (By the way, I won.) Paul also said his mum made a delicious Seville orange sorbet from the oranges so we have included that recipe in Cold (see page 239).

Mrs Bun always warms the sugar so that it dissolves into the fruit and liquid more quickly. Cold sugar brings the temperature right down and for this quantity it takes a long time to get the oranges boiling. As a rough guide, you will need twice the amount of sugar to cooked oranges.

MAKES 3–4KG (6LB 8OZ–8LB 12OZ)

- 1.5kg (3lb 5oz) Seville oranges
- juice of 2 lemons
- approx. 3kg (6lb 8oz) granulated cane sugar

> Scrub the oranges and put them into a preserving pan with the lemon juice. Cover them with cold water and weigh them down with a plate and a weight to keep them submerged, or use a lid. Bring to the boil and simmer for approx. 2 hours or until the skins are soft and tender when poked with a sharp knife or skewer. (This stage can be done the night before and the oranges left to cool overnight.)
> Preheat the oven to 140°C/275°F/gas 1. Remove the oranges from the water one by one and, using a sharp knife, cut them into quarters. Reserve the cooking liquor for later. Separate the skins from the flesh and remove the pips, saving these for later. Cut the skins into thick or fine shreds depending on your preference. I do this by hand, however you can do it in a food processor if you wish. The flesh becomes soft and breaks up but any remaining large pieces should be cut small. Weigh the shredded skin and flesh, along with any juice that came out of the oranges. You will need 2kg (4lb 8oz) sugar and 750ml (1¼

>>>

pints) water to every 1kg (2lb 4oz) fruit. Put the skins, flesh, juice and cooking liquor in a large preserving pan. Put the sugar in an ovenproof dish and warm in the oven for 20–30 minutes.

> Meanwhile, make the pectin stock. Put the reserved pips in a small saucepan with enough water to just cover them and bring to the boil. Simmer for 10 minutes, then strain the liquid into the pan with the oranges.
> Bring the ingredients in the preserving pan to the boil. Add the warmed sugar, ladleful by ladleful, and bring back to the boil. It should dissolve immediately. Skim any scum from the surface. Boil hard until setting point is reached (see pages 42–3). Do not stir or you will only create more bubbles and scum.
> Once your marmalade has reached setting point, remove from the heat and leave it to stand for 10 minutes to allow the fruit to settle. Stir through once to disperse the fruit, and then bottle into warmed, sterilized jars (see page 43).

MERRY MARMALADE

Another of WI jam judge Vivien Lloyd's award-winning marmalades, and too good to miss out. This one is from her excellent book, First Preserves. The colour is vibrant orange with thin-cut skins suspended in a perfect gel. It is 'merry' due to the addition of whisky.

During the 1950s it was fashionable to add alcohol to marmalade. Rum, brandy, Cointreau and even Campari can be added instead of whisky: as a rule of thumb, allow 1 tablespoon of alcohol to each 450ml (16fl oz) jar, stirring it in at the end just before bottling – so you can mix and match as you please. Our favourite is whisky – I like it so much I put 10ml (2 teaspoons) into each jar!

MAKES APPROX. 2.25KG (5LB)

- 675g (1lb 8oz) Seville oranges
- juice of 1 large lemon
- 1.75 litres (3 pints) water
- 1.4kg (3lb 3oz) granulated cane sugar
- alcohol of your choice (optional)

> Cut the oranges in half, squeeze out the juice and combine with the lemon juice and water in a large preserving pan with a lid. Scrape out the inner membranes and pips of the oranges with a small knife; do not remove the bitter pith. Finely chop the inner membranes by hand or use a food processor. Put the chopped membranes, pips and any stray parts of the oranges left on the juicer into a 33cm (13in) muslin square. Tie this up tightly with string and add to the pan, securing it to one of the pan handles.
> Quarter the orange skins, turn them peel-side down and shred them evenly into thin strips with a sharp knife. Add them to the pan. If time allows, cover the pan with a lid and set the fruit aside to soak overnight, which will help soften the peel.
> Bring the lidded pan to the boil, reduce the heat and simmer gently for 2 hours. Meanwhile, warm the sugar in a low oven at 140°C/275°F/gas 1 for 20 minutes. After the marmalade has cooked for 2 hours, remove the muslin bag and squeeze out all the juices into the pan – place it in a sieve and press down hard with a wooden spoon or potato masher to extract all the juices. Check the volume level in the pan – it should have reduced by one-third.
> Add the warmed sugar to the pan and stir over a low heat to dissolve. Bring the pan to a rolling boil and start testing for a set after 5 minutes (see pages 42–3). Once setting point is reached, remove the pan from the heat and set aside to cool for 5 minutes. Remove any scum by pushing

it to the side of the pan with a metal spoon and removing it. Gently stir the marmalade to distribute the peel. Ladle into a jug and pour into warm, sterilized jars or pour directly into the jars using a jam funnel. Add 1 tablespoon of alcohol to each jar and stir in before sealing the jars (see page 43). Store in a cool, dark place for up to a year.

VIVIEN LLOYD'S LEMON AND LIME MARMALADE

We loved the zing of this marmalade as well as the colour. Not only is it zesty enough to grace any breakfast table, but we also find it makes a delicious topping for lemon cheesecake.

MAKES APPROX. 2.25KG (5LB)
- 450g (1lb) limes
- 225g (8oz) lemons
- 1.4kg (3lb 3oz) granulated cane sugar
- 1.75 litres (3 pints) water

> Follow the instructions for Merry Marmalade (see left), using lemons and limes instead of oranges. Shred the lime and lemon skins and set aside to soften in the water and juice for 12 hours before simmering them in water and then boiling with the sugar.

* COMPOTES

A compote is made from whole fruit or pieces of fruit in a sugar syrup. Generally, it is runnier than a conserve or jam, and often it is served with yogurt or poured over ice cream. It can contain nuts and alcohol, and spices are frequently used as flavourings. Compotes were developed in France during the 17th century, when they would have been served in the afternoon with soured cream and biscuits. (A compote is also the name for a long, stemmed dish that holds fruit.) Traditionally compotes used to be very sweet, however as tastes have changed they are more often made with minimal amounts of sugar, meaning they don't last as long and therefore need to be kept in the refrigerator. Because of this they are best made in small amounts. We regularly make them from rhubarb, plums, figs and berries and eat them for breakfast most days with homemade Greek yogurt or porridge.

To turn a compote into a 'fool', a rich and creamy dessert, ripple the compote through softly whipped cream and serve with crumbly shortbread biscuits. My mother's favourite was made with gooseberries. She would add a little grated lemon zest and it was utterly delicious.

FIG AND ORANGE COMPOTE

This is great for breakfast when good figs are in season. In winter, we like it heated for a quick dessert with crème fraîche or whipped cream. If you wish to waterbath the compote use either Kilner or two-part lid jars and do stick to the recipe with the same amount of lemon juice. It is there to increase the level of acidity to make it safe to waterbath.

MAKES APPROX. 500G (1LB 2OZ)
USE EITHER 2 X 250ML (9FL OZ) OR
1 X 500ML (18FL OZ) KILNER JAR OR
TWO-PART LID JARS
- 600g (1lb 5oz) figs (approx. 20 small figs)
- juice of 2 oranges
- 1 tablespoon lemon juice
- 75g (2½oz) granulated cane sugar
- 1 vanilla pod, split

> Trim the hard stalks off the tops of the figs. Peel and cut them into quarters. Remove three long strips of orange zest from the oranges using a vegetable peeler and squeeze out the juice. Put the zest and juice into a saucepan with the figs, sugar and vanilla pod and slowly bring to the boil, stirring to dissolve the sugar. Reduce the heat and stir frequently until the fruit has softened, approx. 10–15 minutes. Spoon into warmed, sterilized jars and seal. Heat-process by waterbathing, according to the instructions on pages 206–7 for 45 minutes for either size of jar and store in a cool, dark place for up to 6 months. (If you choose not to waterbath, store in the refrigerator and consume within 2 weeks.)

VARIATION

RHUBARB AND GINGER COMPOTE

MAKES 600G (1LB 5OZ)

- 500g (1lb 2oz) rhubarb, tough ends removed and cut into 2cm (¾in) lengths
- 1 length of orange zest
- juice of 1 lemon
- 500g (1lb 2oz) soft brown sugar, to taste
- 3cm (1¼in) piece of fresh ginger, grated or stem ginger (see page 63)

> Follow the instructions for the Fig and Orange Compote (see above), using rhubarb instead of figs and flavouring with ginger instead of vanilla.

CRANBERRY SAUCE

My mum always made her cranberry sauce with port and orange. It was rich, sticky and looked just like Christmas, all shiny and red. For this recipe, I followed Glynn Christian's advice and added the sugar after the berries had softened, and I was very pleased with the result.

MAKES 950G–1KG (2LB 2OZ–2LB 4OZ) SAUCE

- 600g (1lb 5oz) fresh cranberries
- 250ml (9fl oz) port or red wine
- thinly sliced zest and juice of 1 orange
- 350g (12oz) dark muscovado sugar

> Combine the cranberries in a medium saucepan with the port and orange zest and juice. Bring to the boil, reduce the heat to a simmer and allow the cranberries to bubble away merrily while you listen to Christmas carols and the skins soften on the fruit and begin to burst, approx. 10–15 minutes. Remove the pan from the heat and add the sugar, stirring to dissolve. If it is very runny, return the pan to the heat and let the sauce boil away rapidly until it thickens to your liking. Allow to cool, then bottle into clean jars and store in the refrigerator for up to 2 weeks.

* JELLIES

Jellies are simple to make. Providing you have the right amount of pectin to set the jelly, you can use a variety of fruits to obtain an array of flavours. Often apples or crab apples are used as a base because they are high in pectin.

TO MAKE A JELLY

Cook the fruit over a low heat with water until it is soft and easily squashed against the side of the pan with a wooden spoon. If there is any resistance, cook a little longer. Seeds, pips and skin can all be left in at this stage. Fruits containing a lot of juice, such as strawberries and blackberries, will need approx. 300ml (½ pint) water per 1kg (2lb 4oz) of fruit. Fruits with less water, such as hard plums and damsons, will need approx. 600ml (20fl oz) water per 1kg (2lb 4oz) of fruit. Harder fruit, such as apples and quinces, simply need to be cooked with just a covering of water (although you can add more if the fruit starts to stick to the bottom of the pan). This initial cooking stage will probably take 30 minutes–1 hour to achieve a soft, wet pulp.

Once the fruit is soft, you need to strain the pulp overnight to remove the pips and skins, etc. You can either use a sterilized sieve lined with two layers of muslin, a clean stocking or a jelly bag suspended over a bowl to catch the drips. I usually set up my muslin or jelly bag and pour through a kettle of boiling water first to sterilize everything before filling it with the fruit pulp.

When the last drip has dropped, do not be tempted to squeeze the bag or you will cloud the jelly. Discard the pulp (or use it to make fruit leather or fruit cheese, see page 112 and pages 57–8) and measure the strained juice to calculate the amount of sugar needed. Traditionally jellies are made with equal parts fruit juice and sugar so for every 100ml (3½fl oz) juice you will need 100g (3½oz) granulated cane sugar (you can use other types of sugar, however they will change the jelly's colour). For a lower-sugar jelly, you can take the ratio down to 75 per cent: for every 100ml (3½fl oz) juice you will need 75g (2½oz) sugar. This may give you a slightly more wobbly jelly.

Pour the juice into a saucepan and bring to the boil, add the sugar and stir to dissolve. Bring the jelly to the boil and boil hard until you achieve a set (see pages 42–3), approx. 10–15 minutes. NOTE: The less you boil the sugar, the lighter in colour your jelly will be; if you boil your jelly long and hard, the sugars will start to caramelize and the jelly could take on a bitter taste. Skim the jelly with a spoon, immediately pour into warm,

sterilized containers and seal (see page 43). Leave to cool and set.

JELLY BAGS

Jelly bags can be bought easily and inexpensively online or from kitchen shops. However, to make your own you simply need a couple of squares of muslin tied over an upturned chair or stool, or use an old but clean pillowcase. Have a bowl ready under your jelly bag to catch the drips. Make sure that you cover the pulp and bag with another cloth to protect it from fruit flies.

HEDGEROW AND PORT JELLY

Blackberries are ideal for making into jelly as the straining process removes all of the annoying pips. For this jelly, you can either use just blackberries or mix them with other foraged fruits from the list below. Crab apples are included to give the necessary pectin for a set. I love this jelly with duck or venison and also use it for sweetening gravy.

MAKES APPROX. 700G (1LB 9OZ)

- 1kg (2lb 4oz) mixed berries and hedgerow fruits, such as blackberries, elderberries, rosehips, bilberries, hips and haws
- 1kg (2lb 4oz) crab apples or cooking apples
- 1 litre (1¾ pints) water
- 200ml (7fl oz) port
- approx. 1kg (2lb 4oz) granulated cane sugar

> Wash the fruit well and remove any stalks. Cut the apples in half and combine them with the rest of the fruit in a heavy-based saucepan. Pour in the water, bring to the boil and simmer until the fruit is really soft and pulpy and can be crushed easily against the side of the pan. Tip into a jelly bag, suspended over a sterilized

bowl, and set aside to drip overnight. For this jelly only, you can gently squeeze the bag to extract all the juices. (Normally we don't advise this as it makes the jelly cloudy, but in this case the jelly is so dark it doesn't really matter, and anyway we hate to waste the valuable hedgerow juice – so go ahead and squeeze!)

> Pour the juice into a measuring jug and weigh out the sugar. You will need the same quantity of sugar as juice and port combined (don't add the port yet).

> Put the sugar and juice into a medium, heavy-based saucepan and set over a low heat to dissolve the sugar. Bring to the boil and boil hard until setting point is reached (see pages 42–3). Remove the pan from the heat, skim the surface and stir in the port. Bottle into warm, sterilized jars (see page 43).

VARIATION

ROSEHIP AND ROSÉ JELLY

Follow the recipe for Hedgerow and Port Jelly (see above), replacing the foraged berries with rosehips. For best results, either freeze them beforehand to soften them or pick after the first frost. Rosehips are full of vitamin C and the finished jelly is supposed to soothe sore throats. The port can be omitted if you wish or substituted with white or rosé wine.

APPLE AND ROSEMARY JELLY

We hate waste and so it seems a really good deal to get lovely gleaming jars of crystal clear jelly in return for a load of peel and cores. We often have apple cores and skins left over from making crumbles and pies. If you don't want to use them there and then, freeze them until you have enough. You can use the whole apple for this, but you won't have the same sense of satisfaction. This jelly is delicious with roast pork and lamb.

MAKES 700G (1LB 9OZ)

- 1.5kg (3lb 5oz) apple peel and cores
- 800ml (1⅓ pints) water
- 2 long sprigs of rosemary
- 3 tablespoons cider vinegar
- up to 1kg (2lb 4oz) granulated cane sugar

> Put the apple bits into a large preserving pan with the water, rosemary and vinegar. Bring to the boil and then reduce the heat to a simmer. Cook gently until the fruit is soft and squashes easily with a wooden spoon. Pour the mixture into a jelly bag, cover with a cloth to keep out flies, and set aside to drip overnight into a container underneath. Measure the strained juices. To calculate the amount of sugar needed and finish the jelly, follow the general instructions on page 55.

VARIATIONS

CHILLI AND APPLE JELLY

Follow the recipe for Apple and Rosemary Jelly, omitting the rosemary and cider vinegar and adding a crushed chilli instead. Taste the jelly towards the end of cooking and add further heat in the form of more crushed chilli as necessary. We love this on a cheese board or with roast pork belly.

QUINCE JELLY

Follow the recipe for Apple and Rosemary Jelly, substituting the apples for quinces – include the skins, flesh, cores, pips and all. Omit the rosemary and cider vinegar and add the juice of 2 lemons at the beginning, when you cook the quinces, to stop them becoming brown.

REDCURRANT JELLY

This bright, ruby-coloured jelly is one of the most beautiful preserves to make. I think I would make it even if I never ate it, just to have a jar sitting on my shelf to look at. Actually it is one of the most useful preserves to have in your storecupboard, so we make a large batch over summer for use in sauces and gravies, or for serving with baked Camembert or Brie. The bittersweet flavour also makes it the perfect partner to accompany lamb or ham.

NOTE: You don't need to include any other fruit with the redcurrants because they are naturally high in pectin.

MAKES APPROX. 600G (1LB 5OZ)

- 1kg (2lb 4oz) redcurrants
- approx. 500ml (18fl oz) water
- approx. 500g (1lb 2oz) granulated cane sugar

> Wash the berries and pick off any long stalks, but don't worry about removing the tiny stems as they will be strained out later.
> Boil the fruit with the water until soft and pulpy. Strain through a jelly bag overnight (see page 55), resisting the temptation to squeeze the jelly bag or your jelly will be cloudy. Weigh the strained juices and calculate the amount of sugar needed, allowing equal quantities of fruit to sugar.
> Return the strained juices to the pan with the sugar and stir over a low heat to dissolve. Bring to the boil and boil hard until setting point is reached (see pages 42–3). Bottle into warm, sterilized jars (see page 43). Store in a cool, dark place for up to a year.

⋆ FRUIT CHEESE

Fruit cheeses are high in sugar and set to a solid consistency similar to soft cheese made with milk. Fruit cheese is one of the earliest preserves. In the 16th century it was traditionally made out of quinces by the Portuguese and called *marmelada*. Fruit cheese can be made using the pulp left over in the jelly bag after making jelly (unless it contains the cores and pips).

Fruit cheese is traditionally potted into moulds and turned out whole, and served cut into slices. You can either use silicone moulds for potting the cheese or individual ramekins. If using ramekins, coat the sides of the container with liquid glycerine beforehand to make them easier to turn out and cover with waxed paper and cellophane; store in the refrigerator for up to 3 months. If you want to keep the cheese for longer than this, bottle into sterilized jam jars and seal with screw-cap lids; store in a cool, dark place for up to a year.

CRAB APPLE AND CHILLI CHEESE

Individual little pots of this fruit cheese make wonderful homemade presents – we often give them as gifts with a wedge of good Cheddar or goat's cheese. The first mouthful of this fruit cheese is soft, sweet and innocent but it is soon followed by a punch of chilli making it irresistible.

MAKES APPROX. 1KG (2LB 4OZ)

- 1kg (2lb 4oz) crab or cooking apples
- 3 red chillies
- approx. 800g–1kg (1lb 12oz–2lb 4oz) granulated cane sugar

> Wash the apples very well and chop them in half. Put them into a saucepan with a covering of cold water and bring to the boil. Reduce the heat to a simmer

and cook for 30 minutes until the fruit squashes easily with a fork and is very soft. Strain through a sieve or a food mill to obtain a purée.

> Measure the purée and put into a saucepan. Add the same quantity of sugar (give or take 100g/3½oz, depending on the tartness or ripeness of the fruit). Put over a low heat, stirring frequently, until the sugar dissolves and the mixture has reduced to a thick paste; this could take up to an hour. If a skin forms during this time, remove it with a spoon and discard. The cheese is done when it is really thick and a line can be drawn across the bottom of the pan with a spoon and it doesn't disappear quickly. Spoon into containers and seal (see page 43). Serve with cheese or roast pork.

VARIATIONS
DAMSON CHEESE
Follow the recipe for Crab Apple and Chilli Cheese (see pages 57–8), omitting the chilli and replacing the crab apples with damsons. You can leave the stones in the fruit to begin with, as they will all be strained out later in the sieve. Warm the sugar in a low oven at 140°C/275°F/gas 1 for 15–30 minutes before adding; this will help it dissolve more quickly. Watch over it as it thickens, approx. 40 minutes. Serve with lamb or duck or layered into a chocolate cake.

QUINCE JELLY
Follow the recipe for Crab Apple and Chilli Cheese (see pages 57–8), omitting the chilli and replacing the crab apples with quinces. To achieve a deep, pink colour, allow the cooked quinces to stand overnight before straining. Serve with roast pork or Manchego or goat's cheese.

* CURDS

Bottle curd into sterilized containers and seal with waxed paper and cellophane to stop it forming a skin. This recipe comes from Stefano Borella, Head Teacher at our cookery school.

STEFANO'S LEMON CURD

This hits the spot where mouth-puckering citrus acidity meets sugary sweetness. We love it stirred into Greek yogurt or ice cream.

MAKES 450G (1 LB)
- 150g (5½oz) unsalted butter
- 200g (7oz) golden caster sugar
- juice and zest of 3 lemons
- 3 eggs and 1 egg yolk

> Put the butter, sugar, lemon juice and zest in a saucepan over a low heat. Meanwhile, whisk up the whole eggs and egg yolk in a bowl with an electric mixer until very smooth. When the butter mixture has melted, pour in the frothy egg mixture. Keep whisking until the mixture starts to thicken, increasing the heat gradually. As soon as you hear the first 'gloop' sound, remove the pan from the heat. Strain the curd through a nylon sieve to obtain a smooth texture. Bottle into sterilized jars, taking care to fill them absolutely full. Press a waxed disc on top, waxed-side down, and set aside to cool. Once cold, seal the pots with cellophane discs and secure with rubber bands. Store in the refrigerator and consume within 2 weeks.

VARIATION
PASSION FRUIT CURD
Follow the recipe for Stefano's Lemon Curd (above), replacing the lemons with the pulp and seeds of 4 passion fruit.

* FRUIT BUTTER

Fruit butter is low in sugar and really delicious spread on toast or hot pancakes. We have given two methods for making it: one on the hob and one in the oven. Both work well, however I do think the oven version gives a slightly better flavour. Either bottle into sterilized glass jars and store in the refrigerator for up to 3 weeks, or heat-process by waterbathing and store in a cool, dark place for up to a year (see pages 206–7).

teaspoonful of the butter on a plate; if it is properly set it shouldn't 'weep' at the edges. Spoon immediately into warmed, sterilized 250ml (9fl oz) Kilner or two-part lid jars, seal and waterbath for 10 minutes using the hot-pack method on pages 206–7. It will keep for up to a year in a cool, dark place. If not waterbathed, store in sterilized containers, after cooling, in the refrigerator for up to 3 weeks.

APPLE AND CINNAMON BUTTER

This butter is spiced with cinnamon and is wonderful served with cheese or as a sauce for roast pork or with homemade British pork and leek sausages (see page 92). Alternatively, spread it onto hot pancakes and top with homemade crème fraîche (see page 180).

MAKES APPROX. 1KG (2LB 4OZ)

- 3kg (6lb 8oz) eating apples
- 200ml (7fl oz) water
- zest and juice of 1 lemon
- 5cm (2in) cinnamon stick
- 4 cloves
- 175g (6oz) dark soft brown sugar

> Quarter the apples, leaving the peel and core intact, and put into a large saucepan with the water, lemon zest and juice and spices. Cover with a lid and simmer until tender, approx. 20 minutes. Put the apple mixture through a food mill or a sieve to strain out the spices and separate the skins and pips from the pulp.

> Combine the purée with the sugar in a heavy-based saucepan, stirring over a low heat to dissolve the sugar. Cook until the purée is really thick and a spreadable consistency, stirring frequently, approx. 1 hour. Check for a set by placing a

ROASTED PEACH AND VANILLA BUTTER

This is a delightful combination that is heightened and concentrated by the roasting of the peaches. I have used the oven method for this recipe, but you can cook it on the hob if you wish. Enjoy it as a base for sponge pudding, mixed into bread and butter pudding or simply on hot toast.

MAKES 600G (1LB 5OZ)

- 1kg (2lb 4oz) ripe but firm peaches
- approx. 25g (1oz) soft brown sugar, to taste
- 1 vanilla pod or ½ teaspoon vanilla extract

> Preheat the oven to 180°C/350°F/gas 4. Wash the peaches and dry them with kitchen paper. Quarter the peaches, discarding the stones, and arrange in an ovenproof dish, skin-side up. Roast in the oven for up to 45 minutes or until the skins have shrivelled and the flesh is soft.

> Remove from the oven and put into a food processor, or use a stick blender, to blitz the peaches to a paste. Taste the purée and sweeten with sugar if you feel it needs it – we normally add approx. 25g (1oz) because we never seem to have really sweet peaches.

> Return the purée to the ovenproof dish and put it back into the oven for a further 30 minutes to reduce some more

>>>

and dissolve the sugar, stirring it halfway through. If the spread is watery after this time, continue to cook until the water has disappeared. Remove from the oven and spoon immediately into warmed, sterilized 250ml (9fl oz) Kilner or two-part lid jars. Seal and waterbath for 10 minutes using the hot-pack method on pages 208–9. It will keep for up to a year in a cool, dark place. If not waterbathed, store in sterilized containers, after cooling, in the refrigerator for up to 3 weeks.

* CORDIALS, COULIS AND ELIXIRS

The term 'cordial' derives from the Latin word *cordialis*, which describes a medicinal drink made from herbs, fruits, honey and often alcohol. Over time, alcoholic cordials have become known as 'liqueurs', while the term 'cordial' is more widely used to describe non-alcoholic syrups diluted with water. One of the most famous cordials is Rose's Lime Cordial, which was patented in 1867 and originally made for British sailors to prevent scurvy.

An elixir or syrup is another name for these sweet, medicinal mixtures. Nowadays all the words seem to be interchangeable, for all of them are fruity and sweet (the sugar content helps them to last). We have grouped all the runny syrups that need diluting together, and called them 'cordials'.

To make a coulis, which is a thin purée served as a sauce, push the fruit through a sieve instead of muslin.

CLEAR AND CLOUDY CORDIALS – TO SQUEEZE OR NOT TO SQUEEZE!

Syrups and cordials are both made by straining the juice through a jelly bag or two layers of muslin. If you want a crystal clear liquid, allow plenty of time to let the juices drip overnight. If you're in a hurry, and not fussed if the resulting liquid isn't crystal clear – and you can't bear the thought of wasting all that precious pulp – the only choice is to squeeze the bag or push it through a sieve with a spatula; this way you will gain more liquid, but it will be cloudy. The choice is yours!

SPICED BLACK FRUIT ELIXIR

Foraging for autumn fruit is always fun, however this recipe also works well with frozen fruits of the forest. In fact, the fruit releases the juice better after being frozen (or after the first frost if picked outside), so you could use a mix of summer and autumn berries.

This elixir is loosely based on an old Antonio Carluccio recipe. It is great heated in a mug with boiling water for a warming winter drink, mixed with prosecco or used as a base for Bramble cocktails. To turn it into a cocktail, combine 2 tablespoons of elixir with 50ml (2fl oz) gin or sloe gin, 1 teaspoon of lemon juice and a little tonic. Serve over crushed ice, garnished with mint leaves (see page 169).

MAKES APPROX. 350ML (12FL OZ)

- 1kg (2lb 4oz) black fruit, such as elderberries, blackberries, blueberries, sloes, cherries
- 500ml (18fl oz) water
- 2 long strips of lemon or orange peel, or 1 of each
- 4 cloves
- 3 cardamom pods

- 6cm (2½in) cinnamon stick
- granulated cane sugar or honey

> Wash the fruit well and remove any stalks. Put into a heavy-based saucepan with the water and flavourings. Bring to the boil and simmer until all the fruit is tender, approx. 30 minutes – it should crush easily when you press it against the side of the pan with a wooden spoon.
> To strain the juice, pour into a jelly bag and leave it to drip overnight. For this recipe, it is perfectly fine to gently squeeze the bag. (Normally we don't advise this as it makes the cordial cloudy, but in this case the elixir is so dark you won't notice it, and anyway it's a shame to waste all that valuable juice.)
> Measure the juice and calculate the amount of sugar needed, allowing 250g (9oz) sugar or 125g (4½oz) honey per 500ml (18fl oz) juice. Combine the juice and sugar or honey in a medium, heavy-based saucepan and stir over a low heat** to dissolve. Pour into warm, sterilized bottles and keep in the refrigerator for up to a month.
> ** To make the elixir last longer, bring the heat up to over 85°C (185°F) when dissolving the sugar, pour into sterilized bottles and waterbath according to the instructions on pages 206–7.

* CORDIALS

RASPBERRY CORDIAL

For a bright, fruity drink, simply dilute this with cold sparkling water. It is also versatile as a base for cocktails – try it mixed with prosecco or cava. For a gin-based drink that tastes like summer in a glass, add a generous dash of raspberry cordial and muddle with crushed ice, a wedge of lime and a few mint leaves. If you leave out the gin it works as a great mocktail for the kids too. Another favourite of mine is Raspberry Gin Fizz – raspberry cordial mixed with a bruised stick of lemongrass, some crushed ice, lime juice, gin and sparkling water.

MAKES APPROX. 350ML (12FL OZ) CLEAR CORDIAL USING A JELLY BAG OR 425ML (15FL OZ) CLOUDY CORDIAL USING A SIEVE

- 500g (1lb 2oz) raspberries
- juice of ½ lemon
- 200g (7oz) caster sugar

> Put the fruit, lemon juice and sugar in a saucepan over a medium heat until the sugar dissolves and the raspberries give up any resistance if you squeeze them against the side of a pan with a wooden spoon, approx. 10 minutes. Strain through a sieve or jelly bag into a sterilized jug or bowl. Pour into a sterilized bottle and keep in the refrigerator for up to 10 days.
> If you wish to make larger quantities of this to keep out of the refrigerator, you will need to waterbath the bottles according to the instructions on pages 208–9.

STRAWBERRY CORDIAL

Follow the method for Raspberry Cordial (see left) with strawberries instead of raspberries. To make a coulis, push the fruit through a sieve instead of through muslin.

RHUBARB CORDIAL

We love our pink rhubarb from the garden. It is one of the first edible plants that greets us with colour and flavour straight after a cold winter. This early rhubarb gives a great colour, but you could also use the later, greener variety too. We mix this with prosecco, pour it over Greek yogurt or ice cream or serve it with vanilla panna cotta.

MAKES APPROX. 750ML (1⅓ PINTS)

- 1kg (2lb 4oz) rhubarb (approx. 10 stalks), roughly cut into 2cm (¾in) chunks
- juice of 1 lemon
- 100ml (3½fl oz) water
- approx. 400g (14oz) caster sugar

> Combine the rhubarb, lemon juice and water in a saucepan and cook until soft, approx. 40 minutes. Strain the liquid through muslin. To achieve a very clear liquid, let it drip through slowly overnight, covered to prevent insects joining it. If you don't mind it being cloudy, push it through with a spatula. Dilute with water if the juice is very thick.

> Pour the strained rhubarb into a saucepan and sweeten with sugar to taste. Boil the rhubarb and sugar together briefly until the sugar dissolves, and then pour into warm, sterilized bottles. Keep in the refrigerator for up to 2 weeks.

ELDERFLOWER CORDIAL

Enjoy this cordial diluted with sparkling water, with a slice of lime and even a sprig of fresh mint. Our friend Hannah's tip is to pour it over ice, using 30ml (1fl oz) gin, 30ml (1fl oz) cordial and a splash of lemon or lime juice and top up with tonic. Try to pick young elderflowers early in the morning when it is dry. Before putting them in the pan, have a good look for insects. Citric acid helps preserve the cordial and adds a pleasant sour flavour.

MAKES 750ML–1 LITRE (1⅓–1¾ PINTS)

- 700g (1lb 9oz) caster sugar
- 600ml (20fl oz) water
- 15–20 elderflower heads (depending on size)
- 1 lemon, juiced and roughly chopped (including the skin)
- 1 tablespoon citric acid powder (optional)

> Boil the sugar and water together in a large pan. When bubbling rapidly, push the flower heads into it, stems upwards. Leave to boil for a few minutes and then add the lemon juice, chopped lemon flesh and citric acid (if using). Remove from the heat and leave to cool in the pan, covered, overnight.

> The following day, strain the syrup through muslin into a jug and then into sterilized bottles. Keep in the refrigerator for up to 3 weeks. To preserve the cordial for longer, reheat after straining until boiling hot. Pour into warm, sterilized bottles and waterbath according to the instructions on pages 208–9.

* CANDYING

Candied fruits, also known as glacé and crystallized fruits, were known in Ancient China but were made popular by the Arabs who served candied citrus fruits at important occasions. Known in Europe since the 16th century candying works by repeatedly soaking fruits in a sugar syrup. The fruit becomes saturated in sugar and is therefore resistant to spoilage bacteria and moulds that cannot survive in a sugary environment.

STEM GINGER

Every year at Christmas our family had a spread of treats adorning the Christmas table including stem ginger in syrup, chocolates and Turkish delight displayed in Victorian glass dishes. I don't remember liking the ginger as a child, but it is definitely something I have grown into. Now we cut the pieces up into small dice and use them and the syrup to flavour ice cream or stir through rhubarb compote. It is spicy and warming when poured over vanilla cheesecake or served with strong cheeses such as Pecorino. It can also be cut into lengths and covered with melted chocolate.

MAKES APPROX. 1.25KG (2LB 12OZ)
- 500g (1lb 2oz) fresh ginger
- 750g (1lb 9oz) granulated cane sugar

> Peel the ginger with the edge of a teaspoon, discarding the rough, dry ends and skin. Cut the ginger into small pieces about the size of a quail's egg, place in a bowl of cold water and set aside to soak overnight.
> The following day, drain the ginger and discard the water. Put the ginger into a saucepan with enough cold water to cover

and bring to the boil. Reduce the heat to a simmer, cover with a lid, and continue to cook until the ginger is tender when poked with a skewer, approx. 2 hours. Add a little more water if necessary to ensure the ginger is always covered. Remove the pan from the heat and set aside to cool overnight at room temperature.

> The following day, remove the ginger from the pan and set aside in a heatproof bowl. Measure out 250ml (9fl oz) of the cooking liquor, making up the amount with cold water if necessary and discarding the rest if too much. Pour into a saucepan and add 250g (9oz) of the sugar. Bring the water and sugar to the boil to dissolve the sugar, and then pour the resulting sugar syrup over the ginger. Set aside to cool overnight. This will allow the sugar to permeate through the fruit and the syrup to become flavoured with the ginger.
> The following day, strain the ginger out of the syrup and set aside. Put the syrup into a saucepan and bring to the boil with another 250g (9oz) sugar; pour over the ginger and set aside overnight.
> Repeat the process again on the fourth day, using up the rest of the sugar. Boil the syrup until you are happy with the consistency, it should be thick but easily pourable. Combine the syrup and ginger in the bowl and bottle immediately into warm sterilized jars (see page 43). Seal with lids and store in a cool, dark place for up to a year.

ORANGE PEEL SPOON SWEETS

This is a recipe from our lovely friend Gloria Mylona who is Greek Cypriot and mother to our friend Soulla. Gloria showed me some of the ways she was taught to preserve fruits by her mother. As a child, she and her siblings would stand on a chair to get into the high cupboard where her mother kept these sticky sweets for special occasions. They would dare to take out a couple each, blaming one another for instigating the stealth if they were ever caught!

Use sweet oranges for this when they are at their best, fresh and young. You can also use watermelon, lemons and grapefruit. Traditionally, these sweets are eaten with strong Greek coffee. This recipe uses the pith of the oranges, which sounds bizarre but it makes great use of an otherwise discarded part of the fruit.

MAKES APPROX. 1KG (2LB 4OZ)

- 6 medium oranges
- approx. 700ml (1¼ pints) water
- approx. 700g (1lb 9oz) caster sugar
- rose geranium leaf (optional)

> Using a vegetable peeler or sharp knife, peel away the dark zest from the oranges leaving the white pith intact; discard. Top and tail the oranges and make four vertical, shallow cuts into the orange pith as if you were about to divide it into quarters. Now carefully peel away the four pieces of pith separating them from the flesh as neatly as possible trying to get smooth surfaces. The flesh can now be eaten or saved for another recipe. Any raggedy edges should be tidied up and cut away. Curl the neatened pieces of pith up tightly into rolls and tie with a length of cotton thread or secure them with a cocktail stick. Soak the rolls in water overnight, changing the water three times to rid them of the bitterness.
> The next day, put the rolls and the geranium leaf into a saucepan and cover with cold water. Bring to the boil and cook until they are tender when poked with a thin skewer, approx. 45 minutes–

1 hour. Remove the pan from the heat and set aside to cool.

> Remove the rolls with a slotted spoon and set aside in a bowl. Pour 700ml (1¼ pints) of the cooking liquor back into a saucepan, discarding the rest. Add 700g (1lb 9oz) sugar to the pan and bring to the boil. Simmer gently for approx. 20 minutes until the sugar syrup thickens, then add the orange rolls. Boil the oranges for 3 minutes, then remove the pan from the heat. Set aside to cool overnight.
> The next day, return the pan to the heat and boil the oranges again for 3 minutes; set aside to cool overnight.
> On the fourth day, boil the mixture again for 3 minutes or until the liquid has reduced to a thick syrup. Spoon the rolls into hot sterilized jars leaving 3cm (1¼in) headroom. Top up with the syrup, making sure the rolls are completely covered. Seal the jars and leave to cool before storing in a cool, dark place for up to a year. Once the jars are opened, consume within a month and store in the refrigerator ensuring the rolls are always covered in syrup.

VARIATION

Do the same with black cherries, flavouring with a cinnamon stick instead of the rose geranium leaf.

MUSTARD FRUITS

Mostarda di Frutta, as this is known in Italian, is a condiment made from candied fruit in mustard syrup that has been made in Cremona, northern Italy, for centuries. It is eaten particularly with cheeses and sliced boiled meats. To make the real thing you need to get hold of mustard essence, also known as mustard oil. This is banned in the US but available from specialist food stores in Europe. We bought ours at a wonderful old pharmacy in Rome called Antica Erboristeria Romana, which is worth a visit just to see the interior dating back to 1752. The owner told us to be really careful of the mustard essence. He told us to open it at arm's length so that you don't breathe too much in and to avoid getting it near your eyes. Apparently mustard oil available from international grocers is just as good but I haven't tried it.

As for the fruits, *Mostarda di Frutta* is made out of a variety of fruits, such as quinces, apricots, oranges, cherries, apples and pears.

MAKES APPROX. 1.5KG (3LB 5OZ)

- 4 large pears, e.g. 'William'
- 1 lemon
- 400g (14oz) mini clementines or kumquats
- 200g (7oz) glacé cherries
- 250ml (9fl oz) water
- 750g (1lb 10oz) granulated cane sugar
- 8–10 drops of mustard essence, according to the strength

> Peel the pears, cut into quarters and discard the cores. Put them in a saucepan and poach until just tender in gently simmering water. Remove the pears from the pan with a slotted spoon, keeping the cooking liquor, and place them in a heatproof bowl. Squeeze over the lemon juice to stop them discolouring and put the hollowed out shells into the pan with the cooking liquor. Make a small cross in the top and bottom of the clementines or kumquats and prick them a few times all over. This ensures that the cooking liquor gets inside. Poach them in the cooking liquor for 5 minutes, remove them with a slotted spoon and add to the pears. Add the cherries as well.

> Measure the cooking liquor and make up to 250ml (9fl oz) with cold water. Return to the saucepan with 250g (9oz) of the sugar and heat to dissolve. Pour the resulting sugar syrup over the fruits. Stir it through and leave the mixture to cool, covered, overnight.

> The following day, drain the fruits from the syrup and set aside. Put the syrup into a pan and bring to the boil with another 250g (9oz) of the sugar to form a thicker sugar syrup. Pour over the candied fruits and stir to combine. Set aside to cool, covered, overnight.

> The following day, repeat the method above using up the remaining sugar. Boil the syrup until you are happy with the consistency, it should be thick but easily pourable. Pour over the fruits and add the mustard essence from arm's length; don't be tempted to have a sniff of it. Take a small piece of fruit out and after cooling taste for the strength of mustard. Add a few more drops if necessary. Immediately pour into warm, sterilized jars (see page 10). Store in a cool, dark place for up to a year. Any leftover syrup can be used to pour over hot gammon or toasted cheese for a delicious combination. If the spicy heat dissipates with time, add a few more drops of essence before serving.

MARRONS GLACÉS

I love to eat these in France or Italy, but wanted to make my own variety with homegrown chestnuts. Our local variety is smaller than the bulging French ones, but none the less sweet and tender.

MAKES APPROX. 4 X 225G (8OZ) JARS

- 450g (1lb) chestnuts
- 225g (8oz) granulated cane sugar
- 150ml (¼ pint) water

>>>

- 225g (8oz) liquid glucose
- 1 vanilla pod, cut into 2.5cm (1in) pieces
- 3 tablespoons brandy

> Pierce each chestnut through the tough brown skin in approx. four places and put into a large saucepan. Cover with cold water and bring to the boil. Reduce the heat to low and simmer for 5 minutes. Remove the pan from the heat, remove the chestnuts one by one and peel off the outer shell and inner skins. Try to do this quickly as possible because they are easier to peel when they have been in the hot water for 5 minutes only. Don't be tempted to remove them all and let them cool or the skin will become like glue and it will be harder to remove.
> Put the sugar, water, glucose and vanilla into a saucepan and bring to the boil to dissolve the sugar. Add the chestnuts to the pan and simmer gently for 5 minutes. Remove the pan from the heat and set aside to stand for 24 hours.
> The next day, return the pan to the heat and simmer the chestnuts for 2–3 minutes. Remove from the heat and set aside to cool overnight.
> On the third day, repeat the process, simmering the chestnuts again for 2–3 minutes in the syrup. Remove the pan from the heat, stir in the brandy and decant the syrup and chestnuts into warm, sterilized jars (see page 10). Store in a cool, dark place for up to a year.

SALT

Salt 'cures' and extends the life of food by stopping bacteria and mould from reproducing. In foods such as bacon, ham and cured salmon it draws out moisture by the process of osmosis, and flavours it at the same time, rendering it delicious as well as long-lasting. Salt curing alters the texture of fish or meat, making it firmer and less delicate to handle, so this process is beneficial for produce that needs to be hung.

Brine (salt mixed with water) can also be used to add moisture to food – for example, to plump up poultry. The purpose of brining poultry is not only to preserve, but to open up the proteins in the meat so that it becomes more sponge-like and can absorb flavours better. In America, most people brine their turkeys before roasting them for Thanksgiving. I tried this and the meat was so tasty and succulent that I couldn't understand why we don't all do it regularly. Now, even when I am going to roast a chicken I leave it in 20 per cent brine overnight and dry it for a few hours in the refrigerator before cooking it. This way, it is just how we like it – flavourful and juicy inside with a savoury, crispy skin.

Nearly all food is salted in some way before being smoked. This adds flavour, makes it firmer in texture and protects it from decay during the smoking process (see Smoke, page 125). The combination of salty and smoky food is quite irresistible – perfect examples are smoked salmon and bacon.

Salting has a long history. It was an ancient and preferred method of preserving food in China, and in the Mediterranean the preservation of fish with salt goes back to 3,500 BC. The process of salting meat – hams in particular – and then hanging them in breezy climates to cure is fundamental to the food of Italy and Spain.

Many of the cured foods were easier to make than we expected, such as smoked salmon and bacon, others took patience and months if not years of experimentation to get right, such as prosciutto. Our advice would be to start small: begin with 1kg (2lb 4oz) of pork belly before you progress to a whole piece, or try a mackerel first rather than a whole salmon until you get used to your new skills and equipment.

WATCH YOUR MEAT!

You will have to tend to your produce almost daily, watching for mould, humidity and temperature changes, so don't start making cured ham before venturing off on a world trip.

WHERE TO CURE

Many smaller items can be cured in your kitchen refrigerator. However, before you undertake any of the large or long-term salt cures in this chapter, such as cured ham or salami, bear in mind that salting is only the first stage of the production process. After curing, you will need somewhere to hang and dry your meat while it cures.

Professional curers are not allowed to hang meat and fish together and logic tells me this should be avoided at home as well, as the flavour of one could taint the other. I have also learned from experience not to hang too many things in my 'curing chamber' (wine refrigerator) at once, as this can raise humidity levels and encourage the wrong sorts of moulds to grow. Air needs to move around the produce easily and so the curing foods should not touch one another. (In the past, I have had to cut out an area of tackiness from a small piece of prosciutto because it was touching another meat and the air couldn't get to it.) Strings of sausages are slightly problematic because they naturally rest against each other, however I find tying them up in between the hooks, rather like a garland, keeps them apart for efficient airflow and drying. Cured foods should be checked daily for mould growth.

Ideally, you want to create your own 'curing chamber' – words that probably conjure up horrible images of torture! In our house, this is our very friendly wine refrigerator that has now taken on the pleasant aroma of a French charcuterie. If you have a larder against a north-facing wall, that is ideal – but we will go into this in more detail in the next chapter, Air, see pages 116–17.

HOW LONG TO CURE FOR?

One phrase that popped up constantly during our quest to learn more about the fine art of curing was 'Well, how long is a piece of string?' Infuriating as it was, that was the response I always seemed to get when I asked various curers how long a piece of meat or fish should be cured for. In my experience, if I cured it for too long it ended up overly salted and if I didn't cure it for long enough it never seemed to preserve properly and then it didn't taste as good either.

We have included approximate curing times in each recipe, however, please be aware that curing is not a precise science. Like many forms of preservation, timings will be affected by many factors, including the temperature of your refrigerator, the size and shape of your joint and whether or not the meat is on the bone. Usually it is better to err on the side of caution and leave your meat in the curing salts or brine for longer to be on the safe side, rather than removing it too quickly. If you find your meat is too salty (as happens to the best of us when we start curing), excess salt can be removed by soaking your joint in cold water for an hour or two; if necessary you can repeat the process several times. However, remember that some salt is always needed to kill bacteria.

SANITATION AND HYGIENE

Cleanliness is next to butchery, as someone once told me. Imagine a shiny-tiled, immaculately scrubbed butcher's shop, and that is what you need to recreate at home. Before you start work, move all your clutter away from the work surfaces, wipe them down with vinegar (I prefer this to breathing in antibacterial sprays) and wash or sterilize your equipment. Keep bowls and equipment cold, where possible, by putting them in the refrigerator. Make sure your hands are washed at all times.

EQUIPMENT

Many of the recipes don't call for anything other than a few containers with lids and some salt. For more complicated recipes, I have listed the equipment at the beginning of each recipe.

LABELS

Always label your meat and sausages before hanging them up to cure. Put what they are, the date you made them and their weight so you can check them regularly and easily.

* THE CURES

There are three basic methods: dry-salting, also known as dry-curing, wet-curing or brining and bag-curing. Dry-curing involves rubbing the food with salt, sometimes with the addition of flavourings, such as black pepper, juniper, cloves, nutmeg, molasses or dark brown sugar (see pages 70–2). Wet-curing involves soaking the food in a salt solution (brine), often with the addition of sugar and spices (see page 72–5). There is also a technique known as bag-curing, which is somewhere between the two, which works well for small things like bacon (see page 76).

WHICH SALT?

Rock salt is found inland from fossilized seabeds, while sea salt comes directly from an existing sea. Table salt is usually sea salt that has gone through an industrial process to refine it to pure sodium chloride.

We originally, and rather romantically, wanted to use flakes of Maldon sea salt, beautiful orange Himalayan rock salt or stunning Hawaiian black salt for all our curing projects. However, we soon discovered it was very expensive and not necessary for an excellent result – although it was fine for using on small items such as fillets of fish.

We recommend using ordinary fine or coarse sea salt for most of the recipes. For best results, look for natural salt without anti-caking agents or iodine. Some recipes specifically call for large grain salt, as it encourages water to leach out more easily and flow away – for example, for making prosciutto and smoked salmon. For other recipes, it is better to use fine sea salt. Many of the meat recipes are cured with specialist curing salts that contain nitrates to control the spread of bacteria.

NITRATES AND NITRITES

Sooner or later when you delve into salt-curing you will come across the words nitrates and nitrites. Nitrates with an 'a' are a form of saltpetre – the original curing salt that was used for centuries and can still be seen in old recipes. Nowadays we know that nitrates can be highly toxic if used in large quantities, so they are no longer sold on their own. Nitrites with an 'i' are what nitrates turn into during the curing process, and since these are far stronger, and much more reliable to use, most curing salts rely entirely on them – though some combine nitrites with a small quantity of nitrates, especially when the salts are required for curing meats like salami, which require longer hanging times. In these cures, the initial nitrites in the curing salts will come to an end more quickly than the nitrates, which will gently keep the process going, producing more nitrites during the long curing.

Ultimately safety is the most important thing, and the safest and most consistent route is to use curing salts, which are a mixture of salt, nitrates and/or nitrites. Curing salts are the only reliable way of eliminating the risk of botulism caused by the bacterium *Clostridium botulinum*. Nitrates prevent *botulinum* spores from transforming into toxins, eliminating the possibility of food poisoning. They also prevent rancidity in the fat. Curing salts preserve the natural, pinky-red colour of the meat that we associate with bacon and salami and give firmness to the food, making it easier to cut.

The two brands of curing salt I recommend are Prague Powder No. 1 and No. 2 and Quickcure (see pages 242–3 for suppliers). The reason I have stuck to these brands is because the percentage of nitrates and nitrites varies between different brands, and I want you to achieve consistent results every time. Other curing salts can be used, but you will have to follow the manufacturer's instructions.

NOTE: Both nitrates and nitrites have endured something of a bad rap in the press over recent years, as people have become concerned with anything chemical that we add to our food. However, it is only fairly recently that we have come to understand the way both nitrates and nitrites work. Today the amounts that can be used in commercial curing are strictly controlled – and actually less than those found naturally in many green leafy vegetables. Ultimately, if you decide not to use curing salts, your cured produce will not last as long and carries a greater risk of spoilage and contamination. Having said that, in some of the recipes we have given instructions for using ordinary sea salt, but this is principally for foods like bacon that will not hang around for long. Saying that, we always use curing salts at

home because we like the texture and colour they impart, but if you don't mind grey bacon and a short shelf-life, then feel free to leave them out.

SUGAR

Sugar can help to balance the salty flavour in cured produce, and since bacteria feeds on sugar its presence helps promote good bacteria at the beginning of the curing process. Once these are established, they will fight off bad bacteria. The drawback of using sugar is it can soften the texture of the product, so this needs to be taken into consideration.

* DRY-CURING

Most artisan curers of bacon and ham will tell you that dry-curing is best, because it allows the salt to dissolve slowly into the meat or fish and cures it from outside to inside, over a period of hours or days, depending on what you are curing, and the size and thickness.

HOW MUCH SALT TO USE?

The amount of salt used in each recipe depends upon its task. When it is used merely for flavour, a small amount can be used, however when it is used to preserve, more is needed. An excess of salt used to keep the food safe during drying or smoking might make the food unpalatable but it can be removed before we eat the results.

A thin fillet of fish that is going to be eaten quickly might only need a light covering of salt to give it flavour and firm up the flesh. It will cure quickly owing to its size.

Salami might have 2.5 per cent salt in it, a low amount. This is because the salt is spread evenly and quickly through the minced meat before it is made into sausages. The salami are preserved partly by the salt but also by their fermentation and drying. Through weight loss the percentage of salt in the finished product could be 3–4.5 per cent.

Bacon by contrast has between 3–4 per cent salt added from the beginning. The salt has to travel from the outside to the middle of the pork. It is only hung for a short amount of time and is not eaten raw.

Conversely a huge ham that is to be cured in a rainy country might have large amounts of salt added to it to carry it safely through the curing and possible smoking stages. English country hams can have as much as 8–9 per cent salt in them but they are traditionally soaked to remove this before cooking or are at least boiled with several changes of water so that the end result is actually rather mild.

LOIN OF PORK

back bacon

x shortest route to the centre = 2.5cm (1in)

7 days for every 2.5cm (1in) to the centre via the shortest route

DRY-CURING – A BASIC GUIDE

TIMING I have indicated approximate curing times in each recipe, however these are a guide only. Actual times will be influenced by many factors, including the temperature of your room/refrigerator, and the size and age of the product you are curing. For more information on dry-curing times, see below.

FEEL Once cured for long enough, the fish/meat will become firmer and take on a bacony texture. Test by prodding regularly with clean fingers to see if it is firm to the touch or still wobbly like jelly.

TASTE It is safe to taste all salted products except raw pork or chicken. If salted correctly, they should have a salty tang but still taste of the product.

WEIGHT LOSS Meat should lose at least 5 per cent of its weight and up to 40 per cent for cured pork such as salami after it has been air-dried. This method of testing is less reliable for fish fillets, which dry out anyway as they age without salting.

PRACTICE Through trial and error you will soon get the hang of curing and there is no better way to practise than on small fish. These cure in minutes, allowing you to see the changes quickly, for example, a floppy fillet of mackerel will become firm and less flexible under a fine covering of salt in 15–30 minutes.

DRY-CURING TIMES

We have worked out the approximate curing times for you, based on the theory learned from our friend Jasper Aykroyd, aka 'The Bacon Wizard', who cures bacon primarily but also most things under the sun. He suggests you work out how long to dry-cure your produce using this simple scale: allow 7 days for every 2.5cm (1in) to the middle of the joint via the shortest route.

The reason Jasper has developed this formula, rather than one based on weight, is because it takes longer for the salt to penetrate to the centre of thicker joints than thinner ones. Using this formula, a standard pork belly, approx. 3cm (1¼in) thick, will usually take approx. 4½ days to cure, whereas back bacon, which is thicker, would normally take approx. 7 days. If the half-day timing falls at an inconvenient moment, midnight say, leave it until the morning and don't worry. Always err on the side of caution, curing for slightly too long rather than too short a time.

* WET-CURING (BRINING)

Most industrial curers employ the 'multi-needle' injection method of curing, which is done on a vast scale and is especially designed to add water. This has the effect of plumping up the meat, which is why bacon that has been cured in this way leaches out that familiar white liquid when it goes into a hot pan. You pay for the water as part of the weight of your purchase – rather expensive water! Some manufacturers even include polyphosphates that form a jelly-like substance at cold temperatures in order to keep the water in there until you cook the product. These modern processes are often done to speed up the whole curing process so that bacon can be made in less than an hour.

Stitch-brining is an older form of curing that involves injecting the meat by hand with a single needle. This is a more skilled technique than the industrial process mentioned above. It can be done at home with a brine pump, and does speed up brining times, however it takes a lot of practice to get uniform results and we have rarely found it necessary.

Traditional wet cures, where the meat is soaked in brine, are something quite different and this method is much older than injection curing. Wet-brining introduces juiciness and flavour during the curing stage. Old-fashioned wet-brining recipes, which vary from region to region, may include flavourings such as black treacle, molasses, brown sugar, bay leaves, juniper, wine, cider or buttermilk with the basic salt and water mixture.

The traditional method of determining whether you have enough salt in your brine is to drop in a potato or an egg: when it floats, there is enough salt. This occurs when the brine is made up of 120g (4¼oz) salt to 1 litre (1¾ pints) water and this is a good all-purpose brine. Today, most people use a brineometer to measure the level of salt, or you can follow the table on page 75.

BRINING – A BASIC GUIDE

TIMING As a rule of thumb, the stronger the brine, the shorter the brining time for the same result. Large pieces of meat and fish take more time to absorb the brine than lean, thin ones.

TEMPERATURE The temperature of the brine is important. Meat and fish must be put into cold brine, approx. 3°C (37°F) is ideal, and this temperature should be maintained throughout the curing process, so leave it in the refrigerator or a cool place below 5°C (41°F).

CONTAINERS For best results, choose a container of a similar size and shape to fit your joint, so that you use as little brine and storage space as possible. Meat or fish should always be submerged below the level of the brine. If necessary, weigh it down with weights to prevent any part from protruding.

PRECAUTIONS If white scum appears on the surface of the brine, this should be removed. If the brine turns milky, blue, slimy or sticky – or smells foul – discard it straight away. Do not reuse brine; discard after one use.

BRINING TIMES

We give curing times with each recipe, but if using strong brine, i.e. in order to cure for preserving, the rule is to allow 4 days for every 1cm (½in) to the centre of the meat via the shortest route. This means a 4kg (8lb 12oz) pork leg could take approx. 1 month; the strength of salt will protect it from decay during this time.

CALCULATING HOW MUCH BRINE YOU NEED

A simple method of calculating the quantity of brine needed is to place your meat/fish in a container that is roughly the same size and shape. Cover with cold water, adding 1 litre (1¾ pints) at a time, until the meat is submerged. Then you know how much brine to make up. As a rough guide, you will need roughly the same amount in litres as the weight of your produce.

HOT BRINE OR COLD BRINE?

There are two methods for making the brine, depending on whether you use hot or cold water. The good thing about cold brine is it can be made up quickly. With this method, the salt isn't heated but gradually dissolves over a few days. The drawback of this method is you have to turn the foods frequently, and stir up the brine, to ensure the salt is evenly distributed around the meat or fish. This method of brining is only suitable for longer brining times – i.e. greater than a day – because the salt needs time to dissolve.

Hot brines need to be made in advance and left to cool before use. With this method, the salt is dissolved in hot liquid (with or without sugar and spices) and then chilled. The advantage of a hot brine is the salt is completely dissolved and any spices have a chance to release their flavour into the brine; the drawback is you need to allow time for the brine to chill (preferably overnight) before use.

METHOD FOR MAKING HOT BRINE

Work out how much brine you need (see page 75) and calculate the correct percentage of water, salt and sugar/flavourings needed. Combine the salt and sugar with 1 litre (1¾ pints) of the water in a saucepan over a medium heat, stirring to dissolve. Herbs and spices can also be included at this stage, since the cooking helps release the flavours. Once the sugar and salt have dissolved, set aside to cool to room temperature (over a bowl of ice to speed things up). Combine with the remaining cold water and transfer the brine to the refrigerator to chill.

ADDING SUGAR AND SPICES

Traditionally, hot brines are flavoured with sugar, herbs and spices – see Bradenham-style Ham, pages 85–6. As a general rule of thumb, allow half the amount of sugar, maple syrup or honey to the amount of salt in the cure. Note that you must always stick to the exact ratio of salt and water stated.

Feel free to experiment with additional flavourings, although in our experience they are never really detectable in the final product. Choose flavourings that go well together out of the following: 2 sprigs of rosemary, 1 tablespoon of crushed juniper berries, 3cm (1¼in) cube of grated ginger, 2 x 6cm (2½in) strips of orange peel, 2 bay leaves, a handful of parsley and 2 crushed garlic cloves to 1 litre (1¾ pints) of water.

BRINING STRENGTHS

These are the three strengths of brine we recommend for the recipes in this book; we refer to them in this chapter and in Smoke.

NOTE: We initially found it very confusing that a so-called 40 per cent brine didn't actually contain 40 per cent salt to water! Instead it is to do with the way brine is measured with using a brineometer or salinometer, which measures the percentage saturated solution of brine in water.

Many curers develop their own preferred brine strengths based on individual tastes. You might decide after experimenting that you prefer a saltier taste to your produce or a longer brining time to suit your schedule. However, bear in mind that if you alter the strength, or the timings, it could affect the shelf-life of your produce.

- WEAK 20 PER CENT BRINE: 55g (2oz) salt to 1 litre (1¾ pints) water.
  This is ideal for already salty foods, such as mussels, or for items that need brining overnight, such as whole turkeys or chickens.

- MEDIUM 40 PER CENT BRINE: 120g (4¼oz) salt to 1 litre (1¾ pints) water.
  This is ideal for curing smallish pieces of meat such as bacon or a small ham. At this ratio, an egg or potato should float in the brine; this was the old way of determining the strength of a brine.

- STRONG 70 PER CENT BRINE: 225g (8oz) salt to 1 litre (1¾ pints) water.
  This will work more quickly than the weaker brines and is useful for smaller pieces of meat or fish – such as pheasant or duck breasts, or whole medium fish – that only need a short curing time, i.e. less than 2 hours.

WET-BRINED TURKEY OR CHICKEN

Wet-brining poultry results in a more flavourful and succulent bird after roasting. You can use large brining or roasting bags for this method – use two just in case one splits – or a sanitized cooler or large, non-reactive container that fits inside your refrigerator. If the weather is cold, you can carry out this process in an outdoor room (providing it stays below 5°C/41°F).

> METHOD Make up a weak, 20 per cent hot brine solution (see left) and set aside to cool in the refrigerator. Place the poultry in a container and top up with the cold brine so that it is completely submerged. Cover the container with a lid or a plate and transfer to the refrigerator to cure for 8 hours or overnight.

> Discard the brine and rinse the poultry briefly under cold running water; pat dry on kitchen paper.

> Set aside to dry on a wire rack in a cool place (covered with a fly net) or in the refrigerator to form a pellicle for a minimum of 3 hours and up to a day.

> To cook, either roast in a conventional oven at 180°C/350°F/gas 4 or hot smoke until the internal temperature reaches 85°C (185°F). Eat straight away or store in the refrigerator for up to 5 days.

WET-BRINED FISH OR SHELLFISH

This method is ideal for fish that are going to be smoked or grilled, as the brining imparts moisture to the fish and stops it from drying out. Brining also affects the texture of the fish, firming it up so the flesh is less likely to fall apart on the grill. It is certainly a great way to get fish seasoned all the way through, and the salt also helps to preserve it. Always make sure the fish is fresh and sustainably caught.

> METHOD Make up a weak, 20 per cent hot brine solution (see left) and set aside to

cool in the refrigerator. Arrange the fish in a single layer, skin-side down, in a large lasagne dish or similar. Pour the cold brine over the fish and cover the container with a plate. If necessary, weigh the fish down so that it is completely submerged in the brine. Transfer the fish to the refrigerator for a period of time, depending on the strength of the brine and the size of the fish, see the box below. Discard the brine and rinse the fish briefly under cold running water; pat dry on kitchen paper.
> Arrange the fish on a wire rack and set aside to dry in a cool place (covered with a fly net) or in the refrigerator to form a pellicle for at least 1 hour and up to a day.
> Cook the fish under a hot grill, flesh-side up, until cooked through. Alternatively, hot smoke until the internal temperature reaches 63°C (145°F). Eat straight away or store in the refrigerator for up to 2 days. For advice on cold smoking, see page 128.

BRINING CHART – A QUICK REFERENCE GUIDE

PRODUCT	% BRINE	TIME	ADDITIONAL FLAVOURINGS
whole turkey, whole chicken, fish	20	overnight	sugar, maple syrup, honey, garlic cloves, parsley, bay leaves, onion
pork chops	40	4 hours	replace half the water with apple juice; rosemary
tuna, mackerel, salmon, white fish	20	1 hour for thin fillets up to 2cm (¾in); 6–8 hours for thicker (over 2cm/¾in)	orange peel, lemon peel, ginger
turkey breast	40	4–6 hours	sugar, maple syrup or honey
chicken or duck breast	40	3–4 hours	sugar, maple syrup or honey; orange peel
prawns, scallops, crayfish	70	15 minutes for small, peeled shellfish; 1 hour for really large prawns	orange or lemon zest, dill – not much time for flavours to penetrate

* BAG-CURING

Bag-curing sits somewhere between dry-curing and wet-curing. Usually when dry-curing meat you leave it on a slope or rack so that the water that is drawn out of it can drain away. However, many recipes use a bag, such as a vacuum or ziplock bag, to hold the meat and its cure instead. With this method, the water is not emptied out; instead the water leaching from the product makes its own brine (sometimes confusingly called 'pickle'). Although the rack method is preferable because it partially dries the product and concentrates the flavour, bag-curing is easy and quick to do. Care needs to be taken when hanging bag-cured produce, as they are more likely to suffer moulds due to their humidity. It is ideal for bacon however as it doesn't have a long hanging time. We make our streaky bacon and Petit Salé using this method. A 1kg (2lb 4oz) of belly will fit perfectly into a medium ziplock bag, I can keep it in the refrigerator easily and turn it daily. The dosages for bag-curing are the same as dry-curing.

* FRUIT

Salting citrus fruit is a method of preserving lemons, limes, grapefruit and kumquats well after their season has expired. This method of preserving was originally used to transport citrus fruit in the days before refrigeration. Indian pickled or salted lemons were regularly brought back from India to Europe by travellers centuries ago. Nowadays, we don't need to preserve these fruits as they are available all year round, but it is the distinct flavour of preserved fruits that we enjoy – especially in Middle Eastern and Indian cuisines. This flavour is partly achieved by the 'healthy' bacteria, lactobacillus, which thrive in the salty environment and ferment the fruit. After a few weeks, the salt draws the water out of the fruit, creating a brine; this can be reused for brining meats – see Duck Breasts Cured with Salted Kumquats on page 100. Preserved citrus flesh and rind can be used in tagines, etc.

SALTED KUMQUATS

We have grown kumquats in the past without ever really knowing what to do with them. These salted kumquats not only look pretty in the jar, but are really delicious in a lamb or chicken tagine. Don't waste the salty brine that collects in the jars; it makes a great citrussy cure for the duck breasts on page 100.

MAKES APPROX. 3 X 350ML (12FL OZ) JARS

- 500g (1lb 2oz) kumquats
- 1 tablespoon black peppercorns
- 5cm (2in) cinnamon stick
- 400–500g (14oz–1lb 2oz) coarse sea salt
- juice of 4–5 lemons

> Wash the kumquats and dry well. Cut off the very end of each kumquat where it was attached to the stalk. Make a cross in each fruit using a small knife, starting at the stalk end and cutting halfway down the side of the fruit; be careful not to cut all the way through. Place the kumquats in a mixing bowl. Lightly crush the peppercorns in a pestle and mortar or pepper grinder and add these to the bowl. Break the cinnamon stick into two or three pieces and add to the bowl with the salt. Mix the ingredients together with your hands, pressing the salt into the cuts in the kumquats to penetrate the flesh. Divide the mixture between sterilized jars and top them up with lemon juice.

Make sure the kumquats are completely covered with the lemon juice and salt to protect them from the air. Put on the lids and transfer to a sunny spot for up to a week. After a week, move to a cool, dark place for approx. 3 months. Salted kumquats will keep for up to a year. Once opened, store in the refrigerator for up to 6 months.

SALTED LEMONS

These are wonderful in Moroccan tagines.

MAKES APPROX. 1KG (2LB 4OZ)

- 500g (1lb 2oz) lemons
- 400–500g (14oz–1lb 2oz) coarse sea salt
- juice of 4–5 lemons

> Follow the method for Salted Kumquats, omitting the cinnamon and pepper.

USES FOR SALTED FRUITS Finely chop the preserved lemons and combine with olives to serve as a canapé.

To make a delicious citrus rub for fish, king prawns or chicken, finely chop them with some spring onions and parsley and combine with olive oil or butter.

Preserved lemons are also used in the impressive Italian topping gremolata for Osso Buco; here they are finely chopped with parsley and garlic.

Marc Frederic, known as the English Charcutier, told us his tip for curing salmon with lemon salt: use one part lemon salt to one part normal salt to impart a delicious citrus flavour.

VARIATION

SALTED LIMES

Follow the recipe for Salted Lemons using limes instead.

* FISH

Few foods go off quicker than fish, which is probably one of the reasons we are sometimes afraid of cooking and eating it as much as we should. Fish has been salted, dried and smoked for centuries to preserve it, and to enable it to travel to areas away from the coast. Although refrigeration has made fresh fish easily accessible, many of us still end up throwing it away occasionally because we haven't used it up quickly enough. However, simply by rubbing salt into fish you can extend its life by a few more days.

Fresh fish contains approx. 80 per cent water, but if it is cured with salt and dried this percentage can be reduced to below 25 per cent, creating a hostile environment for bacteria. If you take the water content down to less than 15 per cent, moulds will struggle to survive. This is the science behind salt cod or *Baccalà*, as it is also known, and this is the way people have preserved fish for centuries.

Most of us are unlikely to try salting a whole cod in the kitchen sink, but it is fulfilling to experiment with fish on a smaller scale.

SALTED COD FILLETS

Salting cod gives the fish a wonderful flavour and texture. It also preserves the shelf-life of the fish. This recipe produces a similar flavour to *Baccalà*, but it is not as intense since less salt is used and the cod is not dried. Use these salted cod fillets in any recipe that calls for salt cod. One of my favourite recipes is simply to steam the fish and serve it with aioli and vegetables. However, do make sure it has had a good soak in cold water beforehand to remove the salt. If you are worried it might be too salty, cut off a small piece and quickly cook it to taste, bearing in mind the outside will be slightly saltier than the inside. This preserving method is also suitable for other fish in the cod family such as pollock.

SERVES 4

- fine sea salt
- 4 x 200g (7oz) cod, haddock or pollock fillets

> Scatter some salt over the base of a shallow dish and put in the fish, skin-side down. Cover the tops and sides of the fish completely with salt so you cannot see the fish – this can be in a thin layer. Cover the dish and set aside overnight in the refrigerator (or a cold place below 5°C/41°F).
> The following day, give the fish a quick rinse under cold running water and pat dry with kitchen paper. Wrap the fish in baking parchment and store in the refrigerator until needed, for up to 1 week. Before use, soak the fish for 24 hours in cold water, changing the water twice during this time.

MARINATED BLACK COD IN MISO

Miso preserves and enhances the flavour of the fish. This is our friend, and Japanese cookery teacher Reiko Hara's recipe. Black cod done in a similar way was made famous by Nobu Matsuhisa at the renowned London restaurant that bears his name. This recipe also works well with mackerel, sea bass and salmon.

SERVES 4

- fine sea salt
- 4 x 100–120g (3½–4¼oz) black cod fillets
- 100ml (3½fl oz) mirin
- 100ml (3½fl oz) sake
- 450g (1lb) white miso

- 250g (9oz) caster sugar
- 1 teaspoon ginger juice (squeezed from grated fresh ginger)
- 4 slices of pickled ginger (see page 23)

> Sprinkle some salt over the base of a large dish, put in the cod fillets, skin-side down, and cover with a thin layer of salt. Set aside in the refrigerator for 1 hour.
> Meanwhile, make the marinade. Pour the mirin and sake into a saucepan and bring to the boil to burn off the alcohol. Add the miso and stir vigorously over a low heat to make a smooth paste, taking care not to let it burn. Add the sugar and stir well to dissolve. Remove the pan from the heat and set aside to cool to room temperature.
> Add the ginger juice to the marinade and mix well. Rinse the cod to remove the salt and pat it dry with kitchen paper. Spread half of the marinade evenly over the base of a large, shallow, rectangular container. Spread a clean piece of muslin over the top, put in the cod fillets and then place another piece of muslin on top. (The muslin stops the miso sticking to the fish.) Spread the rest of the marinade over the muslin, cover with a lid or a plate and set aside to marinate in the refrigerator for 3–4 days.
> To serve, remove the cod fillets from the container and wipe each one with damp kitchen paper. Grill the fish on both sides for a few minutes until golden brown. Serve hot, garnished with the pickled ginger, accompanied by steamed rice.

SALTED ANCHOVIES

Anchovies or sprats are often packed in layers of salt to preserve them for long periods of time, and this is how they have been transported for centuries. The Romans were very keen on anchovies and used the juices released from packing them in salt as a flavour enhancer called *garum*. To this day, anchovies are packed and pressed down in salt in Cetara, on the Amalfi coast of Italy, to release brine called *Colatura di Alici*, which is used to dress spaghetti.

If you want to do this at home, ensure that you use the freshest fish – either anchovies or sprats work well, but don't choose the smallest specimens, which won't stand up to the pressure in the container. Ideally fish should be salted within 12 hours of being caught.

MAKES 1KG (2LB 4OZ)

- a large, sterilized container to hold the fish (either a glass jar or a crock with a lid)
- 1kg (2lb 4oz) anchovies (approx. 50 fish)
- coarse sea salt

> Snap the head off the fish just behind the eyes and pull out the adjoining intestines – if some remain it doesn't matter. Rinse the anchovies briefly and gently in cold water, and then dry them carefully in between layers of kitchen paper.
> Sprinkle some salt in the base of your container and cover with a layer of anchovies. Scatter a thin layer of salt on top and then layer up the rest of the anchovies with the salt in the same way until the container is almost full. Put a weight on top, such as another jar with a flat bottom or a small saucer with a weight on top.
> Cover the container with a plate, or a lid if using a crock, and set aside in the refrigerator or a cold place (below 5°C/41°F) for 6–8 weeks to mature; cooler temperatures will slow down the process. During this time, the salt will draw out the moisture from the fish. The weight on top should ensure that the fish

stay submerged in the brine, however if necessary you can top up the jar with a strong brine to keep them covered at all times (see page 74). Once cured, the fish will take on a flattened, brown appearance. If cured correctly, they will last up to a year in the salty brine.

> To use, remove however many you need from the brine and rinse them carefully in cold water. Pat the anchovies dry on kitchen paper and dress with extra virgin olive oil, finely chopped chilli or onion, lemon juice and parsley. Use on pizzas or in pasta sauces, or in the Bagnetto recipe on pages 152–3. Alternatively, see Marinated Anchovies on pages 23.

* GRAVLAX

Fishermen have made this Nordic dish since the Middle Ages, traditionally salting and burying the salmon in the sand above the high-tide line. *Grav* means 'grave' and *lax* means 'salmon', hence the term *gravlax* meaning 'buried salmon'.

CURED SALMON WITH DILL, MUSTARD AND HONEY SAUCE

I like *gravlax* quite sweet, so I include more sugar than salt in my curing mixture, however you can use less sugar if you wish and reduce the amount of honey in the sauce. If you run out of dill for the sauce, as I did, simply rinse out the dill from the cure and reuse this for the sauce. My first experiments left the salmon too salty, particularly by the tail where the flesh is thinner. To prevent this, put less salt on the tail area. If you do find the fish too salty, soak it for 1 hour in cold water after curing to get rid of some of the saltiness.

SERVES 10 AS A STARTER

- 1.5–2kg (3lb 5oz–4lb 8oz) salmon, filleted

FOR THE CURE

- 100g (3½oz) coarse sea salt
- 150g (5½oz) caster or granulated sugar
- good twist of black pepper
- 75ml (2½fl oz) vodka
- 50g (1¾oz) fresh dill, finely chopped

FOR THE SAUCE

- 3 tablespoons finely chopped dill
- 3 tablespoons runny mild honey
- 2 tablespoons Dijon mustard
- 2 tablespoons cider vinegar
- 2 tablespoons extra virgin olive oil
- salt

> Mix the ingredients for the cure, reserving 25g (1oz) dill. Sprinkle 1–2 tablespoons of the cure in a large lasagne dish and put in one of the fillets, skin-side down. Sprinkle the rest of the cure on top, reserving 1–2 tablespoons. Place the remaining fillet of salmon on top, skin-side up, to make a sandwich and sprinkle over the remaining cure. Cover the dish with a plate and rest some weights on top – I use cartons of UHT juice. Transfer the fish to the refrigerator for 24 hours. Drain off any liquid in the container every 12 hours and turn the fish sandwich over.

> After 24 hours, taste a small piece of the salmon. Note that the thinner tail end will be saltier than the centre, so taste a piece from the middle. If it tastes too salty, soak the fish in cold water for 1 hour. If you are happy with the saltiness, rinse the fish briefly in cold water and pat dry with kitchen paper.

> Scatter the reserved dill over the flesh of the fish and sandwich it back together again. Put the salmon into a clean container and cover with a plate. Store in the refrigerator until you are ready to eat it; it will stay good for approx. 10 days. *Gravlax* can also be frozen.

> To serve, cut the salmon into thin slices on the diagonal with a long, just sharpened knife, starting at the tail end. To make the sauce, combine the ingredients in a bowl and season to taste with salt. Accompany with rye bread and lemon wedges.

* PORK

Pork is surely the greatest meat to salt, as there is so much you can do with it and it is possible to achieve so many different results. Jasper Aykroyd, who makes his living from producing and selling bacon, spent time with me in my kitchen, guiding me through the various processes. He believes that salt curing is alchemy: part science and part magic. It is extraordinary to experience, hands on, the way that time transforms a pig's leg, for example, into a soft, sweet prosciutto, which can be cut into ultra-thin layers that melt in your mouth, delivering the unique tang of umami.

Japanese scientist, Dr Kikunae Ikeda, first identified the so-called fifth taste in 1908 and called it umami after the Japanese word for deliciousness. However, umami wasn't formally recognized until the 1980s. Umami accounts for many of the flavours we love in cured food, which had previously just been considered savoury and delicious. During the processes of curing, drying and ageing, enzymes break down proteins into peptides and an amino acid called glutamate, which has this savoury or umami flavour. Incidentally, Dr Ikeda realized the power of this natural flavour and invented MSG, monosodium glutamate, a processed version of it, which is now used as a flavour enhancer.

In Europe, the annual killing of the pig traditionally took place in November, using the cold months of the year as a natural refrigerator. Nothing from the pig was ever wasted – and we have tried to honour this by including some recipes to use up the valuable offal and some of the unfashionable cuts.

BUYING YOUR PORK

Where possible, choose free-range pigs that have been fed on as much natural produce as possible, as this will result in a better end product. The old breeds have a much better fat content, which makes them ideal for charcuterie. A young pig is better for sausages and bacon, while an older pig is better for charcuterie as it will have more

flavour. A baconer pig is usually approx. 80–90kg (176–198lb) dead weight; a charcuterie pig is approx. 120–160kg (265–353lb) dead weight.

Make sure your butcher knows what you want to do with any cuts you ask for. We once ordered a leg of ham for making prosciutto, only to find the skin had been scored.

* BACON

There is nothing quite like bacon and now we make our own and enjoy it all the more.

You should use middle bacon made from the loin and the belly; it is also known as whole bacon or long back. When separated, they make back bacon and streaky.

Marc Frederic, the British charcutier, recommends that you leave the ribs on when curing bacon, and then butcher it afterwards. The ribs deliver flavour and help the shape of the bacon. These 'bacon ribs' can then be used to flavour stocks or stews, or boiled up and served with mushy peas.

OLD ENGLISH BACON

This traditional Elizabethan recipe by Maynard Davies, famous for his wonderful books on his life as the last apprentice bacon curer, is not usually smoked although the choice is yours.

MAKES APPROX. 900G (2LB)

- 1kg (2lb 4oz) pork loin or belly
- 35g (1¼oz) curing salts: EITHER 9g (¼oz) Quickcure and 26g (1oz) salt OR ½ level teaspoon (2.5g/¹⁄₁₆oz) Prague Powder No. 2 and 32.5g (1⅛oz) salt OR 35g (1¼oz) salt with no cure
- 18g (¾oz) soft brown sugar
- 3g (¹⁄₁₆oz) caraway seeds, lightly crushed
- 3g (¹⁄₁₆oz) ground ginger

>>>

> Follow the instructions for Streaky Bacon, below. If using pork loin instead of belly of pork, increase the curing timing: allow 7 days for every 2.5cm (1in) to the centre of the meat via the shortest route. This bacon can be cold smoked if you wish over mild apple wood smoke, however it already has a subtle flavour so go easy.

STREAKY BACON

This is an easy recipe to start with, as it can all be done in a glass container and stored in the refrigerator. It is how we make our bacon on a regular basis at home now and I nearly always smoke it afterwards. I find that 800g–1kg (1lb 12oz–2lb 4oz) pork belly is a good amount to last a couple of weeks for a family of 4–6.

We have given three measures for salt, depending on whether you use Quickcure, Prague Powder or plain salt with no cure (see page 70). Note that if you use plain salt with no cure your bacon will only last up to 5 days and it will be a brownish-grey colour – that of natural roast pork. **NOTE:** Quickcure recommend a ratio of 40g (1½oz) curing salt to 1kg (2lb 4oz) meat, but I find this a bit salty so I've cut it down to 35g (1¼oz).

Bacon made with curing salts will last up to 2 weeks, stored in the refrigerator. However, all bacon can be frozen. This streaky bacon can be eaten 'green', which means unsmoked, or smoked (see page 133).

Expect 5 per cent weight loss during the curing stage and a further 5–10 per cent during hanging.

MAKES APPROX. 900G (2LB)

- 1kg (2lb 4oz) pork belly, approx. 4cm (1½in) thick
- 35g (1¼oz) curing salts: EITHER 9g (¼oz) Quickcure and 26g (1oz) salt OR ½ level teaspoon (2.5g/¹⁄₁₆oz) Prague Powder

No. 2 and 33g (1⅛oz) salt OR 35g (1¼oz) salt with no cure
- 2 teaspoons crushed black pepper
- 1 teaspoon demerara sugar

> Combine the salt, pepper and sugar for the cure and rub into the meat, allowing approx. 90 per cent for the flesh side and 10 per cent for the skin. Put the belly into a ziplock or vacuum bag, taking care not to let the cure touch the seal if using a ziplock bag. Seal the bag, expelling as much air as you can or use a vacuum machine. Leave the bacon in the refrigerator for 5 days**, turning daily to distribute the juices evenly.

> Remove the meat from the bag and pat dry with kitchen paper; do not rinse. Place the bacon on a wire rack to allow air to circulate and set aside in the refrigerator, or hang in a curing chamber, to dry for 1–5 days. The longer it is left, the more concentrated the flavour; also the texture will become firmer and drier. The bacon is ready when it feels firm to the touch and not jelly-like. If cured correctly, it should have lost 10–15 per cent of its initial weight. If you would like it smoked, see page 133.

> To store, wrap the bacon in baking parchment and keep in the refrigerator for up to 2 weeks. Bacon can also be frozen.

> ** If the belly is thicker than 4cm (1½in), increase the curing timing: allow 7 days for every 2.5cm (1in) to the centre of the meat via the shortest route.

BEER AND CHILLI DRY-CURE BACON

This is Jasper Aykroyd, The Bacon Wizard's recipe for spicy bacon. In his own words: 'it could not be simpler'. Curing salts, dried malt extract and hops are widely available from any homebrew shop, high street or online, and won't break the bank or perish quickly. Light soft brown sugar will work as a replacement for the malt, but it's much more fun to make a dry-beer mix! This can be done with belly or loin of pork.

This makes a wicked and delicious bacon sandwich washed down with a pint of your favourite tipple.

MAKES APPROX. 900G (2LB)

- 1kg (2lb 4oz) pork belly (approx. 4cm/1½in thick) or loin

FOR THE CURE

- 35g (1¼oz) curing salts: EITHER 9g (¼oz) Quickcure and 26g (1oz) salt OR ½ level teaspoon (2.5g/¹⁄₁₆oz) Prague Powder No. 2 and 32.5g (1⅛oz) salt OR 35g (1¼oz) salt with no cure
- 35g (1¼oz) dried malt extract
- 10g (¼oz) dried hops (any will do, but you may have a favourite – Jasper prefers 'Saaz' or 'Cascade')
- 5g (⅛oz) chilli flakes (optional)
- 3g (¹⁄₁₆oz) bay leaf, crushed

> Mix all the ingredients together for the cure and apply liberally to your pork, allowing 90 per cent for the flesh side and 10 per cent for the skin. Massage the cure really well into the meat, leaving no part uncovered. Transfer the pork to a bag or a container with a lid. In this particular recipe, because you want the meat to really absorb the flavours from the cure, it's quite all right to leave it wrapped in a bag or sitting in its juices in a tightly fitting tub. However, if you are a purist, you can elevate the pork in the tub by raising it up on chopsticks or similar and pour off the juices periodically. Allow 5 days in the refrigerator for streaky (belly) bacon or 7 days for back (loin).

> Once the bacon has finished curing, quickly rinse it under a cold tap to wash off the salt and pat dry with kitchen paper. Transfer the bacon to a wire rack or similar with a roasting tray underneath to catch the juices. Dry the bacon for 2 hours at room temperature and then transfer to the refrigerator overnight. Uncovered is best to allow the air to circulate and finish off the curing process, but only do this if you have nothing else in the refrigerator that could taint it like onions or garlic.

> To store, wrap the bacon in baking parchment and store in the refrigerator for up to 2 weeks.

DRY-CURED PANCETTA

Pancetta (air-dried pork belly) is used to flavour dishes such as pasta sauces, soups and stews, and it is one product we couldn't do without in our restaurants. The wonderful flavour of *pancetta* comes from the concentration of herbs and spices used in the dry-cure mixture.

MAKES 750G (1LB 10OZ)

- 1kg (2lb 4oz) pork belly (approx. 4cm/1½in thick)
- 35g (1¼oz) curing salts: EITHER 9g (¼oz) Quickcure and 26g (1oz) salt OR ½ level teaspoon (2.5g/¹⁄₁₆oz) Prague Powder No. 2 and 32.5g (1⅛oz) salt OR 35g (1¼oz) salt with no cure
- 2 teaspoons crushed black peppercorns
- 1 teaspoon demerara sugar
- 20cm (8in) sprig of rosemary, needles removed

> To cure the pork belly, follow the method for Streaky Bacon on page 82, adding the rosemary needles with the curing salts. After the bacon has finished curing for 5–7 days in the refrigerator, remove

>>>

it from the bag and pat dry on kitchen paper. Hang in a curing chamber at 12–16°C (57–61°F) for at least a month and up to 2 months (see pages 116–18). It can be hung for longer, but it will become harder and saltier.

> To serve, slice thinly and wrap around chicken breasts or scallops, or cut into small lardons and use as a flavouring in soups, sauces or *ragùs*. Pancetta can also be minced and included in meatballs. Always remove the skin before cooking, as it is too tough to break down.

VARIATION

To make guanciale, cured pork cheek, follow the recipe for pancetta but cover the surface with finely ground black pepper before hanging – this was traditionally done to keep the flies away.

PETIT SALÉ

The French equivalent of bacon, *petit salé* is also made with belly of pork. Once cured, the salted pork is traditionally boiled and the broth used for cooking pulses such as lentils. *Petit Salé aux Lentilles* is one of my favourite French dishes. It is usually served on top of the lentils along with boiled *saucisson sec* and ham hock, sometimes with *sauerkraut* too.

> METHOD Follow the method for Streaky Bacon on page 82, curing for a week in a bag in the refrigerator; use curing salts if you wish to preserve the pink colour or plain salt for a natural pork colour. Remove from the bag, rinse briefly and pat dry with kitchen paper. To cook, put the petit salé (if you wish with a ham hock and a saucisson sec or two) into a large stock pot two-thirds full with cold water. Bring the water slowly to the boil. Taste

the water and if it is too salty for a stock discard it and start again. From boiling point it should take 40 minutes–1 hour to cook the pork through. The internal temperature of the belly should be 77°C (171°F). Remove from the heat. Gently fry a little roughly chopped carrot, celery and onion in a saucepan until soft. Add the lentils, a couple of bay leaves and a sprig of thyme and stir through, pour over enough ham stock to cover them. Cook until tender, drain and serve topped with sliced belly, sausage and flaked ham hock. Cool and freeze any leftover stock for another day.

LARDING

Larding really improves the texture and flavour of your meat, and smoothes out any hard areas of flesh. It should be carried out after the initial drying process (once the meat has lost 25 per cent of its original weight).

METHOD Mix together lard and flour in equal quantities, depending on the size of your joint. We start with 200g (7oz) flour and 200g (7oz) lard and make up more if necessary (any leftover lard can be stored in the refrigerator in a covered container). Slather the mixture over your meat – this is very therapeutic – and return it to the curing chamber until the meat has lost 30–40 per cent of its original weight.

✳ HAMS

There are two main methods of turning a slab of pork into sweet, pink alluring ham: dry-curing and wet-curing (or brining). Dry-curing involves rubbing the pork with salt and sometimes sugar or molasses; wet-curing involves soaking the pork in a sweet bath of flavoured brine – lucky ham! Both methods can be made with or without curing salts, but without you will not have the traditional pink colour we associate with ham and you won't have the same protection curing salts give against decay and contamination.

During our first experiments, it was easy to see where the cure hadn't penetrated to the inside because when we cut the ham open the centre displayed a circle of grey meat while the surrounding area was pink. This can be corrected when wet-brining by injecting the brine into the centre of the joint with a brine pump. This speeds up the process because the brine enters the meat from the outside and the centre, ensuring all of the meat is evenly cured. Alternatively, you can leave the ham for longer in the brine.

After curing, large hams will always be very salty on the outside and the middle much less so. This is why hams are traditionally hung for at least a month afterwards to equalize the saltiness throughout. Alternatively, they can be soaked overnight in cold water to remove excess salt or boiled in several changes of water.

For dry-curing, allow 100g (3½oz) curing salts per kilo of meat: EITHER 9g (¼oz) Quickcure and 91g (3¼oz) salt OR ½ level teaspoon (2.5g/¹⁄₁₆oz) Prague Powder No. 2 and 98g (3½oz) salt. For wet-brining, allow 100g (3½oz) curing salts per 1kg (2lb 4oz) of curable ingredients – i.e. water and meat combined.

Once the ham has been cured, it can either be left unsmoked or smoked. At home, we smoke our Christmas ham, air-dry prosciutto and smoke and air-dry *speck*.

BRADENHAM-STYLE HAM

This traditional British ham is dry-cured to begin with and then given a sweet bath of wet-brine flavoured with dark beer, stout or porter. The original recipe is protected, but this is a good alternative. The first stage is to make a cured ham – i.e. one that has been treated with curing salts – this will help to preserve it, give it the pink colour and offer protection against bacteria.

SERVES 18–20
- 4kg (8lb 12oz) boned leg of pork

FOR THE DRY-CURE
- 400g (14oz) curing salts: EITHER 36g (1¼oz) Quickcure and 364g (12¾) salt OR 10g (¼oz) Prague Powder No. 2 and 390g (13¾oz) fine salt

FOR THE BRINE
- 4 litres (7 pints) Guinness (use in equal weight to the amount of cured meat and make sure it is fully submerged – you can use half Guinness and half water but there will be a weaker flavour to the end result)
- 400g (14oz) molasses
- 4 bay leaves
- 2 teaspoons juniper berries
- 4 teaspoons coriander seeds
- 4 teaspoons black pepper

TO COOK
- 2 teaspoons mustard seeds
- 3 bay leaves
- 1 teaspoon allspice berries
- honey and demerara sugar, for the glaze

> Mix the curing salts with the salt and divide this mixture in half. You will need half now and the rest in 2 weeks; the remaining half can be kept in a container in a dark place. Rub the mixture into the pork, applying 90 per cent of the

mixture to the exposed meat and fat and 10 per cent to the skin. Place the pork in a container, preferably raised up on a non-metal rack to allow the water that will leach out of the meat to drain off. Alternatively, slope the container so you can drain off the water easily. Cover and store in the refrigerator or in a cold place (below 5°C/41°F) for 2 weeks. Turn daily and pour off the brine periodically.

> Remove the pork from the container and rub the reserved cure mixture into the meat. Rinse out the container, put the pork inside and return it to a cold place to cure for a further 2 weeks.

> Rinse the cured ham under cold running water and pat dry with kitchen paper; wash the container. Put the ham on a wire rack at room temperature to dry overnight.

> Meanwhile, make up the brine by heating the Guinness with the molasses and flavourings; set aside to cool completely.

> Place the ham in the container and pour over the brine. Weigh it down to keep it submerged, if necessary. Set aside in the refrigerator or a cool place (below 5°C/41°F) for 2 weeks, turning every 2 days.

> Remove the ham from the container and discard the soaking liquor. Dry the meat with kitchen paper and hang in a curing chamber at 12–16°C (57–61°F) for 1 month (see pages 116–18).

> Before cooking, soak the ham for 24 hours in cold water. To cook the ham, place it in a pan of fresh water with the spices and bring to the boil. Put on a lid and simmer for 25 minutes per 450g (1lb) or until the internal temperature is 75°C (167°F). Once cooked, remove from the heat and allow the ham to cool and relax in the juices for 30 minutes. It can either be eaten like this or glazed and roasted in a hot oven to finish.

> To glaze and roast the ham, remove the ham from the pan, cut off the skin and discard. Smother the fat side in honey and press on a coating of demerara sugar. Cook in a hot oven, 180°C/350°F/ gas 4, for 30–45 minutes until the glaze has deepened to a rich golden brown. Remove from the oven and allow the ham to rest for 30 minutes before eating. Eat straight away or allow it to cool and store in the refrigerator for up to 5 days.

CHRISTMAS HAM

Christmas wouldn't be the same without a ham bubbling away on Christmas Eve waiting for its skin to be scored into diamonds and stuffed with cloves. I rub ours with homemade marmalade, and this year I decided to cure and smoke it myself. After a few trial runs during the year before the big day, I am happy to say the flavour was wonderful from the start and I will be doing it every year.

SERVES APPROX. 18
• 4kg (8lb 12oz) boned leg of pork leg

BRINE FOR WEEKS 1–2
• 900g (2lb) curing salts: EITHER 81g (2¾oz) Quickcure and 819g (1lb 3¼oz) salt OR 23g (1oz) Prague Powder No. 2 and 877g (1lb 15oz) fine salt
• 5 litres (9 pints) cold water
• 450g (1lb) dark soft brown sugar

BRINE FOR WEEKS 3–4
• 900g (2lb) curing salts: EITHER 81g (2¾oz) Quickcure and 819g (1lb 3¼oz) salt OR 23g (1oz) Prague Powder No. 2 and 877g (1lb 15oz) fine salt
• 5 litres (9 pints) cold water
• 450g (1lb) dark soft brown sugar

> Mix together the first batch of curing salts with the water and sugar to make the brine for the first 2 weeks. Stab the pork a few times with a skewer to help the brine to penetrate and put it into a large glass or non-reactive metal container just bigger than the joint. Pour over the brine and weigh down the meat to keep it submerged – I use a full carton of UHT juice inside a ziplock bag as a weight. Cover the container with a lid or a plate and set aside in the refrigerator or in a cold garage to cure for 2 weeks. Turn the meat daily and ensure it is always completely submerged in the brine.

> After 2 weeks, discard the brine and give the ham a quick rinse under cold running water; clean out the container. Put the ham back into the container and mix up the next batch of brine; pour this over the ham. Transfer the ham, covered, to a cool place for 2 weeks, as before, turning daily.

> After the ham has finished curing, remove it from the brine and pat dry with kitchen paper. Put it on a wire rack to allow air to circulate and transfer it to a cool place (such as a refrigerator) to dry overnight or for up to 2 days before smoking it.

> To smoke the ham, follow the instructions for cold smoking on pages 134.

> If you decide not to smoke the ham, hang it for at least a month in a meat safe in a cool room or in a curing chamber; air-drying improves the flavour and equalizes the saltiness.

> After smoking, allow the ham to come slowly down to room temperature before hanging as above. For best results, hang the ham to allow the smoke flavour to equalize within the ham. Hanging time can be a bit shorter if smoked, 2–3 weeks is fine. After hanging, scrub the ham with a brush and soak overnight before cooking in several changes of water.

> To cook the ham, follow the instructions on page 86. Once cooked, the ham will keep for up to 5 days in the refrigerator.

VARIATION

If you wish, you can flavour the brine with juniper berries, rosemary or bay leaves.

SMALL PROSCIUTTO

Giancarlo and I have enjoyed so much wonderful *prosciutto* from San Daniele in Friuli, the north of Italy, and from Parma in Emilia-Romagna in the centre of Italy, that anything we have been able to produce here in the UK with our climate just doesn't match up. After countless legs of pork being wasted, not to mention time and money, we have come to the conclusion that it is better to leave this product in Italy where it belongs. Instead we have taken great pride in making successful small *prosciutto* that are quicker and easier to prepare and take up less space.

Small (1–2kg/2lb 4oz–4lb 8oz) pieces of pork are a wonderful way to test your curing abilities. With these you will be able to practise larding and wrapping and discover how salty you like your meat. On these smaller pieces you are looking for 30 per cent weight loss before the meat is ready to eat. This will depend upon your environment, but you should be able to make a small *prosciutto* such as this within 2 months. It is really important to weigh the ham at the beginning to calculate the weight loss.

In particularly dry environments, such as Parma and San Daniele in Italy, curing salts are not always used. The combination of salting, rising acidity in the meat (where particular bacteria thrive and cause fermentation) and drying makes an environment where it would be difficult for bad bacteria to grow. However, we do not have such a climate in the UK, and hence there is little tradition of this kind. So when recreating these recipes, we always include the curing salts for safety's sake.

- 2kg (4lb 8oz) lean pork with part skin (taken from the leg joint)
- 200g (7oz) curing salts per 1kg (2lb 4oz) of meat: EITHER 18g (¾oz) Quickcure and 182g (199¼oz) salt OR 5g (⅛oz) Prague Powder No. 2 and 195g (199⅞oz) salt
- 100g (3½oz) demerara or light soft brown sugar

> Remove the skin with a sharp knife, leaving a layer of white fat on the meat. Combine the curing salts with the sugar in a bowl. Rub the curing mixture into the meat all over, with more on the flesh side and less on the fatty side, making sure it is well covered and you haven't missed any crevices. Put into a non-metal container on a plastic rack (or put the container on a slope). Cover and store in the refrigerator or in a cold place (below 5°C/41°F) for 3 days. Turn the meat every day and drain off any water in the container.

> After 3 days, wipe off the cure with kitchen paper and weigh your meat. Rinse under cold running water and wash down with cider vinegar or white wine vinegar. Wrap the *prosciutto* in two layers of muslin and fasten with string. Hang on a butcher's hook in your curing chamber at 12–16°C (57–61°F) until the prosciutto has lost 25 per cent of its weight; this will take approx. 5–6 weeks depending on the size of the meat.

> At this stage, the *prosciutto* should be unwrapped and larded (see page 84) to equalize the cure. Return the larded ham to the curing chamber for a further few weeks until it has lost at least 30 per cent of its original weight, ideally 35 per cent for optimum texture and flavour. When the prosciutto is ready it should feel firm to the touch.

> Now for the exciting part... cleaning off an area of ham and slicing off the first sliver. Slice another and taste it. We were really chuffed with ours, our very own small *prosciutto* – it wasn't San Daniele or Ibérico, but gosh it was sweet, salty and made our mouths water! Once you have cut into your ham, either wrap it in baking parchment and consume within a couple of weeks, storing it in the refrigerator, or re-lard it and hang it back in your curing chamber. The longer you leave it, the harder it will become, so I recommend you use it up within the month.

COPPA

Coppa is made from the nape of the pig, at the top of the shoulder where it joins the loin. The nape usually measures approx. 25cm (10cm)in length and 12cm (4½in) across from an average pig. If you split a boned-out shoulder, you can use the nape for *coppa* and the rest of the shoulder for *speck*. *Coppa* is a relatively easy and quick ham to make and we think it works well in most climates.

This recipe is for a 1.5kg (3lb 5oz) nape of pork. For smaller or larger joints, allow 50g (1¾oz) curing salts 1kg (2lb 4oz) of meat (EITHER 9g/¼oz Quickcure and 41g/1½oz salt per 1kg/2lb 4oz OR 3g/¹⁄₁₆oz Prague Powder No. 2 and 47g/1¹¹⁄₁₆oz salt).

MAKES APPROX. 1KG (2LB 4OZ)

- 1.5kg (3lb 5oz) nape of pork, trimmed
- 75g (2½oz) curing salts: EITHER 14g (½oz) Quickcure and 61g (2oz) salt OR 4g (⅛oz) Prague Powder No. 2 and 71g (2⁷⁄₁₆oz) salt

> Trim and tidy the cut to get rid of any shaggy pieces hanging off the nape. Rub the curing salts into the pork. Transfer the pork onto a rack inside a container with a lid. Set aside to cure in the refrigerator for approx. 7 days. (If your pork is larger than this, allow 7 days per 2.5cm/1in to the centre of the pork via the shortest route.) Pour the water off daily.

> Rinse the cured *coppa* quickly under cold running water (but don't soak it) and pat dry with kitchen paper. Wrap the pork in two layers of muslin and fasten with string. Weigh the coppa and hang in your curing chamber at 12–16°C (57–61°F) until it loses 35 per cent of its weight, checking regularly. In our experience, it took 3 weeks to achieve this. We found it wasn't ready below 25 per cent and it had dried out above 45 per cent.

> Serve finely sliced, preferably cut on a slicing machine or with a very sharp knife. After opening, wrap in baking parchment and keep in the refrigerator. Consume within a couple of weeks.

VARIATIONS

CHILLI, LEMON AND ROSEMARY COPPA

Follow the method for curing the Coppa (see above), adding the following flavourings with the curing salts: finely grated zest of 1 lemon, finely chopped needles of 2 sprigs of rosemary and 10g (¼oz) chilli flakes. After curing, pat dry on kitchen paper and rub the flesh with 2 teaspoons of chilli flakes. Wrap the coppa in muslin and air-dry in your curing chamber as before.

VANILLA COPPA

Marc Frederic's favourite way to make coppa is using vanilla salt, which he makes by infusing vanilla pods in his curing salt for a few weeks before using.

LOIN OF PORK

Loins can be cured in the same way as *coppa*. Loin of pork is a great joint to start with because it doesn't take long to cure. For maximum flavour, try covering it with smoked paprika or black pepper before drying in your curing chamber.

SPECK

Speck is a method rather than a cut that comes from the Austro-Italian border. *Speck* can be made either using the shoulder or leg of pork. According to the Italians, it must not be smoked with resinous woods such as pine – however, the Germans and Austrians say it should be!

Traditionally *speck* is not larded, but we have found this useful. For speed, we chose to cure a small shoulder rather than a large leg. Often curing salts are not used, but we prefer to use them for safety.

MAKES APPROX. 2KG (4LB 8OZ)

- 2 bay leaves
- 5 teaspoons juniper berries
- 1–2 teaspoons freshly ground black pepper
- 150g (5½oz) curing salt: EITHER 27g (1oz) Quickcure and 123g (4½oz) salt OR 8g (¼oz) Prague Powder No. 2 and 142g (5¼oz) salt
- 2 garlic cloves, finely chopped
- 3kg (6lb 8oz) boned pork shoulder, neatly trimmed

> Whizz the herbs and spices in a spice grinder or crush in a pestle and mortar; mix with the curing salt and garlic. Rub the mixture over the meat and place, skin-side down, in a container. (It doesn't need to be on a rack, as the mixture will form a pickle that the meat sits in.) Put on a lid and set aside to cure in the refrigerator

for approx. 10 days. As a rule of thumb, allow 7 days per 2.5cm (1in) to the centre of the meat via the shortest route.

> Remove the cured pork from the container and rinse it quickly under the tap. Pat dry on kitchen paper and place on a wire rack to dry at room temperature for an hour or two (provided it isn't a hot summer's day).
> Cold smoke the *speck* over beech wood – this will take 7 days over gentle smoke in an open smoker or 3 hours in a Bradley smoker, where the smoke is more concentrated.
> After smoking, weigh your *speck* and hang in a curing chamber at 12–16°C (57–61°F) for approx. 5–6 weeks until it has lost 25 per cent of its weight. After this, the *speck* should be larded (see page 84) and rehung for a further 6 months.
> At this point, you can try a slice from one end, just in from the outer edge, and see if it is ready eat it. If it seems soft or not tasty enough, re-lard that end and rehang for a further month. Serve cut into wafer thin slices with pickled gherkins and sourdough rye bread.

* SAUSAGES

Sausage-making is a giggle, at least the first time – it causes an infernal amount of teenage innuendo but it really is fun to do. Sausages are really not that difficult to make and can be cooked and eaten straight away or allowed to dry – I know that if you cook and eat them immediately this isn't strictly food preservation, but if you have all the equipment why not make use of it? Sausagemeat can be made into patties or meatballs if you cannot get hold of casings or a sausage machine.

We alter the stuffings frequently as you can see from some of our favourite recipes.

EQUIPMENT
- MINCER with approx. 7mm (⅜in) holes – or buy coarsely ground mince from your butcher
- SAUSAGE-MAKING MACHINE – this is essential if you are making more than a few sausages (although you could try filling the casings with a funnel). Some food mixers, such as Kenwood, come with a sausage-making attachment.
- SAUSAGE PRICKER, corn-on-the-cob skewer or thick pin
- BUTCHER'S STRING
- PROBE THERMOMETER to check the internal temperature of cooked foods
- BUTCHER'S HOOKS

SAUSAGE-MAKING TIPS
- HYGIENE Keep everything super clean and refrigerator cold. Work in a cold environment. When we worked with the butchers in Lazio, I have never been so cold in my life! Your hands might hurt when mixing cold meat, but it will help keep the bacteria from growing.
- SALT As a rule of thumb, allow 15–18g (½–¾oz) salt per 1kg (2lb 4oz) of meat for regular sausages and 23–25g (1oz) per 1kg (2lb 4oz) for cured sausages that will hang, such as salami.
- MIXING Mix the ingredients together really well with your hands until thoroughly mixed. Remove any glands and bloody parts you see.
- TASTING YOUR MIXTURE Take a little of the mixture out and fry it in a pan to check the seasoning before filling the casings.
- FILLING THE CASINGS Keep the skins wet while on the nozzle, dabbing them with cold water frequently. Ease them off with one hand, while guiding the

sausage with the other. Prick the skins straight away if you see an air bubble. Sausages don't need to be pricked unless you see a lot of air bubbles.

- **TWISTING OR TYING?** For British sausages, twist the sausages a few times at the desired lengths after you have finished filling the casings. For cured sausages, such as salami, don't twist in the normal way (or the air won't be able to circulate properly around them during hanging). Instead, fasten them at intervals with butcher's string. For best results, hang like a garland in the chamber so that they don't rest against each other.
- **HANGING** For cured sausages, wipe the finished sausages with vinegar to make them shiny and attractive. This should deter insects if you are hanging them, but don't rely on this.
- **RESTING IN THE REFRIGERATOR** Allow British sausages to rest in the refrigerator overnight before cooking them. This helps meld the flavours together.
- **COOKING** Cook British sausages over a low heat in a frying pan or in the oven at 180°C/350°F/gas 4, turning frequently in the pan or twice in the oven. Make sure they are cooked through to the centre; a temperature probe is ideal for this. They should have an internal temperature of 72°C (162°F).

WHICH CASINGS?

There are a variety of natural casings available. The standard ones for sausage-making are hog casings made from pig intestines. Small sausages, such as merguez, are frequently made with lamb intestines, and these are useful if you are not a pork eater, however these are more delicate and can tear easily. Large skins made from beef middles are used for salami-making; these should be removed before eating. Extra-large casings made from beef, known as ox bungs, are used for huge sausages like *mortadella*. Natural casings are kept in salt in bags or they can be frozen. They don't smell great and should be washed before use. Avoid using discoloured or grey casings, and throw them away if they smell really bad or break easily.

Collagen casings, made from animal hide, are not as pleasant to eat as they are made from intestines. However, they are convenient because most of them don't require soaking before use (check the manufacturer's instructions) and they are usually sold ready to transfer straight from the spool onto the machine spout.

MAKING SAUSAGES

All natural casings should be soaked in water with a little vinegar for 1 hour (up to overnight) in the refrigerator before use to soften them. Allow time to unravel the lengths. To help them open, so that they glide easily onto the machine, pour a little cold water into the open end to lubricate it from the inside. A good tip is to thread them onto the spout of a tap and let the water run through; cut the end off where it came into contact with the tap for cleanliness. This will push the impurities out and show up any holes.

Combine the ingredients for the filling in a stainless-steel or glass bowl until they are thoroughly mixed. It is important to include a minimum of 20 per cent back fat to stop the mixture from drying out; I prefer 30 per cent as a general rule for a better flavour and texture. We prefer to cut the fat by hand as we find it softens and creams in the mincer. Always taste some of the filling by frying it in a pan before filling your casings to check for seasoning. Go easy on the garlic; we have learned from experience that a little goes a long way.

TRADITIONAL PORK AND LEEK SAUSAGE

After much experimentation, we LOVE these sausages. The addition of leeks just gives them a lick of sweetness, which marries so well with the pork. We used belly of pork mixed with shoulder meat, as between them there is a good mixture of fat and lean meat. We regularly make a batch and eat some straight away (even though they are better after a day resting in the refrigerator). The rest we freeze in fives, the number in our family, tightly wrapped in baking parchment in two layers.

MAKES APPROX. 20 SAUSAGES, 13CM (5IN) LONG

- approx. 4m (13ft) hog casings
- 2.5kg (5lb 8oz) mixed belly and shoulder of pork with fat and lean bits
- 200g (7oz) leeks, finely chopped
- 2 tablespoons extra virgin olive oil
- 370g (13oz) stale white breadcrumbs
- 42g (1½oz) fine salt
- 1 teaspoon ground white pepper
- 1 teaspoon grated nutmeg
- 1 small garlic clove, grated

> Prepare the casings as on page 91.
> Meanwhile, put the meat through a coarse mincer or ask your butcher to mince it for you. Set aside in the refrigerator to cool. Cook the leeks in the oil over a medium heat until soft but not brown. Set aside to cool completely.
> To make the filling, mix all the ingredients together in a large bowl. Cover with a plate and transfer to the refrigerator while set up the sausage stuffer.

> Fill the canister of the sausage-maker with the prepared meat mix. Put a length of hog casing onto the nozzle and tie a knot in the end. Turn the handle to start filling the sausages. Filling is easier when there are two of you, so that one person is turning the handle at the correct speed while the other helps guide the casings off the end of the nozzle, watching out for air bubbles and pricking them when they appear. Finish a length either when the casings run out or when the meat does. Link or tie the sausages as necessary (see page 91) and set aside in a container in the refrigerator to rest for 24 hours. Either eat straight away or 'open' freeze on trays in your freezer and pack into ziplock or vacuum bags once frozen. Frozen sausages should be consumed within 3 months.

ITALIAN FENNEL SEED SAUSAGE

These taste really authentic and Tuscan. When we first made them, they brought tears to Giancarlo's eyes as he remembered home!

MAKES APPROX. 18 SAUSAGES, 13CM (5IN) LONG

- approx. 3–4m (10–13ft) hog casings
- 3 garlic cloves, peeled
- 75ml (2½fl oz) white wine
- 2.4kg (4lb 12oz) pork (⅓ back fat and ⅔ lean meat), coarsely minced
- 60g (2¼oz) salt
- 1 teaspoon whole fennel seeds, very lightly crushed
- 1 teaspoon ground white pepper

> Prepare the casings as on page 91.
> Mince the garlic with the white wine in a food processor, then mix with the remaining ingredients. To fill the casings, follow the instructions for Traditional Pork and Leek Sausage (see left).

VARIATION

Substitute 500g (1lb 2oz) of the pork with 500g (1lb 2oz) minced pork liver and leave out the fennel seeds. We saw this done in Lazio, where the sausages were called *salsicce neri* or black sausages, since they become dark from the livers. I am not an offal fan, but I thought the flavour was outstanding – rich, more meaty and slightly softer in texture. This recipe is a great way to use up the liver. You can include the heart and spleen too, but I felt it would make the sausages too strong in flavour.

SMALL COTECHINO-STYLE SAUSAGE

Cotechino is usually a large salami-style Italian sausage, but we saw individual ones on a recent trip to Turin and decided to make our own. Often the large ones are sold ready-cooked as this can take hours.

This recipe makes great use of the scraps of pork, such as the skin, ears and tougher cuts, which are left behind after the main pieces have been removed for making *prosciutto* or salami. The long, 1½-hour boiling time softens the texture, resulting in a tender, savoury sausage that melts in your mouth.

MAKES 24 SAUSAGES, APPROX. 13CM (5IN) LONG

- approx. 4–5m (13–16½ft) hog casings
- 2kg (4lb 8oz) pork (35 per cent back fat; the rest should be made up of lean meat and scraps, see above), finely minced
- 60g (2¼oz) curing salts: EITHER 18g (¾oz) Quickcure and 42g (1½oz) salt OR 5g (⅛oz) Prague Powder No. 2 and 55g (2⅛oz) fine salt
- 1 teaspoon freshly ground black pepper
- 1 teaspoon freshly grated nutmeg
- ½ teaspoon ground cloves

> To make the sausages, follow the method for Traditional Pork and Leek Sausage (see left). Do not prick them, as they will be boiled. To cook the sausages, put them into a saucepan of cold water and bring to the boil; reduce the heat immediately to a simmer and cook for 1½ hours.

FRENCH SAUCISSON

This recipe is a mixture of the *Saucisson de Ménage* (or *de Campagne*) and the *Saucisson à l'Ail* from Jane Grigson's wonderful book, Charcuterie and French Pork Cookery. It is a really versatile sausage with a lovely garlicky flavour that just gets better with time. Eat them after a day boiled or fried, or hang them in a curing chamber for up to a month to dry them out (see pages 116–18) and enjoy like salami. They are also great smoked (see pages 132–3). Boiling them gives a great stock, which you can use for cooking lentils or in soup. Jane Grigson uses *quatre épices*, a pre-mixed blend chosen from four spices: allspice, cloves, cinnamon, ginger and white pepper.

MAKES APPROX. 12–15 SAUSAGES, 15CM (6IN) LONG

- 3–4m (10–13ft) hog casings
- 2kg (4lb 8oz) pork (⅓ fat and ⅔ lean meat)
- 4 garlic cloves, pounded in a pestle and mortar
- 50g (1¾oz) curing salts: EITHER 18g (¾oz) Quickcure and 32g (1oz) fine salt OR 5g (⅛oz) Prague Powder No. 2 and 45g (1⅝oz) fine salt
- 2½ teaspoons ground black pepper
- 1½ teaspoons *quatre épices*, made up from a pinch each of allspice, cloves, cinnamon and white pepper
- 4 teaspoons golden caster sugar

>>>

> To make the sausages, follow the method for Traditional Pork and Leek Sausage on page 92. If eating fresh, rather than curing, twist the sausages at the desired length and store in the refrigerator overnight before cooking.

> For cured sausages, *Saucissons sec*, fasten the sausages at intervals with butcher's string and hang in the curing chamber at 12–16°C (57–61°F) for 1 month (see pages 116–18). Eat as salami, slicing them thinly. Store cured sausages in the refrigerator, wrapped in baking parchment, and consume within a couple of weeks as they will continue to dry out.

> For smoked sausages, fasten the sausages at intervals with butcher's string and hang in your refrigerator (or curing chamber at 12–16°C/57–61°F) for 24 hours to form a pellicle. Cold smoke over oak or apple wood for 2–3 hours (see pages 132–3). Either eat immediately or hang in the curing chamber at 12–16°C (57–61°F) to dry for a further month. The sausages can be frozen at any stage, but should be consumed within 3 months.

SOBRASADA-STYLE SPREADING SAUSAGE

The traditional *sobrasada de Mallorca* has a protected name, meaning that it cannot be called that if it is produced outside Mallorca (where it is made from the local pigs). *Sobrasada* has been made for centuries, its first mention being in the 17th century. It is the same size as salami and also made from pork with paprika, salt and spices as flavourings. It is cured but not hardened, meaning it can be cut open and spread on hot toast – usually topped with a slice of Manchego cheese – or stirred into pasta sauces or casseroles. Our version is small to give a faster curing time. In the dry climate of Mallorca these sausages do not traditionally contain curing salts, but we have added them and suggest you do as a precaution against bad bacteria forming during the short hanging time.

MAKES APPROX. 20 SAUSAGES, APPROX. 12CM (4½IN) LONG

- 1.3kg (3lb) belly pork
- 100g (3½oz) paprika
- approx. 3–4m (10–13ft) hog casings
- 700g (1lb 9oz) lean pork meat
- 48g (1¾oz) curing salts: EITHER 48g (1¾oz) fine salt OR 18g (¾oz) Quickcure and 30g (1oz) fine salt OR 5g (⅛oz) Prague Powder No. 2 and 43g (1⅝oz) fine salt
- 1 teaspoon freshly ground black pepper
- 1 teaspoon dried thyme
- 1 teaspoon dried oregano

> Mince the meat through a mincer using a 3–5mm (⅛–¼in) diameter grinder disc. To make the sausages, follow the method for Traditional Pork and Leek Sausage on page 92. Tie the individual sausages at intervals with butcher's string instead of twisting.

> Hang the sausages in a warm room overnight (18–24°C/64–75°F) to kickstart fermentation. Then transfer to the curing chamber at 12–16°C (57–61°F) for a further 2 weeks (see pages 116–18). Eat straight away or wrap in baking parchment and store in the refrigerator for up to 2 weeks where they will continue to harden.

CHORIZO

According to Spanish chef, José Pizarro, every town in Spain has its own recipe for chorizo – and that is just the ingredients. Some chorizos are spreadable in consistency, some are firm, some are for cooking, others for slicing for tapas, some are fresh, others are air-dried and some are smoked or made with smoked paprika. In the following recipes we used a mixture of sweet paprika (pimentón dulce) and hot paprika (pimentón picante) to give just the right degree of pungency. Paprika is made from ground dried red peppers (see pages 127–8 for how to make it yourself).

SPANISH FRESH CHORIZO

This recipe, and the following one for dried *chorizo*, comes from chef and writer Nick Sandler. Nick likes to use a 2-year-old pig for *chorizo*, preferably a Black-Footed Pig; this has a good amount of shoulder and back fat as well as a good flavour. This fresh *chorizo* is great crumbled into rice dishes, put onto pizza or simply fried and served with eggs.

MAKES 30–35 SAUSAGES, 12–15CM (4½–6IN) LONG

- approx. 6–7m (19½–23ft) hog casings
- 4kg (8lb 12oz) belly pork, minced through an 8mm (⅜in)-gauge mincer
- 80g (2¾oz) fine sea salt
- 40g (1½oz) garlic, peeled and pounded to a paste
- 120g (4¼oz) Spanish paprika (80g/2¾oz *pimentón dulce* and 40g/1½oz) *pimentón picante*)

> Prepare the casings as on page 91.
> Put gloves on (or the mixture will dye your hands) and combine the ingredients really well in a bowl for 5 minutes. To fill the casings, follow the method for Traditional Pork and Leek Sausage (see page 92); store in the refrigerator for 24 hours. Either use straight away, store in the refrigerator for up to a week or freeze for up to 3 months.

SPANISH DRIED CHORIZO

This dried version will last longer than the fresh *chorizo* because it contains curing salts. Over time it will become firm enough to slice. Nick prefers to mix the meat with the curing salts and flavourings the night before making the sausages to kickstart the curing process. He then chills the mixture in the refrigerator overnight so that it is properly chilled before it goes in the casings.

MAKES 12 SAUSAGES, APPROX. 30CM (12IN) LONG

- approx. 4–5m (13–16½ft) hog casings
- 2kg (4lb 8oz) back and belly fat
- 4kg (8lb 12oz) lean pork, minced through an 8mm (⅜in)-gauge mincer
- 150g (5½oz) curing salts: EITHER 54g (2oz) Quickcure and 96g (3½oz) fine sea salt OR 15g (½oz) Prague Powder No. 2 and 135g (5oz) fine salt
- 180g (6½oz) Spanish paprika (90g/3¼oz *pimentón dulce* and 90g/3¼oz *pimentón picante*)
- 36g (1¼oz) ground garlic, pounded in a pestle and mortar

> Prepare the casings as on page 91.
> Cut the fat into 1–2cm (½–¾in) cubes with a sharp knife. Put gloves on (or the paprika will dye your hands) and combine the fat with the remaining ingredients in a large bowl. Cover the bowl with a plate and transfer to the refrigerator overnight.
> Make the sausages following the method for Traditional Pork and Leek Sausage on page 91, tying them at 30cm (12in) intervals with butcher's string. Weigh your sausages. (If you wish to smoke the *chorizo*, see pages 132–3.)
> Hang the sausages in a curing chamber at 12–16°C (57–61°F) until they have achieved 30 per cent weight loss; ours took approx. 28 days. Make sure that

>>>

the air can circulate freely and that none of them are touching. Check on the sausages daily and wipe off any moulds that aren't white with strong alcohol – we use Grappa.

> Once dried, the *chorizo* can be stored in the refrigerator for up to a month or frozen for up to 3 months.

NORTH AFRICAN MERGUEZ

These spicy sausages are usually made with lamb and/or beef. They are stuffed into sheep intestines, which are smaller than typical hog casings and are very delicate to work with. If your casings split, don't despair: keep the good ones and either put the stuffing through again from any that have broken or shape into balls and fry like meatballs – they will taste just as good! *Merguez* are spiced with harissa paste, a fiery paste made from chilli. They are wonderful grilled and eaten with couscous or in a tagine.

MAKES APPROX. 12–15 SAUSAGES, APPROX. 12CM (4½IN) LONG

• 3–4m (10–13ft) sheep casings
• 750g (1lb 10oz) finely minced lamb
• 250g (9oz) finely minced beef
• 500g (1lb 2oz) beef or lamb fat, finely minced
• 38g (1½oz) salt
• 100g (3½oz) harissa or rose harissa paste (see pages 153–4)

> Prepare the casings as on page 91.
> Combine the minced meat in a bowl with the rest of the ingredients and mix really well with your hands. Make the sausages following the method for Traditional Pork and Leek Sausage on page 92. Cook straight away or rest overnight in the refrigerator.

> Serve with citrus couscous: combine some couscous with lots of olive oil, plenty of salt and pepper and loads of mixed citrus juice (lime, orange and lemon), stir in some dried fruits and raw onion and pour over enough water to cover. Leave overnight to fluff up and serve with the *merguez* and some fried chicken.

SOUTH AFRICAN BOEREWORS

These are often cooked on a South African *braai*, a barbecue, accompanied by fried onions and sweet chutney and, of course, a Southern African beer or two. They are filling and spicy and great in a soft bun. Try them with one of our chutneys on pages 27–34.

MAKES 20 BOEREWORS, APPROX. 15CM (6IN) LONG

• 4–5m (13–16½ft) hog casings
• 8 teaspoons coriander seeds
• 1 teaspoon cloves
• 1kg (2lb 4oz) fatty pork (this could be from really fatty belly or neck and/or cheek), coarsely minced
• 2kg (4lb 8oz) coarsely minced beef
• 2 teaspoons ground allspice
• ¼ nutmeg, grated
• 150ml (¼ pint) cider vinegar
• 3 teaspoons honey
• 60g (2¼oz) fine sea salt
• 3 teaspoons freshly ground or crushed black pepper

> Prepare the casings as on page 91.
> Toast the coriander seeds and cloves in a dry frying pan to release their fragrance and grind until smooth in a pestle and mortar or spice grinder. Combine with the remaining ingredients. Mix really well with cold, clean hands – it will hurt as your fingers get cold, but try to keep

going for at least 5 minutes to ensure the meat is really well blended with the flavourings. To make the sausages, follow the method for Traditional Pork and Leek Sausage on page 92. Store in the refrigerator and consume within 5 days or freeze and consume within 3 months.

ITALIAN SOPRESSATA

This reminds me of British haslet, in that the meat is pressed. It is a great way to use up non-prime cuts of meat, including the skin of pork – this releases gelatine during the cooking process, which helps to hold the shape of the *sopressata* together.

MAKES APPROX. 2–3KG (4LB 8OZ–6LB 8OZ)

- 5kg (11lb) pork trimmings, such as skin, bones with flesh on, etc. – one-third of this should be lean meat
- ½ teaspoon ground nutmeg per 1kg (2lb 4oz) of cooked meat
- 1 teaspoon ground black pepper per 1kg (2lb 4oz) of cooked meat
- 1 teaspoon crushed fennel seeds per 1kg (2lb 4oz) of cooked meat
- ½ teaspoon ground cinnamon per 1kg (2lb 4oz) of cooked meat
- 15g (½oz) salt per 1kg (2lb 4oz) of cooked meat

> Put the meat and bones in a large saucepan. Cover with cold water and simmer for 2 hours or until the skin is tender. Drain through a colander, discarding the stock, and set aside to cool slightly.
> Once the pork is cool enough to handle, pick the flesh from the bones and set aside with any pieces of boiled skin. Discard the bones. Chop the cooked flesh and skin into 2cm (¾in) pieces and place in a large bowl; you should be left with approx. 2–3kg (4lb 8oz–6lb 8oz) edible meat and skin. Weigh the contents and calculate the salt and spices. Add these to the bowl and mix well. Put the mixture into a double layer of muslin and squeeze tight. Tie with string at both ends to form a very large fat sausage shape. Hang in the refrigerator or curing chamber overnight. The next day it will have set so that it is firm enough to slice. To serve, unwrap the sausage and cut into thin slices. Enjoy with other cured meats as antipasti or with salad, or serve with pickles and warm bread.

* SALAMI

Salami is a cured sausage that is fermented and air-dried. The word 'salami' comes from the Italian *salare*, meaning 'to salt'. Roman soldiers were often paid with salt, hence the term 'salary', and they used this to preserve meat such as salami to offer a valuable source of protein in times when fresh meat was unavailable.

SALAMI-MAKING TIPS

MEAT Choose shoulder meat and back fat for salami-making. Avoid using white fat from belly of pork as it will smear; back fat is firmer and holds its shape better.

CURING TEMPERATURE Monitor the temperature in your curing chamber regularly with a thermometer.

For fermented meats, such as prosciutto and salami, it is necessary to introduce slight warmth (up to 24°C/75°F) during the first couple of days of air-drying to encourage fermentation. This provides a friendly climate for good, salt-tolerant bacteria, such as *Lactobacillus* and *Leuconostoc*, to flourish. In turn, these produce lactic and acetic acids that lower the pH value of the salami from 6 to 4.5; this is too acidic for most harmful bacteria to survive. After a couple of days in the warmth, the salami should be transferred to a cooler temperature to finish curing (12–16°C/57–61°F is fine).

INTRODUCING GOOD BACTERIA To encourage friendly bacteria and moulds to grow, it is a good idea to place a previously made salami in the curing chamber with your homemade salamis.

HUMIDITY Monitor the humidity in your curing chamber regularly with a hygrometer and check your salami daily for unwanted mould and any stickiness. If patches of slight tackiness are found, you may have a humidity problem. Wipe off the stickiness with vinegar and kitchen paper and re-hang before this becomes a problem. Real stickiness is a bad sign and it is best to discard your salami.

PRECAUTIONS The harmless white mould found on the outside of salami helps the fermentation process and is nothing to worry about. However, any other coloured mould is dodgy; if you catch it very early on you can wipe it off with kitchen paper dipped in vinegar.

CURING TIMES Allow 2–3 months in the curing chamber. Some people cure their salami for longer to acquire a stronger flavour and firmer meat; others prefer it softer and milder. In a professional environment, the temperature can be kept low to allow a controlled and slow-maturing process. However, at home this is rarely possible and you have to follow the ebb and flow of temperatures; this is often a process speedier than 3 months.

Giancarlo remembers making salami as a child. When Riccardo Cappelli, a visiting chef from Castello Banfi in Tuscany, came to our restaurant they had a wonderful time creating this Tuscan salami and recreating a little of Giancarlo's past.

MAKES 6 SALAMI, APPROX. 25–27CM (10–10¾IN) LONG

- 2–3m (6½–10ft) ox casings
- 3kg (6lb 8oz) lean pork shoulder, coarsely minced
- 300g (10½oz) white back fat, cut into 1cm (½in) cubes
- 2 fat garlic cloves, green stems removed, peeled and crushed to a smooth paste
- 88g (3¼oz) curing salts: EITHER 30g (1oz) Quickcure and 58g (2¼oz) salt OR 8g (¼oz) Prague Powder No. 2 and 80g (3oz) salt
- ½ teaspoon ground cinnamon
- ½ teaspoon ground nutmeg
- 1 tablespoon whole black peppercorns
- 100ml (3½fl oz) red wine

> Wash the casings with water and vinegar and leave to soak while you prepare the mixture. Keep the meat in the refrigerator until you are ready to use it.

> Combine the minced pork with the fat in a bowl. Add the garlic, curing salts, spices and red wine and mix thoroughly by hand for 10 minutes – it will change colour from pinky-red to brown.

> Fill each sausage to 25cm (10in) and then fasten with butcher's string. Make sure the meat really fills the casings; there should be no air holes and the filling should be really compact inside. Continue filling the rest of the casings with sausagemeat, tying at intervals with string. (If you tear a skin, squeeze out the mix and put it through again into a new skin.)

> Use a pricker (or corn-on-the-cob holder) to prick the sausages all over, and then massage them smooth with your hand to release any air bubbles trapped inside.

> Hang the sausages in your curing chamber at 24°C (75°F) for 2 days, and then move them to a cooler place (at 12–16°C/ 57–61°F) to finish curing. Curing will take 2–3 months. For more information on salami-making, see pages 97–8.

> The salami will continue to harden if left in the curing chamber, so don't leave them too long before eating. Once cut, wrap the cut end tightly in baking parchment and store in the refrigerator for up to 6 weeks.

VARIATION

FENNEL SALAMI

Omit the black peppercorns and replace with the same amount of fennel seeds.

∗ OTHER MEATS

RHUBARB-CURED HAUNCH OF VENISON BY PAUL BURTON

The story of this cure is that a culled hind was given to Paul just as forced rhubarb was coming into season. Seeing the two in his kitchen, he decided to marry them together. The high acidity of the rhubarb, and its enzymes, have a preservative and tenderising effect on the meat.

MAKES APPROX. 700G (1LB 9OZ)

- 500g (1lb 2oz) (4–6 sticks) forced rhubarb (unforced is more bitter so add a teaspoon more sugar)
- 1 teaspoon juniper berries
- ½ teaspoon cloves
- 1 teaspoon black peppercorns
- 1 teaspoon allspice berries

- 8g (¼oz) demerara sugar
- 68g (2½oz) curing salts: EITHER 14g (½oz) Quickcure and 54g salt (2oz) OR 4g (⅛oz) Prague Powder No. 2 and 64g (2⅜oz) salt
- 1kg (2lb 4oz) cannon of venison (trimmed loin)

FOR THE RUB

- 2 teaspoons juniper berries (optional)
- 4 rounded teaspoons black peppercorns
- 35ml (1fl oz) gin

> Roughly chop and crush the rhubarb either in a food processor or using a meat mallet on a chopping board. Grind the spices with the sugar and curing salts in a spice grinder. Combine the rhubarb with the spice mixture in a container and add the venison. Rub the rhubarb/ spice mixture all over the venison to coat it well on all sides and then put a lid on the container. Transfer the venison to the refrigerator or a cold room at 2–5°C (36–41°F) to marinate for 5 days, turning every other day.

> Rinse the cured venison under the tap and pat dry on kitchen paper. Put on a wire rack, resting on a roasting tray and set aside in a warm room at 24°C (75°F) to start the fermentation process.

> The following day, make up the rub: grind the spices in a spice grinder and combine them with the gin in a small bowl. Sprinkle the mixture over the venison and press down with your fingers to coat it on all sides. Return the meat to the rack for a further 24 hours before smoking.

> Smoking flavours the venison and allows the natural enzymes and lactic beasties (Paul's words, not mine) to do their work. We also find it disguises the metallic tang that can sometimes be detected in less well aged examples. If you don't have

a smoker, go to the next step. To smoke the venison, place it over fruit wood such as apple for 24 hours in gentle smoke; we did ours in the barbecue smoker. For more information on Smoking, see pages 134–5.

> After smoking, wrap the venison in muslin and hang in a curing chamber for 2 weeks at 12–16°C (57–61°F). Serve thinly sliced with bread and sliced pears. To store, wrap tightly in baking parchment and keep in the refrigerator for up to 1 month.

CURED DUCK AND GOOSE BREASTS

Cured duck and goose breasts have an intense gamey flavour after hanging. They are delicious cut into thin slices and eaten at room temperature as part of an antipasti platter. If the game is wild, freeze it first to kill any parasites.

• 1kg (2lb 4oz) duck or goose breasts
• 50g (1¾oz) curing salts: EITHER 9g (¼oz) Quickcure and 41g (1½oz) fine salt OR ½ teaspoon (2.5g/¹⁄₁₆oz) Prague Powder No. 2 and 47.5g (1¹¹⁄₁₆oz)fine salt

> Rub the curing salts into the duck or goose breasts, rubbing it more generously over the thicker areas and using less on the thinner areas and skin. Put onto a rack or a couple of chopsticks inside a container so that the juices can leach out. Transfer to the refrigerator to cure for 1–3 days. A small duck breast will only need a day but a large, fat goose breast could need the full 36 hours.
> Rinse the breasts briefly under cold running water and pat dry on kitchen paper. Leave them to dry on a rack at room temperature for a couple of hours.
> Hang the duck breasts in a curing chamber at 12–16°C (57–61°F) to dry

for a further 10 days to lose weight and concentrate the flavour. Eat straight away or wrap in baking parchment and keep in the refrigerator for up to 6 weeks.

DUCK BREASTS CURED WITH SALTED KUMQUATS

For this recipe, we cured the duck breasts in the citrus brine from the Salted Kumquats on pages 76–7. The duck flavour is intensified by the salting and drying process and the orange flavour is subtle but delicious.

SERVES 4

• 9g (¼oz) Quickcure and 7 tablespoons brine from the Salted Kumquats (see pages 88–89) OR ½ level teaspoon (2.5g/¹⁄₁₆oz) Prague Powder No. 2 and 8 tablespoons of brine from the Salted Kumquats (see pages 76–7)
• 1kg (2lb 4oz) duck breasts

> Combine the curing salts with the kumquat brine. Pour a little of the salty brine into the bottom of a small container. Put in the duck breasts, skin-side up, and cover with the rest of the salty liquid. Put on a lid and set aside to cure in the refrigerator for 36 hours.
> Remove the duck breasts, discarding the cure. Rinse them briefly under cold running water and pat dry with kitchen paper. Hang in a curing chamber at 12–16°C (57–61°F) to dry for 10 days, or put on a wire rack, uncovered, in the refrigerator. Serve thinly sliced. Accompany with a few thinly sliced pieces of salted kumquat, some rocket leaves and warm bread and butter.

DRY-CURED BRESAOLA

Bresaola is made in the north of Italy and is usually dry cured. It is full of iron and low in fat. We serve it as part of our antipasti boards in our restaurants, but I like it at home as a canapé rolled with rocket and shaved Parmesan inside.

- 1.5kg (3lb 5oz) silverside or top rump (it could be in 2–3 pieces)

FOR THE CURE

- 10cm (2in) sprig of rosemary, needles removed
- 1 teaspoon juniper berries
- 1 teaspoon cloves
- 1 teaspoon black peppercorns
- 2 bay leaves
- 42g (1½oz) curing salts: EITHER 14g (½oz) Quickcure and 28g (1oz) fine salt OR 4g (⅛oz) Prague Powder No. 2 and 38g (1⁷/₁₆oz) fine salt
- 25g (1oz) caster sugar
- 1 level teaspoon orange peel powder (optional, see pages 111–12)

> First, make the cure. Whizz the herbs and spices in a spice grinder or crush in a pestle and mortar. Combine with the curing salts, sugar and orange peel powder in a bowl. Rub half of the cure into the meat; the rest should be stored in a container in a dark place. Put the meat into a ziplock or vacuum bag and set aside to cure in the refrigerator for 7 days, turning daily.

> Remove the meat from the bag and rinse quickly under the tap. Dry carefully on kitchen paper and rub in the remainder of the cure. Put the meat in a clean ziplock or vacuum bag and return to the refrigerator for a further 7 days, turning daily.

> Remove the meat from the bag and wipe off the cure with kitchen paper.

Weigh the meat. Wrap the meat in two layers of muslin and hang in a curing chamber at 12–16°C (57–61°F) until it has lost 30–35 per cent of its weight; this will take approx. 5–6 months. Check on the meat every week and wipe off any spots of mould that are not white using kitchen paper dipped in vinegar. Once fully cured, the meat should feel firm to the touch with a slight give on the inside.

> Once the beef has lost one-third of its weight it is ready to taste. Remove a small piece of meat, bearing in mind that the outside will be very strong, and see if you like the flavour. If necessary, you can rewrap and hang the meat until it is dried to your liking.

> After air-drying, wipe down the meat with vinegar and store in clean muslin in the refrigerator. Use within a few weeks; as it will carry on hardening.

SALT BEEF

This recipe makes the most of a cheap cut. Brisket has plenty of connective tissue and a covering of fat which offer flavour and break down during cooking. You can make this without curing salts, but it will lose the bright red colour associated with salt beef.

MAKES APPROX. 3KG (6LB 8OZ)

- 3kg (6lb 8oz) beef brisket

FOR THE CURE

- 4 litres (7 pints) water
- 268g (9¾oz) curing salts: EITHER 63g (2½oz) Quickcure and 205g (7¼oz) fine salt OR 18g (¾oz) Prague Powder No. 2 and 250g (9oz) fine salt
- 210g (7¼oz) soft brown sugar
- 2 medium dried chillies
- 1 teaspoon crushed juniper berries
- 1 teaspoon whole allspice

>>>

FOR THE STOCK

- 1 fat carrot, cut in half lengthways
- 1 onion, cut in half
- 1 bay leaf
- 1 sprig of rosemary
- 1 sprig of thyme
- 2 celery sticks, including leaves
- 4 garlic cloves, crushed with the flat of a knife
- 10 black peppercorns

> Combine the water, curing salts and sugar in a large saucepan and bring slowly to the boil. Skim off the scum and add the spices. Simmer for 4 minutes, stirring to dissolve the sugar; remove the pan from the heat and set aside to cool to room temperature.

> Pour the curing liquor into a glass container with a lid and chill in the refrigerator. Once cold, add the meat and weigh it down with weights; cover with a lid. Transfer the container to the refrigerator for 7–10 days, turning the meat twice during this time.

> After the beef has finished curing, remove it from the container, discarding the curing liquor. Rinse briefly under cold water and put into a large saucepan. Cover with fresh water and add the carrot, onion, bay leaf, rosemary, thyme, celery sticks, garlic and peppercorns. Bring to the boil, cover with a lid and then reduce the heat to low. Simmer for approx. 2–3 hours or until the meat is very tender when prodded with a skewer. Serve hot straight away (or reheated in its broth). Alternatively, set aside to cool and serve sliced with pickled gherkins, rye or sourdough bread, sauerkraut and mustard. Store any leftovers in the refrigerator, wrapped in baking parchment, for up to a week.

Pastrami can be made from mutton or venison, however beef brisket is the most well-known version. Ask your butcher for a trimmed brisket with a very thin layer of fat.

SERVES 20

- 3kg (6lb 8oz) beef brisket, mainly trimmed but with a thin covering of fat

FOR THE RUB

- 1 tablespoon black peppercorns
- 1 tablespoon pink peppercorns
- 1 tablespoon coriander seeds
- 1 tablespoon paprika
- 2 tablespoons soft brown sugar
- 3 fat garlic cloves, crushed

> To cure the brisket, follow the curing instructions for Salt Beef.

> Rinse the cured beef quickly under cold running water and pat dry on kitchen paper. Crush the spices for the rub in a pestle and mortar or spice grinder and mix with sugar in a bowl. Massage the garlic all over the meat, and then coat with the spice mixture. Transfer the meat to a large plastic bag, seal the top of the bag and suck out as much air as possible using a straw. Marinate in the refrigerator for 24 hours, turning it a couple of times. Then remove it from the bag and discard the juices. Allow the meat to dry for a few hours in the fridge before smoking.

> Hot smoke over oak until the internal temperature reaches 70°C (158°F) – as a guide ours takes 4–5 hours at 105°C (221°F) in a Bradley smoker. Remove from the smoker and eat straight away or leave to cool. To store, wrap in baking parchment and keep in the fridge for up to a week. Serve thick or very thinly sliced in sandwiches or on an antipasti platter.

AIR

If we dry any food, so that it loses two-thirds of its original weight, we can halt bacterial growth. Without water, micro-organisms that cause decay are unable to survive. We can remove the water using a number of processes – from leaving the food out in the hot sun to dry to using a dehydrator, a machine especially designed to dry food.

Preserving food by dehydration has been carried out in almost all cultures since the dawn of man. Probably the first dried foods were discovered by accident – perhaps dates fallen from the tree, or meat hung in thorn bushes to keep it safe from animals, only to be discovered much later dried and edible. We know that ancient Egyptians dried fish and poultry in the hot sun as far back as 12,000 BC and ancient Japanese made pots to gather shellfish for drying in 10,000 BC. Much later, Native Americans mixed dried meat with fat and dried fruit to make a high-energy food known as pemmican. This had a long shelf-life and contained virtually all the nutrients needed for survival, making it perfect for taking with them on their travels.

Today, of course, we don't rely on this method of preserving food for our survival, but it is still a good way of improving the flavour of certain foods and introducing an appealing texture. Many foods that are preserved by drying take on an intense, concentrated and complex flavour – think of the difference between biting into a crisp, slightly tart fresh apple and chewing on a sweet, dried apple ring or the contrast between a fresh tomato and a chewy, intensely flavoured sun-dried tomato, or raw beef and jerky. Through drying, we can play with the layers of flavour and alter the mouthfeel.

For those who follow a raw food or living food diet, drying is treated as a necessity. Dehydrators provide a way of preserving and changing food without compromising the goodness it holds, since enzymes, vitamins and nutrients are kept intact; these can be destroyed at the high temperatures used to cook food in the traditional manner.

* SUN-DRYING

Sun-drying must be one of the earliest ways of preserving food known to man. In its simplest form it involves leaving the food outside in the hot sun to dry – for example think of sun-dried tomatoes from hot, sunny Italy. When I went porcini picking in Italy, I noticed that the locals used a thorny bush to dry their mushrooms. The mushrooms were picked early in the morning, pierced onto the branches of the bush and left to dry in the hot sun during the day.

Since our ancestors had no choice, they would sun-dry all foods from meat for jerky, fruit for pemmican and fish for use another day. I have successfully used the sun (when we see it) to dry all types of food and it is free. However you do need a warm day, no sign of rain, protection against insects and no animals around, which can limit you.

METHOD In hot, dry weather, scatter your fruit or vegetables on a rack, cover with a fine net to keep off insects and place outside in direct sunlight. At the first sight of rain, or at night, you should bring the rack inside. Drying should take 2–3 days, depending on temperature and humidity. To speed up the process, place your fruit or vegetables behind a pane of glass or inside a warm greenhouse. In wet weather, bring your produce indoors and leave to dry on a sunny windowsill – if necessary, move the food around the house to maximize the heat from the sunshine.

SOLAR-DRYING FRAMES If you enjoy drying your own produce, it is well worth constructing a purpose-built frame. This should be enclosed with netting on all sides, to keep out insects, and fitted with a tilted pane of glass or Perspex on top to speed up the drying process. Make sure the frame is large enough to accommodate a roasting tray – that way, you can finish off the drying process in the oven afterwards (see below) if the weather deteriorates.

* OVEN-DRYING

An oven can be used for all types of food but it is the most costly method and takes the longest amount of time. Part of the reason for this is that there is not much air blowing across the food despite the fan in the oven. If you think of fish drying in the sun in a hot country such as Sri Lanka, the sun is accompanied by a strong sea breeze or hams drying in San Daniele in Italy, which are in a building that catches the light mountain and sea winds through vents in the narrow windows. For this reason, I prefer to use the oven for drying foods that don't need long, such as fruit leathers or apple rings. Forget plums into prunes and dried fish, it takes too long. Check your produce frequently and move trays around as ovens can have hot spots.

METHOD Preheat your oven to a low setting, 55–65°C/130–150°F/gas ¼ is ideal. A fan oven is perfect; if using a conventional oven, leave the oven door slightly ajar. Arrange your loose fruit or vegetables on a wire rack to allow air to circulate or, if making fruit leathers, spread on a baking or roasting tray (see page 112). For temperatures and drying times, see individual recipes.

* DEHYDRATORS

An electric dehydrator is a sensible investment if you plan to do a lot of drying. Not only does it dry the food in half the time compared to a conventional oven, but is more energy efficient and produces more consistent results. Most models come with a thermostat to control the temperature and a timer, as well as silicone mats suitable for drying liquids such as fruit purées. We also use our dehydrator for rising bread if we are in a hurry and incubating yogurt and cheese.

I first heard about dehydrators a few years ago when a friend built one when he was on a raw food diet. I thought dried food sounded horrible and couldn't understand why you would want to dehydrate fresh food. Three years later we own a dehydrator and we love using it – sometimes it's good to be proved wrong! We lent our dehydrator out recently and one of our sons demanded it back saying he missed the rolls of sweet fruit leather.

There are plenty of foods that can be preserved in a dehydrator – from fruit leathers (see page 112) and herbs to kale crisps and pungent, earthy dried mushrooms. On the following pages are just a few ways to dry our favourite foods but there are so many possibilities.

DRYING FOOD IN A DEHYDRATOR

Only use produce in good condition and pick over it, checking for insects. Wash the food well and dry in a salad spinner or on clean tea towels. Remove any tough stalks that would take much longer to dry than the attached leaves, for example, and cut produce into even-sized pieces so that it all has roughly the same drying time.

As a general guide you should dehydrate herbs at 35°C (95°F), vegetables at 52°C (125°F), fruits at 57°C (135°F), and meat and fish at 68°C (154°F).

DRYING TIMES AND STORAGE

These vary considerably, depending on what you are drying. As a general guide, the safe maximum percentage of water left after drying is 10 per cent for vegetables, 20 per cent for fruit and no more than 20 per cent for meat. Weight loss can be measured by chemist's digital scales but I must admit we don't do that as the amounts we make are so small. The point of measuring is to make sure your produce has lost enough water to last a long time but if you are going to consume it relatively quickly weight loss is not an issue.

It is down to personal choice as to whether you dry foods to a crisp or semi-dry them to a leathery stage. Crisp foods, such as the hard, brittle banana chips that you can buy in health food stores, will have almost no moisture left inside them, so can be stored for up to a year and maybe longer. Personally we prefer them dried to a semi-dried or leathery state, even if they will only last a matter of weeks. You can tell when the produce has dried enough by allowing it to cool and cutting through the centre. There should be no visible sign of moisture. If it is darker inside, or obviously wet, you need to dry it more. You can test fruit by squeezing it: if no moisture comes out, it is ready. Fruit leather should feel leathery when done.

Vacuum-packed foods, where there is very little air inside the package, will last longer than those in an airtight tin where there is still some air inside. Vacuum-packed foods can be frozen to last longer still. All foods should be inspected regularly for signs of moisture and mould. Trust your eyes and nose and if you are suspicious throw it away.

∗ HUMIDITY

Humidity will affect your drying time enormously i.e. on very damp days it will take longer to dry your food than on dry days. If you want to measure it you will need a hygrometer. However, for simple fruit drying you just need to be aware that drying times will differ day to day and throughout the seasons.

* EQUIPMENT

For general drying of fruit and vegetables no specialist equipment is necessary unless you want to invest in a dehydrator. For drying outside you will need fly nets to stop insects landing while drying. Most dried foods can be stored in airtight jars or vacuum bags. For drying meat for charcuterie these are some of the things you may need:

- A hygrometer: a device for measuring humidity
- Thermometer
- A small fan
- Racks or homemade devices such as chopsticks over a dish to dry food

* DRYING FOOD – A BASIC GUIDE

FRUIT

Always choose good-quality fruit that is fresh but not soft or overripe. All fruits that can be thinly sliced – such as apples, bananas, mangoes, coconuts, apricots, figs, strawberries, pears and peaches can be successfully dried (see below for individual fruits). All of these make delicious snacks. They can also be used in cooking; the strawberries add great flavour and texture to biscuits and chopped dried apple is great in granola. There are some fruits that have such a large water content, and cannot be sliced easily, which take far too long in my opinion to be worth drying whole, such as grapes. Raspberries and blackberries should be carefully broken into pieces by hand. Alternatively, you can purée the fruit to make fruit leathers (see page 112 for recipes). Crisply dried fruit can last up to a year.

NOTE: Drying times for individual fruits vary according to the water content of the fruit and the humidity on the day, so don't rely on your previous experiences. Approximate drying times are given below and right, these are a guide only, check your dehydrator or oven regularly to see when your fruit is to your liking.

APPLES AND PEARS Core the fruit and cut into rings or slices 3mm (⅛in) thick; it's up to you whether you leave the skin on or off. Brush or dip in lemon juice or citric acid to prevent discolouration if you wish. I skip this step because I don't mind my fruit discoloured, and anyway dried fruit never lasts long in our house – not because of any bacterial growth, just because it is so moreish! Arrange the fruit on a rack and dry at 57°C (135°F) for 5–7 hours in a dehydrator or 65°C/150°F/gas ¼ in an oven for 6–12 hours or until pliable. Pack into airtight containers or vacuum bags and store in a cool, dark place for up to a year.

PLUMS For fruit with tough skins, such as plums, blanch in boiling water or steam for 3 minutes beforehand. This process will help to crack the skins so that water can be lost more easily. After blanching, plunge into ice-cold water to cool quickly and then pat dry on kitchen paper. Cut the fruit into halves and remove the stones. Arrange the fruit on a rack in the dehydrator and dry at 57°C (135°F) for up to 24 hours or until pliable and leathery. Pack into airtight containers or vacuum bags and store in a cool, dark place for up to a year. Use in any recipe that calls for prunes, such as the Spiced Red Onion Marmalade on page 32.

BANANAS, PEACHES AND MANGOES Cut into uniform slices, approx. 3mm (⅛in) thick. Arrange on a rack in the dehydrator and dry at 57°C (135°F) for 4–6 hours or use an oven at 65°C/150°F/gas ¼ and dry for approx. 6–8 hours until leathery. Pack into airtight containers or ziplock bags and store in a cool, dark place for up to a year.

STRAWBERRIES Cut into slices approx. 3mm (⅛in) thick – you can make them thinner or thicker if you wish, but in my experience wafer-thin slices tend to stick to the mats. Arrange on a rack in the dehydrator and dry at 57°C (135°F) for 5–7 hours or use an oven at 65°C/150°F/gas ¼ and dry for approx. 7–9 hours until leathery and crisp. Store in ziplock bags in a cool, dark place for up to a year.

FIGS AND APRICOTS Cut figs into quarters and apricots in half, removing the stones. Flatten and arrange on a rack in a dehydrator at 57°C (135°F) and dry for up to 30 hours until pliable. Dried figs are delicious soaked in brandy and then dipped in chocolate, Calabrian style, or included in cake and biscuit recipes, see the Pan de Higo on page 111.

VEGETABLES

ONIONS AND GARLIC Peel and finely slice the onion and peel and roughly chop the garlic. Scatter onto the racks or mats in a dehydrator and dry at 55°C (130°F) for 5–6 hours. Alternatively dry on a roasting tray in the oven at 65°C/150°F/gas ¼ for 6–7 hours or until crisp. Pack into airtight containers or ziplock bags and store in a cool, dark place for up to 6 months. Dried onion pieces are great in homemade bread or for dressing a Thai curry.

To make onion or garlic powder, grind the dried onion/garlic pieces in a spice grinder; store in an airtight container. Onion and garlic powder make ideal flavourings for crisps, potato wedges, fried chicken, jerky, batters and rubs for meat and chicken.

MUSHROOMS This method is suitable for drying all sorts of mushrooms. At home, we collect fresh porcini and dry them to really concentrate the flavour.

Cut into slices 2mm (¹⁄₁₆in) thick and dry on a rack in a dehydrator at 57°C (135°F) for

3 hours. Alternatively, spread on a wire rack in the oven and dry at 65°C/150°F/gas ¼ for 5 hours or until crisp. Store in an airtight container or vacuum bag in a cool, dark place for up to a year.

To make mushroom powder, grind the dried mushroom pieces in a spice grinder. Store in an airtight jar in a cool, dark place for up to 3 months. This gives an earthy, umami punch to cooking. Rub into steak with sea salt and extra virgin olive oil, stir into gravy or stock, scatter through roast vegetables before cooking, mix into bread dough and savoury biscuits.

To rehydrate dried mushrooms, soak in warm water for up to 30 minutes until soft. Reserve the soaking liquor for flavouring sauces etc., however, make sure you sieve it carefully to remove any grit. Rehydrated mushrooms are great for the Mushroom Ketchup on page 35.

KALE Dehydrated kale leaves make great crisps when dried and lightly salted. To make kale crisps, cut away the leaves (cut into quarters if leaves are huge), discarding the core, sprinkle lightly with salt, chilli powder or onion/garlic powder and toss gently with your fingers. Spread on wire racks and dry in an oven or dehydrator until crisp. This is one method of drying where the oven is quicker. Cavolo nero or curly kale will take 1–2 hours in an oven at 65°C/150°F/gas ¼ or 3–4 hours in a dehydrator at 57°C (135°F). Store in an airtight container in a cool, dark place for up to a year.

To make kale crisps in a hurry, sprinkle the finely shredded kale with sea salt and drizzle with extra virgin olive oil. Spread on a wire rack in the oven at 200°C/400°F/gas 6 and bake for 5 minutes or until crisp. These make a great snack with drinks before a meal, especially if you have the oven on anyway. Eat straight away.

TOMATOES, COURGETTES, PEPPERS AND CHILLIES It might be a romantic thought but I do think the natural combination of drying in the sun and air gives a better flavour to these fruits and vegetables than drying in an oven with a fan.

Lay halved cherry tomatoes or quartered large tomatoes onto racks and scatter over a generous pinch of fine sea salt, caster sugar and a little thyme (fresh or dried). Lay 3mm (⅛in) courgettes slices, finger-width slices of peppers and halved chillies onto racks. Dry in the sun, covered with fly nets ,for up to several days, bringing the food inside in the evenings when humidity rises and the temperature drops.

Alternatively, you can dry tomatoes on a rack in a dehydrator at 57°C (135°F) for approx. 5-8 hours or in the oven at 65°C/150°F/gas ¼ for 6-9 hours, depending on the size of the fruit. Either store in airtight containers or under oil (see pages 148-9). Courgettes and chillies can be dried in a dehydrator at 55°C (130°F) for 2-3 hours or in the oven at 65°C/150°F/gas ¼ for 3-4 hours. Courgettes and chillies should not be stored under oil as they have little or no acidity. Instead store in airtight containers or vacuum bags for up to a year.

We dry halved chillies and small hot peppers in a basket in our kitchen or outdoors in the sunshine and sometimes smoke them afterwards (see pages 127-8). Once dried, they can be ground for dried chilli powder, or smoked and then ground for paprika. Chillies are best ground in a spice grinder as the dust particles can affect your eyes if you use a pestle and mortar.

Courgettes can be rehydrated or used in a semi-dried state and fried briefly, scattered with salt and dried mint and served as chips. Or use them in the *Courgettes alla Poverella* on page 149.

BEANS

BEANS AND PEAS These can be dried on the plant and then stored in jars. However, beware, dried beans can be susceptible to bean weevil, which means you could find adults emerging in your stored beans! To break the life cycle of the weevil, either freeze the dried beans for 5 days or keep in the refrigerator for a minimum of 7 days. After that they can be stored in a cool, dark cupboard until needed for up to a year. They should be rehydrated before use. Beans can be kept in sealed glass jars or vacuum bags.

POPCORN Hang whole corn cobs in a sunny, draughty place until well-dried. Remove the kernels with a sharp knife and store in airtight containers or vacuum bags in a cool, dark place for up to a year. Use for making popcorn.

SEEDS AND FLOWERS

Many growers dry seeds from their favourite plants to sow the following year. However, any spare seeds taken from plants such sunflower, pumpkin, fennel or coriander are great to use in cooking. To dry them, simply scatter them over a sheet of baking parchment and put in a warm place to dry.

MUSTARD SEED Tie bunches with string and hang upside down inside a large paper bag to catch the tiny seeds. Do this in a warm, well-ventilated room to encourage the seed pods to open. If the plant is not already dry, you should make a few holes in the bag around the top to allow air to circulate.

FLOWERS AND LEAVES FOR TEA Chamomile and certain types of jasmine flowers (if not from a plant treated with pesticides) can be preserved for tea. Pick the flowers early in the morning and dry as soon as possible. Dry the flowers on a sunny windowsill, or put in a dehydrator at 43°C (109°F) for 6-8 hours; alternatively, microwave on high for 30-second bursts. Young blackberry leaves can be dried slowly in a paper bag. Give them a shake daily before use.

PUMPKIN AND SUNFLOWER SEEDS Dry in a dehydrator or oven at 50°C (122°F) until brittle. Use in breads and cakes.

POPPY SEEDS The best seed to cultivate is the bread seed poppy, *Papaver somniferum*, whose seeds do not open to disperse, making them easier to harvest. I pick poppies from my garden and simply shake the seeds from the dried pods into bread and cakes, or use them as a garnish.

HERBS

Although we love fresh herbs there are some that are just as good, if not better, dried. Oregano is usually sold dried in bunches in Italy. The flavour is more intense and so a little goes a long way. It makes a huge difference to our pizza sauce when we use our own home-dried oregano rather than a bought dried version or fresh leaves. Dried oregano and thyme are wonderful rubbed into meat or chicken before cooking, with a little olive oil and salt. Dried mint is perfect for Harissa Paste (see pages 153–4).

OREGANO, MINT AND THYME On a warm day, these herbs can be left to dry on a wire cake rack on the kitchen windowsill. Alternatively, you can hang them in bunches upside down. Once dried, put the herbs into a clean bag and rub them to loosen the leaves. Discard the stems and store in airtight jars in a cool, dark place.

Soft-leaved herbs such as basil and mint can be dried efficiently in a microwave. Lay individual leaves between sheets of kitchen paper and put into the microwave on high for 30-second bursts until crisp and dry. Once dried, store in airtight jars in a cool, dark place for up to a year.

STORAGE OF DRIED FOODS

Containers should be thoroughly cleaned and have secure lids to keep out moisture and insects. Glass jars with lids or Kilner-style jars are ideal, as are vacuum or ziplock bags. Always store dried foods in a cool (10–16°C/50–61°F), dark place away from moisture.

PEPPER AND ALMOND CRACKERS

These terracotta-coloured crackers are deliciously sweet and salty. They are a great way of using up a glut of red peppers, which I love in almost any form. This recipe is based on one from the Preserve it Naturally cookbook, which normally comes with an Excalibur dehydrator. It is a fascinating book to read, especially if you are interested in raw and living food diets.

These crackers take a long time to make, so it is worth drying other items in the dehydrator at the same time. They are delicious topped with hummus, guacamole or cream cheese and Debi's Tomato, Chilli and Ginger Jam (see page 30). I have only given the method for making these in a dehydrator, as I think they would take forever in the oven.

SERVES 4–6 AS A SNACK
- 2 tablespoons raisins
- 100ml (3½fl oz) warm water
- 1 red pepper, destalked and seeded, cut into quarters
- 100g (3½oz) whole or ground almonds
- pinch of dried thyme
- pinch of salt
- pinch of ground chilli (optional)

> Soak the raisins in the water for 30 minutes; drain, reserving the water. Put all the ingredients into a food processor with 2 tablespoons of the raisin water

and blitz until smooth; if you prefer a chunky texture, leave slightly coarse. Mix to a spreadable paste with a little more of the raisin water, if necessary. Taste and adjust the seasoning.

> Spread the mixture onto a silicone sheet and dry in a dehydrator at 52°C (126°F) for 4 hours. Once dry enough to handle, peel off the paste and place upside down on a plastic or metal rack to dry out the other side. Reduce the temperature of the dehydrator to 41°C (106°F) and bake until crisp, approx. 4–6 hours. Once the cracker is brittle and dry all the way through, break it into pieces and eat straight away or store in an airtight container for up 5 days.

TARHANA – TURKISH HOMEMADE INSTANT VEGETABLE SOUP

Tarhana is said to be the first instant soup, invented by the Turks of Central Asia. Apparently this soup was served to the Sultan when he was a guest at a poor peasant's house, hence the name tarhana, deriving from the Turkish *dar hane*, meaning 'poor house'. Tarhana was traditionally prepared by the women of the village in summer using the glut of seasonal vegetables and stored throughout winter to make into soup. There are many variations of this dried soup including a Cypriot version made with yogurt, wheat and mint. Feel free to experiment with your own flavourings: ground cumin, coriander or paprika all work well.

MAKES APPROX. 1KG (2LB 4OZ)/SERVES 4

- 150g (5½oz) tomatoes, peeled
- 150g (5½oz) red pepper, deseeded
- 150g (5½oz) onions, peeled
- 150g (5o½z) cooked chickpeas, mashed
- 150g (5½oz) thick Turkish or Greek yogurt
- 7g (⅛oz) sachet of fast-acting yeast
- 700g (1lb 9oz) strong white flour
- a handful of parsley, finely chopped
- 1 tablespoon dried or finely chopped fresh mint leaves
- 3 tablespoons olive oil
- 1 tablespoon dried oregano
- 1–2 teaspoons salt

> Use a food processor to finely chop the tomatoes, red peppers and onions, or do this by hand. Combine the chopped vegetables in a bowl with the rest of the ingredients and mix to a firm paste with a little water. Bring together in a ball and turn out onto a clean work surface, scraping the bowl clean. Knead until the mixture is smooth and soft, and then return to the bowl. Cover with a plate or foil and set aside to ferment in a cool place, such as a refrigerator, for at least a day (up to 10 days). The length of time you leave the dough to ferment is up to you; the longer you leave it, the stronger the fermented flavour. We prefer it after just 3 days. Knead the dough every day for a few minutes and return to the bowl.

> Once the dough has fermented to your liking, flatten it onto trays and set aside to dry at room temperature or in the oven at 60°C/140°F/gas ¼ or a dehydrator at 57°C (135°F) until the outside is dry and the inside is still slightly moist, approx. 6–8 hours. Turn the flatbreads every few hours so that they dry evenly on both sides. Crack them into pieces to help the air to circulate.

> Once dry, grate the flatbreads into crumbs on the coarse side of a grater or push through a sieve onto a clean tea towel. Collect up the crumbs and spread them out on a baking tray to dry.

Transfer to a warm place (not outside or in a dehydrator or they will blow away!), moving the crumbs around from time to time to ensure they dry uniformly.

> You now have your instant soup granules, your tarhana. Traditionally they are kept in cotton bags, but you could store them in glass jars. They will last up to a year, stored in a cool, dry place.

TO REHYDRATE YOUR SOUP

Put 100g (3½oz) tarhana granules in a bowl with 500ml (18fl oz) water and set aside until the grains have swelled and there are no hard lumps, approx. 30 minutes. Tip into a large saucepan, stir in 1 litre (1¾ pints) chicken, meat or vegetable stock (or water) and bring to the boil. Season to taste with salt and stir in 1 tablespoon of tomato purée if you wish. Ladle the soup into bowls, crumble some halloumi cheese or cooked roasted red peppers over the top and garnish with shredded mint leaves. Finish with a swirl of extra virgin olive oil.

PAN DE HIGO – FIG AND NUT CAKES

This dense and gooey fig and nut cake is traditionally served in Spain with Manchego cheese and honey. It can either be made as a whole cake, served sliced, or made into balls and either wrapped in vine leaves or rolled in sesame seeds. *Pan de higo* is a good use of your dried fruits and stores well.

MAKES 18–20 BALLS

- 500g (1lb 2oz) dried figs
- 100g (3½oz) dried apricots
- 200g (7oz) walnuts or almonds
- ½ teaspoon ground nutmeg
- ½ teaspoon ground cinnamon
- ½ teaspoon ground cloves
- 2 tablespoons honey

- 2–4 tablespoons sweet wine or brandy
- 100g (3½oz) sesame seeds, for coating

> Remove any stems on the fruits. Put them in a food processor with the nuts and spices and pulse to a coarse paste; alternatively, finely chop everything by hand. Scoop the mixture into a bowl, adding the honey and enough wine to bring the mixture together in a ball. It should be firm but malleable. Break the mixture into golf-ball-sized pieces and shape into individual balls. Scatter the sesame seeds onto a plate and roll the balls in the seeds to coat them. Arrange on a wire rack and set aside at room temperature to harden for a day or two. Eat straight away or once hard, store in a tin with a lid in a cool, dark place for up to 3 months.

CITRUS POWDER

Instead of throwing away peel from oranges, limes and lemons, turn it into citrus powder. Our patisserie chef Dawid scatters a little citrus powder over dessert plates and on ice creams; I use it to flavour almond biscuits (see page 225).

> METHOD Peel the coloured zest only away from the fruit, leaving the white pith behind. Either leave in finger-width pieces if you are going to grind it later or use a zester to get long thin strips that will dry more quickly. Dry until crisp – either outside in the sun or in a dehydrator at 57°C (135°F) for 2–4 hours, or in a low oven. I often put mine in the oven overnight if I have been cooking; the residual heat cooks the peel for no extra energy. Grind the brittle strips into powder using a spice grinder or pestle and mortar.

> To make a zingy lemon salt for grinding over fish or into casseroles, zest a lemon

>>>

onto a thin bed of coarse sea salt. The essential oils will spray onto the salt. Dry as above and then crush with a pestle and mortar, a salt grinder or your fingers.

✳ FRUIT LEATHERS

These shiny, sweet strips of fruit make your mouth water and pucker with flavour. Whenever the kids make them they are swiftly eaten within the day as they are just so moreish.

Fruit leathers can be made from most puréed fruits, provided their water content is not too high – which rules out fruits such as citrus or rhubarb on their own, although these can be mixed with other fruits such as apple or banana. Ideal fruits are apples, berries, grapes, pears, peaches, plums, tomatoes, mango, pineapple and more. Always choose fruit in a good condition that is not bruised or overripe. Sweeten with sugar or honey to taste, although this isn't always necessary because the drying process concentrates the natural sugars anyway. Flavourings can be added such as vanilla to banana, chilli to pineapple and cinnamon to apple. Adding nuts or oats gives an interesting texture and ultimately makes the leather more filling for snacks. Tear or cut into strips in a pasta machine.

FRUIT LEATHER RECIPES

MAKES 1 LEATHER APPROX. 35CM (14IN) SQUARE

MANGO LEATHER

• 1 large mango

RASPBERRY AND BANANA LEATHER

• 2 bananas
• 200g (7oz) raspberries
• juice of ½ lemon

APPLE LEATHER

• 4 apples
• juice of ½ lemon

> Cut the fruit with or without the peel into chunks and purée in a food processor or blender. Pour the purée onto silicone mats. Make sure the pool of purée doesn't go over the edge of the trays; smooth out by shaking and tilting the tray to make it spread out. The purée should be no thicker than 3mm (⅛in).

> Dry in the dehydrator at 57°C (135°F) for 4–6 hours, or in the oven at 60°C/140°F/ gas ¼ for 6–8 hours. Fruit leathers are ready when they are not sticky to the touch, but can be peeled easily from the mat. Lift the edge, which will adhere lightly to the surface, and peel it back. If it peels back easily, it is ready.

RHUBARB AND STRAWBERRY LEATHER

• 2 long rhubarb sticks, roughly chopped
• 4 tablespoons caster sugar
• 8 strawberries

Cook the fruit with the sugar until it is soft and pulpy. Push through a sieve to remove the pips and tough fibres, and then dry following the method above.

✳ CHICKEN

FLAVIO'S CHICKEN FAJITA RUB

Once a week we eat fajitas with ours sons, Flavio and Giorgio. I was cautious about buying packets of pre-mixed rubs and salsa so we started to make our own. After a lot of fun experimenting, this is the version we liked most. Use as a marinade for chicken and serve with tortillas and Giorgio's Salsa (see pages 209–10).

MAKES APPROX. 4 PORTIONS (EACH PORTION IS ENOUGH RUB FOR 6)

- 6 tablespoons coriander seeds
- 6 teaspoons cumin seeds
- 1 tablespoon dried oregano (see page 109)
- 1 teaspoon saffron (not the terribly expensive kind as this is more for colour)
- 1 dried red chilli
- 2 teaspoons salt
- ¼ teaspoon ground nutmeg
- 6cm (2½in) cinnamon stick
- 1 heaped teaspoon pink peppercorns

> Heat the coriander and cumin seeds in a dry frying pan until they just start to pop; remove from the heat and cool. Put into a spice grinder with the remaining ingredients, in two batches if there isn't room, and grind until you have a powder. Store in a small glass jar for up to 3 months. It will keep for longer but the intensity of the spices fades with time. To use, coat diced chicken in the powder and leave to marinate for 30 minutes or up to 2 hours in a bowl in the refrigerator. As a guide, 1 tablespoon of powder will coat two diced chicken breasts. Fry the chicken in a little extra virgin olive oil until cooked through and use to fill soft warm tortillas with Giorgio's Salsa on pages 209–10.

✳ FISH

Only the freshest fish should be dried and, if it has not been salted first, the quicker it is done, the better before it starts to go off. Fish are 80 per cent water. If they are dried to hold only 25 per cent water, bacterial growth is halted. If they are dried to under 15 per cent water, moulds cannot grow.

In Sri Lanka, we saw stalls selling all types of dried seafood – from tiny prawns to slabs of tuna. The hot sun and sea breezes quickly dry the fish, after gutting first, while it is still on the boats. Dried fish is used to enhance complex flavours in many dishes.

As a general rule, lean fish such as cod and shellfish dry better than oily fish, since the fats in these can oxidize and become rancid.

Stockfish – usually cod – was traditionally freeze-dried in the cool, windy climate along the Norwegian, Swedish and Icelandic coastline, but it is now produced in factories. It has a strong, pronounced flavour of umami (see page 81), which I love but Giancarlo dislikes in fish. Stockfish should be soaked for a few days in several changes of water to prevent bacterial growth as it rehydrates. It can then be pounded to a creamy paste or poached in portions and cooked like fresh cod only with more flavour. *Baccalà* is similar but it is salted before drying.

AIR-DRIED MACKEREL FILLET

This delicious Japanese method of drying fish was shown to me by cookery teacher Rieko Hara. Air-dried mackerel has a rich, sweet taste with a hint of saltiness. Herring and sardines can also be dried in this way.

SERVES 4

- 4 mackerel fillets
- fine sea salt
- 50ml (2fl oz) mirin
- 50ml (2fl oz) sake
- 80ml (2½fl oz) Japanese soy sauce
- 50g (1¾oz) caster sugar
- 2 tablespoons white sesame seeds
- thinly sliced cucumber and radish dressed in sweet vinegar, to garnish

> Sprinkle the mackerel fillets with salt. Cover with a plate and set aside in the refrigerator for 1 hour.
> Meanwhile, make the marinade. Place the mirin and sake in a saucepan and bring to the boil to burn off the alcohol. Add the soy sauce and sugar and stir well over a low heat to dissolve the sugar, taking care not to burn. Set aside to cool to room temperature.
> Rinse the mackerel fillets in cold water and pat dry with kitchen paper. Pour the marinade into a large shallow container and add the fish, making sure the fillets don't overlap. Cover the container with a plate and set aside to marinate in the refrigerator overnight.
> The following day, lift out the fillets and dry carefully on kitchen paper. Sprinkle the sesame seeds over the flesh side of the fillets to coat them evenly. Arrange the fillets on a wire rack, sesame-side up, and set aside to dry in a cool place such as a north-facing room or garage, taking precautions to keep flies away, for 5–6 hours or until the surface is firm and no longer sticky. Either cook straight away (see below) or pack into freezer bags and store in the freezer for up to 3 months.
> To serve, grill the mackerel fillets for 3–4 minutes on each side until slightly brown and the sesame seeds are toasted. Serve with a cucumber and radish salad.

* MEAT

BEEF JERKY

Jerky as it is called today originates from Peru, where ch'arki (as it was known in the Inca language) was traditionally made using leftover meat from a hunt. It was originally created from wild game, however as farming methods grew it was made more and more from beef. Its popularity spread into North America, where jerky became the survival food for the pioneers as it could be taken on long journeys to provide vital nutrition.

Jerky should be made from lean, if tough, cuts of meat as fatty cuts are more susceptible to rancidity. Beef, lamb, venison or wild boar are all good. Jerky is high in protein and so it makes a nutritious and filling snack.

BEEF JERKY

Our son Giorgio loves jerky but it is expensive to buy so we make our own; this is his recipe. One of the joys of making jerky is experimenting with different flavours. However, do write down your experiments to repeat or avoid them next time. We recommend the following flavourings: spices such as coriander, curry powder or chilli; powders such as garlic and onion (see page 107), or sauces such as soy sauce, teriyaki, Worcestershire or Mushroom Ketchup (see page 35). If you wish you can finish your jerky in a smoker after drying.

MAKES 500G (1LB 2OZ)

- 1kg (2lb 4oz) beef such as rump, flank or top round

FOR THE MARINADE

- 500ml (18fl oz) soy sauce
- 1 tablespoon crushed coriander seeds
- 1 tablespoon dark brown sugar
- 2 garlic cloves, finely chopped
- 1 teaspoon chilli flakes
- ½ teaspoon freshly ground black pepper
- 2 heaped teaspoons grated fresh ginger

> If your meat is tough, put it in the freezer and partially freeze it; this makes it easier to cut.

> Cut the beef into 5mm (¼in) slices, cutting with the grain if the meat is tender or against the grain if it is not. If necessary, put the slices between sheets of baking parchment and bash with a meat mallet to tenderize them and make them all the same thickness. Cut any large pieces in half so they are all a similar size. Very roughly 12–15cm (4½–6in) in length and 4cm (1½in) in width is ideal.

> Mix together the ingredients for the marinade and pour into a large lasagne dish or similar. Add the beef strips, turning them so they are evenly coated in the marinade. Cover the dish with a plate and set aside to marinate in the refrigerator for at least 6 hours (preferably overnight).

> The following day, take out the meat strips and pat dry on kitchen paper. Arrange the meat on racks and dry at 68°C (154°F) in a dehydrator for 4–8 hours or in the oven at 60°C/140°F/gas ¼ for up to 8–10 hours. The jerky is ready when it feels dry and leathery; you should be able to bend it without snapping. Store in an airtight container or vacuum bags in a cool, dark place for up to a month or in the refrigerator for up to 6 months. It can be also frozen in vacuum bags and kept for up to 6 months.

VARIATION

Follow the instructions above with fresh salmon for salmon jerky but there is no need to bash out the pieces.

BILTONG

South African biltong and chilli pork loin strips can be made in a dehydrator, oven or purpose-built biltong box. The Bantu men of Africa originally taught the skill of drying meat to the Boers. Salt and air preserved the meats, which were hung out to dry; coriander seed was used as a flavouring or possibly as an insect deterrent. Eventually when the Boers settled they added saltpetre to the mix, which preserved the red colour of the meat and enabled it to be stored for longer. This recipe was given to me by Grant Fletcher, who now lives in the UK. He misses his biltong so much that he has resorted to making it himself in his own purpose-built biltong box.

MAKES APPROX. 500G (1LB 2OZ)

- 1kg (2lb 4oz) beef – a roasting joint such as top rump or a similar cut of venison
- rock salt
- 500ml (18fl oz) cider vinegar
- approx. 2 teaspoons freshly ground black pepper
- approx. 2 teaspoons ground or crushed coriander seeds

> Cut the beef into steaks, approx. 2cm (¾in) thick and the same length as the cut of meat. Put a scattering of rock salt into the base of a dish. Layer up the steaks, placing a sprinkling of salt in between each layer and covering with more salt on top. Set aside for approx. 20–30 minutes, during which time the meat will sweat as the salt starts to draw out the moisture.

> Pour the cider vinegar into a bowl and mix the spices into it. Grant's tip (or confession!) is that he never measures the spices – he says he just throws them in for good measure!

> After 30 minutes, remove the steaks from the dish and scrape off as much salt as possible from each one using the back of a knife. Dip the steaks in the vinegar and spice mixture, coating them on each side; this should wash off the salt and give them a nice coating.

> Hang the steaks in a biltong dryer (see

>>>

below) for 3 days or in a dehydrator at 68°C (154°F) for approx. 6 hours. To check it is fully dry, and ensure that it has lost enough water to preserve it, you can weigh the bundle. If dried correctly, the biltong should have lost half its original weight and the strips should snap when you bend them.

BILTONG BOX
This is designed to mimic the African climate where biltong is traditionally made. You can make a dryer yourself from a small cabinet or cupboard fitted with rails at the top from which you hang your biltong to dry. Biltong dryers are usually fitted with a light inside to drive off humidity and provide a little warmth, and a fan at the bottom. Two light bulbs and a computer fan are ideal.

CHILLI PORK STRIPS

Although these are made in a similar way to biltong, it is important to use specialist curing salts because pork is potentially more dangerous than beef.

MAKES APPROX. 500G (1LB 2OZ)
- 1kg (2lb 4oz) lean pork (leg meat is good)
- 35g (1¼oz) curing salts: EITHER 9g (¼oz) Quickcure and 26g (1oz) coarse salt OR 3g (⅛oz) Prague Powder No 2 and 32g (1⅛oz) coarse salt
- 250ml (9fl oz) cider vinegar
- 2 level teaspoons chilli powder
- ½–1 teaspoon chilli flakes
- 1–2 teaspoons fennel seeds, lightly crushed
> Follow the instructions for the Biltong (see pages 115–16), using curing salts and coarse salt instead of rock salt and chilli powder instead of the pepper and coriander. After dipping the meat in the vinegar, scatter with a few chilli flakes and fennel seeds (sparingly), pressing them into the surface of the meat. Dry as before.

* HAMS, SALAMI AND SAUSAGES

Most dried pork products, particularly hams, are salted first before being air-dried. In regions such as Parma and San Daniele in Italy, drying is traditionally done using the gentle local breezes.

WHERE TO CURE

After curing sausages and meat with salt, the next stage is to dry them so that they slowly lose moisture. This reduction in water content combined with the increased salt levels this creates prolongs the shelf-life and improves the flavour.

Although fermented charcuterie such as cured sausages need a little warmth to kickstart fermentation, after that they need to be moved somewhere cool. Similarly, hams and any other cured meats need to be stored somewhere the temperature does not exceed 16°C (61°F).

Before refrigeration, meat was cured in the coldest months of the year and hung in the coolest areas of people's houses. This might have been in a larder against a north-facing wall, with a small window for ventilation (but not a direct draught) and this is still viable today if you are lucky enough to have one. We have also had success with a curing box. By this I mean an old kitchen cupboard that has had a new door fitted onto it with a window and fly mesh attached. This stands in our garage where the badly fitted garage doors allow air to circulate. The box keeps the meat away from direct draughts and the fly mesh stops the insects. The temperature and relative humidity (see right) is fairly stable in our garage during the winter months and can be monitored from the warmth of our kitchen with a remote sensor.

However, conditions including temperature, humidity and air flow should always be monitored and controlled and this is hard to do in a large space like a garage. For this reason it makes life easier to create a small environment where this can be done easily, where you are in control. At home I have successfully cured bacon, salami and small hams in my wine refrigerator, which has a fan to circulate air, racks for hanging and a built-in temperature control. A small portable weather station available at most garden centres will tell you the temperature and humidity. The humidity can then be altered by not hanging too much in the space and by the saturated water (see Altering the humidity levels, right).

Alternatively, an old refrigerator can be adapted for this purpose. To increase air circulation, a computer fan can be put inside. It needs to have a small, thin lead to ensure the door shuts properly and the door seal is not disrupted. You can buy gadgets that control temperature and humidity and a humidifier can be employed to adjust this. There are plenty of plans and more detailed ideas of how to do this online.

Make sure wherever you choose to dry your charcuterie is scrupulously clean and has no traces of mould. You only want to encourage certain moulds for your meat. Hanging is better than putting meat on a rack as air can distribute easily and there are no marks or imprints left on the food.

HUMIDITY

Humidity is measured with a hygrometer. If you are going to start curing and drying, this is an essential gadget to have. We have a digital one that was not expensive and measures temperature as well as relative humidity (known as RH). It also has a remote sensor that I use in my garage or Wendy house when cold smoking.

The ideal humidity for curing meats is RH 75 per cent, however anywhere between RH 65–80 per cent is acceptable; in fact you will always have some variance during the day unless you are using a refrigerator. At the beginning of the curing period, RH 80 per cent is fine to encourage fermentation to take place and to kickstart the nitrates.

ALTERING THE HUMIDITY LEVELS

The humidity in an enclosed space such as a refrigerator can be altered using saturated salt in a container. Pour an amount of water, say 4 litres (7 pints), into a large saucepan and set it on the hob to boil. Add salt a little at a time and stir to dissolve. At some point you will not be able to add any more – you will see that it won't dissolve – this is when the solution is saturated. Allow the solution to cool and place in the curing chamber. Some crystals of salt will develop on the bottom of the bowl but don't worry about these. The solution has the ability to raise and lower the humidity as needed.

NOTE: If your chosen area is too dry or draughty your meat may develop 'case hardening' – this is when the outside of the sausage hardens. If this is allowed to form, the sausage will not cure properly on the inside and will remain soft. If this happens the sausage should be discarded.

TEMPERATURE

Curing is historically done in the winter when the foods, equipment and storage areas are naturally cold. By curing foods at lower temperatures we slow down the growth of bacteria, extending the shelf-life. The temperature surrounding the curing meat should be monitored at all times using a thermometer.

For fermented meats such as prosciutto and salami, etc. slight warmth (up to 24°C/75°F) for the first couple of days at the beginning encourages fermentation. However, this should always be followed by a long period in cooler conditions (12–16°C/54–61°F is fine). It is perfectly fine to cure bacon in a normal refrigerator at a temperature of approx. 4°C (39°F). All meats should be kept in the dark while they are curing.

FERMENTATION CULTURES

Fermentation happens at the beginning of making cured salami and sausages when the temperature is often a little higher to encourage it. All meat contains lactose, a type of sugar; bacteria eat this and make lactic acid. It is this enzyme activity that creates amino acids, which give us the unique flavour we enjoy in cured sausages. In a way it is a form of controlled rotting, which sounds unpleasant, but is in fact the natural breakdown of meat; this is why we like 28-day-hung steak rather than fresh.

MOULDS – GOOD AND BAD

Most white, dry, powdery moulds are good and help starve out other moulds; they form either as small white spots or as a fur. To prevent white moulds from completely swamping your meat, wipe them off regularly with vinegar or a strong spirit such as Grappa on a piece of kitchen paper. Before eating, it is advisable to clean off any moulds with a nail or toothbrush; keep the brush only for this task.

Most green moulds are bad and if these form you are better to err on the side of caution and discard the meat. However, a spot or two of green or blue mould can be cleaned away with vinegar and the meat re-hung.

Slimy grey or black, yellow, orange and red moulds definitely mean throw the meat away.

Many suppliers such as Weschenfelder sell fermentation kits with existing cultures in them to be included in sausage and salami mixtures. Some curers hang a sausage from a previous batch in with the new batch to introduce the right moulds.

SMOKE

It is good to know that you can create some really stunning smoked food with very basic equipment. At its simplest, food is smoked by putting it into a contained space with a smoky fire lit near it. Our ancestors have been doing this since they first learned to light a fire, without the use of any gadgetry such as internal temperature gauges, timers and briquettes.

What is fascinating is that there is something called 'the smoke line' – which neither Giancarlo nor I had heard of until we went to Friuli in Italy to research curing and smoking ham. It was explained to us that Friuli, which is situated just below the Alps, is on the border of this latitude that extends around the world. Areas above this latitude traditionally smoke their foods, while areas below it generally air-dry. This is due to the humidity in the atmosphere that makes food difficult to dry in regions above the smoke line – instead food is traditionally smoked as well in order to ensure it is properly preserved. Fascinating! It just demonstrates how humans all over the world have learned to adapt to their environment in order to make food last, using whichever method works best with the natural conditions.

I suggest you start with some very simple techniques such as smoking a piece of cheese (see page 127) to get the feel of what you are doing, and then you can progress to things like cold smoking bacon and hot smoking fish. Once you get confident – and hooked – you can begin to tweak the basic methods and experiment with different woods, etc.

Just one word of caution: research suggests that smoked foods should be eaten in moderation since they can damage your health in large quantities. However, whereas smoke used to be applied in a much more heavy-handed way, to ensure foods would last, nowadays foods tend to be smoked for flavour, more than as a preservative, so a lighter approach can be adopted.

HOW SMOKING PRESERVES FOOD

Wood smoke contains compounds that inhibit the growth of micro-organisms, slow down the rancidity of fats and provide a flavour that most of us find really moreish. Smoking also deters insects. As smoking only tends to penetrate the surface of the food, most foods are salted first and dried as a further preservative (see Salt and Air chapters for more information). Drying forms a pellicle, which is a slightly tacky film on the surface of the food. If you press your finger against the surface it will 'snap' as your finger is removed. This slight stickiness will help the smoke stick or cling to the food. And, of course, foods that are salted, dried and then smoked have a wonderful flavour, since drying helps to concentrate the flavour of the food and salt enhances it: think of smoked bacon, smoked salmon or peppered mackerel.

HOT AND COLD SMOKING

There are two types of smoking: hot and cold. Cold smoking is a gentle process, which takes place at a low temperature. Cold smoking dries out the food, preserves it and gives it a smoky flavour, without cooking it. Hot smoking takes the temperature much higher, and so it does actually cook the food. Strictly speaking, hot smoking in itself does not preserve food for long. However, if the food has been salted first it will keep for longer – Peppered Mackerel (page 138) and Hot Smoked Chicken (page 142), for example, can be enjoyed for days longer than their fresh counterparts. Also, hot smoked food tends to be eaten hot from the smoker, or fairly soon afterwards. Hot smoking originally gave shelf-life to fish that went off quickly, such as herrings that were turned into kippers. With refrigeration, this is now unnecessary, so some smokers prefer to cold smoke only as it gives a gentler flavour; the food can then be cooked afterwards. In cold weather most foods can be cold smoked as long as they have been salted first.

WOOD CHOICES

A variety of woods are available from specialist suppliers in the form of dust, chips or logs, all of which are ideal for smoking. Hard woods, such as oak and beech, should always be used since the sap in soft woods is not good for us – although certain recipes, such as German *speck*, are bizarrely smoked over pine (however, we don't recommend this).

Ideally you want to keep the temperature down and the humidity levels high. Larger pieces of wood should be green – that is, not completely wet and just cut, but not dried out either. Logs cut and left for approx. 6–9 months are ideal. This way, the wood will smoulder well. However, you can soak older logs and wood chips first to slow the burning time and make smoke, not fire. Sawdust can be sprayed with a water spray to do the same.

For cold smoking, milder flavours such as apple, cherry, oak and beech are often used, whereas for hot smoking a quick blast of a strong flavour such as hickory or mesquite is more effective over a short time.

Enthusiasts such as David at www.hotsmoked.co.uk agree that smoking should be about the food not about the smoke, so it is important to enhance the flavour of food, not disguise it. Saying that, certain woods do complement particular foods – for example, beech and salmon, or cheese and apple wood.

Indigenous North American cooked salmon over thin planks of wood soaked in water. This gives a subtle flavour. The food sits on top and as the wood steams the flavour is forced through the food. Planks are produced commercially for smoking or you can make your own but ensure that the wood hasn't been treated with chemicals.

Peat has been used for centuries in smoking to give a unique flavour. Traditionally, peat was popular in areas where there was little firewood. Environmentally, many people are against using peat as it is not sustainable.

CHOICE OF WOOD

This is a rough guide to the various woods and the suggested foods they should be married with.

ALDER A light, versatile, slightly sweet flavour – good with fish, seafood, poultry and game birds.

APPLE Mild and fruity, slightly sweet – good with cheese, bacon, poultry and pork.

BEECH A good all-rounder – ideal for fish, bacon and poultry.

BIRCH Medium strength, similar to maple – good with fish, poultry and pork.

CHERRY Mild and fruity, versatile – good all-rounder with fish, poultry, pork and beef.

CITRUS Light and fruity – good all-rounder.

HICKORY Strong – good with beef and lamb.

JUNIPER Spicy branches of juniper add flavour to Eastern European sausages.

MAPLE Fruity and sweet – good with pork, poultry, vegetables and cheese.

MESQUITE Strong flavour, good for hot smoking.

OAK A good all-rounder.

PEAR Light and sweet – good with poultry and pork.

WALNUT Heavy flavour – good with game and beef.

COLD DAYS AND HIGH HUMIDITY

Smoking has long been a tradition in mountainous areas where the high altitude and low humidity has created the perfect conditions for this form of food preservation. The outside temperature, humidity and breeze all influence smoking. It is better not to cold smoke in warm or humid weather, as you could inadvertently create the ideal environment for bacteria to breed. For cold smoking, the temperature inside your smoke chamber should be 10–30°C (50–86°F), with the ideal being 22–26°C (72–79°F); humidity should be no more than 85 per cent. Fish starts to cook above 30°C (86°F), so you need to keep the temperature well below this for safety. To be absolutely safe, I always do my cold smoking in cold weather and I enjoy the fact it has become a seasonal activity. If it is very cold outside you can heat the smoking chamber in an electric smoker, such as a Bradley, to approx. 25°C (77°F). I know from experience trying to cold smoke salmon for Christmas dinner in the snow that it took longer than normal to get the smoke to adhere to the fish.

Humidity is good when hot smoking to prevent the foods drying out; often water, or in some cases beer or wine, are introduced into the drip tray of the smoker to increase humidity. In the case of hot smoked Arbroath smokies, humidity is increased by splashing water onto the fire in the barrel before the fish are suspended over it. Wet sackcloth seals the top of the barrel so that, effectively, the fish are steamed in smoke – which creates a wonderfully moist result.

HOW AND WHERE TO SMOKE?

There are many ways to smoke food, using containers such as cardboard boxes, old refrigerators, or barrels to professional smoke chambers and purpose-built smokehouses, some of which develop a wonderful layer of tar on the inside to enhance the flavour. The smoky flavour of food is affected by many factors, including the density of smoke it is exposed to, the external and internal temperature of the smoking space and the fire temperature generated by the heat source.

We now have five different methods of smoking in and around our house and we use them all, depending on what and how much we want to smoke. Each method has its own pros and cons, however you really don't need five – just pick one or two that suit your surroundings and lifestyle.

∗ COLD SMOKERS

THE EXTERNAL FIRE SOURCE

Enthusiasts usually prefer to have an external fire source, which means you don't get smoked yourself while tending to your fire, and there is no chance of the flames and the heat being too close to your food. DIY fanatics often make their own using a length of ducting to channel the smoke from the fire source to the smoking chamber. My nephew Jamie has made his own, low-cost cold smoker, which he loves and tends to like a child. As far as he is concerned, it is all part of the joy of smoking to wake up in the middle of the night and relight the fire! If you fancy going down the DIY route, there are all kinds of forums, websites and books devoted to building your own model: take your pick!

MULTI-PURPOSE SMOKERS – THE BRADLEY SMOKER

For not a lot of money, and a lot less time spent scratching your head over calculations and drawings, you can simply buy a Bradley smoker, which plugs in and uses purpose-made bisquettes. We have one of these and it is great for both cold and hot smoking, as it has an element inside to control the heat. The beauty of a Bradley smoker is that it also has a timer and an oven control so it will keep going for hours without any fuss. The downside is that you have to buy the bisquettes, which makes it the most costly method of the five we recommend – although you might choose the ease of using it over the effort required for other methods. Our tip would be to learn to use the air vent (called the damper) on the top of the smoker effectively, since it is important to control the flow of smoke around the food because a high density of smoke will result in a very strong flavour. To get the most out of the cost of the fuel it is worth smoking as much as you can at the same time.

Heat the chamber to temperature first when hot smoking. Use the drip tray not only to collect fat and juices falling from the food but also to induce some humidity where necessary. Often wine, beer, juice or water is poured into it. See the instruction manual with your Bradley for more information or their website (see page 242).

THE OLD BARBECUE

Our barbecue broke years ago and was waiting for a trip to the dump. However, it now has a new lease of life as a cold smoker. Where once there was charcoal, we now have a ProQ Cold Smoke Generator in it. This is a maze made of wire mesh that contains enough fine sawdust to let out small wafts of smoke for 10 hours, so it produces slow, gentle cold smoke to give a subtle flavour. It is also available as an economical and eco-friendly smoking chamber consisting of a cardboard box fitted with a generator, shelves and drip trays. We have had wonderful results with our old barbecue, using it for smoking whole sides of salmon, cheese, tomatoes and more – it is absolutely my preferred method for cold smoking salmon and bacon. I can buy all sorts of dust easily, so I can have fun experimenting with flavour, and the whole process is inexpensive.

THE WENDY HOUSE – GARDEN SMOKEHOUSE

The kids lost interest in the Wendy house long ago, so now it has a greater purpose in life: a smokehouse for cold smoking. Any outhouse or shed will also suit this purpose, it doesn't have to be completely airtight as a gentle flow of air through the building is ideal. If there aren't already gaps you can drill holes low down in the door, for example, to allow air in and further holes opposite and high up for the smoke to exit. This helps carry the smoke up and through the food.

A garden smokehouse has the big advantage of being low tech, inexpensive and offers space for smoking plenty of food. The flavour of the food is greatly influenced by the density of the smoke it is exposed to; therefore this method of smoking using logs gives a mellow and perhaps less acrid taste to the food than other techniques. A small garden shed (approx. 1.8 x 1.1m/6 x 3½ft) is ideal.

In one corner, we light a small fire from tinder and logs in a fire bowl – a purpose-made, heavy-duty metal bowl for outdoor use – which sits on paving slabs to prevent the spread of heat onto the wooden floor. If you don't have a fire bowl, a metal box or

disused woodburner is ideal. Over the fire is a metal sheet, which limits the air supply to the fire to keep down the flames and heat. The food to be smoked is in another corner, high up on a rack resting on poles. While the fire smoulders gently and eventually burns out, we monitor the temperature and humidity from inside our kitchen using a remote sensor fitted on the rack. I occasionally use the smoke generator part of a Bradley in here to give more gentle smoke in a large area, especially when smoking lots of produce. For photos and videos of us hot-smoking at home see www.caldesi.com.

* HOT SMOKERS

THE DUSTBIN

Cheap, simple, unsophisticated and it works! This is our version of the barrels used to make Arbroath smokies. We light a fire, using kindling and birch logs, in a small grate in the bottom of a galvanized dustbin, and wait until it has subsided to embers. We spray these with a water-spray and then put a rack over the top on which the food sits, then we put the dustbin lid on. A wet towel over the top helps trap the smoke inside.

Iain Spink, a fourth-generation smoker from the Scottish coastline, demonstrated the traditional process of hanging Arbroath smokies over the fire, which is done in a particular way so that they do not fall into the embers. After numerous attempts to reproduce this system at home, I decided on the rack idea instead and we can now hot smoke mackerel, haddock and lean, smaller cuts of chicken in this way. This method should not be used to hot smoke fatty cuts of meat over a long period of time, since dripping fat could re-ignite the flames underneath. I love this method: it is cheap to construct and I can move my dustbin around wherever I want it – although I make sure it stands on a paving slab or some tiles, so it doesn't burn the lawn or decking. The process doesn't take long and is simple and not fiddly to get right. You just have to lift the lid to see if the food is done.

THE WOK

Many people smoke in a wok lined with foil but we have never been pleased with the results and ruined a wok in the process!

THE CAMERON STOVETOP

A favourite with our kids, this is small and portable so we can use it indoors on the hob under the extraction fan, or outdoors with the spirit burner to take on picnics. It is also economical, as a spoonful of dust is all it takes to create enough smoke to flavour foods such as salmon or mackerel.

HOW LONG TO SMOKE FOR?

As with so many of the processes in this book, this is probably the toughest question to answer. Invariably the experts I talked to would all begin with: 'well, that depends!' Smoke density, outside temperature, humidity and draught all affect the process, as does the freshness and size of the food to be smoked. You have to be the judge of when it is done and how smoky you want it to be.

Commercial smokers, who need consistent results, will take a more mathematical approach and measure weight loss. However, for home smoking the best way to tell is to use your senses: Move the product away from the smoke and give it a few minutes, then smell it for the strength of aroma.

- Touch it to feel the firmness and the loss of weight. Bill and Sukie Barber taught us to smoke. Bill explained that properly smoked food should feel like a block of jelly from a packet before it is made up with water: firm with a very slight give; it becomes quite translucent too.
- Look at the colour – often smoked foods will take on a golden appearance, particularly for eggs or mozzarella, where it shows up against the milky white of the food. However, dark meats do not show the colour change at all.
- Cut a small piece and taste it – either raw for salmon or cheese or cooked for chicken or pork. The outside of the food will be most affected by the smoke, so taste a second slice further in.
- Always use a probe thermometer for checking the internal temperature of hot smoked meats.

NOTE: The timings we give are just a guide, as humidity, temperature and wind will alter the smoking to an extent. Over time you will build up a feeling and an instinct for when your food is done. I found this happened quite quickly, particularly when you repeat the same process with the same food. We love our smoked salmon and it wasn't long before I felt confident to produce great results each time. I think it is like bread-making, how do you know when your loaf is done? After a while you just know; trust your instincts.

CAPTAIN'S LOG

Like the good old Captain Jim on the starship Enterprise, make a log. Note your smoking times, wood choice, humidity, outside temperature and results so that next time you are not guessing what to do. Experiment with small amounts of food and time them in the smoker for, say, 20 minutes, 30 minutes, and so on – preferably on the same day so the external conditions are the same. This way you will have a record of previous smoking times so you can improve or repeat the success! Don't forget, though, that outside conditions will affect your results.

WHAT HAPPENS WHEN THE FIRE GOES OUT?

Often food is actually drying in the smoker, as well as smoking, so it doesn't matter if the fire goes out while you are cold smoking; you are still helping concentrate the flavour of the food at the same time. This is a good reason why you should always make sure the weather is cold when you are smoking, since in warm weather it could be dangerous to leave the food in the smoker for too long. For hot smoking, it is important to have a constant and reliable heat source.

BRINING AND SALTING

Before smoking food should be cured with salt. This can be in the form of dry salt or salt and water sometimes mixed with sugar known as wet brining. The food is cured to extend its life, harden the flesh making it better for handling during smoking and for flavour. For more information on this, see the Salt chapter.

DRYING BEFORE SMOKING

As I mentioned at the beginning of this chapter, foods are often dried before smoking but this is a matter of individual choice: some people prefer very dry and heavily smoked food while others prefer it hardly dried at all, so it is still juicy and succulent with just a gentle hint of smoke. Many smokers will dry the food only briefly and allow it to drip-dry as it smokes – this also creates moisture in the air. This is often the case with fish such as Arbroath smokies. Size and oiliness matters: salmon can be left to dry for up to 24 hours, while a thin duck breast may only need a couple of hours; trout and eel are best not dried at all as they are already dry.

WHERE TO DRY THE FOOD BEFORE SMOKING

In the days before refrigeration, food was hung to dry in a breeze in a cool spot or in a larder before being smoked. This might still be appropriate in high altitude where there are no flies and fresh mountain air can circulate around your food. However, for many of us insects and higher humidity are a problem, so drying is better done in a refrigerator, larder or curing chamber.

Initially some foods made with curing salts such as Christmas Ham (see pages 135–6), bacon, venison and beef benefit from being hung at a higher temperature (up to 24°C/75°F) so that good bacteria can flourish and a degree of fermentation can begin. At most this would be overnight and the curing salts will help protect the food. Salami is further protected by its skin. If you can do this in an area of low humidity and be sure insects cannot get to the food, you may well achieve a better result but for safety's sake we recommend drying in the contained environment of a refrigerator, larder or curing chamber.

* COLD SMOKING RECIPES

The timings below are approximate and only given as a guideline based on timings taken in our garden in England on a cool, calm day. With a little trial and error you will soon be the judge of when your food is ready. Begin with some easy produce such as nuts, cheese and eggs or a small piece of fish. All should be rested on metal racks unless specified in the recipe.

All the products below should be cold smoked on a cold day when the temperature is low – 21–31°C (70–88°F)is ideal – so that it does not warm the produce. Very low temperatures may extend the smoking time – in snowy weather or strong cold winds I have smoked salmon for two days – be prepared for external conditions to affect timings.

COLD SMOKED NUTS

Shelled almonds and walnuts are delicious smoked and these are good, small things to put in while you are smoking something else so as not to waste space. After smoking they can be salted or tossed in maple syrup, butter and sugar or spice rub and baked in a conventional oven for 15 minutes at 180°C/350°F/gas 4.

Olives and coarse sea salt can also be smoked in this way.

> PREPARATION Place the nuts on foil, which has had a few holes perforated into it with a skewer to let the smoke through, or a fine mesh tray.
> WOOD CHOICE Alder, beech, oak.
> TIMING Cold smoke for 4–8 hours in a barbecue or garden smokehouse; 2 hours in a Bradley smoker.
> STORAGE Eat straight away or store in an airtight container up to 2 weeks.

COLD SMOKED EGGS

Vary the smoking time according to the size of your egg.

> PREPARATION Hard-boil the eggs and shell them. If you wish you can brine them before smoking for a salty flavour: soak in medium brine (see page 74) for 15–30 minutes, depending on their size.
> WOOD CHOICE Oak or beech.
> TIMING Cold smoke for 2–3 hours for quail eggs or 4–5 hours for hen eggs in a barbecue or garden smokehouse; 1–2 hours for quail eggs or 3–4 hours for hen eggs in a Bradley smoker. The eggs should take on a light golden hue when ready.
> SERVING SUGGESTION Smoked quail's eggs are delicious served with a small pile of celery salt to dip them in.
> STORAGE Put into a sealed container in the refrigerator and consume within 48 hours.

COLD SMOKED BUTTER

Smoked butter is really delicious in mash, jacket potatoes or hot toast. For extra satisfaction, use your own homemade sea salt butter (see pages 161–2 for a recipe).

> PREPARATION Cut a 250g (9oz) block of butter into four pieces. Put onto foil, which has had a few holes perforated into it with a skewer to let the smoke through, or a fine mesh tray.
> WOOD CHOICE Beech or fruit wood.
> TIMING Cold smoke for 10 hours in a barbecue or garden smokehouse; 3–4 hours in a Bradley smoker.
> STORAGE Wrap in baking parchment or baking parchment and store in the refrigerator. Consume within a couple of weeks.

COLD SMOKED CHEESE

Cheese is a good indicator of temperature: if it is too hot inside the smoker the cheese will melt. This method is suitable for most cheeses, including hard cheese such as Cheddar and soft cheese such as mozzarella; the smaller the piece of cheese, the quicker the smoke will penetrate, so you can chop a block of cheese into quarters if you prefer as this will increase the surface area for the smoke. If smoking Cheddar, it is best to smoke a largish piece approx. 300–500g (10½oz–1lb 2oz) and store it in the refrigerator after smoking for several weeks before sampling to allow the smoky flavour to really penetrate the cheese.

> PREPARATION If smoking mozzarella, pat dry on kitchen paper before smoking.
> WOOD CHOICE Fruit wood such as apple or oak.
> TIMING Cold smoke for 2–3 hours in a Bradley smoker for Cheddar, depending on size, and 1 hour for mozzarella. Cheddar will become a deeper yellow when done; mozzarella should become slightly golden.
> SERVING SUGGESTION Smoked mozzarella is gorgeous on pizza or cubed and stirred through hot pasta.
> STORAGE Smoking will increase the shelf-life of most cheese by approx. 3 days. Store hard cheeses such as Cheddar in beeswax paper or a glass container is ideal for at least 3 weeks before sampling. Store smoked mozzarella wrapped in baking parchment in the refrigerator for up to 4 days.

COLD SMOKED TOMATOES

Cherry tomatoes are a real treat when smoked.

> PREPARATION Cut the tomatoes in half around the equator (rather than pole to pole) and lay them on a wire rack. Scatter over a little salt and white sugar and dry them in a low oven at approx. 50°C/122°F/gas ¼ for approx. 4 hours until shrivelled but still holding some moisture.
> WOOD CHOICE Alder, beech, birch, oak.
> TIMING Cold smoke for 10 hours in a barbecue or garden smokehouse; 4 hours in a Bradley smoker.
> STORAGE Once smoked, put the tomatoes into a sealed container as they are, or put under extra virgin olive oil and keep in the refrigerator for up to 10 days. For best results, allow them to come to room temperature before serving.
> SERVING SUGGESTION Serve with cheese and crusty bread or stir them through hot pasta.

COLD SMOKED RED PEPPERS AND CHILLIES

Use cold smoked peppers and chillies anywhere you would use unsmoked ones to enhance the finished dish. To intensify the flavour blacken in a hot oven and peel before cooking.

> WOOD CHOICE Alder, beech, oak, maple.
> TIMING Cold smoke for 10 hours in a barbecue or garden smokehouse; 4 hours in a Bradley smoker.
> STORAGE Put the peppers and chillies in a bag or container and store in the refrigerator up to 4 days.
> USES Make your own smoked paprika by drying the peppers and chillies after smoking and grinding them in a spice mill.

* COLD SMOKED FISH AND SHELLFISH

GENERAL ADVICE

Most fish can be cold smoked and then cooked later, like kippers, so don't worry if you only have a cold smoker. Oily fish such as mackerel, salmon and herring are ideal, however other firm fish such as tuna (although in short supply so best avoided), haddock and trout also work well.

As I mentioned previously, as far as I am concerned, hanging fish inside your smoking area is for the professionals. However, if you want to have a go bear in mind that the fish might drop as they smoke. I think it is far easier to smoke delicate foods such as fish on a rack. Whichever system you choose, make sure the fish are gutted. If you smoke them unfilleted, prop open their bellies with cocktail sticks so the smoke can circulate.

NOTE: It is important to use produce that is as fresh as possible for smoking. Wild fish should be frozen first to kill any parasites.

COLD SMOKED SALMON

You will need a pin-boned side of salmon; avoid trimming the fat off the edges.

> PREPARATION Wash the fillet carefully in cold water and remove any blood; pat dry on kitchen paper. Sprinkle some salt over a tray and lay the fillet on top, skin-side down. Scatter the surface of the fish with more salt, very lightly on the tail and more on the thicker parts. You can either use large grain or fine salt. Expect to use approx. 3 tablespoons for an average side of salmon. Absorption of salt on the skin is minimal – it is the skin that stops the salt water becoming a brine

to the fish and sucking water out of it at sea – so apply just 10 per cent of the salt to the bottom of your tray and more to the top. Set aside to cure for 10–12 hours in the refrigerator, sloping the tray so that the brine can run off freely. The length of time the fish takes to cure will depend on the thickness and freshness of the fish, and the amount of salt. It should feel lightly firm to touch when ready. A large, thick side of salmon could take 15–16 hours.

> Remove the fillet and rinse briefly under cold water, discarding the brine. Pat dry on kitchen paper and place, skin-side down, on a wire rack to dry for up to a day to form a pellicle. This could be in the refrigerator or in a larder protected from insects.

> WOOD CHOICE Oak or beech.

> TIMING Cold smoke for 14–17 hours in a barbecue; at least 24 hours in a garden smokehouse; 4–8 hours in a Bradley smoker with the vent (damper) wide open. NOTE: I normally smoke fish overnight over a cold smoke generator in our barbecue. If after 10 hours, the length of time it takes for the maze to burn through, the fire has gone out – or I am not happy with the smell and feel of the fish – I will set it to smoke for longer. I normally allow 14–15 hours for a medium fillet of salmon.

> NOTE: If the salmon tastes too salty or too smoky after this time, you can always soak the fish in cold water for a few hours afterwards, changing the water once. It won't be great smoked salmon, but you could always flake it up for pâté or add it to pasta dishes.

> STORAGE Wrap in baking parchment and set aside in the refrigerator for a day before eating. It will last up to 2 weeks in the refrigerator.

> SERVING SUGGESTION Cut into thin slices, starting from the tail. Serve with wedges of lemon and brown bread and butter.

COLD SMOKED TROUT

Bill Barber, a smoker and teacher in the Borders, showed us how he cold smokes trout fillets.

> PREPARATION Scatter some fine sea salt over the base of a lasagne dish or similar. Arrange the trout fillets, skin-side down, on top and sprinkle over a light covering of salt. Set aside in the refrigerator to cure for up to 20–30 minutes or until the fish feels firm to the touch. Rinse briefly afterwards and smoke straight away. Pat dry on kitchen paper. There is no need to air-dry trout after curing, as with other fish, because it is already a dryish fish.
> WOOD CHOICE Alder or oak.
> TIMING Cold smoke for 6 hours in a barbecue or garden smokehouse; 2 hours in a Bradley smoker.
> COOKING INSTRUCTIONS Poach in gently simmering water for 5–7 minutes, depending on their size. Once cooked they can be made into the Smoked Trout Pâté on pages 159–60.
> STORAGE Wrap the cooled cooked or uncooked fish in baking parchment and store in the refrigerator for up to 10 days or freeze and use within 3 months.

KIPPERS

Smoked herrings are called kippers. To 'kipper' something used to mean to smoke it. As this was frequently done to the herring, the words became interchangeable. Kippers are traditionally butterflied before smoking to expose the maximum area to the smoke. They are usually eaten at breakfast

time with brown toast and a poached egg. 'Bloaters' are whole herrings; 'red' herrings are those that have been smoked for a long time or been dyed.

Choose your fish carefully, making sure they are plump and fresh – this will depend upon their reproductive cycle as after spawning the fat content drops greatly – there is no point in going to the effort of smoking them if there is nothing but bones to eat!

> PREPARATION Make up a strong 70 per cent brine (see page 74) and set aside to cool.
> Butterfly the herring or ask your fishmonger to do this for you. To do it yourself, cut the fish open along the belly from tail to head. It should be open from the top to the bottom on one side so that it opens out fully. Discard the guts and gently rinse the fish inside and out under the tap, being careful not to break the skin. Leave the backbone and head in place. Remove the gills and guts and wash well under cold running water, scraping away any blood.
> Brine the fish for approx. 15–20 minutes, depending on the size of the herring (I have had tiny fillets of herring that were delicious but only needed 7 minutes in the brine). Pat dry on kitchen paper and hang or leave on a rack to dry in the refrigerator or a cool room for a few hours to form a pellicle.
> WOOD CHOICE Beech or oak.
> TIMING Cold smoke for 8 hours in a barbecue or garden smokehouse; 2–4 hours in a Bradley smoker (with the damper open wide).
> STORAGE Wrap in baking parchment or pack in vacuum bags or sealed containers. Store in the refrigerator for up to 10 days or in the freezer for up to 3 months.

COLD SMOKED ANCHOVIES AND OTHER SMALL FISH

Smoking even small fish will extend their shelf-life for a few days. As fillets of tiny fish such as anchovies or sprats tend to be delicate, it is better to dry-cure them whole – without gutting them – before smoking.

> PREPARATION Scatter some fine salt over a tray and lay the whole fish on top. Sprinkle the surface with a fine layer of salt and set aside to cure in the refrigerator or in a cold room for up to 15 minutes or until the fish are the same texture as hard jelly. Rinse under cold running water and pat dry on kitchen paper. Arrange the fish on a wire rack and set aside in the refrigerator or a cool breeze for 30 minutes to form a pellicle.
> WOOD CHOICE Alder, beech, birch, oak.
> TIMING Cold smoke for 1 hour in a barbecue or garden smokehouse; 30 minutes in a Bradley smoker.
> STORAGE Smoked anchovies can be stored under oil in a sealed container in the refrigerator up to 2 weeks. Serve as a mouthwatering appetizer.

COLD SMOKED MUSSELS

I was hesitant about the idea of smoked shellfish but actually I couldn't have been more wrong. Mussels look stunning when you remove them from the smoker – all plump and orange sitting in their slate grey half shells.

> PREPARATION Debeard and remove any bits of barnacle from 2kg (4lb 8oz) of mussels. Throw away any if they have broken shells. To cook the mussels, heat a large frying pan or saucepan and when hot add the mussels to the pan and put on the lid. Cook for a few minutes, shaking the pan regularly, until the mussels have opened. Discard any mussels that don't open. Drain and set aside while you make up the brine and until the shells are cool enough to touch.
> Make up a weak brine solution using a ratio of 50g (1¾oz) salt per 1 litre (1¾ pints) of water; set aside to cool to approx. 3°C (37°F). To speed things up, we use a little boiling water to dissolve the salt and make up to the full amount with cold water.
> Open the shells and throw one half away, leaving each mussel in a half shell. Layer up the mussels in a lasagne dish and pour over the cold brine. Cover with a plate and set aside in the refrigerator or a cool place for 10 minutes. Remove the mussels from the brining liquor, shake off any excess brine and arrange in a single layer on the rack inside your smoker.
> WOOD CHOICE Oak, birch or beech.
> TIMING Cold smoke for 2 hours in a barbecue or garden smokehouse; 15–30 minutes in a Bradley smoker.
> STORAGE Remove the mussels from their shells and transfer them to a sealed container with a lid. Store in the refrigerator for up to 24 hours.
> SERVING SUGGESTION Enjoy as they are as part of a shellfish antipasti, or make into Sukie Barber's delicious pasta dish.

TAGLIATELLE WITH CREAMY SMOKED MUSSELS

SERVES 6

- 2kg (4lb 8oz) cold smoked mussels (see left)
- 200g (7fl oz) double cream
- 480g (1lb 1oz) pasta, such as tagliatelle or spaghetti
- a small handful of fresh chives and

their flowers
- juice of 1 lemon
- freshly ground black pepper
- fine salt (optional)
- 2 courgettes (optional)

> Heat the smoked mussels in the double cream and leave in a warm place for 30 minutes for the smokiness to flavour the cream. Put the pasta into a saucepan full of lightly salted boiling water. While the pasta is cooking, reheat the creamy mussels and at the last moment add the chives. Season with freshly ground black pepper and lemon juice. It probably won't need any salt as the smoked mussels will have a hint of salt, but taste to make sure.

> Thinly slice a courgette lengthways using a mandolin or a potato peeler, then cut each piece down the middle to create tagliatelle-shaped pieces with a green edge down one side. Add these to the pasta water just before it is cooked for approx. 30 seconds. Drain the pasta and add to the pan with the sauce. Toss together and serve straight away scattered with a few chives and their flowers.

COLD SMOKED PRAWNS

Eating prawns with your hands straight from the shell with a squeeze of lemon, some crusty bread and a glass of Pouilly Fumé is my idea of heaven. It doesn't happen often enough, but I savour moments like this. We first ate smoked prawns at Cley Smokehouse in Norfolk. They were so delicious we went back for more and enquired how they made them. To get around the problem of overcooking them, we were told to use cooked frozen prawns instead of fresh ones.

I would only do these in a Bradley smoker or similar that has strong smoke – so the frozen prawns smoke quickly – since you don't want to have the prawns sitting around too long.

> **PREPARATION** You will need frozen king or tiger prawns in their shells for this. Lay the frozen prawns on the rack inside your smoker, spacing them apart so that the smoke can swirl around them.
> **WOOD CHOICE** Oak or beech.
> **TIMING** Cold smoke for approx. 3 hours in a Bradley smoker, depending on the size of the prawns. In cool weather they will just defrost in that time and take on the flavour and yellowish colour from the smoke.
> **STORAGE** Store in the refrigerator and eat within 24 hours.
> **SERVING SUGGESTION** Serve with crusty bread and wedges of lemon. In my opinion, keep it simple and don't be tempted to disguise the wonderful flavour with sauces.

ANDREW FAIRLIE'S COLD SMOKED LOBSTER

This was the late Michelin starred Andrew Fairlie's signature dish at his restaurant in Gleneagles. I had heard that Andrew was keen on smoking and curing, so we took a trip to his kitchen to find out more. He was keen to use local Scottish lobster, which is tender and sweet, on his menu and had seen smoked lobster before in France. To smoke a whole lobster would spoil the tenderness of the flesh, so he and his Head Chef, Stephen McLaughlin, came up with this method after much experimentation. In this way only the shells are smoked. I am not exaggerating when I say this is one of the most delicious foods I have ever tasted. There is no wonder he won *The Times* UK Best Restaurant of the Year 2012.

SERVES 4

- 4 lobster, weighing approx. 950g–1kg (2lb 2oz–2lb 4oz)
- juice of ½ lemon
- juice of ½ lime
- 2 tablespoons double cream
- 250g (9oz) unsalted butter
- good pinch of salt
- freshly ground black pepper
- 2 tablespoons finely chopped mixed fresh herbs, such as chives, tarragon and parsley

> Cook the live lobsters in boiling water for 8 minutes or until the shells are pink. Remove them from the water and cut the shells along the belly with kitchen scissors or a knife. Carefully remove the flesh as neatly as you can without tearing it. Split the shells and put them on the rack of a Bradley smoker. Cold smoke for 40 minutes over oak or beech wood. Remove them from the smoker and set aside to cool. Store in the refrigerator until needed.

> To make the sauce, pour the citrus juice into a small saucepan and bubble away over a low heat until it has almost disappeared. Add the cream and shake the pan to amalgamate. Cut the butter into 2cm (¾in) lumps and add to the sauce, one lump at a time, stirring constantly to amalgamate each lump before you add the next. This will take approx. 15 minutes; don't rush it. Season with salt and black pepper to taste.

> Arrange the lobster meat in the smoked shells. Put the meat from the knuckle in the head and the claw meat on top to raise it up. Trim away the messy end from the tail and slice the meat on the diagonal. Put this into the tail. It is sliced to stop it twisting as it heats and to ensure the heat penetrates quickly to stop it drying out. The meat should be tightly packed

inside the shells. Spoon 3 tablespoons of the sauce over each lobster so that it goes into the crevasses. Transfer the lobsters to the refrigerator, covered, until you are ready to eat.

> To serve, transfer each lobster into an individual roasting tray, adding 2 tablespoons of water under the shells. Wrap the trays very tightly in foil, 'drum-skin tight', as Steve told me in his Scottish accent. Place over a high heat on the hob so that the water boils quickly to produce puffs of steam – these will penetrate the smoky flavour of the shell and transfer the smokiness into the flesh. Once the foil puffs up, after approx. 1 minute, take the lobsters off the heat and set aside to rest for 3 minutes while you finish the sauce.

> Put the sauce over a low heat to reheat and stir in the cooking juices from the roasting trays along with the chopped herbs. Transfer the lobsters to a plate and dress with the butter and herb sauce. Serve straight away.

* COLD SMOKED MEAT

COLD SMOKED SAUSAGES

Smoked sausages are popular in many regions of the world, especially in areas above the smoke line (see page 119). Some people mimic the flavour of smoking with smoked paprika or smoke essence, but we think the real thing is sublime. Use a strong flavoured sausage made with curing salts such as the French *Saucisson* on pages 93–4 or the Spanish Dried *Chorizo* on pages 95–6.

Straight after making the sausages, hang them in a garland to dry at room temperature overnight (or for 8 hours) so that the air can circulate around them. The sausages are then ready to smoke.

After smoking they can be eaten straight away or hung to cure longer in a curing chamber at 12–16°C (54–61°F) until they have achieved up to 30 per cent weight loss; ours took approx. 28 days. Make sure that the air can circulate freely and that none of them are touching. Check on the sausages daily and wipe off any moulds that aren't white with strong alcohol – we use Grappa.

> WOOD CHOICE Oak or apple wood.
> TIMING Cold smoke for 6–8 hours in a barbecue or garden smokehouse; 2–3 hours in a Bradley smoker.
> STORAGE Once dried, the sausages can be stored, wrapped in baking parchment in the refrigerator for up to a month or frozen for up to 3 months.

COLD SMOKED BACON

We have given three recipes for cured bacon in the Salt chapter, see pages 81–3, and all of these are suitable for smoking. Note that smoking is always carried out after curing. It is important to hang the bacon for at least a day before smoking to form a pellicle.

> PREPARATION Follow the recipes on pages 81–3 for curing the bacon. Rinse off the cure under cold running water and pat dry on kitchen paper. Set aside to dry for 24 hours on a rack at room temperature under a fly net, in the refrigerator or cool room before smoking. After smoking eat straight away or for a firmer texture hang in a curing chamber to dry for 1–5 days. The longer it is left, the more concentrated the flavour; also the texture will become firmer and drier. The bacon is ready when it feels firm to the touch and not jelly-like. If cured correctly,

it should have lost 10–15 per cent of its initial weight.

> WOOD CHOICE Beech, apple or maple.
TIMING Cold smoke for 8–10 hours in a barbecue or garden smokehouse; 4 hours in a Bradley smoker.
> STORAGE To store, wrap the bacon in baking parchment and keep in the refrigerator for up to 2 weeks. Bacon can also be frozen.

COLD SMOKED PIGEON, GOOSE AND DUCK BREAST

We used to buy smoked goose breast for our restaurants for the antipasti platters of cured meats. Now we make our own. A wet brine with curing salts is good for inducing a little moisture into the breasts before smoking. Be prepared to experiment with the timings given below for the curing and smoking of the breasts. Write down your results so you can repeat the process. We actually forgot our cured and smoked duck breasts in the refrigerator while we went on holiday. We tasted them when we came home and the extra time had made all the difference! Ideally we should have left them in the curing chamber as they became case hardened in the refrigerator but the flavour was still there. It took us quite a few trials at this as there are various stages to the finished process, but the result is wonderfully soft meat with layers of flavour that melts in your mouth. The flavour of the salt, the smoke and the meat should be equal, with none dominating. If you are doing this for the first time it is a good idea to cut a little of the flesh off the breast and cook it briefly to taste for saltiness. The outside will be saltier than the inside, so bear that in mind. If it is really salty, soak the breast in water for a few hours, pat dry on kitchen paper and then dry as before. The same applies if the breasts are too smoky.

> PREPARATION For 1kg (2lb 4oz) of either pigeon, duck or goose breasts make up a medium 40 per cent brine solution using 120g (4¼oz) curing salts (either 18g/¾oz Quickcure and 102g/3½oz salt or 5g/⅛oz Prague Powder No. 2 and 115g/4⅛oz salt) to 1 litre (1¾ pints) of boiling water. If you wish, you can flavour the brine with up to 120g (4¼oz) sugar per 1 litre (1¾ pints) of red wine – substituting it for part or all of the water and a few sprigs of herbs or 1 tablespoon of crushed juniper berries per 1 litre (1¾ pints) of water. Set aside to cool, then chill in the refrigerator.
> Put the breasts into the cold brine and set aside to cure in the refrigerator for approx. 2 hours for pigeon breasts, 8 hours for duck and goose. You may need to weigh them down so that they are fully submerged. Take out the breasts and pat dry on kitchen paper.
> Place the breasts on a wire rack and transfer them to the refrigerator to dry a little and form a pellicle, approx. 2–4 hours is enough for the pigeon and up to 24 hours for the duck and goose. Alternatively, you can leave them in a cool place, such as a larder, covered with netting.
> WOOD CHOICE Cherry, apple, maple.
> TIMING Cold smoke in the barbecue overnight (approx. 14 hours); or for 2–4 hours in a Bradley smoker, depending on the size of the breasts.
> STORAGE Wrap in baking parchment to stop them drying further and keep in the refrigerator, eat within 3 days.
> SERVING SUGGESTION Eat as soon as they are smoked, leave on a rack or hang in a curing chamber to lose weight. Ours were at their best after 10–12 days but I have heard of an artisan Italian curer who leaves his goose breasts for 60 days. Serve raw, cut into thin slices with Pickled

Nectarines (see page 20) or Peach, Grape and Vanilla Chutney (see pages 190–1).

COLD SMOKED HAM, BEEF AND VENISON

Large cuts of meat require a lot more time for the smoke to penetrate. If you research the traditional methods for smoking meats, you will discover they were often smoked for a matter of days or weeks. This wouldn't necessarily be over a continuous fire but one that went out and was lit again, maybe hours later, or the next day. During this time the meat would also be drying out in the smoky atmosphere – which could be up a chimney or in an external smokehouse where it was also cold. Most meats would have been salted first. To preserve a piece of bacon, for example, four methods of preservation would have been used – salting, drying, smoking and chilling – and this is what prevented the meat from becoming bad.

As a general rule of thumb when brining and smoking your own meat at home, allow for an overall weight loss of 15 per cent (with 10 per cent lost during brining and 5 per cent during smoking). We have successfully smoked Christmas ham, venison and beef in our Wendy house during cold weather over 3 days. For reasons of self-preservation (avoiding food poisoning), I would recommend using curing salts for large cuts. This will safely carry them through the curing, smoking and drying stages.

COLD SMOKED VENISON CARPACCIO

We love this recipe. It is easy and relatively quick to do as the loin is lean and slim so absorbs the brine and smoke quickly. We haven't suggested using curing salts for this recipe as the timing in the smoker is short and the meat is frozen after rather than hung. The result is soft, juicy slices of raw smoked venison that melt in your mouth and have a much more interesting flavour than regular carpaccio. We make this using a 500g (1lb 2oz) venison loin, but you could use the same method for smoking a fillet of beef.

> **PREPARATION** Make up a 20 per cent brine (see page 74) and submerge the loin in it overnight, weighing it down if necessary. Remove from the brine, pat dry with kitchen paper and set on a rack to dry in a refrigerator or in a cool larder covered with fly netting for a day to form a pellicle.
> **WOOD CHOICE** Alder, beech, birch, oak, juniper and any fruit wood.
> **TIMING** Cold smoke smaller cuts (under 1.5kg/3lb 5oz) in a Bradley smoker for 4 hours.
> **STORAGE** Remove the meat from the smoker and wrap it in baking parchment. Transfer it to the freezer for a day to equalize the flavour of the smoke throughout the meat and make it easier to cut. If the venison is wild, freezing will also kill any parasites.
> **SERVING SUGGESTION** Lean, smoky venison makes a sumptuous carpaccio served with rocket salad dressed with lemon and olive oil. For carpaccio it is easier to cut the meat into really thin slices while it is still frozen. Alternatively, cut into thicker slices and fry briefly for fantastic steaks.

HAM HOCKS AND HANDS

Pork hands or hocks are small, inexpensive cuts of meat to experiment with before you tackle larger projects, such as smoking your own hams. Ready-cured hocks are available from butchers or you can cure your own.

> **PREPARATION** Remove the skin from the hocks and discard. Place the hocks in a container and cover them with a layer of fine salt. Set aside to cure for approx. 1 hour. Remove the hocks, rinse briefly under cold running water and pat dry on kitchen paper. Set aside on a wire rack to dry for 2–3 hours until a pellicle is formed. This can either be done in the refrigerator or in a cool pantry, covered with netting.
> **WOOD CHOICE** Alder, beech, birch, oak, maple and any fruit wood.
> **TIMING** Cold smoke for 3 hours in a Bradley smoker.
> **COOKING INSTRUCTIONS** After smoking, boil the hocks until cooked through and the meat is falling from the bone. Change the water at least once to get rid of the initial smoky taste. The cooking water can then be used as a stock.

CHRISTMAS HAM

The timings here are suitable for a 4kg (8lb 12oz) cured leg of ham. You can either follow the recipe on pages 135–6 for curing the ham or buy one that has already been cured for you (also known as a 'green' ham).

> **PREPARATION** To cure the ham, follow the recipe for Christmas Ham on pages 135–6. Remove the ham from the brine and pat dry on kitchen paper. Place it on a wire rack in the refrigerator or a cool larder covered in a fly net to dry overnight or up to 1 day to form a pellicle.
> **WOOD CHOICE** Oak, beech, maple.
> **TIMING** Cold smoke in intense smoke in a Bradley for 4–6 hours; over gentle smoke in a barbecue for approx. 10 hours; or for 2–3 days in a garden smokehouse. The

>>>

longer the process, the more the ham will dry out, concentrating the flavour. If you are concerned it is over-smoked it can be scrubbed and soaked before cooking.

> COOKING INSTRUCTIONS To cook the ham, place it in a saucepan of cold water and bring to the boil. Taste the water to see if it is overly salty and replace with fresh cold water if necessary. Bring to the boil and simmer for 25 minutes per 450g (1lb) or until the internal temperature is 72°C (162°F). You can add flavourings such as carrots, bay leaves and an onion to the water if you wish. Remove the ham from the pan, cut off the skin and discard.

> Preheat the oven to 180°C/350°F/gas 4. Using a sharp knife, dipped in hot water, make diagonal cuts in the outside fat and poke a clove into each diamond. Put the ham in a roasting tray, slather on 350ml (12fl oz) marmalade and bake in the hot oven for 30–45 minutes until the glaze has deepened to a rich golden brown. Remove from the oven and rest for 30 minutes before eating.

> STORAGE The cooked ham will keep, wrapped in baking parchment or in a covered container, for up to 5 days in the refrigerator.

SPECK

Speck is often served in Italy as part of antipasti, or with pickled gherkins and sourdough rye bread for those north of the Austro-Italian border.

> PREPARATION To cure the pork, follow the instructions for *Speck* on pages 89–90. After curing, rinse the meat under cold running water and pat dry on kitchen paper. Hang up to dry at room temperature (providing it isn't a warm day) for 1–2 hours.

> WOOD CHOICE Alder, oak, beech, birch

> TIMING Cold smoke for 7 days over gentle smoke in a Wendy house or barbecue. Alternatively, use a Bradley smoker for approx. 3 hours.

> CURING INSTRUCTIONS After smoking, hang the pork in a curing chamber at 12–16°C (54–61°F) for 5–6 weeks until it has lost 25 per cent of its weight. Remove the *speck* from the chamber and follow the instructions for larding on page 84. Return the larded *speck* to the curing chamber for a further 6 months.

> At this point, you can sample a slice from one end – just in from the outer edge – to see if it is ready. If it seems soft or not tasty enough, re-lard that end and rehang for a further month.

> SERVING SUGGESTION Serve cut into wafer thin slices with pickled gherkins and sourdough rye bread.

> STORAGE Once the *speck* is cut into, wrap that end in baking parchment tightly and store in the refrigerator. It will keep for weeks if not months more but will continue to dry out and harden.

* HOT SMOKING RECIPES

Hot smoking involves cooking the food at the same time as it smokes. Smoking dries out the meat, so by introducing water into the smoker you end up partly steaming the food as well as heating it, resulting in juicy, savoury, finger-licking good food.

There are several ways of introducing humidity into your smoker. If it has a drip tray, this can be filled with water (or beer); if you are smoking over an open fire, this can be dampened down with wet cloths or water sprays. If your hot smoker has a vent, this can be closed or partially closed to keep humidity inside. Another trick is to brush food such as fish with extra virgin olive oil during smoking to help prevent it from drying out.

Hot smoking should be continuous and temperatures monitored carefully. A probe thermometer is essential so that you can safely tell when your food is done. Some probes can be left in the product and read from outside the smoking chamber – a good investment, we think, so that you don't have to keep opening the door and losing valuable heat and steam. There are also gadgets available that will read the internal temperature of the food in the smoker and inform you on your phone when you have reached the target. Amazing when you are in the pub and waiting for your pulled pork to be done.

The Big Green Egg and Weber barbecues are both excellent for hot smoking. All of the following recipes will work in them but follow the manufacturer's instructions for temperature and timings.

HOT SMOKED AUBERGINE

Hot smoking the aubergine gives a wonderful smoky flavour that you just don't get by roasting it in the oven or scorching it over a flame. Smoked aubergine is delicious puréed and made into Baba Ghanoush also known as Moutabal, a Middle Eastern dip (see right). Alternatively, cut the smoked aubergines open and serve warm as a side dish with lemon juice, salt and pepper.

> WOOD CHOICE Alder, oak, beech, maple.
> TIMING Hot smoke halved or sliced aubergines for 30–40 minutes in a Cameron smoker; whole aubergines should be smoked for 1–2 hours in a Bradley smoker at the maximum temperature.

> TO MAKE MOUTABAL Allow the smoked aubergine to cool and scrape out the flesh; chop finely or blitz in a food processor. Combine with 2 tablespoons of tahini, 2 tablespoons of plain or Greek yogurt, 1 tablespoon of lemon juice and a good pinch of salt. Serve as a dip, sprinkled with paprika and toasted chopped walnuts, with pitta bread for dipping.

HOT SMOKED TOMATO AND RED PEPPER SOUP

Hot smoking tomatoes, peppers and chillies is easy to do and gives really impressive results in little time. The tomatoes become soft quickly and get a deep, smoky flavour that is wonderful on toast or with an English breakfast. Peppers and chillies take longer but offer a typically Spanish flavour of spicy smoked paprika to stews and salads. Use either the Cameron stovetop smoker or a Bradley hot smoker. If you don't have round tomatoes, cherry tomatoes are fine too. It is a great way to use up slightly soft tomatoes and if left thick makes a sublime and intense sauce for pasta or gnocchi.

SERVES 6–8

- 2 red peppers, roughly chopped
- 1 red chilli, cut in half lengthways, deseeded
- 1kg (2lb 4oz) round tomatoes, cut in half
- sea salt and freshly ground black pepper
- 1 teaspoon caster sugar
- 4 tablespoons extra virgin olive oil
- 2 red onions, finely chopped
- 2 garlic cloves, peeled and lightly crushed
- 2 medium potatoes (approx. 400g/14oz), peeled and diced into 1cm (½in) cubes
- 2 tablespoons tomato purée
- 2 litres (3½ pints) vegetable or chicken stock
- basil leaves, to serve

>>>

> Smoke the peppers and chilli first for 10 minutes before adding the tomatoes, cut-side upwards. Scatter a little salt and the sugar over them before replacing the lid on the smoker. Continue to smoke for a further 20–30 minutes or until the tomatoes and chilli are all soft. Remove from the heat and set aside to cool.
> Meanwhile, heat the oil in a heavy-based saucepan and fry the onion and garlic cloves for approx. 10 minutes or until translucent. Take care not to burn them. Add the potatoes and stir through. Continue to fry for a couple of minutes so that the cubes of potato become coated with oil.
> Cut the chilli roughly and taste it for heat. Add some or all of it to the pan, depending on the heat, followed by the tomatoes and peppers. Stir through and add the tomato purée. Now add 1.5 litres (2½ pints) of stock and bring to the boil. Reduce the heat to simmer slowly. Cook the soup, partially covered, for approx. 1 hour, stirring frequently.
> Put the soup through a sieve or food mill or blitz with a stick blender to get rid of the skins. Pour into another pan to warm. Taste and add salt and pepper as necessary. Add the rest of the stock as necessary until you are happy with the consistency. Serve bubbling hot in warm bowls with basil leaves, a swirl of extra virgin olive oil and a twist of black pepper.

PEPPERED MACKEREL

I had no idea these were so easy. Mackerel is inexpensive and good for you, and so I have eaten a lot of it over the years. In light of its recent change in sustainability, it is best to look for line-caught mackerel. Our favourite method of hot smoking them is using our dustbin smoker. It looks fun and is quick and effective.

> **PREPARATION** You will need mackerel fillets for this. Put the mackerel fillets in a dish and sprinkle over a thin layer of fine sea salt. Cover with a plate and set aside in the refrigerator to cure for 15–30 minutes, depending on the size and freshness of the fish, or until they are firm to the touch. Rinse off the salt and pat dry on kitchen paper. Arrange the mackerel on a wire rack and set aside to dry either in a cool breeze, covered with netting, or in the refrigerator for 1 hour to form a pellicle. Now is an ideal time to build the fire. Scatter the flesh side only with crushed black peppercorns and press down well with your palm.
> **WOOD CHOICE** Oak or beech.
> **TIMING** Hot smoke medium-sized fillets over a medium fire for approx. 30–40 minutes in a dustbin smoker; or over a low heat for approx. 20–30 minutes in a Cameron stovetop smoker. To tell if they are cooked through, press down on the fish with your index finger; they should feel firm to the touch.
> **SERVING SUGGESTION** Serve hot in a bap with lemon juice and parsley, or cold with brown bread and homemade Horseradish Sauce (see page 22).
> **STORAGE** To keep, allow the mackerel to cool and wrap in baking parchment. Store in the refrigerator and eat within 5 days or freeze and consume within 3 months.

ARBROATH SMOKIES

This method involves steaming whole gutted haddock in smoke, which is what makes Arbroath smokies so succulent. Iain Spink is one of the few smokers left to smoke haddock in the traditional way in old whisky barrels in the small fishing town of Arbroath on the west coast of Scotland. He is a fifth-generation smoker and we went to meet him to see how he smokes these famous fish. He told us that traditionally it was the fishwives who would clean, gut and smoke the fish while the fishermen were out at sea. Our dustbin smoker is ideal for making these because it is based on the barrel method of smoking.

If you want to try Iain's method, tie similar sized whole gutted haddock together by the tails with string, making sure that it is neither too tight or too loose – Iain explained that if the string is too tight it goes through the bone and if not tight enough the fish will fall into the fire. He wasn't kidding; we tried this several times at home and each time they fell. Now we lay the fish on a rack and use large fillets rather than whole fish.

This is how Iain Spink smokes his Arbroath smokies: he makes a fire in the bottom of a barrel that has been buried in the earth or on the pebble beach. When the fire is hot, after approx. 20 minutes, he sprays it down with water and then suspends his fish over the top to cook for approx. 40 minutes–1 hour. The belly of each fish is held open with a small stick so that the heat and smoke can permeate throughout. Iain places wet hessian sacks over the top of the barrel to introduce humidity and also starve the fire of oxygen so that it cannot take hold again. After they are cooked, he squeezes the fish from side to side and the fish pops off the bone.

Down the road at Gleneagles, the chefs told us of their visit to Arbroath. They thought that this hot smoked fish, fresh from the barrel, was just outstanding. Iain had some ready as we arrived with our children. On a chilly October morning we devoured hot, salty, smoky fish with our fingers. The chefs were right; it is one of life's experiences not to be missed.

> PREPARATION To follow our method, you will need small (approx. 500g/1lb 2oz) haddock. Buy them ready filleted or do it yourself. Gut the fish and remove the heads; split them in half leaving the backbone in one side. Remove the black membrane that runs along the backbone of the fish, if it is still there. Sprinkle some fine sea salt over a large lasagne dish or similar and arrange the fish on top in a single layer. Cover with a thin layer of salt and repeat this process to give more layers of fish and salt. Set aside in the refrigerator to cure for 2–10 hours, depending on the freshness and size of the fish – we allow approx. 30 minutes–2 hours as they are fillets rather than whole fish. They will be firm to the touch when done.

> Rinse off the salt briefly under cold running water, pat dry on kitchen paper and allow the fish to dry for 1 hour to form a pellicle. Iain ties them in pairs by their tails and hangs them over sticks to dry in the open air, but you could lay them on a wire rack in a cool breeze covered in a fly net. After drying, they can be smoked.

> I struggled with Iain's traditional method of hanging the fish in pairs over triangular lengths of wood in the smoker and now prefer to lay them side by side on a rack inside our dustbin smoker instead.

> WOOD CHOICE Oak or beech.

> TIMING Hot smoke medium haddock fillets for 30–40 minutes over a medium fire in a dustbin smoker; or for 2–4 hours

in a Bradley smoker at 160°C (320°F) with the damper just open.

> **SERVING SUGGESTION** I am not going to write a 'serve with...' because you just shouldn't! At most they need brown bread and butter and maybe a squeeze of lemon. After they are cold, you can use the smoked haddock in fish pies, Scottish Cullen skink soup or pâté.

> **STORAGE** Keep wrapped in clingfilm or in a covered container in the refrigerator and consume within 7 days or freeze for up to 3 months.

HOT SMOKED SALMON

I still remember the first time I ate this at Billingsgate market, it was around 6am and the fishmonger broke a piece up for us to try. The flavour was so sweet, salty and smoky; I licked the oil from my fingers not wanting to waste a drop. We have also seen it being prepared in Arbroath: we watched a smoker start a fire in a large, well-tarred box. When it was really burning fiercely, he splashed water over it to take the fire down to smouldering embers and introduce steam. He quickly laid trays of salmon portions on racks inside and closed the lid. After 1½ hours he lifted the lids and the most incredible, rich aroma flowed out of the box. The salmon was ready; hot and juicy, it flaked apart easily as we ate it straight away with our hands. This is one of the easiest recipes to make.

> **PREPARATION** You will need salmon fillets for this. The size doesn't matter – thicker pieces will take longer than thin. Sprinkle a thin layer of fine sea salt over the base of a lasagne dish or similar and arrange the salmon fillets, skin-side down, on top. Sprinkle some more salt over the surface

of the fish, cover the dish with a plate and set aside to cure in the refrigerator for approx. 1 hour.

> Rinse the fillets briefly under the tap and pat dry on kitchen paper. Arrange on a wire rack in the refrigerator or a cool room to dry for approx. 30 minutes or so to form a pellicle.

> **WOOD CHOICE** Alder, maple, beech or oak.

> **TIMING** Hot smoke for approx. 20 minutes in a Cameron or dustbin smoker; 45 minutes–1 hour in a Bradley smoker at 105°C (221°F). Once the fish is cooked it should feel firm to the touch.

> **SERVING SUGGESTION** Enjoy hot, straight from the smoker. Alternatively, cool it down and have it with watercress salad and crème fraîche dressing (see page 180). Also see Pasta with Hot Smoked Salmon, Cream and Chilli Vodka (right).

> **STORAGE** Keep wrapped in clingfilm or in a covered container in the refrigerator and consume within 7 days.

VARIATION

HOT SMOKED SPICY SALMON

After salting, rub the flesh side of each portion with ½ teaspoon of finely chopped chilli and garlic. Smoke as before.

PASTA WITH HOT SMOKED SALMON, CREAM AND CHILLI VODKA

There is a well-known recipe in Italy that combines smoked salmon with penne and vodka bound together with cream. I am not sure of its origin, as neither salmon nor vodka is found traditionally in Italy. However it is a wonderful combination whatever the origin and even better when made with your own produce. I love to serve each person a shot glass of chilli vodka to drink with their pasta – it adds a real kick and a giggle to the meal.

SERVES 8–10

- 600g (1lb 5oz) rigatoni or penne pasta
- 1 white onion, finely chopped
- 2 garlic cloves, peeled, lightly crushed but left whole
- 2 tablespoons extra virgin olive oil
- 100ml (3½fl oz) chilli vodka (see page 171)
- 300g (10½oz) hot smoked salmon (see page 140)
- 600ml (20fl oz) double cream
- salt and freshly ground black pepper
- roughly chopped fresh parsley, to serve

> Cook the pasta in a large saucepan filled with boiling salted water. Meanwhile, fry the onion and garlic in the olive oil in a large frying pan over a medium heat until soft but not coloured, approx. 5 minutes. Add a pinch of salt, bearing in mind that the salmon will be salty already, and a generous pinch of black pepper. Pour in the chilli vodka and ignite if you wish (stand back) or simply leave for a couple of minutes to burn off the alcohol. Flake the salmon into the pan and pour in the cream. Cook over a low heat until the sauce has thickened and the pasta is al dente. Drain the pasta through a colander and add to the pan with the salmon and cream. Toss through gently so as not to break up the salmon any more and serve with a sprinkling of fresh parsley.

* RUBS FOR HOT SMOKING

A good way of introducing extra flavour to your smoked foods is to rub them with spices before smoking. This is a great way to introduce complex flavours to mingle in with the smoke.

PASTRAMI

See page 102.

CHINESE HOT SMOKED DUCK BREASTS

Our children love stir-fried noodles and Peking duck with plum sauce and pancakes. This recipe for hot smoked duck has all the lovely spiciness you would expect from Peking duck but the flesh is soft and juicy.

SERVES 2

- 2 duck breasts (approx. 440g1lb each)
- 1 tablespoon fine salt
- 2 tablespoons dark brown sugar
- 3 teaspoons Chinese five spice powder
- 1 teaspoon ground Sichuan pepper

FOR THE GLAZE

- 3 teaspoons honey
- 3 teaspoons dark soy sauce
- 3 teaspoons rice or white wine vinegar

> PREPARATION Put the duck breasts in a bowl. Mix together the salt, sugar, five spice powder and Sichuan pepper and rub well in to the duck flesh. Cover the bowl with a plate and set aside to marinate in the refrigerator overnight.

>>>

> The following day, wipe off the cure with kitchen paper. Combine the honey, soy sauce and vinegar in a small bowl and brush half of the mixture over the duck breasts.
> WOOD Oak, beech, birch, fruit woods, walnut.
> TIMING Hot smoke for 30–40 minutes in a Cameron smoker; 40 minutes– 1 hour in a Bradley smoker – or until the internal temperature reaches 54°C (129°F) for medium rare.
> SERVING SUGGESTION Serve sliced on the diagonal in a noodle stir-fry with the Chinese Plum Sauce on pages 34–5. Alternatively, cut into strips and serve in pancakes with hoisin sauce, cucumber batons and slivers of spring onion.
> STORAGE 3–4 days in the refrigerator.

HOT SMOKED PHEASANT BREAST

This is an excellent way to cook pheasant when in season and plentiful.

> PREPARATION Make up enough medium 40 per cent brine (see page 74) to cover the breasts and set aside to cool. Transfer to the refrigerator to chill. Put the pheasant breasts into the cure for 1 hour. Remove from the brine, pat dry on kitchen paper and set aside on a rack to dry in the refrigerator or in a cool room temperature for 2 hours to form a pellicle.
> WOOD CHOICE Alder, Oak, beech, birch, fruit woods.
> TIMING Hot smoke for 20–30 minutes in a Cameron smoker; approx. 30–45 minutes at 160°C (320°F) in a Bradley smoker.
> SERVING SUGGESTION Lovely hot served with bread sauce and buttery cabbage, these can also be served cold and sliced in a sandwich with mayonnaise, lemon juice and black pepper.

> STORAGE Keep in the refrigerator and consume within 3 days. Freeze wrapped in baking parchment and consume within 3 months.

HOT SMOKED CHICKEN

This is one of those dishes that you need to eat with your fingers. There are all sorts of rubs you can try, but really if you buy a good free-range chicken that has seen approx. 6 months of life it will reward you with enough flavour naked.

A whole chicken wouldn't fit in the Cameron stovetop smoker or the dustbin smoker so we hot smoked ours in the Bradley.

> PREPARATION You will need a 1.6kg (3lb 8oz) free-range chicken. Make up a weak 20 per cent brine allowing 200g (7oz) fine salt to 2 litres (3½ pints) of water, and set aside to cool (see page 74). Immerse the whole bird in the cold brine and transfer to the refrigerator for 8 hours.
> Remove the chicken from the brine, pat dry on kitchen paper and place on a wire rack to dry for 8 hours in the refrigerator to form a pellicle.
> WOOD CHOICE Oak, beech, alder, mesquite, hickory or cherry.
> TIMING Hot smoke in a Bradley smoker at 120°C (248°F) for 3–4 hours or until the internal temperature reaches 85°C (185°F).
> SERVING SUGGESTION Serve with bread and salad. If you want to serve some sauce on the side, try it with Southern Sweet Mustard Sauce (see page 145) or a dash of Debi's Tomato, Chilli and Ginger Jam (see page 30).
> STORAGE 3–4 days in the refrigerator.

HOT SMOKED CURRIED LAMB

I love to do this when entertaining. It means that I can prepare all the side dishes in advance, except the rice, and then have the lamb cooking slowly outside to bring in when we are ready, with the aroma circling around the kitchen. I like the addition of the extra spices, but this is equally delicious smoked plain.

We hot smoke ours in the Bradley due to the size of the lamb, filling the drip tray with water to introduce some steam into the smoke chamber.

SERVES 4–6

• 1.8kg (4lb) butterflied leg of lamb
• 1 portion of Manjula Samarasinghe's Sri Lankan Spice Paste for Meat and Chicken Curries (see page 234)

> PREPARATION Rub the lamb with the spice rub and set aside in the refrigerator, covered, to marinate overnight. The following day, remove the lamb from the refrigerator and allow it to come to room temperature.

> WOOD CHOICE Alder, oak, beech, birch or fruit wood.

> TIMING Hot smoke for 4–5 hours at 125°C (257°F) in a Bradley smoker or until the internal temperature is 60°C (140°F). Set aside to rest, covered with foil, for 20–30 minutes before serving. It will be juicy, tender and full of flavour.

> SERVING SUGGESTION Serve with rice, Green Bean Curry (see page 219), Mango Chutney (see page 29) and yogurt and mint raita.

> STORAGE Store any leftover meat in the refrigerator, covered, for up to 4 days.

BOSTON BUTT BARBECUE

Our friends Margaret and Mike, from Georgia, USA, make this Boston Butt twice a year for family and friends at holiday time. Although the cut of pork used is known as a Boston butt (possibly because it is shaped like the butt of a rifle), it is actually the shoulder – and sometimes the shoulder, hand and spring – that is used. A large shoulder can be cut into two pieces, one known as the Boston butt and the other as the 'picnic' ham.

This is definitely not a meal in a hurry, as it can take up to 17 hours of slow cooking to achieve the meltingly soft strands of meat. However, this quantity makes a large amount of pulled pork once complete, which is wonderful for feeding a huge crowd. And as it can be eaten hot, cold or reheated (or frozen for later use), the waiting time is well worth it. Many Americans like to eat the pork inside a huge bun, however Margaret loves hers in a toasted baguette sandwich, while Mike likes his with coleslaw and potato salad.

VARIATIONS

There are an infinite amount of recipes for this dish as every Southern region and family puts their own twist on it. Recipes for the sauce also vary with many different names such as 'Kick Ass' or 'Slap yo mama'; Mike's very own version is 'Wild and Wicked' according to him! In Carolina they often make a vinegary 'mop sauce' to inject into the pork before cooking and then regularly use a small mop to moisten it further during the cooking, but personally I think there is enough going on with the rub and barbecue sauce without giving yourself any further work.

Boston butt has now become a family favourite of ours. This is our tried and tested version based on Margaret and

Mike's recipe. Feel free to experiment with your own flavourings – just remember to write down the quantities you used for next time. Additions you might consider are squeezy American mustard smeared all over the pork before you add the rub. I quite like this, despite my loathing of ready-prepared sauces, as I like the sweetness it gives.

My chilli powder is quite hot, so I have limited it to 2 teaspoons and it still has enough kick – but, again, it is up to you.

SERVES 12–14

- 3kg (6lb 8oz) shoulder of pork on or off the bone

FOR THE RUB

- 75g (2½oz) muscovado sugar
- 3 tablespoons paprika
- 1 teaspoon coarsely ground black pepper
- 1 tablespoon fine salt
- 2 teaspoons chilli powder
- 2 teaspoons mustard powder
- 3 fat garlic cloves, finely chopped

> **PREPARATION** Mix the ingredients together for the rub and, using your hands, massage it into the pork. Put the pork into a large container and marinate in the refrigerator for 24 hours. Remove the meat from the refrigerator and allow it to come up to room temperature.

> For a large joint of meat such as this I would recommend using a Bradley smoker, Big Green Egg or a Weber barbecue, however many people successfully smoke their pork butts in customized barbecues. Light the smoker and bring up the heat in the chamber to 100°C (212°F). Remove the marinated pork from the bag and set it on the rack in the smoker.

> **WOOD CHOICE** Hickory, maple, mesquite.

> **TIMING** If I have people coming for Sunday lunch or early dinner I marinate the shoulder from Friday night through to Saturday night. I then get the smoker ready and smoke overnight and through Sunday until around lunchtime. The pork will then need to rest for 1 hour before eating. It shreds better after resting for an hour and, if necessary, can be reheated in a covered dish in the oven.

> Leaving the bone in adds flavour to the joint, but removing it speeds up the cooking time: the 'choice is yours', as my friends say whenever I try to pin them down on recipes and cooking methods.

> The butt will need approx. 2 hours per 500g (1lb 2oz) in the smoker at 100°C (212°F); I would allow approx. 12–17 hours for a joint such as this, as sometimes you can encounter 'the stall'. This is when a large joint of meat, such as this, stops rising in temperature. It is thought that this is due to the evaporating moisture from the meat cooling down the chamber temperature. To stop this happening, when the internal temperature reaches approx. 65°C (150°F), wrap the joint in foil, adding a couple of spoons of apple juice, cider or water to the parcel, and put it back in the smoker. The temperature should start to climb slowly after this time until it reaches 75°C (167°F), which is when the meat is safe and ready to eat. Another way to get over the stall, if it happens, is to whack up the temperature of the smoker. Alternatively, you can remove the pork and transfer it to a hot oven (180°C/350°F/gas 4) to finish cooking. Always use a temperature probe to check the internal temperature; the pork is cooked when it reaches 75°C (167°F).

> At this point, remove the foil (if you have used it) and transfer the pork to a conventional oven at 180°C/350°F/gas

4 for approx. 30 minutes to crisp up the 'bark'. This is the crisp outside of the joint, which should become really black in colour and lined with deep crevasses. It is fantastically tasty and regularly causes fights in our family, as we can't wait to pull pieces off as soon as it is out of the oven. To make the bark even more delicious, glaze with some of the Wild and Wicked Barbecue Sauce (see right) before putting it in the oven.

SOUTHERN SWEET MUSTARD SAUCE

Serve this with the pork at the table.

SERVES 8

- 75g (2½oz) salted butter
- 5 tablespoons extra virgin olive oil
- 3 large white onions, finely chopped
- 4 tablespoons Dijon mustard (smooth or seedy)
- 4 tablespoons muscovado sugar
- 4 tablespoons cider vinegar
- salt and freshly ground black pepper

> Heat the butter and oil in a medium saucepan. Add the onions and fry over a medium heat until really soft and translucent, approx. 10–15 minutes. Add the remaining ingredients and stir through, allowing them to splutter. Simmer gently for 5 minutes. If the sauce is very thick, thin with a little water and heat through until you have the consistency you like. Taste for seasoning and serve warm with the pork.

WILD AND WICKED BARBECUE SAUCE

SERVES 20

- 450ml (16fl oz) tomato ketchup (see page 36)
- 2 tablespoons black treacle
- 3 tablespoons Worcestershire sauce
- 3 tablespoons cider vinegar
- few drops of Tabasco sauce
- generous pinch of salt and freshly ground black pepper

> Mix the ingredients together in a small saucepan and bring to the boil, then turn the heat down and simmer gently for approx. 10 minutes. Taste and adjust the seasoning if necessary.
> We use half of the sauce as a glaze (see left) and the rest as an accompaniment. If you have any left over, you can store it sterilized glass jars in the refrigerator and use within 2 months.

THE TWO G'S
HOT SMOKED PORK RIBS

Giancarlo and Giorgio love to get the fire going and enjoy the smoky, sweet flavour on these ribs. Eat them with your hands and enjoy licking your sticky fingers. Precooking the ribs in foil makes the meat soft and utterly irresistible without hours of cooking time. These work really well in our dustbin smoker. They are also excellent cooked in a Weber barbecue or a Big Green Egg but it is better to refer to their manufacturer's instructions for temperatures and timings.

SERVES 4

- 2 racks baby back ribs (approx. 1kg/ 2lb 4oz)

FOR THE RUB

- 3 fat garlic cloves, finely crushed to a paste
- 2 tablespoons extra virgin olive oil
- 50g (1¾oz) muscovado sugar
- ½ teaspoon crushed black peppercorns

FOR THE SAUCE

- 125g (4½oz) tomato ketchup (see page 36)
- ½ teaspoon Tabasco sauce
- 1 tablespoon Worcestershire sauce
- 75ml (2½fl oz) soy sauce
- 75g (2½oz) dark muscovado sugar
- 50g (1¾oz) demerara sugar

> Mix the ingredients together in a small saucepan and bring to the boil, then turn the heat down and simmer gently for approx. 10 minutes. Taste and adjust the seasoning if necessary.

OIL, FAT & BUTTER

Walk into any delicatessen or food hall and you will see trays of tempting roasted peppers, sun-dried tomatoes, olives and garlicky mushrooms coated in oil. Oil prevents the oxidization of food by stopping it from coming into contact with air. This protects it from natural decay, airborne bacteria and moulds.

Preserving food in oil is most popular in Mediterranean countries where olive trees grow. Olive oil is the preferred oil for the task as it takes on the flavour of the food and can be used as a dressing afterwards. Extra virgin olive oil is a delicious, if costly, way to preserve and is suitable for a variety of foods including peppers, artichokes, aubergines, tomatoes, onions, asparagus, mushrooms, fish, lemons and shellfish, to name but a few.

Sometimes a layer of oil, butter or fat is added on the surface of a product to protect the food underneath from oxidizing. This method is used for Fermented Tomatoes (see page 191) and Sun-dried Tomato Pesto (see page 152), as well as *Bagnetto* (see pages 152–3) and Smoked Potted Chicken (see pages 157–8). In the case of confit, animal fat is used both to cook and store the food, which is completely encapsulated by the fat and so protected from the air.

While oil and fat are good at preserving foods, they cannot be relied on to do the job on their own. This is because bacteria such as *Clostridium botulinum* can exist without oxygen. Foods with low acidity in particular, such as artichokes or aubergines, require an additional measure to protect them from decay – usually another preservative in the form of an acid like vinegar or lemon juice. This acidity, combined with the oil, creates an inhospitable environment where bacteria cannot survive. How can this be, I hear you ask, when sun-dried tomatoes are preserved in oil and they don't taste of vinegar? Tomatoes are usually high in acid and if dried their acidity is increased so that the pH of the tomatoes goes from 4.6 to 4 (a level where bacteria cannot survive), so there is no need for the vinegar.

PH VALUE AND PH TESTING STRIPS

The pH value of a product is a measure of its acidity. Foods with a pH below 4.6 are generally too acidic for bacteria to breed; these foods don't usually require the addition of any extra acid to make them safe to preserve. Foods that need to be treated with caution are low-acid foods such as aubergines, courgettes and peppers. These foods should always be supplemented with vinegar, citric acid or vitamin C before bottling to maintain the right levels of acidity and prevent the growth of harmful bacteria.

If you follow the recipes in this chapter, you shouldn't encounter any problems – especially if you stick to the quantities of vinegar listed and follow the instructions carefully regarding waterbathing. However, if you start playing around with your own flavours, it is always safest to test the acidity levels of your product before bottling. pH testing strips are straightforward to use and are available online (see page 242 for suppliers).

GARLIC IN OIL WARNING

Garlic is a low-acid vegetable which, since it is grown in the ground, could contain traces of *Clostridium botulinum*, the bacteria that causes botulism, a potentially fatal form of food poisoning. When exposed to oxygen the spores of the bacteria cannot develop, but when put under oil they are in the perfect environment for reproduction. It is with this in mind that recipes for storing low-acid vegetables under oil are better made without garlic. However, it is perfectly safe to add a little finely chopped garlic to any of these recipes just before eating.

* PRESERVING VEGETABLES UNDER OIL

Marinated vegetables look very pretty, taste gorgeous and make great antipasti in a hurry served with mozzarella and fresh basil. For years Italians have bottled their vegetables in oil but this is no longer deemed safe as some bacteria can survive under oil. I know we are going to upset the groups of people who have been doing this for years without harming anyone but we prefer to err on the side of safety and recommend you make these in small batches and keep them for less time in the refrigerator. Originally preserves under oil would have been kept in a cantina or cellar, which was dark and cool all year round. Nowadays our homes are warmer with central heating and the cool conditions necessary for these products are not available. There are recipes that use large amounts of vinegar to ensure the vegetables are safe to eat as high-acid environments make it impossible for these bacteria to survive. These have to be waterbathed and can then be kept out of the refrigerator but actually I don't enjoy the flavour when that much vinegar is present. So here is our version of these typical antipasti favourites to be made in small quantities, kept in the refrigerator and easily on hand when you need them. Alternatively, these recipes can be frozen for up to 3 months. Defrost in the refrigerator overnight and consume within a week.

GENERAL GUIDELINES FOR PRESERVING VEGETABLES UNDER OIL

OIL Use extra virgin olive oil of a medium quality; don't waste your favourite single estate stuff.

AFTER OPENING If you remove some of the vegetables, always top up the container with more oil so the vegetables are submerged in oil at all times.

Don't throw away the precious oil after you have eaten your vegetables. Use it for frying or for drizzling over salads, etc. It will have a wonderful flavour.

TROUBLESHOOTING

BULGING LIDS: If the lid on a container of food preserved in oil is bulging, or oil is leaking from it, your food has probably become contaminated. Don't attempt to eat it; throw it away immediately.

MOULD: If you discover mould growing on your food, throw it away; likewise, if it is starting to fizz. Always trust your nose – if the food smells bad, discard it.

Sometimes garlic turns green or blue in the jar. This is due to the acidity of the product and is nothing to worry about.

SUN-DRIED AND SMOKED TOMATOES UNDER OIL

I like the flavour of tomatoes without any vinegar and am happy to prepare them in small amounts to eat up fairly quickly. To keep semi-dried or Cold Smoked Tomatoes (see page 127), submerge them in oil in sterile containers and store in the refrigerator; consume within 10 days. The flavoured oil is delicious and can be used for cooking and dressing foods.

COURGETTES ALLA POVERELLA SOTT'OLIO

We grow courgettes in our garden and always end up with a glut of them in summer. I picked up this idea from our niece Pierangela, from Puglia, southern Italy. The flavours of the mint, vinegar and oil are evocative of summer and the semi-drying stops the courgettes becoming soggy and helps them last longer.

MAKES APPROX. 600G (1LB 5OZ)

- 1kg (2lb 4oz) courgettes, washed and sliced into 5mm (¼in) rounds
- first-pressed rapeseed oil or beef fat, for frying
- 300–400ml (10–14fl oz) extra virgin olive oil
- 2 tablespoons red or white wine vinegar
- a handful of mint leaves, roughly chopped
- fine sea salt

> Dry the courgettes according to the instructions on page 108 to the point where they have lost some of their water, are dry to the touch but are still flexible. They should not be crisp. This can be speeded up if dried on racks in the oven at 100°C/212°F/gas ¼ for 1 hour; as they will be cooked it is not essential to dry them slowly.

> A deep fat fryer is perfect for cooking the courgettes but if you don't have one use a large frying pan with 6 tablespoons of oil fine instead. Heat the oil until a piece of bread sizzles when lowered in. Fry the courgettes briefly until lightly browned. Remove from the oil with a slotted spoon and drain on layers of kitchen paper. Scatter them with salt to taste and layer them with the olive oil, vinegar and mint leaves into a container with a lid. Eat after a day and store in the refrigerator for up to 10 days, making sure the surface is covered with a layer of oil.

VARIATION

AUBERGINES UNDER OIL

Follow the method for Courgettes alla Poverella Sott'olio (see left) but be prepared to use more oil for frying as aubergines are more absorbent than courgettes.

ROASTED RED PEPPERS WITH THYME

This is an Italian way of preserving these bright red beauties under oil. Our friend Livia makes them regularly during summer. She uses her homegrown peppers and her husband Nello's olive oil. For this recipe, we bought all of the ingredients from our local supermarket and were very pleased with the result. Serve with steamed fish, cold meats or cheese, stirred into hot pasta with a dash of cream or as an ingredient in stir-fries, sauces or casseroles.

MAKES APPROX. 800G (1LB 12OZ)

- 8 red peppers
- 3 tablespoons lemon juice
- 4 sprigs of thyme
- 2 bay leaves, torn into two
- approx. 250ml (9fl oz) extra virgin olive oil
- fine sea salt

> Preheat the oven to 200°C/400°F/gas 6. Roast the peppers whole on a tray until black, approx. 30–40 minutes. Using tongs, transfer the peppers to a large bowl and cover with a plate, set aside to cool. The peppers will sweat inside the bag, loosening the skins. When cool enough to handle, peel off the skins, discard the seeds and rinse the flesh briefly under cold running water to remove any black bits. Pat dry on kitchen paper.
> Pack the peppers into a container or jar with a lid, interspersing each layer with the lemon juice, salt and herbs. Top up with the olive oil, making sure that the peppers are fully submerged before putting on the lid.
> Store in the refrigerator for up to 3 weeks. If you don't want to eat them all in one go, remove the amount you need and make sure the rest are covered in oil. Bring to room temperature before serving.

SALVO'S ARTICHOKES UNDER OIL

Salvatore has an allotment here in the UK and grows small violet coloured artichokes. This is his way of preserving them. His method is to prepare the artichokes and then cook them in one-third vinegar to two-thirds salted water.

MAKES APPROX. 1KG (2LB 4OZ)

- 1.5kg (3lb 5oz) artichokes
- 2 lemons
- white wine vinegar, salt and water for the poaching liquor (see recipe introduction)
- a few black peppercorns
- a few sprigs of dried thyme
- extra virgin olive oil, to cover

> Trim the hard leaves and tough stems from the artichokes and remove the fluffy chokes with a small teaspoon. Cut them into quarters and rub with a cut lemon to stop them becoming black. Put into cold water as you cut them, along with the used lemons. Boil the artichokes until tender in the correct proportions of vinegar to water ratio (see recipe introduction). Drain with the stems pointing upwards on a clean tea towel for several hours or overnight.
> Sterilize the jars and lids according to page 10. Heat the oil with the peppercorns and thyme over a medium heat. Pack the artichokes into the jars and cover with warm oil dividing the flavourings between them. Seal and when cooled to room temperature put them into the refrigerator or a cool, dark place. They will keep like this for up to 3 months but once opened use within 10 days and make sure the surface is always covered with oil. Serve at room temperature with mozzarella, use on pizza or griddle until hot and drizzle with balsamic vinegar.

ASPARAGUS UNDER OIL

For a while after the asparagus season is over you can enjoy these tender spears with a poached egg, salad, chopped into pasta or simply warmed on their own.

MAKES APPROX. 1 LITRE (1¾ PINTS) JAR

- 500g (1lb 2oz) asparagus
- 300ml (½ pint) white wine vinegar
- 200ml (7fl oz) water
- a few sprigs of thyme
- a few black peppercorns
- 500ml (18fl oz) extra virgin olive oil

> Trim away any woody ends of the asparagus and cut into lengths to fit inside your jar with enough headroom that they can easily be covered in oil. Cook them in the vinegar and water until just tender, then drain until dry on kitchen paper. Griddle, if you like, to add a roasted flavour and black lines. Warm the oil with the flavourings and sterilize the jar(s). Pack the spears into warm sterilized jar(s) and cover with the warm oil. Add the flavourings and seal. When cool transfer to the refrigerator and store for up to a month. Once opened, make sure the asparagus spears are always covered with oil.

CYRUS TODIWALA'S LIME PICKLE – LIMBU MARCHA NU ACHAAR

This simple chilli and lime pickle is certainly very popular with Cyrus's customers in his restaurants Café Spice Namasté and Mr Todiwala's Kitchen. Cyrus was keen to point out that there is no point making miniscule quantities of pickle and chutney as they need time to mature for the flavours to develop fully. They should always be made when the fruit or vegetable is abundant and in season. Pickles made well should last a long time, providing you ensure that the

pickle is submerged beneath the oil. Wipe down the sides of the jar with kitchen paper each time you remove some.

This simple recipe is very versatile and can be made with lemons, marrows, courgettes, rhubarb or asparagus. My advice is don't 'freak out' at the quantity and strength of the chillies at the beginning. Wait. After just a week, even though I was supposed to leave it longer, the flavours really mellow. This pickle is delicious served with curries or alongside grilled white fish. I am so glad Cyrus told me to make loads of it.

MAKES 3 X 500ML (18FL OZ) KILNER JARS

- 500g (1lb 2oz) large green chillies (or red chillies in season)
- 10 limes
- 500–600ml (18–20fl oz) first-pressed rapeseed oil
- 15–20 garlic cloves, peeled
- 5 heaped tablespoons English mustard powder
- 50g (1¾oz) salt
- 1 heaped teaspoon ground turmeric
- 1 teaspoon asafoetida

> Heat the rapeseed oil in a pan to smoking point; set aside to cool to room temperature. Wash the chillies and dry. Remove the stems and cut the chillies into approx. 1cm (½in) pieces. Wash the limes, trim off the ends and dice into 1cm (½in) pieces, skins and all. Place the chillies and limes together in a large bowl.
> In a blender, purée half the oil with the garlic, mustard, salt, turmeric and asafoetida. Scoop the purée into the bowl with the chillies and limes and mix well with a large spoon so everything is well coated. Reheat the remaining oil until hot, and then pour over the mixture in the

>>>

bowl. Stir well for 1–2 minutes, then wipe down the sides of the bowl with kitchen paper. Push down any chillies or limes that float to the surface; you might need to heat some more oil if necessary to cover them completely. Cover the bowl with a cloth and set aside in a warm place for a couple of days to ferment, checking regularly to make sure everything stays submerged to protect it from the air.

> Spoon the pickle into sterilized jars and top up if necessary with more oil. Cover the tops of the jars with a small circle of muslin, fastened with string or a rubber band, and then transfer them to a sunny windowsill. Leave the pickle to mature for 2 weeks before tasting. (If it is not sunny, leave it for up to a month.) During this time it will undergo lacto-fermentation (see Fermentation for more details on this, page 186). Expect to see a few bubbles, but wait for them to stop before you bottle. After that time the jars can be sealed with non-reactive lids and stored in a cool, dark place. The pickle will keep for up to a year.

✳ PASTES AND PESTO

We believe the best way to preserve the flavour of fresh basil is in frozen pesto cubes (page 227). However, here are some alternative pastes, and a tomato pesto sauce, which keep well in the refrigerator under oil.

SUN-DRIED TOMATO PESTO

This spicy little number is great spread onto hot crostini and topped with goat's cheese. Alternatively, stir it into hot pasta and grate over your favourite hard cheese. You can also try it stirred into couscous with some of the Roasted Red Peppers on page 150. For maximum flavour, use homemade dried or semi-dried tomatoes.

MAKES APPROX. 1 X 300ML (½ PINT) JAR

- 100g (3½oz) sun-dried or semi-dried tomatoes (see page 108)
- 1 garlic clove, peeled
- 25g (1oz) whole almonds, toasted until golden in a hot oven for a few minutes
- ½ teaspoon salt
- ½–1 whole dried red chilli, to taste
- 1 tablespoon lemon juice
- 150ml (¼ pint) extra virgin olive oil, plus extra to top up your jar with at the end

> Mix all the ingredients together with a stick blender or in a small food processor until you have a paste. I like to stop before it becomes completely smooth as I prefer a coarse texture. Taste and adjust the salt and chilli accordingly. Spoon into a sterilized jar, top up with some extra virgin olive oil and put on the lid. Store in the refrigerator for up to a month, keeping the top covered with a layer of olive oil at all times to stop oxidization.

BAGNETTO – PIEDMONTESE SAVOURY SAUCE FOR FISH AND CHICKEN

Imagine looking in an Italian mamma's refrigerator in Piedmont, northern Italy. There you are bound to discover a little pot of sauce that doesn't look or taste like anything you have experienced before, but you love it. It is umami – salty and savoury and full of things that you can't quite place, but you know you want more. It is so well balanced that not one flavour dominates and the result is something you want to spread on hot toast, drizzle onto pan-fried fish or scoop from your plate onto roast or poached chicken. This recipe was given to me by such an Italian mamma, Giorgina Vogliolo, who stills cooks with a passion at the age of 89. I am eternally grateful to her and I am sure I will be making *bagnetto* into my eighties if I am so lucky.

In Italy they eat this with *Bollito Misto*, the famous dish of boiled meats that is pushed around on a trolley in old-fashioned restaurants by waiters in white jackets and black bow ties. Giorgina's daughter, Luisa, is a friend of ours and told us the reason it is so good is that you have to make it with care. Her mother only uses salted capers, which she wipes free of salt with kitchen paper first, and she only uses anchovies under salt. Apparently she even keeps a special little spoon to serve it with so that it never takes on any other flavours.

MAKES 100G (3½OZ)

- 2 tablespoons capers
- 2 tablespoons chopped Salted Anchovies (see pages 78–9)
- 6 tablespoons finely chopped parsley
- 2 tablespoons tomato purée
- 2 tablespoon Dijon mustard
- 6 tablespoons extra virgin olive oil, plus extra to top up your jar with at the end
- 1 tablespoon red wine vinegar
- ½–1 teaspoon freshly ground black pepper
- ½ teaspoon freshly ground dried red chilli or chilli flakes
- 1 teaspoon caster sugar, to taste

> Chop the capers and anchovies finely by hand with a *mezza luna* (a half-moon-shaped knife), or a large cook's knife, grouping them into a pile on a large wooden chopping board. Transfer to a bowl with the remaining ingredients and mix well. Alternatively, put all the ingredients in a food processor and blend until smooth. Taste and adjust the seasoning as necessary. Spoon into a small jar and top up with extra virgin olive oil. Store in the refrigerator and consume within 2 weeks.

HARISSA PASTE

This recipe is from Moroccan chef, Ghalid Assyb. Harissa is strong, powerful stuff usually made with a mixture of chillies in different strengths – some dried and some fresh. Ghalid uses a mix of jalapeño, Scotch bonnet, bird's eye and Serrano. I have my own long red chillies that I dry (see page 108) and so used a mixture of those and some fresh red chillies to make up the amount to 100g (3½oz). Ghalid told me harissa should have a smokiness about it, so he blackens not only the peppers but also the fresh chillies and garlic too. We eat this on roast chicken, stir it into couscous or just use it as a condiment when we want a bit of spice.

MAKES APPROX. 250G (9OZ)

- 100g (3½oz) mixed chillies (see above) consisting of 25g (1oz) dried and 75g (2½oz) fresh
- 2 red peppers
- 2 fat garlic cloves, still in their skins
- ½ teaspoon cumin seeds
- ½ teaspoon coriander seeds
- ½ teaspoon caraway seeds
- 3 tablespoons lemon juice
- 50ml (2fl oz) extra virgin olive oil, plus extra for topping up the jar at the end
- 1 tablespoon tomato purée
- fine sea salt

> Preheat the oven to 200°C/400°F/gas 6. Soak the dried chillies in cold water for approx. 30 minutes. Place the peppers on a roasting tray in a hot oven for 20 minutes, then add the fresh chillies and garlic cloves and return to the oven for a further 10–15 minutes until the peppers and chillies start to blacken. Using tongs, transfer the roasted vegetables to a mixing bowl, cover with a plate, and set aside to sweat.
> Meanwhile, toast the spices in a dry frying pan until they release their fragrance;

>>>

set aside to cool and then grind to a powder in a spice grinder or pestle and mortar.

> Once the peppers and chillies are cool enough to handle, peel away any blackened areas of skin. It is a good idea to do this wearing thin gloves as the heat can stay on your fingers for a while afterwards and it can burn your eyes.

> Drain the dried chillies through a fine sieve, discarding the liquor. Squeeze the garlic cloves from their papery skins and place them in a blender or food processor. Add the chillies and peppers along with the remaining ingredients and blend to a smooth paste.

> Spoon the paste into a sterilized jar and cover with a layer of olive oil. The harissa will keep in the refrigerator for up to a month.

VARIATION

To make the wonderfully scented Rose Harissa add a large handful of fresh edible or dried edible rose petals to the paste, adding a little more extra virgin olive oil to make a paste. Make sure the petals have never been sprayed with pesticide and have a good natural perfume.

* FISH UNDER OIL

MARINATED SALTED ANCHOVIES

These are made using the Salted Anchovies on pages 78–9.

MAKES APPROX. 300G (10½OZ) (SERVES 8–10 AS A CANAPÉ OR STARTER)

- 200g (7oz) Salted Anchovies (see pages 78–9)
- juice of 1 lemon
- 200ml (7fl oz) white wine vinegar
- 100–150ml (3½–5fl oz) extra virgin olive oil

TO SERVE

- 1 red onion, finely chopped
- 1 garlic clove, finely sliced
- ½ chilli, finely sliced
- juice of 1 lemon
- 3 tablespoons extra virgin olive oil
- 1 tablespoon roughly chopped parsley

> Remove the anchovies from the salt and wash them in cold water. Place them in a glass container, squeeze over the lemon juice and pour in the vinegar. Set aside to soak for 30 minutes.

> Wash the anchovies again and squeeze them gently between sheets of kitchen paper to remove any excess moisture. Put them into a small container, such as a sterilized jar, and cover with the oil. Put on a lid and store in the refrigerator for up to 2 weeks.

> To serve, lay the anchovy fillets on a serving dish and dress with the onion, garlic, chilli, lemon juice, oil and parsley. Eat with toasted bread.

* CONFIT

The term confit comes from the French word *confire*, meaning to produce, make or prepare. Confit was originally used to describe fruits that had been cooked slowly in sugar or honey, hence the French word confiture, meaning jam, and the English word 'confection' for sweet treats. Today the term is used to describe any food prepared for preservation by immersing in a liquid and by being cooked slowly.

Confit-making as we know it today began during the 18th century in south-west

France, where fattened geese and ducks were salted and then cooked very slowly in their own fat, which rendered down during the cooking process. This method was designed to preserve meat throughout the winter.

Traditionally salt or saltpetre was used in the recipe to keep the meat pink and help to protect it from bacteria. However, this isn't necessary today if you keep the confit in the refrigerator, as the long, slow cooking process tenderizes the meat and kills off any unwanted bacteria.

The process of confit works so well as over time the collagen in the meat, usually the tough legs of goose and duck, is broken down. More recently in his book *Cooking for Geeks*, Jeff Potter writes about tests that have been done to show that actually it is this length of time that softens the meat, not the fat, so you could cook the meat in olive oil to save the cost of the duck fat. The duck-flavoured olive oil can also be used up afterwards and has a lot more uses than the expensive duck fat.

If done properly, this process is a simple and effective way of preserving meat. To reheat the meat, simply pull out the duck legs from the jar and cook until crisp. The flesh should be meltingly tender, while the fat can be used for flavourful roast potatoes.

CHRIS TERRY'S DUCK CONFIT

Crispy skin and soft, melting meat that falls from the bone, this is how confit of duck should be. Before writing this book I had never attempted this dish thinking it was too complicated. However our photographer friend, Chris Terry, had perfected the recipe and showed us how easy it was. Now it has become a staple dish we make at home for entertaining. We can prepare it in advance and cook it in the oven when the guests are present knowing we are going to get a fantastic result. We serve it with roast potatoes cooked in the fat or oil from the duck and a jar of Peas in Sweet Brine (see pages 214–15). The fat or oil can be used two or three times for another confit, after that it becomes too salty.

This recipe is also just right for using in the Cassoulet in Heat (see pages 217–18).

SERVES 4

- 1 head of garlic, broken into cloves and peeled
- 1 tablespoon juniper berries
- 1 tablespoon crushed black peppercorns
- 1 tablespoon fresh thyme leaves, plus a couple of sprigs
- 150g (5½oz) coarse sea salt
- 1 tablespoon bay leaves, roughly chopped with scissors
- 4 duck legs
- 800g (1lb 12oz) duck fat or goose fat or 1–1.5 litres (1¾–2½ pints) extra virgin olive oil

> Lightly crush three garlic cloves, the juniper berries, peppercorns and thyme leaves in a pestle and mortar. Add this mixture to the salt and cut bay leaves. Lay the duck skin-side down in a ceramic or glass container, preferably raised off the bottom so it doesn't sit in the brine. You could use a plastic rack for this or a few chopsticks laid down will do. Layer the duck legs with the salt and the flavourings between them. Put the lid on the container and transfer to the refrigerator or a cool place below 5°C (41°F) for 12 hours or overnight.

> Preheat the oven to 100°C/212°F/gas ¼. Brush the majority of salt off the duck and then give it a really brief rinse under the tap to remove the rest. Thoroughly pat dry on kitchen paper. Warm the duck fat or olive oil in a heavy ovenproof casserole

>>>

then add the fresh thyme sprigs and the remaining garlic cloves that should be lightly crushed.

> Lay the duck skin-side up into the fat or oil, making sure it is submerged and put the casserole into the oven. Cook for 4 hours or until a skewer slides into the meat with little or no resistance. During this time it is a good idea to measure the temperature with a digital probe, as it should never go above 100°C (212°F) in the fat or oil. Although small bubbles will appear in the oil or fat it should never boil. Although the oven is set at 100°C (212°F), the temperature in the casserole rarely gets to around 90°C (194°F).

> The duck can be eaten straight away but to preserve it, it should be stored in the fat. To do this put the legs into a heatproof container and carefully pour over the fat or oil but not the liquid at the bottom. (This will make duck jelly when set, which is excellent as a base for a stock or gravy.) The meat should be completely submerged in the fat or oil. The duck will keep for up to a month in the refrigerator like this. If you eat only one or two duck legs at a time make sure the remaining legs are covered in fat to protect them from oxidization.

> To reheat the duck legs preheat the oven to 180°C/350°F/gas 4. Lay the duck legs onto an ovenproof dish skin-side up and roast for 30–40 minutes, turning halfway through. This gives a delicious crispy result to the skin.

BOTTLING TIPS Jane Grigson recommends putting two sterilized sticks (one-third of a chopstick will do) in the bottom of each jar so that the meat is completely encircled by the fat. Other recipes suggest a scattering of salt at the bottom of the jar. Jane also recommends that you put a little circle of foil on top of the fat, pressing it down well on the surface, so it cannot become contaminated by air.

ANTONIO'S CONFIT OF TOMATOES

Head Chef, Antonio Sanzone, taught me this recipe. During the summer my family had arranged to come for lunch. It was a beautiful sunny day and, although I had made some fresh bread, I spent the morning lazing around in the garden letting time slip away. When my family suddenly appeared, I realized I had to think fast and prepare something to eat. I remembered Antonio's tomato confit in the cupboard. This is just what the idea of preserving is all about, I thought – rustling up a quick meal from your cupboard. I roughly tore up some mozzarella and laid it onto a serving dish. Then I cut up the tomatoes from the jars and laid these over the cheese, followed by most of the oil from the jar and some fresh basil. The result was delicious, and so simple served with warm bread, but none of my family realized I hadn't spent all morning preparing it!

Do pick very flavourful tomatoes for the best result. Tomatoes grown out of season in polytunnels just won't hit the spot.

MAKES 2 X 500ML (18FL OZ) KILNER JARS

- 500ml (18fl oz) extra virgin olive oil
- 1 banana shallot or 3 small shallots, thinly sliced
- ½ teaspoon fine sea salt
- 12 medium round, flavourful tomatoes
- 2 sprigs of rosemary
- 2 sprigs of marjoram
- 4 sprigs of mint
- 2 sprigs of thyme
- 2 leafy stems of basil
- 20 fennel seeds
- 2 star anise
- 10 black peppercorns
- 4 tablespoons lemon juice

> Heat a couple of tablespoons of the oil in a frying pan and soften the shallots over a

low heat for a few minutes with the salt. Meanwhile, skin the tomatoes: make a cross in the bottom of each one and cut out the core; drop into a pan of boiling water for 12–15 seconds (30–40 for San Marzano as the skins are tougher), and then plunge into ice-cold water; peel off the skins.

> Make sure your sterilized jars are completely dry. Divide the herbs and spices between the jars, placing them in a layer at the bottom. Some tomatoes have a visible ridge on them running from stalk to bottom. If this is the case, cut the tomatoes along this part, so that the seeds are trapped inside. Each tomato should be cut into quarters. Transfer the tomatoes to a large bowl and put in the softened shallots along with the oil and lemon juice. Toss everything together gently with clean hands, and then spoon the shallots and tomatoes into sterilized jars. Top up the jars with oil so the tomatoes are completely submerged. Cut out two discs from baking parchment to fit inside the jars and press down well to form a seal. Put on the lids and process the jars for 45 minutes using the waterbathing technique on pages 206–7. If waterbathed correctly, the tomatoes should keep in a cool, dark place for up to a year.

* POTTED PÂTÉS AND TERRINES

In medieval times, chopped meat and fat was pressed and cooked either inside an earthenware pot with a pastry lid or was completely encased in pastry. This is where the French term pâte, meaning pastry, comes from. Over time the French did away with the pastry and pâté as we know it today was born.

A terrine is a coarser version of a pâté, although both were traditionally made using raw meat that was pressed and cooked slowly in a waterbath. They were often weighted down to make them even more compact and expel the air.

English potted meats, shrimps and salmon are usually made with cooked meat and fish – making them an excellent way of using up leftovers – and they are traditionally preserved under a layer of clarified butter.

Today these historic terms for preserved meat have become interchangeable. Ingredients range from chicken and trout to game or rabbit – but they always contain a high percentage of fat. Flavourings are as luxurious as foie gras and truffle, but can be as simple as leek and rosemary. Terrines can be made in elegant layers that are visible only when sliced or blended until smooth and scooped out with a spoon. Either way, hot toast is essential as is a selection of pickles. Try them with the Swedish Pickled Cucumbers on pages 17–18.

POTTED SMOKED CHICKEN

Potted meats were traditionally made using leftovers to create another meal. This recipe can be made with other cooked meats such as ham, beef, pork, rabbit or other game. It has a lovely flavour from the smoking, although it isn't essential to use smoked chicken if you are looking for a way to use up the cooked meat from a Sunday roast. Experiment with the flavourings – try tarragon or lemon zest with unsmoked chicken, sage with pork, or add a little chilli or mustard seed with beef. In the past, we have used the leftover wing and leg meat from a roast chicken for this (after eating up all the breast meat first). Go easy with the thyme; it can easily overpower the flavour of the chicken.

- 120g (4¼oz) salted butter
- 1 white or brown onion, finely chopped
- 300g (10½oz) smoked cooked chicken or plain roast chicken
- ½ teaspoon chopped thyme leaves
- 1 tablespoon finely chopped fresh parsley
- 100ml (3½fl oz) chicken or vegetable stock or hot water
- 100ml (3½fl oz) clarified butter (see right)
- fine sea salt and freshly ground black pepper

> Melt the salted butter in a frying pan over a low heat and gently cook the onion until soft and translucent. Roughly chop the chicken either in a food processor using the pulse button or with a large kitchen knife. Tip the chicken into the pan, add the herbs and stock (or water) and cook for 5 minutes until heated through. Season with salt and pepper to taste. Divide the mixture between six ramekins and set aside to cool to room temperature; don't let them sit out any longer than 1 hour. Heat the clarified butter and pour some over each pot to form a thick protective layer. Transfer the ramekins to the refrigerator to set. They will keep for up to a week in the refrigerator.

VARIATION

POTTED SALMON

This recipe can also be made with leftover cooked salmon instead of chicken. Omit the thyme and instead add the juice of ½ lemon and some lemon zest to taste.

POTTED CHEESE

You can use any kind of cheese for this. I learned this recipe in Italy from our chef friend Gino Borella, who made it with pecorino and Parmesan, but I have since tried it with a mixture of leftover British cheeses, including some blue cheese from my refrigerator, and it worked brilliantly. Either enjoy it plain or introduce your own flavourings, such as a pinch of chilli powder or grated nutmeg, some dried herbs or lemon rind. This is lovely spread onto hot crostini, stirred into pasta or served on a cheese board with chutney.

MAKES 225G (8OZ)/ENOUGH FOR 10–12 CROSTINI

- 150g (5½oz) mixed cheeses of your choice
- 3 tablespoons extra virgin olive oil, plus extra to cover
- 4 tablespoons white wine

> Grate the cheeses either by hand or using the grater attachment in a food processor. Combine with the remaining ingredients in a bowl and beat until smooth. Either use straight away or spoon into a standard-sized jar and press down well. Cover the surface with a layer of oil and store in the refrigerator for up to a month.

POTTED CHICKEN LIVER AND PORT PÂTÉ

This pâté can be served straight away or covered tightly in baking parchment and kept refrigerated for a day before serving. To make it last longer cover it with clarified butter to stop it oxidizing and becoming bitter. It can be served in small jars for individual portions or from a kilner jar. For example it fills two 500g (1lb 2oz) Kilner jars. The amount of clarified butter you need depends on your containers but you should allow a depth of 3mm (⅛in) of butter to seal the pate.

SERVES 10, YIELD IS 1KG (2LB 4OZ)

- 800g (1lb 12oz) chicken livers
- 250g (9oz) butter
- 1 onion, roughly chopped
- 2 garlic cloves, roughly chopped
- 1 tablespoon thyme leaves
- 1 heaped tablespoon chopped sage leaves
- 1 teaspoon salt and plenty of black pepper
- 250ml (9fl oz) port, sherry, Madeira or Marsala
- 2 tablespoons double cream
- clarified butter (see below), to cover

> Clean the livers of any obvious green tinged areas and tough membrane, set aside. Heat 125g (4½oz) of the butter in a large frying pan. Add the onion and fry gently for 10 minutes or until softened. Add the garlic, livers and herbs until there are no signs of pink inside them. It will take approx. 10–15 minutes over a medium heat; be careful not to cook the livers too much or they will crispen.

> Add the alcohol and let it bubble and the sharp smell disappear. Add the cream and stir through. Remove from the heat and allow to come to room temperature. Transfer the mixture to a food processor and add the remaining butter in cubes. Blend the mixture until smooth. Taste and adjust the seasoning as necessary.

> Transfer the pate to sterilized containers (see page 10) and pack it down tightly so that there are no air bubbles. Pour the clarified butter over the top and let it set firm to seal it. Keep refrigerated for up to a week or freeze for up to 3 months.

> NOTE: To make **clarified butter**, melt butter in a small saucepan over a gentle heat. Leave to stand for 10 minutes, then spoon off the white foamy top layer. Slowly pour the clear butter into a jug and discard the salty particles at the bottom. Keep in or out of the refrigerator for up to a fortnight.

SMOKED TROUT PÂTÉ

This is Tim Lobb's recipe from Brookleas fish farm on the Ginge Brook at Ludbridge, Oxfordshire. Tim breeds trout, smokes them and sells them at local farmers' markets. Brookleas is a beautiful farm on the site of an old mill on the river. We love taking the children there because we can fish for trout and hot smoke it afterwards on our little Cameron smoker. With a bottle of chilled Sauvignon nestling in the hamper and happy children, it's a perfect day out! The pâté can be made with any smoked fish – in particular, it is a good way of using up broken or overcooked pieces of fish left over while learning to smoke your own fish.

SERVES 6

- 300g (10½oz) smoked trout (approx. 2 trout, filleted)
- 75ml (2½fl oz) low-fat yogurt, double cream or crème fraîche (see page 180)
- juice of ½ lemon
- ½ teaspoon paprika
- a few drops of Tabasco
- pinch of fine sea salt
- freshly ground black pepper
- clarified butter (see left), to seal

> Put all the ingredients apart from the butter into a food processor and blend until you have the consistency you like. Giancarlo prefers his pâté smooth, but I like mine chunky and a bit rough, so stop blending as you wish. Season to taste and serve straight away or store in the refrigerator in one or individual containers sealed with clarified butter as in the recipe for Potted Smoked Chicken (see page 157) for up to 5 days.

RILLETTES

My family used to holiday in Normandy every year and I remember my mother buying tubs of rillettes to slather onto warm baguettes. As we were a large family, we always did picnics and travelled with all the necessary items including freshly ground black pepper and sharp knives. Rillettes were eaten with gorgeous ripe tomatoes and black pepper. This is the French version of British potted meat using shredded rather than chopped meat.

This recipe is based on one shown to us by Marc Frederic, who has been inspirational in getting us into charcuterie. Rillettes can also be made with rabbit and pork fat or duck and goose with their own fat. Poultry fat melts at a lower temperature than pork fat so the end result is more spreadable. Always serve rillettes at room temperature like a good wine or cheese.

MAKES 4 X 340G (11¾OZ) JARS

- 500g (1lb 2oz) pork back fat, cut into small pieces
- 1kg (2lb 4oz) pork from the shoulder or belly
- 125ml (4fl oz) white wine
- 2 garlic cloves, finely chopped
- ½ teaspoon ground nutmeg
- 1 teaspoon freshly ground black pepper
- 1–2 teaspoons salt

> Put the fat into a heavy-based saucepan or a slow cooker over a low heat to melt. Meanwhile, cut the pork into 4cm (1½in) cubes. Add the pork to the warm melted fat and pour in the wine. Add the garlic, nutmeg and black pepper. Bring to the boil, cover with a lid and then cook over a very low heat for 3–4 hours until the meat is tender and falling apart.
> Strain the meat through a sieve over a heatproof bowl to collect the fat. Tip the meat out onto a chopping board and shred it finely between two forks. Place the shredded meat in a clean bowl and gradually pour in some of the warm fat, little by little, until it reaches the consistency, according to Marc, of a peat bog – if you press down on the shredded meat the juices should rise to the top – not that I've ever been to a peat bog, but I think he means it should be really, really thick with the juices just visible with pressure! Season with salt to taste.
> Spoon the mixture into sterilized jars or ramekins and set aside to cool. To seal your jars, melt some of the remaining fat in the pan and pour a thick layer of the top of each jar to cover the surface completely. Put on the lids and store in the refrigerator for up to 2 weeks. Serve with hot toast or bread, Swedish Pickled Cucumbers (see pages 17–18) and ripe juicy tomatoes.

WILD GARLIC PESTO

To me, the sight and smell of wild garlic growing in our local woods heralds the first sign of spring. I love making this wild garlic pesto, which is delicious stirred into hot pasta or spread over fish before grilling.

SERVES 4–6

- 50g (1¾oz) young wild garlic leaves
- 50g (1¾oz) pine nuts, almonds or cashews, toasted in a hot oven for 3–5 minutes
- 125ml (4fl oz) extra virgin olive oil, plus extra to cover
- 25g (1oz) Parmesan or Grana Padano cheese, finely grated
- freshly ground black pepper
- pinch of salt

> Rinse the garlic leaves in cold water and pat dry on kitchen paper. Blend to a

paste with the nuts and pepper in a food processor or a pestle and mortar. I like my pesto fairly coarse, but keep grinding if you prefer it smooth. Pour in the oil and pulse quickly to blend. Scoop the pesto into a bowl and stir in the cheese. Season to taste with salt if necessary. Spoon the pesto into clean jars with lids, top up with extra virgin olive oil to cover and store in the refrigerator for up to 2 weeks.

* BUTTER

If you have ever over-whipped cream, you will know how easy it is to make butter. By churning cream, we can separate the fat in the form of butter grains from the water-based part of the cream, called buttermilk.

Traditionally butter producers use the evening milk, which is 4 per cent higher in fat than morning milk, because it is produced over a shorter period so it is more concentrated. Butter can be made out of fresh or fermented milk or cream. The colour of butter varies depending on the cow's feed; manufactured varieties often contain colourings such as carotene.

TO MAKE BUTTER

This can be done very simply in a glass jar with a tight-fitting lid. Pour double cream into a jar and add a couple of ice cubes. Shake the jar vigorously until the fat has separated into a ball that floats in the buttermilk. To speed up the process, churning can also be done in a food processor with a tight-fitting lid. Whip the cream until it becomes very thick. Eventually it will separate into lumps of butter and buttermilk.

After churning, whether you have used a jar or a food processor, it is essential that you wash the lumps of butter in a sieve under very cold water to get rid of any buttermilk,

which will make it spoil. Break up the lumps with your hands to remove any traces of buttermilk that could cause spoilage. Once the water runs clear, the butter can be pressed together. This is traditionally done with butter pats, which have ridges down them to leave a pattern but also to encourage the water to run away. Failing that, you could press the butter with your hands or roll it into a sausage shape in a piece of baking parchment.

After pressing, you can flavour the butter if you wish with fine or coarse sea salt, chilli or herbs. Shape into logs, wrap in baking parchment and keep chilled until ready to use. Butter will keep for a couple of weeks in the refrigerator.

TO MAKE CULTURED BUTTER

In small dairies, milk was traditionally collected over several days before being made into cream or butter and by this time it had started to ferment. During fermentation, cream naturally sours as bacteria convert milk sugars into lactic acid. This fermentation is what gives the resulting 'cultured' butter its strong flavour and today cultured butter is attracting lots of attention from chefs and the public alike. Nowadays, cultured butter is usually made on a large scale from pasteurized cream, which has been fermented with the addition of bacteria cultures such as *Lactococcus* and *Leuconostoc*. However, it is possible to make cultured butter at home.

METHOD First, you need to ferment the cream. Put a couple of tablespoons of live yogurt into 500ml (18fl oz) double cream and set aside, covered, in a warm place for 24 hours. Alternatively, mix in the tip of a teaspoon of Mesophilic starter (from cheese-making suppliers, see page 242) and set aside in a warm place for 12 hours.

To turn your fermented cream into butter, follow the method for making butter (see page 161) using 3 parts double cream to 1 part fermented cream. As before, it is essential that you rinse the butter really well in plenty of cold water before seasoning it with salt. Store as for fresh butter.

⋆ FLAVOURED BUTTERS

These versatile little pastes make wonderful toppings for baked potatoes, hot steak or burgers, or they can be stirred into pasta, or melted onto hot sourdough toast, chicken or fish – I told you they were versatile!

Bring a 250g (9oz) packet of butter to room temperature. Put the softened butter in a bowl and use a fork to mash in your chosen flavourings (see below); season with salt and pepper. Spoon the butter onto a piece of baking parchment and roll up into a log shape. Put the flavoured butter in the refrigerator to harden and then cut into slices if you wish, wrapping them individually in baking parchment. Store in the freezer for up to 3 months or keep in the refrigerator for up to a week.

FLAVOURINGS

WILD GARLIC Add 6 heaped tablespoons of finely chopped wild garlic leaves. Use on steak or in jacket potatoes.

TRUFFLE Add a generous grating of fresh truffle or ½ teaspoon of truffle oil. Melt over hot pasta.

TARRAGON Add 6 heaped tablespoons of finely chopped fresh tarragon. Melt over hot roast chicken or stuff under the skin before cooking. Alternatively, add a cube to hot steamed carrots before serving.

PORCINI Soak a small handful of dried porcini mushrooms in hot water to rehydrate them, and then drain well. Pat dry on kitchen paper and finely chop. Fry briefly in extra virgin olive oil with a finely chopped garlic clove. Drain from the oil and allow to cool. Mix into the butter. Melt over hot pasta, steak or stir into mashed potato.

CHILLI AND GARLIC Add 2–3 teaspoons of finely chopped fresh or dried red chilli and 5 teaspoons of finely chopped garlic. Stir into rice, melt over chicken or spread on hot thick toast for garlic bread.

⋆ FLAVOURED OILS

Oils flavoured with fresh herbs and spices do not have a long shelf-life. There is also a small risk of inviting unwanted bacteria into your oil via the additional flavourings – there have been a few cases of botulism coming from garlic preserved in oil. We prefer to make Spice Cubes for cooking, see page 227, or we make small amounts of flavoured oil and keep them refrigerated for use within 3 days.

CHILLI OIL

> Pour 200ml (7fl oz) of extra virgin olive oil into a clean bottle or jug and stir in 2 teaspoons of dried chilli flakes. (To make these yourself see page 108.) Cover and store in the refrigerator and consume within 3 days. Chilli oil is delicious drizzled over pizza or stir-fries where you want a dash of heat and others don't.

HERB OIL

Mix the oil with 1 teaspoon of dried thyme, 1 teaspoon of dried oregano and 2 chopped bay leaves as above. Pour this over steak, grilled chicken or lamb.

BASIL OIL

This is a great way to use up the dried leaves of basil that appear on a plant when it has been in the sun. Put a handful into the oil as above and store in the refrigerator overnight. Strain and use as a dip for hot bread. Store in the refrigerator and consume within 3 days.

ZHUG

This coriander and chilli paste originates from the Yemen and Yemenite Jews introduced it to Israel. *Zhug* is now popular all over Israel on falafel stalls. Green *zhug* is made from green chillies and red *zhug* is made from red ones. *Zhug* looks like a sort of Middle-Eastern version of pesto, as it also contains plenty of fresh herbs blended with oil. I love Middle Eastern cooking and so use it quite frequently with couscous, harissa, North African merguez sausages (see page 96) or over halved boiled eggs and roasted vegetables. It is really versatile and you can alter the strength of the heat by adding or subtracting chillies as you like.

MAKES 175G (6OZ)

- 60g (2¼oz) fresh coriander
- 40g (1½oz) parsley
- 2 green chillies
- 3 garlic cloves, peeled
- 2 tablespoons lemon juice
- 4 tablespoons extra virgin olive oil, plus extra to cover
- 1 teaspoon coriander seeds

- ½ teaspoon cumin seeds
- ½ teaspoon cardamom pods
- 4 cloves
- ½ teaspoon fine sea salt

> Wash the herbs and pat dry on kitchen paper. Discard any large tough stalks from the coriander and parsley (you can freeze the parsley stalks for use in stocks). Place the herbs, chillies, garlic and lemon juice into a food processor with the olive oil and blitz to a paste. Grind the spices and salt to a powder in a pestle and mortar or spice grinder, discarding the cardamom husks once they have released their seeds. Add the spices to the food processor and blitz again – it doesn't have to be completely smooth, I prefer mine a little chunky. Use straight away or spoon into a sterilized jam jar and top up with olive oil. Store in the refrigerator for up to a week but the flavour is better before 5 days. Alternatively, freeze cubes of zhug in an ice-cube tray for up to 3 months.

FETA IN OIL

Look out for proper feta that is sold in a tub of brine from a deli. The flavour and acidity will be superior to the plastic-wrapped variety. This is a great way to use your dried herbs (see page 109). Don't add garlic cloves if you wish to keep the cheese for more than a week.

MAKES 1 X 500ML (18FL OZ) KILNER OR LE PARFAIT JAR/SERVES APPROX. 6

- 300g (10½oz) feta
- 1 teaspoon dried thyme
- 1 teaspoon dried oregano
- 1 teaspoon dried chilli flakes
- 1 strip of lemon zest (optional)
- 250ml (9fl oz) extra virgin olive oil

>>>

> Cut the feta into 2cm (¾in) dice and put into a clean jar, interspersed with the herbs, chilli and lemon zest (if using), leaving 2cm (¾in) headroom. Pour over the oil, moving the cheese around gently with a chopstick to ensure that there are no air bubbles left and that the cubes are completely submerged in oil.

> Wait a day before eating to let the flavours infuse. If you remove some cheese, make sure the remainder is completely covered in oil. It will keep for up to 2 weeks in the refrigerator. Make a Greek salad from your marinated feta with large cubes of tomato, cucumber and olives, using the oil as the dressing. Alternatively, toss with slices of roast aubergine or mix with cubes of watermelon, fresh mint, the oil from the jar and a splash of balsamic vinegar.

ALCOHOL

Bottling in alcohol is one of the oldest, simplest and definitely most pleasurable ways of preserving fruit. Boozy fruits, as my mother used to call them, make wonderfully sweet, yet citric, desserts. And then, of course, there are plenty of spirits you can enhance with the addition of some hedgerow fruits, such as sloes or blackberries.

We are a family of foragers who have been picking sloes from our thorny bushes for years now to make sloe gin. However, since writing this book summer lunches in the garden have been brightened by peaches in rosé wine and chilly winter nights have been warmed by shots of damson whisky – my new favourite nightcap – and blackberry gin.

Many of these recipes double up as boozy fruit or fruity booze. We lift out the fruits and serve them with crème fraîche or whipped cream, and then drink the liquor that is left afterwards – either on its own over crushed ice, as a base for cocktails or in a Champagne flute topped with prosecco or Champagne. Boozy fruits are incredibly versatile – you can add them to apple or pear crumbles or pies, or spoon them over porridge or muesli – or you can use both the fruit and the liquor together in trifles, or purée them together to make a sauce for meat, add to gravy or pour them over ice cream.

The only downside to the recipes in this chapter is that you need to wait 2 weeks for the quickest result, and up to a year for the slowest – but it is worth having patience!

WHICH ALCOHOL AND WHAT FLAVOURS?

As long as the alcohol is strong – i.e. above 37.5 per cent proof, such as gin, vodka, rum, etc. – you can mix and match to suit your preference. However, don't be tempted to economize and use poor-quality spirits, as you will definitely taste the difference in the end result.

You can add extra flavourings such as cinnamon sticks, allspice berries, vanilla pods and star anise, but remember the flavours will increase in strength over time so don't go overboard with the spicing.

STERILIZING BOTTLES AND JARS

Wash bottles and jars in the dishwasher or with hot soapy water and rinse well so that there is no inherent smell or taste. Put in the oven at 140°C/275°F/gas 1 for 30 minutes to sterilize. If you are filling them with hot liquid, leave them in the oven until the last minute so that you are pouring hot into hot to avoid cracking. If you are filling with cold liquid, cool the jar or bottle upside down on a rack after sterilizing. Make sure you use non-reactive lids, sterilized before use by boiling them separately for a few minutes; leave in the water until you need them.

FILLING YOUR BOTTLES

Sterilized funnels should be used to fill bottles. The fruit should be completely covered with alcohol to stop spoilage.

STORAGE

Unless you are using dark coloured jars or bottles, store your fruity booze in a cool, dark place away from the light.

A NOTE ABOUT SWEETENING

The usual way to make sloe gin and similar drinks is to put the fruit, sugar and alcohol together in the bottle, and then gently shake it every other day for the first week until the sugar dissolves. The advantage of this method is that the job is done all in one go and all you have to do is sit back and wait for it to be ready. However, the only problem with this method is sometimes the resulting drink turns out to be sweeter than you would like – as much depends on the sweetness of your fruit, which can vary from one season to the next. Now, thanks to Jared Brown of the artisan distillers Sipsmith, I have discovered a better method, which allows you to control the sweetness. Jared recommends that you sweeten your drink after it has matured using sugar syrup, which you can add to the bottle little by little until you have the sweetness you like. If you are concerned about diluting your spirit, you can always make up a more concentrated version using two-thirds sugar to one-third water – however, add it cautiously because it will be really sweet.

SUMMER FRUITS IN BRANDY

This method is suitable for preserving all sorts of summer fruits, including berries, plums and apricots. The boozy fruit should be ready to eat within 2 weeks, however you can leave it to mature for longer if you wish.

Our favourite way of serving the boozy fruits is with ice cream, yogurt or sponge cake. The fruity brandy is delicious served hot in shot glasses, or mixed with red wine for a variation on mulled wine. Alternatively, purée the fruits with their liquor and use as a sauce for desserts or with game dishes.

MAKES APPROX. 4 X 340G (11¾OZ) JARS
- 1kg (2lb 4oz) summer berries or stone fruits
- 400g (14oz) caster sugar
- 1 litre (1¾ pints) brandy

> Wash the fruit and pat dry on kitchen paper. Stone and halve the stone fruits. Divide the fruit and sugar between the sterilized jars and top up with brandy. Seal and set aside in a cool, dark place for at least 2 weeks, turning the jars upside down every day until the sugar dissolves. Store for 3 months before sampling, although it can be matured for up to a year in a cool, dark place.

and screw on the lids tightly. Store in a cool, dark place and gently shake the jars every day until the sugar dissolves.

> After 2 weeks, fish out the peaches from the liquid and eat. You can either serve the wine at the same time – we like it chilled as an aperitif – or leave it to mature for up to a year in a cool, dark place, by which time you will be ready to make some more!

PEACHES IN ROSÉ

This drink is just gorgeous on a sunny day. Instead of drinking plain rosé wine, I like this at lunchtime as an aperitif. The wine only requires a couple of weeks to take on the flavour of the peaches, so this is a great one to do over summer – although it will keep into winter for when you want a reminder of the sun. The peaches are great served with vanilla ice cream or crème fraîche – we fish them out after 2 weeks, leaving 1 litre (1¾ pints) of enriched wine to drink later.

MAKES APPROX. 2 X 1 LITRE (1¾ PINTS) JARS

- 4 ripe peaches
- 200g (7oz) granulated sugar
- 750ml (1⅓ pints) rosé wine
- 100ml (3½fl oz) grappa, eau de vie or vodka
- 2 small bay leaves

> Put the jars into the oven to sterilize, see page 166. Make two small crosses in the top and bottom of each peach. Drop them into boiling water for 2 minutes. Remove and immediately put into iced water to cool them down quickly. Peel the peach and cut into quarters, discarding the skin and stone.

> Divide the peaches and the remaining ingredients between the sterilized jars

CARAMELIZED ORANGES IN BRANDY

These remind me of when I first met Giancarlo. He had an ancient, slightly squeaky sweet trolley in his restaurant that would wobble as it was pushed around, loaded with typical Italian desserts. The sticky bittersweet oranges in brandy were in a big glass bowl at the bottom and were always my favourite. As sweet trolleys went out of fashion and customers began eating fewer puddings we stopped making them – until I started writing this book. Now I have been reminded of how much I love them, I have a jar permanently on standby ready to serve with whipped cream and toasted almonds, whenever friends arrive, or, if time allows, I can pour them over a base of sponges and top with homemade custard to make a trifle.

MAKES 2 X 1 LITRE (1¾ PINTS) JARS

- 12 small oranges (700g/1lb 9oz without peel and pith)
- 2 x approx. 5cm (2in) cinnamon sticks
- 2 teaspoons allspice berries
- 800ml (1⅓ pints) cold water
- 300g (10½oz) sugar
- 200ml (7fl oz) brandy

> Preheat the oven to 140°C/225°F/gas 1. Sterilize your jars, see page 166. Prepare a waterbath, see pages 208–9.

>>>

> Using a potato peeler, cut away the zest from two of the oranges in long pieces (try not to get any of the white pith) and set aside. Cut away the pith from all the oranges and set them aside. Discard the pith. Put the peel into a large saucepan with the cinnamon, allspice berries and water and bring to the boil. Reduce to a simmer.

> Put the sugar into a large saucepan and over a medium heat. Without stirring let the sugar caramelize until it is golden brown. At arm's length, slowly pour this molten sugar into the water with the peel. It will splutter, so take care. Stir through, add the oranges and cook for 10 minutes. Remove the pan from the heat.

> Use a slotted spoon to remove the peel and the oranges from the syrup and put into the jars. Add the brandy to the syrup and stir through. Pour into the hot jars dividing the cinnamon sticks and allspice berries between them. Screw on the lid and process in a waterbath following the hot-pack method for 30 minutes (see pages 208–9). Allow to cool for 5 minutes, remove from the water with jar lifters and cool to room temperature. Label and store in a cool, dark place for at least a month and up to a year.

peaches, nectarines, apricots, currants and cherries. Plums and apples become rubbery, bananas are too sweet and melon is too watery.

> METHOD You need approx. 500g (1lb 2oz) caster sugar for 1kg (2lb 4oz) of fruit. Wash all the fruit gently and dry on a clean tea towel. Sterilize a crockpot, large glass jar or ceramic casserole dish and put in the first layer of fruit – either a single variety or a mixture. Cover with a layer of sugar and pour over enough dark rum to cover the fruit by at least 2cm (¾in), so none of it is sticking out. Put a lid on the pot and set aside in a cool, dark place. As different fruits come into season, you can build up further layers of fruit, sugar and rum until your jar is full. Sample after 6 weeks or leave to mature for up to a year.

> Once matured, the boozy fruit can be eaten as a potent dessert with cream or you can drop individual berries into glasses and top them up with prosecco for a Berry Fizz. Alternatively, mix into crumbles or pies. The flavoured rum can be served neat in shot glasses or mixed with sparkling wine as an aperitif.

RUMTOPF

I can remember my mother making this wonderful German concoction in an old crockpot. I love the fact that there is no set recipe and you can keep adding to the layers of fruit throughout the season, starting with the first strawberries of the year and continuing until the last blackberry is plucked from the brambles.

The key is to pick perfect, just ripe fruit. However, some work better than others. I would go for strawberries, raspberries, blackberries, blueberries, grapes, pears,

RUM PLUM COMPOTE

This idea was given to us by our friend, and keen home-brewing expert, Debi King. The compote doubles as a gorgeous sweet drink, best served in shot glasses, or a rich sauce to pour over ice cream. It could also be made with brandy or kirsch instead of the rum.

MAKES 6 X 250G (9OZ) JARS

- 1.6kg (3lb 8oz) Victoria or other plums
- 350g (12oz) demerara sugar
- 300ml (½ pint) amaretto
- 300ml (½ pint) rum

> Halve and stone the plums and put them in a large saucepan with the sugar. Set over a low heat, stirring frequently to dissolve the sugar, and cook until the fruit is soft and pulpy, approx. 20 minutes. Push through a sieve into a clean bowl, discarding the skins. Put the purée into a saucepan and bring to the boil stirring constantly. When bubbling, remove from the heat and add the alcohol. Stir through and pour into hot sterilized jars. Put on the lids and process in a waterbath following the hot-pack method for 10 minutes (see pages 208–9). Store in a cool, dark place for up to a year.

SLOE GIN

My favourite gin and tonic has now been supplanted by sloe gin and tonic, which has a pretty pink glow.

Sloes are the berries of the blackthorn tree, which have a bluish hue to them, making them appear like small dark grapes. Watch out for the slender thorns on the tree when you pick them, and never take all you can see – leave some for the birds. This year I took advice from Jared Brown from the artisan distillers Sipsmith, who make their own excellent sloe gin. This is what he suggests:

Ideally pick the berries after the first frost, because this freezing tenderizes the skins. However, don't pick them before they are ripe. You can tell when they are ripe by gently squashing them between your fingers. If they are rock hard, leave them on the tree. If they ripen before the frost, pick them and then put them into the freezer overnight. There is no need to prick the berries provided they have been frozen – either by the frost, or in your freezer. A lightly crushed almond added to the bottle with the sloes gives a subtle marzipan flavour.

Add the sugar syrup to taste just before you want to drink the gin. This allows the natural flavours of the fruit to be extracted and developed by the alcohol alone, and will prevent the finished drink from becoming too sweet.

MAKES 2 X 1 LITRE (1¾ PINTS) BOTTLES
- 600g (1lb 5oz) ripe sloes
- 1 litre (1¾ pints) gin
- 2 almonds, lightly crushed (optional)

FOR THE SUGAR SYRUP
- 200g (7oz) granulated cane sugar
- 200ml (7fl oz) water

> Wash the fruit and dry between two clean tea towels. Unless the berries were picked after the first frost (see left), put them in a container in the freezer overnight.
> The following day, bring the fruit out of the freezer and let it defrost. Divide the berries between sterilized jars and top up with the gin. Drop an almond into each jar (if using). Put on the lids and transfer the jars to a cool, dark cupboard. Shake the bottles gently every other day for the first week, and then leave them alone for at least 3 months to mature.
> After a year, you can strain out the sloes and discard them. You can then return the liqueur to the same bottle to mature for several years before sampling; it will mellow with time.
> Once you are ready to start drinking your sloe gin, prepare the sugar syrup. Dissolve the sugar in the water in a saucepan over a medium heat, then set aside to cool. Add the concentrated sugar syrup to the bottle, little by little, stirring thoroughly and tasting regularly until you are happy with the sweetness – you may not need it all. Store in a cool, dark place for up to a year.

VARIATIONS

DAMSON GIN

What a lovely tipple. On a freezing cold night in January, my father and I decided to sample all the hedgerow liqueurs I had made. This was my favourite, and we both found it warming, welcome and delightfully moreish. It had so much flavour I didn't like to dilute it with tonic and ice, so instead I would recommend serving it in shot glasses.

> METHOD Follow the recipe for Sloe Gin (see page 169), substituting the sloes for damsons. Ignore the note about freezing the fruit.

BLACKBERRY GIN

This adds not only colour, but also sweetness and a wonderful berry flavour to the gin.

> METHOD Follow the recipe for Sloe Gin (see page 169), substituting the sloes for 300g (10½oz) blackberries and using 500ml (18fl oz) gin. Ignore the note about freezing the fruit. Make the sugar syrup with 150g (5½oz) caster sugar and 150ml (¼ pint) water.
> SERVING SUGGESTION This is great for making a version of the cocktail called Bramble, which is usually made with blackberry liqueur. Just muddle some of the blackberries from the finished gin in a glass with a dash of lemon juice, add a large shot of the blackberry gin, 1 teaspoon of sugar and some crushed ice. Garnish with a mint leaf and enjoy!

DAMSON WHISKY

Our friend Chris Terry gave this idea to me. During our tasting nights, my late father decided this was his favourite. He loved the strength of the whisky (I used a single malt!), followed by the sweetness of the sugar and damsons – so we renamed it Papa's Medicine!

> METHOD Follow the recipe for Sloe Gin (see page 169), substituting the sloes for 300g (10½oz) damsons and using 500ml (18fl oz) whisky (preferably single malt) instead of the gin. Ignore the note about freezing the fruit. Make the sugar syrup with 150g (5½oz) caster sugar and 150ml (¼ pint) water.

VIN D'ORANGE

Choose a dry white wine that you like to drink for this – don't be tempted to use a really cheap one or the result won't be as good.

MAKES APPROX. 2.25 LITRES (4 PINTS)

- 2 x 750ml (1⅓ pints) bottles of white wine
- 4 oranges
- 450ml (14oz) vodka, eau de vie or grappa
- 200g (7oz) icing sugar
- 1 cinnamon stick

> Wash the oranges and cut into quarters, leaving the peel on. Put into a large, sterilized container such as a lidded bucket, a ceramic crock or divide into several Kilner or Le Parfait jars. Add the remaining ingredients and stir through to dissolve the sugar. Put a saucer or two on top of the oranges to keep them under the level of the wine. Put on the lid(s) and leave in a cool, dark place for 2 weeks, stirring every other day.
> Strain the liquor from the container and discard the oranges. Taste and add a little more sugar if you prefer it sweeter. Pour through a funnel into sterilized bottles and fit a cork into each. Store in the refrigerator for up to 6 months.

PINEAPPLE VODKA OR RUM

This can be used in cocktails or served with dessert. Serve pineapple vodka neat over crushed ice; pineapple rum makes a great cocktail mixed with sugar syrup and coconut milk.

MAKES 2 X 1 LITRE (1¾ PINTS) JARS

- 1 medium ripe pineapple (approx. 1.5kg/3lb 5oz)
- 1 litre (1¾ pints) vodka or white rum

> Cut the pineapple into triangles, discarding the skin and core along with any black areas. Divide the pineapple pieces between the sterilized jars and pour over the vodka or white rum to cover. Put on the lids and set aside in a cool, dark place for a week.
> Pour the contents of the jars into a blender and purée until smooth. Sweeten to taste with sugar syrup using a ratio of equal parts sugar to water (see Sloe Gin, page 169). If you wish it to be clear, you can strain it through muslin. Pour the sweetened purée into a cold sterilized bottle and store in the refrigerator until needed. It will keep for up to 3 weeks. Serve chilled in martini glasses.

VARIATIONS

WATERMELON VODKA

> METHOD Remove the seeds and skin from a small watermelon and cut the flesh into chunks. Put the chunks into a large sterilized jar and top up with vodka. Put on a lid and set aside in a cool, dark place for 5 days.
> After 5 days, strain through a fine sieve lined with muslin, squeezing the juice from the melon chunks as you do so. Serve over crushed ice in martini glasses or use as a base for cocktails.

VODKA WATERMELON

Not exactly preserving, but this is good fun.

> METHOD Make a hole in your watermelon the same size as a cork and pour in the contents of a bottle of vodka, little by little each day over a period of 5 days, blocking up the hole with a cork. To serve, either cut the boozy watermelon into wedges and enjoy as it is, or purée and strain the watermelon through a sieve lined with muslin to collect the juices and serve as a drink over crushed ice.

CHILLI VODKA

Surely the easiest recipe in the whole book. I love the herbiness and heat the chillies bring to the vodka, and we have had such fun drinking it. Our favourite way of serving it is in Pasta with Hot Smoked Salmon, Cream and Chilli Vodka (see page 141) – and to cut through the fat, we serve a shot of chilli vodka on the side. It's a real ice-breaker, try it! Chilli vodka also makes a wicked Bloody Mary.

> METHOD Open a 700ml (1¼ pints) bottle of vodka, put in a whole red chilli, screw on the lid and wait at least 6 weeks. Over time the chilli will lose its colour.

FERMENTING

Fermentation is a really exciting area in the world of food. It has been practised all over the world throughout history and has formed a valuable, if not essential, part of our diet for centuries. Georgians are reputed to have produced wine for up to 8,000 years, Babylonians have made fermented drinks since 5,000 BC and Egyptians started fermenting in 3,150 BC. In Japan, miso apparently existed during the Neolithic Age, and it has been used as a preservative and flavouring for generations. Miso is made by fermenting soybeans, rice, barley or a mixture of soy and one of the other grains with the yeast mould known as koji and salt. We know that Roman soldiers existed on a diet of slowly fermented sourdough and apparently Inuits traditionally wrapped whole orks (seabirds) in sealskins and buried them underground. Months later they dug them up to eat the delicacy that was fermented bird... yum! We also know that early settlers carried sourdough starters across America and Captain Cook's sailors took sauerkraut to sea to provide a vital source of vitamin C on long voyages.

You might think that we don't need these fermented foods any more, since we have refrigeration and polytunnels to provide us with fruit and vegetables all year round – and anyway, we have vitamin pills. And it is true that since industrialization, fermented foods have been on the decline. This is partly due to the fact that fermentation gives variable results and it is hard to produce fermented foods on a large scale. In order to make food safe and increase shelf-life, it has become far easier for manufacturers to turn to other methods of food preservation such as pasteurization, canning or using large amounts of vinegar and salt as a preservative. Today you can't just grab a jar of sauerkraut off the supermarket shelf and assume you are eating something really nutritious; it will most likely contain vinegar to get the typically acidic flavour and will have been pasteurized. If you really want to benefit from the health-giving properties of fermented foods, you will have to make them yourself.

Fermentation is exciting because it not only appears to have incredible health benefits, but also by fermenting everyday food we can bring really interesting flavours and textures into our diet.

HOW FERMENTATION WORKS

Fermentation works by encouraging certain good bacteria and fungi (including yeasts and moulds) to flourish, outcompeting the bad ones that would normally cause spoilage. While all the other chapters in this book deal with killing or halting the development of micro-organisms, this one sees us positively encouraging them. Food that has been fermented not only lasts longer, but the benefit to the consumer is that this method also preserves most of the beneficial vitamins and enzymes.

For food to be fermented, it must contain carbohydrate or have it added in the form of sugar – say for Kombucha (see pages 199–200). Micro-organisms such as yeasts, bacteria and mould eat this carbohydrate and produce either lactic, ethyl or acetic acid. These micro-organisms could be in the form of an added culture, such as a small quantity of live yogurt being added to milk to make more yogurt, or they could be bacteria already present in the food or in the air around the food to kick off fermentation. The latter is known as wild fermentation, and this is the method used to make sauerkraut and sourdough starters.

HEALTH BENEFITS OF FERMENTATION

We need certain bacteria to stay alive – we are made up of more bacteria than human cells – and most of these are found in our intestines. We know that these natural floras are easily upset by changes to our diet, illness, antibiotics, stress and other factors. However, it is believed that certain fermented foods containing 'good' bacteria can help with digestive recovery – and if our gut is healthy, it has a better chance of absorbing the nutrients in the foods we eat.

In recent years, nutritionists have identified that fermented foods have a beneficial effect on the bowel and can help treat leaky gut syndrome, also known as intestinal hyperpermeability, a much hypothesized condition. Although science is lagging behind, it is believed that a whole raft of other illnesses, including autism, coeliac disease, irritable bowel syndrome and multiple sclerosis are all linked to damage to the gut lining. Probiotic foods such as kefir are thought to help repair this damage, allowing beneficial nutrients to be absorbed into the body.

Today, in the United States, fermentation is a buzzword that is sweeping the country like a fashion craze. According to American writer and 'fermentation fetishist' Sandor Ellix Katz, author of *The Art of Fermentation*, almost every culture in the world originally had a fermented product in their diet that promoted good gut health. 'In the normal scheme of things,' he writes, 'we'd never have to think twice about replenishing the bacteria that allow us to digest food. But since we're living with antibiotic drugs and chlorinated water and antibacterial soap and all these factors in our contemporary lives that I'd group together as a "war on bacteria", if we fail to replenish [good bacteria], we won't effectively get nutrients out of the food we're eating.'

While most of us consume cheese, sauerkraut and pickles, we usually eat pasteurized versions – or bastardized ones that use vinegar rather than the naturally occurring living solution produced by the foods themselves. The drawback of modern processing methods is they end up destroying the 'live' content of our foods, which is why we end up having to substitute our diets with little bottles of probiotics containing strains of lactic-acid bacteria to counteract the imbalance. This shouldn't be necessary, as they should be present naturally in our diet.

While many people shy away from eating unpasteurized or fermented foods, they shouldn't be something to be scared of unless you are pregnant or suffering from ill health.

* KEFIR

This fermented probiotic, enzyme-rich food is filled with friendly micro-organisms that promote gut health by feeding it good bacteria such as *Lactobacillus acidophilus*. These friendly bacteria inhibit the growth of harmful bacteria in the gut and, more specifically, they are thought to help with yeast infections, poor health suffered after a course of antibiotics and peptic ulcers.

Kefir is simple and inexpensive to make at home. The grains are thought to originate from the Caucasus Mountains – kefir is a popular drink throughout the Middle East and Russia – and you can buy them from some health food stores or online (see page 243). At home, we drink milk kefir on its own in small glasses or mix it with fruit such as mango in smoothies. I have given two recipes: water kefir and milk kefir; water kefir is made from small transparent water kefir grains fermented in sweetened water, and milk kefir is made from milk kefir grains, which are cream in colour and resemble cauliflower florets, fermented in milk.

A note of caution: do not let your kefir grains come into contact with reactive metals such as copper, brass, zinc, iron or aluminium as they are acidic and can react with certain metals. To be on the safe side, use a plastic sieve, or cheesecloth and wooden or silicone utensils for making kefir.

WATER KEFIR

When I had my first glass of sparkling water kefir (see right), served over ice with a slice of lemon, my mind and body felt completely refreshed. I now have a jug fizzing quietly in the corner of my kitchen for when I feel exhausted or just need a little awakening.

Water kefir is a lightly sparkling probiotic drink that is refreshing, good for you and economical to make. It is made with water kefir grains, a culture of bacteria and yeast, in sugary water. The basic recipe can be flavoured with different herbs or fruit to produce different flavours (see Variations, right).

MAKES APPROX. 1 LITRE (1¾ PINTS)

EQUIPMENT

- 1 litre (1¾ pints) (or larger) glass jar or jug with a lid
- wooden or plastic spoon
- plastic sieve
- sterilized bottles for storage

INGREDIENTS

- 65–70g (2¼–2½oz) golden caster sugar*
- 1 litre (1¾ pints) filtered, non-chlorinated water (leave boiled water to stand overnight to remove chlorine)
- approx. 100g (3½oz) water kefir grains (available online or from health food stores)
- 3 tablespoons organic raisins or other unsulphured dried fruit
- juice of ½ organic lemon
- 1 thin slice of fresh ginger, peeled

* Do not use honey in place of sugar; honey has antimicrobial properties that will damage the water kefir grains or delay their proliferation.

> Stir the sugar into the water in a clean glass jar or jug using a non-metal spoon.

174

Add the kefir grains, raisins, lemon juice and ginger and stir to combine.

> Cover the jar loosely with a cloth or lid (don't tighten it at this stage) and set aside to ferment at room temperature for 24–72 hours, depending on the strength you prefer and the temperature of your home. The warmer your home, the faster the water kefir will brew. As the kefir ferments, it will take on a distinct and pleasant aroma that becomes more vinegary the longer you leave it. In time you will know what it should smell like when it is ready for you. I don't like it too strong, so a couple of days is usually enough for me.

> Strain the liquid through a sieve lined with muslin and bottle into smaller containers. Save the grains for another batch, but discard the added fruit. Put on the lids, but don't tighten them at this stage, and set aside at room temperature for a further 24–48 hours to complete the fermentation and produce natural carbonation. After this time, you can tighten the lids.

> Store the kefir water in the refrigerator, where it will keep for up to 1 week. Serve cold with ice and a slice of lemon or lime or add flavourings such as lemon juice, fruit juice, cucumber or mint.

VARIATIONS

Some people replace the ginger with fresh mint, star anise or cardamom, while others substitute the raisins with figs, mango, prunes, strawberries or dried cherries for a lovely rosy-hued water kefir. Dried fruit can be left to infuse for a week, however fresh fruit should be changed daily. For best results, keep the fruit pieces large or put them into a muslin bag so they are easy to remove and don't become tangled in the kefir grains.

REUSING YOUR WATER KEFIR GRAINS

Once you have strained the grains, don't throw them away. Simply put them back into a clean jar and repeat the process again. They can be used indefinitely.

If you need a break from tending to your grains – for example, if you are going on holiday – store in a small amount of the sugar/water mixture in the refrigerator for up to several weeks. Strain them when you come back to make a new batch of kefir.

MILK KEFIR

Milk kefir is made with live kefir grains (available online or from health food stores – see page 243 for suppliers). It is more nutritious than yogurt and supplies protein, essential minerals and valuable B vitamins. As a source of nourishment it is good for all of us, but particularly those with compromised immunity and bad gut health. It can be drunk on its own or mixed with fruit such as mango or date and vanilla seeds for rich and delicious smoothies. Milk kefir can be used for any recipe that calls for yogurt; it is excellent in salad dressings, cucumber and mint raita or frozen yogurt desserts.

Fellow fermentation enthusiast Sarah Moore gave my milk kefir grains to me. We transferred a small jar of these amazing grains from handbag to handbag over lunch. As soon as I was home I put them into a clean jar and added milk – within days I was enjoying fresh kefir at home.

When you first receive your grains in their milk solution they will be hard to see, however they are there! After the first brew they will have grown in size and quantity. If cared for correctly, you will have a lifetime supply of kefir grains. A little goes a long way!

> **METHOD** Put approx. 1 heaped tablespoon of live or dried milk kefir grains into a clean glass jar (a 600ml/20fl oz or 1 litre/1¾ pint jar is best). The quantity of grains doesn't matter, it will just take longer to ferment the milk with less. Fill the container with raw or pasteurized milk until it is two-thirds full. Cover the jar with a clean tea towel and put it in a cupboard at room temperature out of direct sunlight. Set aside to stand for at least 24 hours (sometimes it can take 48–72 hours) or until it has separated and reached the desired sourness. Occasional rocking/stirring is helpful as it helps the grains absorb all the nutrients from the milk. As with many forms of fermentation, making kefir is not a precise science; many people find the kefir a little too sour once separation has occurred and prefer to bottle their kefir much faster. We use ours after just a day in the warmth of our kitchen.

> To serve, strain the kefir through a nylon sieve into a clean jar and transfer it to the refrigerator to chill. (You can reuse the grains for another batch, see right.) If you want to make your kefir fizzy, place the strained liquor in a sealed bottle and set aside at room temperature for 1–2 days. This will make very sour, fizzy kefir.

REUSING YOUR MILK KEFIR GRAINS

Once you have strained the grains, don't throw them away. Simply put them back into a clean jar and repeat the process again. They can be used indefinitely.

If you need a break from tending to your grains – for example, if you are going on holiday – put the grains in a jar with milk (as you would to make kefir), cover with a tight-fitting lid and store in the refrigerator; the low temperature will slow down the fermentation process of the grains, causing them to go into a semi-dormant state. Every week or two, change the milk and drink the kefir that you have made in your refrigerator. Your grains may survive longer than this, so if you do neglect them for a time it's always worth trying to rejuvenate them before deciding you have killed them completely. Make a batch or two of kefir and see how they do.

* YOGURT AND STRAINED YOGURT

We worked with cheese-maker Christine Ashby, who has been making yogurt and cheese for many years and teaches her passion to others. Making your own dairy produce is very rewarding as you are in control of its contents and you can tailor their flavour and texture as you wish.

YOGURT

Yogurt is derived from the Turkish word *yoğurt*, meaning coagulated milk. Pliny the elder, writing in Roman times, described how 'barbarous nations' knew how to thicken milk into a substance of 'agreeable acidity'. The lactic acid produced by lactic bacteria in heated milk is what gives its tangy, slightly sour flavour. These same cultures give you the healthy dose of 'live' probiotic bacteria known to balance the intestines. Yogurt is versatile, usually low in fat, high in protein and calcium and rich in vitamins B6 and B12. It is also inexpensive and easy to make. We know you can buy good yogurt easily, however somehow it tastes better made at home. Use the type of milk you like: cow's, goat's or sheep's milk work equally well.

CHRISTINE'S TOP TIPS FOR YOGURT-MAKING

HYGIENE is critical; milk will support the growth of undesirable micro-organisms. Make sure your surrounding area is clean and any equipment coming into contact with your yogurt or is sterilized. Put muslin cloths through the washing machine and dry properly; just before use, pour boiling water from a kettle through the cloths in a sieve.

MILK Raw milk is good to use, but only if you are used to drinking it. We always prefer to use organic milk if available.

TEMPERATURE The area you work in must be warm, ideally above 20°C (68°F).

Heating the milk should be slow and involve indirect heat, if possible, e.g. using a double boiler, since excessive heating will damage the milk proteins. Giancarlo and I don't have a double boiler, however we do have very heavy-based pans and an induction hob, both of which conduct the heat well. The temperature of the milk is critical so it is worthwhile investing in a probe thermometer.

WHERE TO INCUBATE YOUR YOGURT

Incubation of the yogurt can be done in a host of ways and you don't need to rely on specialist equipment to keep it warm. For example, you could sit covered pots of yogurt around a warm kettle overnight, you could wrap the bowl in blankets, sit it in the airing cupboard or a low oven or inside an insulated cooler, or use a wide-mouthed vacuum flask or electrically heated pad. My kitchen is pretty warm after an evening's cooking and although the temperature drops below 35°C (95°F) it does work to set the yogurt, albeit slowly.

YOGURT-MAKING EQUIPMENT

You don't need any specialist equipment to make yogurt; just make sure that everything is scrupulously clean. Here is what you need:

- **thermometer**, preferably a probe thermometer
- **saucepan**
- glass, plastic or china **bowl**
- some sort of **warming devices**
- **cloths** to keep it warm
- **Milton sterilizing fluid** to clean your equipment beforehand

THICK, CREAMY YOGURT

Traditional Greek or Turkish yogurt is made with sheep's milk and it is strained afterwards to thicken it. It has a strong flavour, which is great in cooking, but I prefer a version made with cow's milk. Instead of straining it you can add cream beforehand as we have done. To get ours started we used a starter culture bought from an online supplier, but you could add a previously made or shop-bought live Greek yogurt. If you wish you could leave out the milk powder and make it with milk and cream alone, but it won't be as thick and creamy.

MAKES APPROX. 2.3KG (5LB 2OZ)

- 2 litres (3½ pints) whole homogenized milk
- 150ml (¼ pint) double cream
- 175ml (6fl oz) skimmed milk powder
- starter culture (available from cheese-making suppliers, see page 242) – follow the manufacturer's instructions for how much you need OR 3 tablespoons live yogurt

> Sterilize all your equipment either an oven, see page 10, or with sterilizing liquid such as Milton's, following their

>>>

instructions. Warm the milk and cream to 30°C (86°F) in a large, heavy-based saucepan, stirring constantly so that the mixture doesn't catch on the bottom. Remove from the heat and add the skimmed milk powder. Whisk thoroughly until well blended.

> Return the pan to the hob and heat to 90°C (194°F), using a probe thermometer for accuracy. Stirring constantly, keep it at this temperature for 5 minutes. Remove the pan from the heat and cool to 44°C (111°F). The best way to do this is to sit your pan in a sink of cool water and stir it constantly until the temperature drops. Add the starter culture and whisk for 5 minutes. Transfer the mixture to a sterilized bowl and cover with a plate. Wrap the bowl up in a blanket and set aside in a warm place (ideally at 35°C/95°F) overnight. See page 177 for ideas on where to incubate your yogurt.

> The following morning, the yogurt should be set and taste pleasantly sour. If it is still runny and not strong enough in flavour, set it aside for a bit longer. I often leave mine for another few hours to obtain a flavour that we enjoy. When you are happy with the set and the flavour, give the yogurt a really good whisk to blend out any lumps. It should be smooth and glossy. At this point you can spoon it into small, clean plastic or glass containers or jars and transfer them to the refrigerator. You can also flavour the yogurt with fruit and sugar if you wish. We like to put fruit compote such as the Rhubarb and Ginger Jam (see page 46) at the bottom of a jar and top it up with yogurt. You can use a jam jar lid to seal it before storing in the refrigerator.

> Our yogurt lasts for up to 3 weeks – if we haven't eaten it by then – but trust your nose and if it smells or tastes unpleasant or has a fizzy sensation throw it away. Also discard it if any mould or fuzz appears on the surface. Only good yogurt should be used to start a new batch.

VARIATION

NATURAL YOGURT

This yogurt is lower in fat because there is no added cream. It is not as thick because there is no added skimmed milk powder. To make natural yogurt, follow the instructions for Thick, Creamy Yogurt (see pages 177–8) omitting the cream and skimmed milk powder.

STRAINED YOGURT – LABNEH

In the Middle East, yogurt is often strained to separate the curds from the whey and the resulting yogurt is known as *labneh*. Depending on how long it is strained for, and how much whey comes out it, *labneh* can be very thick but soft and creamy, or firmer like cream cheese. This is Anissa Helou's recipe for *Labneh bil-Zeyt*, a delicious way of preserving strained yogurt under oil. You can enliven the taste of the *labneh* balls by flavouring the oil with crushed chilli pepper and/or sprigs of dried thyme. It is important that you mix in enough salt with the strained yogurt before shaping it into balls to preserve it.

NOTE: This recipe is made with shop-bought yogurt, but you could use your own homemade yogurt (see pages 177–8) made using cow's, ewe's or goat's milk.

MAKES 12–14 BALLS, APPROX. 2.5CM (1IN) IN DIAMETER

- 450g (1lb) pot of goat's, sheep's or cow's milk yogurt (this will give approx. 150g/5½oz strained yogurt and approx. 150ml/¼ pint whey)
- 1 teaspoon fine sea salt

- fresh or dried herbs
- 1 dried red chilli (optional)
- extra virgin olive oil

> Place a clean muslin in a sieve and pour boiling water over it to sterilize it. Lay the muslin in a double layer over a sieve or colander and pour the yogurt into it. Gather the edges to make a pouch and tie with string. Hang the filled pouch on the tap over the sink, or anywhere else, over a receptacle to receive the draining liquid (whey); set aside to drain overnight.
> The following day, scoop the strained yogurt into a bowl and beat in the salt – don't stint on the salt as you need it to preserve the yogurt. The whey can be used in place of water when making a sourdough starter (see pages 181–2) or for fermented fruits (see pages 190–1), or for making scones.
> You can either eat the labneh as it is, mixed with some fresh herbs such as chives or thyme (leaves and flowers), or shape it into balls and store under oil.
> To make labneh balls, spread out a clean tea towel on a tray. Pinch off little pieces of strained yogurt and shape into balls the size of a small walnut. Arrange the balls on the cloth and set aside to dry at room temperature for 24–48 hours or until firm to the touch. Cover them with a fly net or drape some muslin over the top, propped up on a few tins to allow the air to circulate underneath.
> Once the balls are set, carefully pack them into a 1 litre (1¾ pints) sterilized glass jar and top up with extra virgin olive oil. Flavour the oil with a dried chilli and some sprigs of dried thyme if you wish and seal the jar. Store in the refrigerator and eat after 3 days and before 1 month, making sure the balls are always covered with oil.

> Mix the strained yogurt with salt and crushed dried chilli flakes before shaping into balls. Roll in sesame seeds and dry for a day in a warm room or until firm to the touch. Store in olive oil in the refrigerator for up to 3 weeks. To serve, crush gently and mix into lettuce or couscous salad.

WHAT TO DO WITH YOUR YOGURT

Turn it into thicker-style yogurt by straining it; if it is really thick it can be rolled and flavoured, and then preserved in oil and spices (see *Labneh*, left).

Mix it with the Tikka Masala Curry Paste on page 235 and use as a marinade for chicken.

Use it in smoothies (see pages 238–40).

Enjoy as an accompaniment to smoked aubergine purée (see Moutabal, page 137).

Layer it up with sliced banana and raspberry jam as a dessert.

Mix it with chopped cucumber, a little sugar, finely chopped mint leaves, salt and crushed toasted cumin seeds to form a raita to serve alongside Indian or Middle Eastern dishes.

Blend it with fruit to form fruit yogurt: sweeten the fruit first with icing sugar, and then push it through a sieve to form a purée before mixing in the yogurt. Alternatively, **cook** the fruit briefly in a saucepan on the hob or in a bowl in the microwave until the fruit has softened and the sugar has dissolved. Wait until it is cool before stirring in the yogurt. I like to leave mine not completely stirred in so you end up with bursts of sweet fruit mixed with tangy, creamy yogurt. For 1 litre (1¾ pints) yogurt, allow 200g (7oz) fruit and 25g (1oz) icing sugar.

CRÈME FRAÎCHE

This is absolutely delicious, better than anything you can buy from a supermarket and totally irresistible. I love crème fraîche with compotes or with a dollop of low-sugar jam. It is also creamy and luscious in the tarragon chicken recipe on page 12.

Crème fraîche is produced in a similar manner to soured cream, although the end result has a higher fat content and is less sour in flavour. Made with cream and culture, crème fraîche remains stable when heated, which makes it ideal for adding to soups and sauces. This recipe is from our Scottish cheese-maker friend Katy Rodgers, whose beautiful old dairy we visited. She uses the farm's own milk to make this product, which is used in her popular café and tearoom based in Stirlingshire, Scotland.

MAKES APPROX. 1.2KG (2LB 10OZ)

- 250ml (9fl oz) whole milk
- 1.25 litres (2 pints) double cream (36 per cent fat)
- 60g (2¼oz) skimmed milk powder
- 1 heaped tablespoon live yogurt OR the tip of a teaspoon of crème fraîche starter culture OR 3 tablespoons crème fraîche from a previous batch

> First, sterilize all your equipment. Mix the milk with the cream and heat to 37°C (99°F) in a large bowl set over a saucepan of gently simmering water – this way you can control the temperature more easily. Stir in the skimmed milk powder to dissolve. Once the skimmed milk powder has dissolved, bring the mixture up to 80°C (176°F). Now place the bowl in a sink of cold water and cool it back down to 30°C (86°F). Whisk in the yogurt or starter culture (or some crème fraîche from a previous batch).

> Pour the mixture into sterilized plastic or glass pots and transfer them to an incubator, low oven or warm room for approx. 12 hours, or until the cream has set; the ideal temperature is 30°C (86°F), however as long as the temperature is between 18–30°C (64–86°F) it will work. Find the warmest room in your house, an airing cupboard or somewhere with underfloor heating. If the crème fraîche is not firm enough for your liking, it can be whipped thicker with an electric mixer. Put on the lids, cover and transfer the pots to the refrigerator for a further 24 hours before use. Store in the refrigerator for up to 5 days.

> To make a simple dressing, mix the crème fraîche with lemon juice or tarragon vinegar, a pinch of salt and sugar and some chopped chives. The acidity cuts through oily fish such as salmon beautifully, see Hot Smoked Salmon on page 140.

* SOURDOUGH

Making sourdough bread is more a case of alchemy and practise than a precise science. From working with bakers and keen enthusiasts, it is clear everyone has their own methods, which can be confusing when you are trying to learn. I believe it takes a particular kind of person to make sourdough; you will need patience and perseverance to perfect your technique and allow the various stages of fermentation need to fit into your life, so if you have an erratic schedule, it may not be for you. You need to nurture your starter culture as you would a pet. You will feed it, give it water, keep it warm, or help it cool, arrange for who will look after it while you go on holiday and generally cater to its every need all in the name of making precious loaves of sweet-smelling bread.

Here we have given the recipe for a simplified version of making sourdough from starter to loaf. We have added all the ingredients in one go rather than separated them into stages, removed the use of a peel (to shunt the dough into the oven) and used a Dutch oven (casserole with lid) which we believe gives more consistent results. There are many of stages of fermentation that can be added in to increase the flavour and airiness of your loaf but this is a good way to start. After mastering this simple way you can submerge yourself in a world of other people's way of doing it from books, YouTube and TikTok videos to your heart's delight. In the meantime, watch our method of breadmaking via our videos on www.caldesi.com/video-gallery.

FLOURS

There are so many brands of flour – from mass-industrial suppliers to small artisan mills. I would stick to an organic one, particularly for the starter. I would also stick more or less to the same brand, especially at the beginning, as different brands give different results. Once you are confident with the basic technique, you can start experimenting with new ingredients and ratios.

EQUIPMENT

Although you can improvise with equipment it is a good idea to know what you will need in advance. You will need:
- 500ml (18fl oz) Kilner jar for your starter
- A large mixing bowl
- A dough scraper (or rounded edged tool for scraping dough)
- A round or rectangular banneton (ridged bread mould) or linen cloth lined bowl for proving
- A linen tea towel
- A shower cap, plastic shopping bag or a linen tea towel for covering the dough
- A piece of baking parchment just bigger than the base of the casserole
- A large enamel or ceramic casserole with a lid or Dutch oven

FIRST STAGE – MAKING THE STARTER

So precious is a starter that migrant travellers to foreign countries were known to take theirs with them among their treasured possessions, so fearful were they of losing part of their heritage and way of life. Sourdough has a big following in the US, and there are known to be sourdough starters as old as 170 years. A starter is also known as a 'mother' or *madre* in Italy.

A starter is the initial mixture of fermented flour and water that kickstarts the fermentation process of making bread. It should be bubbly, lively and have a pleasant acidic smell to it. You may know someone who can give you some of their established starter or it can be bought or made at home. Sourdough starters can also be used successfully in anything that requires baker's yeast, including pancakes and pizza bases. Our pancake recipe on page 185 is for Sri Lankan Hoppers. If you leave the batter to ferment overnight, your pancakes will result in bubbling light versions.

If you want to make your own, use an organic wholemeal rye as it is the most reliable and fastest method. You can always feed a rye starter with white flour once it is started. Make sure it is organic so that the yeasts can grow easily uninhibited by any chemicals and the water should be pure spring water or non-chlorinated. (You can boil water for 20 minutes in a pan or leave a jug out overnight and by morning most of the chlorine will have evaporated away).

FOR THE STARTER

MAKES APPROX. 400G (14OZ)
- organic wholemeal rye flour
- tepid spring or non-chlorinated water

> STAGE ONE Combine 50g (1¾oz) flour and 60ml (4 tablespoons) warm water in a bowl and stir well with a spoon. It should be thick but drop easily from the spoon so add a splash more water if necessary. Transfer the mixture to a medium (500ml/18floz) Kilner jar. Close the lid and set aside in a warm place, out of direct sunlight, for a day. Stir the starter and replace for one more day.

> NOTE: Fermenting times may vary considerably depending on the weather. In warm weather your starter will begin to bubble within a day; in cold weather fermentation will be slower and could take a couple of days.

> STAGE TWO When you notice bubbles occurring add 50g (1¾oz) flour and 50ml (2fl oz) water and stir through. Close the lid and set aside in a warm place, out of direct sunlight, for 1–2 days, stir each day.

> STAGE THREE When the starter is bubbling, repeat the step above.

> STAGE FOUR When the starter is bubbling, discard half the mixture. Feed the remaining mixture with 50g (1¾oz) flour and 50ml (2fl oz) water. If you wish to turn a wholemeal starter into a white one, this is a good time to do this as the starter has become established. Close the lid and set aside in a warm place, out of direct sunlight, for 1–2 days until bubbling.

> By now your starter should be active, lively and bubbling, and the consistency should be that of a very thick batter.

At this point, your starter can be used straight away or transferred to the refrigerator in the closed Kilner jar to slow down fermentation until you are ready to use it, or it. NOTE: If storing in the refrigerator, you will need to refresh your starter regularly (see right) to keep it alive.

CARING FOR YOUR STARTER

You can keep your starter alive in the refrigerator indefinitely or put it to sleep in the freezer for up to a year. If you make bread regularly (I bake once a week), it makes most sense to store your starter in the refrigerator. I always keep at least 300g (10½oz) starter on standby in my refrigerator – this way, I have enough to use and keep. Even if you are not using it, you must keep feeding your starter with more flour and water at least once a week (preferably every 3–4 days) to keep it going. (I feed my starter a day before baking so it is fresh and bubbling when I need it.)

Note that after your dough has been refreshed a couple of times in the refrigerator, its strength will increase. A young starter will often lack strength and structure to begin with, but after it has had time to mature it will take on a distinctive flavour.

METHOD TO FEED YOUR STARTER Assuming you have approx. 300g (10½oz) starter in your refrigerator, weigh out half of it and discard (or use or freeze or give it to a friend). Mix in 100g (3½oz) flour and 80–100ml (3–3½fl oz) water (less for white and more for wholemeal flour) to give the consistency of a very thick batter. WHAT IF YOU GO ON HOLIDAY? If you go away, either feed your starter as above and store in the refrigerator for up to 2 weeks or transfer it to the freezer – I have frozen mine successfully before (for

2 years!) and once defrosted it smelled as sweet as the day I froze it. Alternatively, and this is perhaps the safest option, divide your starter into two and freeze half and store the other half in the refrigerator. You can then use some, discard some and feed it again on your arrival at home. If you find the starter collects a pool of grey water on the surface, pour this away and feed it regularly to refresh it. A strong alcoholic smell will dissipate with regular feeding. However, if the starter has gone mouldy it is best to throw it away and start again.

SECOND STAGE – MAKING THE DOUGH

This stage is best carried out early evening before you go to bed so that it is ready to bake in the morning.

MAKES 1 LOAF

- 150g (5½oz) starter, fed the day before
- 300g (10½oz) strong white flour
- 200g (7oz) strong wholemeal flour
- 325ml (11fl oz) tepid water
- 10g (¼oz) fine salt
- rice or other flour, for dusting

> Place the ingredients in a large bowl and stir together with a spoon until well blended. Now hold the bowl in one hand and cup the fingers of your other hand around the dough to lift it up and over itself trapping air inside. Keep doing this in the bowl for 2 minutes, turning the dough between the folds. Clean the sides of the bowl with a dough scraper and cover it with a shower cap, plastic bag or linen cloth. Set aside until it has doubled in size and there are plenty of bubbles on the surface. To see when your dough is doubled in size you can pull off a small piece and press it into a jam jar. An elastic band is then placed over the jar with the level matching the level of the dough. Cover the jar with a plate. Once the small piece has doubled in size over the elastic band line, your main dough will have done the same. You can add the small piece back into the dough. Once you are practised at making sourdough, you will quickly recognize the puffy look to the dough – it appears stretched and domed, with a few bubbles on the surface.

CONTROLLING THE FERMENTATION TIME

The timing in sourdough fermentation making is never a precise science – types of flour vary, temperatures and humidity levels change depending on the room in your house and the time of year. It takes a while to get this timing correct, but practice makes perfect so have patience. If you run out of time and bake your bread too soon, don't worry; the flavour won't be as acidic, the characteristic holes won't be as large and the texture won't be as moist as perfect sourdough but it should taste fine. On the other hand, there is always the chance of your sourdough overproving if it is left too long in a warm house, and then the texture will become soft and lacking in structure.

You can do this stage slowly in a cool larder or refrigerator overnight for more acidity from a long fermentation and more holes in your loaf, or you can speed things up to 2–4 hours by leaving the dough in a warm place at a temperature of 28–32°C (82–90°F) although you will have a closer grain and less acidity. Putting dough into the refrigerator to rise also helps if you are getting tired and it's getting late – you can continue in the morning.

THIRD STAGE –
SHAPING THE DOUGH

> Prepare your banneton or bowl lined with a linen cloth by scattering it lightly with rice or other flour. Use a dough scraper to gently coax the dough out of the bowl onto a lightly floured worksurface. There should be plenty of stretched bubbles to see in the dough and a pleasant acidic aroma. For a rectangular loaf, wet your hands and gently push the dough into a rough rectangular shape, trying not to expel the trapped air. Wet your hands again and fold one long side into the centre, repeat with the other long side. Dampen your hands again and now take the top of the loaf and stretch it upwards a little. Fold this over towards you and keep folding it forming a spiral. Set aside. To make a round loaf, gently shape the dough, with wet hands, into a circle. Pull one edge into the centre, then repeat approx. eight times so that all of it has been folded in.

> Lightly dust a clean area of worksurface and place either shape smooth side upwards. Dust with flour and leave it to rest under a linen tea towel for 30–40 minutes until puffy and risen. Do this twice more, allowing the dough to rest in between. On the last time you need to create tension on the surface. To do this, bring the shaped loaf towards you by using the dough scraper while keeping it on the work surface. You will see the top become taut.

> Change direction and do this a couple of times again. Watch our video at www.caldesi.com/video-gallery for further instructions. You should have a puffy, bouncy shaped loaf shape of dough. Use the dough scraper to lift it up and place smooth, domed-side down into the floured banneton or lined bowl. Leave the loaf until it passes the 'poke' test.

FOURTH STAGE –
BAKING THE LOAF

> This is probably the most important part of baking sourdough – judging its readiness for the oven. Wet your finger with water and poke it into the dough by approx. 2cm (¾in). If the dent bounces back to the touch, it isn't ready. If it slowly returns, leaving a shallow dent, the loaf is ready to be baked.

> Preheat the base of the casserole or Dutch oven in the oven at 230°C/450°F/gas 8 for 30 minutes.

> Cut a piece of baking parchment approx. 5cm (2in) larger than the base of your casserole. Lightly flour the top of the loaf and place the paper over the top. Place your palm flat over the paper and invert the loaf onto it. Place it onto a work surface and gently lift off the mould. Slash the top of the loaf cleanly a couple of times with a razor blade, Stanley knife or sharp serrated knife to a depth of 4cm (1½in). This will allow the dough to expand easily.

> Remove the casserole base from the oven and carefully lower in the loaf on the baking parchment, taking care not to touch the sides of the hot casserole. Use your fingers to splash a little water over the loaf and put the lid on. Use oven gloves to transfer the casserole to the oven. Bake for 30 minutes before removing the lid. Continue to bake for 15–20 minutes or until the crust is dark brown in colour. Take the casserole out of the oven and carefully remove your loaf from it using the paper – it should feel light. Set aside to cool on a wire rack.

VARIATION

BEETROOT SOUGHDOUGH

Sourdough specialist and author of *How to Bake Bread*, Emmanuel Hadjiandreou gave me some great ideas to incorporate root vegetables and dried produce into my sourdough. Emmanuel bakes deep pink loaves which he makes by adding grated raw beetroot into the dough (roughly 200g/7oz to 750–800g/1lb 10 oz–1lb 12oz dough – half the mixture at the Third Stage). The same can be done with parsnip and celeriac, which add a herby sweetness to the bread. You can also use some of your dried produce to flavour your bread such as oregano, rosemary, onions, porcini mushrooms, apples or dill, nigella and poppy seeds.

SOURDOUGH HOPPERS

Hoppers are Sri Lankan pancakes also known as *appa*. They are made from a fermented batter of rice flour, coconut milk and a little toddy. The toddy helps to ferment them and gives them their characteristic slightly sour flavour. We make hoppers using the sourdough starter on pages 181–2 (although you could use baker's yeast). Hoppers are traditionally made in a small domed pan. However, I have tried the same mixture in my crêpe pan with great success.

MAKES 16–20

- 500g (1lb 2oz) rice flour
- 2 teaspoons palm or caster sugar
- 100g (3½oz) sourdough starter or a pinch of baker's yeast (approx. 4g/⅛oz)
- 600ml (20fl oz) tepid water
- approx. 200g (7oz) coconut milk
- 1 teaspoon salt
- a few teaspoons oil, for frying
- eggs (optional)
- salt and black pepper (optional)

> Combine the flour, sugar, starter (or yeast) and water in a large bowl. Pour in the coconut milk a little at a time and whisk to a loose pancake batter. Cover the bowl with a tea towel and set aside to ferment at room temperature for 6–8 hours. When the surface is covered with bubbles, and the mixture has almost doubled in size, it is ready to use. Add the salt and stir well to combine.

> Heat a little oil in a pan and wipe it over with kitchen paper to achieve just a thin film. The pan should be hot but not smoking hot when you pour in the batter or it will cook too quickly and not move around in the pan. Drop a ladleful of batter into the pan and swirl it around to cover halfway up the sides. (If you would like an egg in it, crack it in now, followed by a little salt and pepper.) Keep the pan over a medium heat and put the lid on. Cook for just a few minutes or until the pancake is golden brown around the edges and cooked through in the centre. Slide it out with the help of a spatula onto a plate and serve immediately or set aside while you cook the rest.

* LACTO-FERMENTED VEGETABLES

There is a dispute as to which came first, kimchi or sauerkraut, but in fact the earliest recorded details of fermented cabbage exist in China. It is thought that the workers were given kimchi to eat during the construction of the Great Wall. Kimchi is regarded so highly in Korea that employers give a grant to their employees to make their own supply. It preserves tradition and keeps their workforce healthy. Fermentation pits for preserving tropical fruit have been used in Fiji for centuries and traditionally a new husband's pits would be inspected by the bride's parents before they were allowed to marry.

Vegetables and fruit mixed and left with salt will begin a process called lacto-fermentation (see Salted Kumquats Salted and Lemons on pages 76–7). Sauerkraut and kimchi are traditionally made from cabbage, but this method of fermentation is suitable for preserving almost any vegetable or fruit. Salt physically draws out water from the produce to make a brine. This brine is so concentrated that harmful bacteria cannot survive in it, however many beneficial bacteria thrive in these conditions. Lacto-fermented foods are higher in vitamin C than their unfermented counterparts.

CONTAINERS

Our German friends kindly brought us a huge sauerkraut crock on their last visit. The smooth, straight, shiny insides make it easy to push the weights that came with it down onto the food to keep it submerged in the brine. It has a cleverly designed lid to allow a small amount of gas to come out and a rim that is filled with water to stop insects getting in. If you aren't lucky enough to own such a crock, you could use a large glass jar with a rubber seal or a non-reactive lid.

NOTE: Avoid using metal containers or utensils as the acids produced by the fermentation process could react with them. Cover your containers with vinegar-proofed lids as ordinary lids will corrode.

CLEANING AND PREPARATION

As with all methods of preservation, hygiene is important. I wash my jars and crocks in the dishwasher or with very hot soapy water, rinse them thoroughly with water to dispel any soapy aromas and then allow them to cool and dry upside down on a clean rack. Avoid using chemical sterilizers that might leave traces in the jars, as you don't want to destroy the good bacteria you are trying to encourage.

WEIGHTS

These are essential to keep your vegetables fully submerged in the brine solution, otherwise moulds will be able to grow and your kraut will rot. A plastic bag filled with brine works – the reason I suggest filling it with brine, rather than water, is in case the bag leaks. Alternatively, a small sterilized stone works well. You can collect various sizes on a trip to the beach, scrub them well with hot soapy water, then boil them for 30 minutes in a saucepan of water and dry them out before use. An upturned plastic lid (with holes bored into it) or a glass jar smaller than the diameter of the opening of your jar will also help to keep the vegetables or fruits submerged and not trap air underneath. Boil it in hot water for 10 minutes, then cool before use.

TROUBLESHOOTING
- SCUM A thin white scum of mould can sometimes appear on the surface of your fermenting fruit or vegetables. If

it has only just appeared, and it is very thin, you can simply stir it back in. However, if there is fuzzy or coloured mould on the surface, you should discard the batch and start again.

- **AROMA** Lacto-fermented foods should have a clean, slightly sour smell. Discard any that are cloudy or smell 'off' and unpleasant. Trust your nose.
- **GAS** Be aware that gases can build up during the fermentation process and these need to be released from time to time. Ferments are living things that cannot be ignored!
- **BRINE** Your produce should be fully submerged in brine at all times. If necessary, top it up with fresh brine to keep it undercover. It is especially important to keep an eye on the brine in cold weather when the vegetables will produce less juice.
- **WHEN TO EAT** This is up to you, many people really enjoy the fizziness of fermented fruit and vegetables while others prefer to put the ferments into the refrigerator after a few days to limit this occurring.

SAUERKRAUT

Roman writer Pliny the Elder wrote about *sauerkraut* and apparently Julius Caesar was fond of pickles. Popular in Germany and most of Eastern Europe, *sauerkraut* can be made from white cabbage alone or red and white cabbage, carrots and garlic. Traditionally many people eat *sauerkraut* with sausages and salt beef but it is also lovely mixed into a salad with grated carrot, olive oil and walnuts, in coleslaw, stir-fries, combined with batter to make into pancakes or used to fill spring rolls or Polish dumplings.

MAKES 1 LITRE (1¾ PINTS)
- 900g (2lb) organic white or red (or mixed) hard cabbage
- 20g (¾oz) fine salt

FOR THE BRINE
- 4 tablespoons salt dissolved in 1 litre (1¾ pints) filtered water

> Discard the outer cabbage leaves if they are very damaged. Cut the cabbage into quarters from tip to root, and cut out and discard the hard core in the centre. Shred the cabbage either using the grating mechanism on a food processor or by hand. Place the cabbage and salt in a large bowl and mix together thoroughly with your hands. Squeeze the cabbage quite hard as you mix to encourage it to start weeping; keep going until all of it has been squeezed.

> Transfer the cabbage into a crock or clean Kilner jar and pour in the juices from the bowl. Push the cabbage down well with another smaller jar or a potato masher to expel most of the air inside. Add a weight on top so that the vegetables are completely submerged in the liquor. If they aren't fully covered, top up the jar with some of the fresh brine, making sure you leave 3cm (1¼in) headroom to allow the cabbage to expand as it ferments. Close the lid and set aside at room temperature for a week. Check on your sauerkraut daily: skim off any scum that forms on the surface and push down the vegetables so they remain below the line of the brine.

> You will notice some bubbling occurring as the fermentation gets underway. When this has died down, after a few days, your sauerkraut is ready to eat. You can either enjoy it young, fresh and crisp after approx. 5 days or leave it to mature for

longer, when it will become more sour in flavour and softer in texture. Store in a cool, dark place (under 16°C/61°F is ideal). For maximum health benefits, do not heat the sauerkraut but enjoy it raw.

VARIATIONS

Mix in some grated onion, carrot, garlic or celeriac, or flavour with 1 teaspoon of caraway, cumin or fennel seeds or some juniper berries. Probably my favourite sauerkraut is cabbage, apple pieces and freshly ground black pepper.

KIMCHI

This hot and spicy delight is usually served with Korean and Vietnamese meals. We love it with barbecues, roast pork or grilled chicken and fish, too. The juice can be poured out and used in place of hot chilli sauce, such as Tabasco, on oysters or to spice a Bloody Mary.

MAKES APPROX. 2KG (4LB 8OZ)

- 2 litres (3½ pints) cold water
- 150g (5½oz) fine salt
- 2kg (4lb 8oz) mixed vegetables, such as carrots, pak choi, spring onions, green beans, cabbages, peppers, daikon, mangetout
- 3 garlic cloves, roughly chopped
- 3 tablespoons chopped fresh ginger (approx. 50g/1¾oz)
- 40–50g (1½–1¾oz) Korean red pepper powder
- 2 teaspoons caster sugar (optional)

> Make up the brine by mixing the water with the salt. Wash, peel if necessary, and cut all of the vegetables into bite-sized pieces. Put them into a bowl with the garlic and brine solution and mix thoroughly with clean hands. Weigh the vegetables down with a clean plate, so they are fully submerged in the brine solution, and cover with a cloth. Set aside at room temperature for at least 6 hours or overnight if possible.

> Drain the vegetables through a colander, reserving the brine, and taste. If they taste too salty, rinse them in very cold, non-chlorinated water; if they taste to your liking there is no need to rinse them. If they are not salty enough, mix in a little more salt (up to a couple of teaspoons should be sufficient).

> Combine the ginger, red pepper powder and sugar (if using) in a bowl. Add a little of the brine and mix to a smooth paste. Combine this mixture with the vegetables and mix thoroughly with clean hands.

> Pack the vegetables into large Kilner jars and press down thoroughly with a wooden rolling pin. If there is still space at the top of the jar, add some more vegetables and squeeze down again. Top up the jars with some of the reserved brine so that the vegetables are fully submerged, leaving 3cm (1¼in) headroom to allow for expansion. Put on the lids and store in your kitchen for a few days and up to a week. Taste the kimchi every day and push the vegetables back down with clean fingers so they are totally submerged in the brine; if necessary, weigh the vegetables down. Once the kimchi has stopped fizzing, and if you are happy with the flavour, move it to the refrigerator or a cool room below 16°C (61°F) where it will keep for several months. Traditionally kimchi is stored buried in the ground to keep it cool or in a cellar to last throughout the winter.

HAKUSAI NO TSUKEMONO OR JAPANESE PICKLED CABBAGE

This is similar to the *sauerkraut* and kimchi recipes in that cabbage, in this case Chinese long cabbage, is the main vegetable of choice. *Kombu* is dried seaweed which gives a particular flavour to the cabbage but if you can't find it, leave it out. Yuzu is a citrus scented fruit, like an intense lime-y lemon. Use a lemon if you can't find them. *Tsukemono* are good to eat on their own, as a side dish to fried foods or with rice and spicy dishes.

MAKES 1 PICKLED CABBAGE

- 1 Chinese long pale green cabbage
- 1 tablespoon fine sea salt
- 4 spring onions, roughly chopped
- juice of 1 yuzu or lemon
- 1 tablespoon fermented soy sauce
- 20cm (8in) long dried kombu, cut into finger widths (optional)
- 1 teaspoon chilli flakes

> Pull away the outer leaves of the cabbage and reserve for later. Cut away the hard core from the end and then slice the cabbage lengthways into quarters. Now put the cabbage onto a tray and put into sunlight or the warmest part of your house. Leave for approx. 5 hours in sunshine or overnight if no sun. This will concentrate the flavour of the cabbage and make it sweeter.

> Meanwhile, find a container that will hold the cabbage; I use a rectangular plastic container with a lid. I can fit a smaller one inside it that I fill with water to act as a weight. The Japanese have pickling pots called *tsukemonoki* with screw-top lids that are perfect for this.

> Scatter the cabbage quarters with the salt over the container so that any surplus drops inside. Layer the cabbage with the remaining ingredients and then put the weight on top. Cover the container and leave at room temperature for up to a week. When the juices run from the cabbage, push the weight down to make sure that they are submerged. If there is not enough juice, add brine (using the Kimchi recipe left) to cover them. Turn the cabbages a couple of times to make sure the flavourings and salty brine are equally distributed. When you are happy with the flavour, transfer to the refrigerator and consume within a month.

CUCUMBERS IN BRINE

One of the easiest and most satisfying fermented vegetables has to be Jewish pickled cucumbers. Vinegary versions are available everywhere and you can make them as described on pages 17–18 but they won't have the fermentation health benefits of this recipe. Here they are made from cucumbers, salt and water. If you want a little more acidity and a vinegary taste, you can add 2 tablespoons of cider vinegar but no more as it will halt the process of the lactic-acid producing bacteria you are trying to encourage.

How to keep the crisp snap of a pickled cucumber is a subject of endless debate between pickling enthusiasts. Some use leaves, others believe the addition of a few carrot batons helps and others swear by blanching the cucumbers briefly first. I believe mine are better if small, left whole and moved to the refrigerator as soon as fermentation has started.

Typical flavourings such as dill, garlic, chilli or pickling spices such as mustard or caraway seeds can be added as you wish. Depending on the size of your cucumbers you can choose your container accordingly. Little cucumbers fit into short, squat, tubby jars and long ones fit into tall jars. I use a 1.5 litre (2¾ pints) Kilner jar for five cucumbers approx. 18cm (7in). Water for fermenting should not be chlorinated, so leave tap water to stand overnight for the chlorine to evaporate. Alternatively, use bottled or filtered water.

MAKES 1.5 LITRES (2¾ PINTS)

- approx. 700g (1lb 9oz) small cucumbers or gherkins
- 2 tablespoons fine sea salt
- 1 litre (1¾ pints) cold, non-chlorinated water
- a small handful of dill
- 1 tablespoon pickling spice
- 2 garlic cloves
- 1 horseradish or grape leaf or a few oak leaves (optional)

> Wash the cucumbers in cold water, taking care not to bruise them. Remove any blossoms from the end but try not to pierce the skin. Make up the brine by stirring the salt into the water. Put the cucumbers into your clean container and pour over the brine, followed by the flavourings and leaves (if using). Put a weight over the cucumbers to keep them submerged under the brine. Fasten the lid, making sure the rubber seal is present and leave at room temperature for up to 7 days. Sunlight, if you are lucky enough to have any, helps keep the mould at bay through the ultra-violet rays. Release the pressure by opening the lid at least once a day. When you are happy with the taste and texture, move the cucumbers to the refrigerator or a cool room below 16°C (61°F) and consume within a few months.

VARIATION

PICKLED CARROTS WITH CARDAMOM

Most vegetables can be fermented in this way with varying results. Do the same with batons of carrot and flavour them with crushed cardamom pods.

∗ LACTO-FERMENTED FRUITS

This is a new and exciting world for us. Before writing this book and reading about fermented foods, I would have instantly thrown away fizzy or bubbly foods. Yet having read books by Sandor Ellix Katz, Sally Fellon and fermenting bloggers' experiments I have understood this whole neglected world so much more. Over recent months I have begun to ferment peaches, apples, grapes and have loved the results. Fruit ferments quickly as we know from leaving fruit bowls untouched for days. By adding a small amount of salt to chopped fruit you can encourage the good bacteria to do their job of breaking down the fruit and offering us a store of *Lactobacillus acidophilus* to consume, not to mention new flavours and textures to enjoy. For a good breakfast I now open my jar of fermented peaches with grapes and vanilla and enjoy a few tablespoons of it with natural live yogurt. It is filling and satisfying and a healthy alternative to the wheat-based snacks that I would previously have turned to.

PEACH, GRAPE AND VANILLA CHUTNEY

This is a naturally sweet and delightful mixture of fruits that are fermented to make a healthy chutney that can be kept in the refrigerator. The fermentation can be hastened by the addition of a small quantity of whey (see page 179). Depending on the sweetness of the fruit and your taste, the added sugar is optional. However, don't be tempted to add honey instead as its antibacterial qualities are not what we need in this case. The salt encourages the healthy bacteria – you can use fine sea salt or the citrus salt from Salted Kumquats or Salted Lemons (see pages 76–7). Once made, this recipe makes a quick dessert or breakfast with yogurt, or it can be used as a chutney to enjoy with cold meats, cheeses and bread.

MAKES JUST LESS THAN 1KG (2LB 4OZ), YOU WILL NEED A 1KG (2LB 4OZ) KILNER JAR

- 650g (1lb 7oz) soft fruit such as peaches, plums, nectarines
- 100g (3½oz) grapes, seeded or raisins or sultanas (optional)
- 1 tablespoon light brown muscovado sugar (optional)
- 6cm (2½in) cinnamon stick
- 1 vanilla pod, split lengthways in two or ½ teaspoon organic vanilla extract
- 50ml (2fl oz) whey (optional)
- finely grated rind and juice of 1 lemon or 2 limes
- 1 level teaspoon fine salt or 1 heaped teaspoon finely chopped Salted Kumquats or Lemons (see pages 76–7)

> Wash and prepare the fruit, discarding the stones but keeping the skins on the fruit. Chop into bite-sized pieces. Mix all the ingredients together in a bowl. Pack into a sterilized and cooled Kilner jar allowing 3cm (1¼in) headroom. Push the fruit down under the juice with a plastic spoon or wooden rolling pin. If the juice doesn't cover it, add a little non-chlorinated water to make sure it is submerged. Add a weight to make sure the fruit stays down. Close the lid tightly and stand in a warm place out of direct sunlight. It should

start to bubble as it ferments. Leave for 2–3 days, lifting the lid daily to allow any gases to escape. When you are happy with the taste (it should be slightly sour and may have some fizziness), transfer the jar to the refrigerator where it will keep for up to a month. It will keep slowly fermenting and continue to soften in the refrigerator and may become fizzy and smell of alcohol. All of these effects are fine, simply eat it how you like it.

FERMENTED TOMATOES

This is a very simple way of preserving the wonderful sweet tomatoes we get at the end of summer. In this way they hold their texture and flavour for up to a year. You need to be brave and persevere through the initial aroma and fizziness but it is really interesting to watch the transformation they undergo. They can be used in cooking for tomato sauce, soups and casseroles or to preserve their goodness use them raw in salsa.

MAKES APPROX. 2.5KG (5LB 8OZ)

- 2.5kg (5lb 8oz) organic, flavourful tomatoes (can be a mix of round and cherry)
- 2 level tablespoons salt
- 250–500ml (9–18fl oz) non-chlorinated or filtered water
- extra virgin olive oil

> Wash the tomatoes and cut roughly into bite-sized pieces, discarding any hard cores and the part where they were attached to the stems. Put them into a clean crock or large non-reactive bowl. Mix the salt with 250ml (9fl oz) of water and pour this over the tomatoes, using clean hands to combine. Push the tomatoes down, releasing their juice and

making sure they are covered with water. Top up with more water if necessary. Cover the crock with a clean tea towel or muslin so that the tomatoes can breathe but insects can't join them.

> Leave in a warm place out of direct sunlight for a few days. The tomatoes might begin to smell awful, yes, awful! (This doesn't always happen, some batches ferment quickly in warmer weather and don't go through this.) However, you must stir them through at least twice a day, preferably three or four times. There should be small bubbles as the fermentation takes place. Watch for a surface film of white mould, this should be stirred in if very thin or removed if thick. If you see a green or black mould discard the batch and start again.

> After two or three days the aroma will change to a really pleasant fresh smell and any bubbling will dissipate. Wait until the good aroma has been there a day and there are no obvious bubbles. Be brave and taste your tomatoes, you will be surprised how they taste as if just picked and cut. If they smell, taste and look good with no evidence of fizzing, they are ready to bottle. The process so far should have taken approx. 4–5 days, depending on the temperature around them. Ladle the tomatoes into clean Kilner jars leaving 3cm (1¼in) headroom. Put the lids on but do not tighten them. This way you will stop insects getting in but let any gases out. Leave for a couple of days in a cool, dark place below 16°C (61°F) until you are sure the bubbling has stopped. Now pour a layer of oil approx. 1cm (½in) thick over the surface and close the lids. Keep an eye on the jars for the first week, loosening the lids every so often to allow any gases to escape, then close. The tomatoes can be left like this for up to a year.

∗ ALCOHOLIC DRINKS

The pleasures of alcohol have been enjoyed since our hairy ancestors realized eating fermented fruit from trees made them giggle. Since then almost every culture has perfected the art of fermenting fruit into alcohol. My early experiences of making wine date back to when I was a student, when I used to make it for parties from packs bought at the local chemist. I hadn't touched wine-making again since, but now I am really hooked. At home we take lots of pleasure in the 'country wines' we produce – the sort you make simply from foraged or homegrown produce such as damsons and raspberries. Crushing fruits with a meat tenderizer or your hands and dealing with large amounts of bubbling berries in a vat is lots of fun. We love to watch the yeast become activated and the smell is incredible. Our damson wine is rich, full-bodied and delicious. Our elderflower champagne was ready for popping at New Year, we discovered its sweet perfume went perfectly with our rich orange trifle on New Year's Day.

What we cover in this chapter is very much at entry level into wine-making. If you like what you make, read C J J Berry's brilliant book *First Steps in Winemaking* and Andy Hamilton's books for many other wonderful recipes. To help us on our way into wine-making, I have enjoyed the help of friend Debi King who has been making wine for years and Doctor Maslin who is also a keen wine-maker. We haven't touched on grape wines or beer-making in this chapter, as they should really go in a book by themselves because there is so much to write about and we don't grow our own grapes.

INGREDIENTS

FRUIT

Most fruits, edible flowers and some vegetables can be used to make wine with the addition of sugar, yeast and yeast nutrients.

YEAST

Wine is made from fruit, which is crushed and allowed to ferment with the addition of yeast. The process of fermentation converts the sugar in the fruit to alcohol. By adding a carefully chosen yeast, the wine-maker can control which yeast forms. (The natural yeasts that are present on the skins of the fruit or in the air are impossible to control and don't provide a reliable method of wine-making.) Alcohol is the by-product of the yeast's reproduction, which begins to happen as soon as the yeast is put into the right conditions for it to thrive.

SUGAR

Like any other living organism, yeast needs warmth, liquid and food to survive – so the sugary solution made by crushed grapes that is full of natural glucose is ideal. The sugar is converted approx. half into alcohol by weight and half into bubbles of carbon dioxide. Professional wine-makers working with grapes are not allowed to add sugar (as there is enough in the grapes), but for country wines it is nearly always added – which is why country wines can be made from fruits that are low in sugar.

Any golden or brown sugar will affect the colour and, less so, the flavour of the wine – so some people choose this to improve the appearance of their wines. Caster, granulated, beet or cane sugar give the same result, so the choice is yours. C J J Berry recommends 'when starting a wine off it is always better to use little sugar rather than too much, because dry wine can always be sweetened, but there is little you can really do about a wine which is oversweet,

other than blend it with a dry one of the same type'.

Sugar is often added in stages to boost the activity of yeast when it drops. You can calculate the amount of sugar to add using a hydrometer (see page 194); consult specialist wine-making books and online charts to find out more. We had to add more sugar to our damson wine to get the fermentation going again after it slowed down; this was because the berries were not sweet enough that season. This secondary dose of sugar boosted the flavour and strength.

YEAST NUTRIENT

This additive will give the yeast a much-needed boost. As we have said before, pure grape juice provides all the elements yeast needs to thrive, but when other fruits are used a nutrient is required to provide the correct doses of nitrogen and phosphate. It also enables the yeast to work for longer so that more of the sugar is turned into alcohol, which is a great help in the production of dry wines. It is less important for fruit wines but more important for flower wines, which have less 'substance' for the yeast to thrive on.

PECTIC ENZYME

This is needed for fruit and vegetables that are naturally high in pectin, such as damsons and parsnips. It speeds up the breakdown of the fruit and ensures a clear wine. If using pectic enzyme add it to the fruit when it is cool, 24 hours before the yeast.

CAMPDEN TABLETS

These are used to kill off any naturally occurring yeasts on the fruit before you add the wine yeast to your brew. This way, only your chosen yeast will be the one that reproduces. Campden tablets are also used at the end, after fermentation has finished, to kill the added yeast so as to avoid unwanted secondary fermentation in the bottle. Some wine-makers do not like to add them as they contain sulphites.

EQUIPMENT

You will need a fermentation bucket, a probe thermometer, a wine-straining bag, a funnel, a length of plastic tubing, a long-handled plastic spoon, a wine strainer or strong large sieve, some demijohns, bungs with fermentation traps (see below), bottles, corks and a cork fitter. You will also need a room thermometer to work out the best place to ferment your brew (see right). Thermometer strips are also useful for monitoring the temperature of your individual demijohns or bottles. A hydrometer isn't essential but it is helpful for determining the amount of sugar in the liquid, from which you can also discover the alcohol content.

STERILIZING EQUIPMENT

Specialist sterilizers are available from home-brewing suppliers, however I have used both Campden tablets and Milton fluid with success. Make up the sterilizing solution in your fermenting bucket and put in all the equipment you will need including the long plastic spoon and a sieve if necessary.

UNWANTED VISITORS AND FERMENTATION TRAPS

A visiting fruit or vinegar fly will more than likely cause your wine to turn to vinegar. These annoying flies appear as soon as fruit begins to overripen. This is where the name *vinaigre* comes from in French, meaning 'sour wine'. To prevent unwanted visitors, always make sure your wine is covered. In the first stage this could be with a cloth or plastic lid. In the second stage you will need an airlock or fermentation trap to prevent flies and bacteria from contaminating your wine; these also control the air supply to the yeast and allow carbon dioxide to escape. Airlocks are controlled by a small amount

of water filling the U-bend of the trap. A good tip is to place a piece of crushed Campden tablet into this water so that if a fly does enter it cannot contaminate the water, which occasionally drips into the wine when the trap is removed. Alternatively, a small piece of cotton wool stuffed into the top of the trap will prevent flies from entering.

After fitting the trap and adding the water to it, you will see and hear bubbles of carbon dioxide coming through it. It is a delightful sound and sight and will continue for some months as the fermentation progresses.

FERMENTATION

Fermentation occurs in two stages. The first, lasting up to 6 days, is aerobic (with air) and is usually frothy and obvious. The second, which can go on for months, is anaerobic (without air); it is subtle and often barely visible. As the process of fermentation continues the alcohol content rises, usually stopping approx. 15–16 per cent. At this point the yeast cannot reproduce in such an environment. This means that any leftover sugar that hasn't been converted into alcohol will remain.

TEMPERATURE

Temperature is crucial for the yeast to work efficiently, and at the right pace, to ensure a good flavour to the wine. At temperatures above 38°C (100°F) the yeast will die; too cold and it will reproduce very slowly or not at all. Fermentation should begin within the first few days when the fruit and yeast are held at 21°C (70°F). I have found our kitchen to be the perfect environment for stage one, and it means the vat is in front of me so I remember to check on it regularly. During the second stage of fermentation, the wine should be held at approx. 16°C

(61°F). My garage is ideal for this, providing the wine is stored off the floor and away from the draught by the door. As a rule of thumb, fermentation that takes place slowly produces better wine than wines produced in a hurry. Your finished wine should be kept at a fairly constant 10–13°C (50–55°F).

RACKING

Wines often remain cloudy in their first few months due to the yeast suspended in them. However, after time, the solids sink to the bottom to form a thick, brownish visible layer and clear wine above. This is when you are ready to rack. Racking involves siphoning off your wine from the demijohn, leaving the lees (the sediment from the yeast) behind, and putting it into new demijohns or bottles.

BOTTLING

It is essential you use clean sterile bottles for bottling. Either buy new ones or thoroughly clean old wine bottles. Never be tempted to use bottles that have had another strong flavour inside; it will spoil the flavour of your finished wine. Some people prefer not to bottle their wine and instead leave it in the demijohns with their safety bungs in place (in case it starts to re-ferment). They can then pull it off at the last minute into a bottle or decanter, thereby avoiding the stage of sterilizing bottles, corking and labelling.

MAKING WINE FROM FRUIT AND FLOWERS

It is wise to understand a few basics before you embark on fermenting your fruit. Here is the process in a nutshell:

- Extract the flavours by pressing, soaking or boiling.
- Add sugar and yeast, plus nutrients/citric acid/pectic enzyme depending on the type of fruit or flower.
- Set aside to ferment in a bucket in a warm place (20–25°C/68–77°F) for up to 10 days.
- Strain off. Put the resulting liquid into a fermentation container with a fermentation trap (to let the carbon dioxide out and nothing else back in).
- Set aside to ferment in a cooler place (16°C/61°F) until bubbling ceases.
- 'Rack' several times (i.e. siphon off the wine, discarding the yeast debris or 'lees'). Return the wine each time to a fermenting container with a fermentation trap until fermentation is over. After this time, the wine can be safely bottled without exploding; this usually takes place after approx. 6 months.

DOCTOR MASLIN'S DAMSON WINE

This recipe is based on C J J Berry's recipe for plum wine from his book First Steps in Winemaking; he describes it as 'a beautiful, satisfying wine'. Doctor Maslin, a homemade wine enthusiast, advises that you taste the damsons for sweetness first. The good doctor is lucky enough to have a damson tree in his garden, and so he can choose precisely the right moment when the fruit is ripe enough to use without having to compensate by adding lots of sugar. Our fruit was quite unripe, as the season had not been a good one, so we added a further amount of sugar to the demijohns later to get the fermentation going once it had slowed down (see page 193).

MAKES 9 LITRES (15¾ PINTS)

- 4.5-5kg (9lb 13oz-11lb) firm, ripe damsons (the higher amount for good body)
- Campden tablets (optional, see pages 193-4)
- 3-3.5kg (6lb 8oz-1lb 10oz) golden caster or granulated sugar, depending on the sweetness of the damsons
- 12.5 litres (22½ pints) boiling water
- pectic enzyme (pectolase) – refer to the manufacturer's instructions for quantity needed
- cooled, boiled water
- burgundy or red wine yeast – refer to the manufacturer's instructions for quantity needed
- yeast nutrient – refer to the manufacturer's instructions for quantity needed

> Pick over the fruit, discarding any rotten damsons along with the stems and leaves. Give the fruit a wash with cold water and put into a sterilized fermentation bucket. Add the crushed Campden tablet (if using). Using a large sterilized rolling pin, mush up the fruit with half of the sugar and the boiling water. Stir with a sterilized spoon to dissolve the sugar.

> Put the lid on the bucket and set aside to cool to 35°C (95°F), testing with a sterile probe thermometer. Mix the pectic enzyme with 100ml (3½fl oz) cooled, boiled water and stir into the cooled fruit. Set aside at room temperature (20-25°C/68-77°F) for 24 hours, stirring every few hours with a sterile plastic spoon. At this point, your house should fill with the intoxicating smell of boozy fruits.

> Prepare the yeast and yeast nutrient by stirring them into a little cooled, boiled water or refer to the manufacturer's instructions. Pour the mixture into your fruit and stir through. Set aside at room temperature (20-25°C/68-77°F) for 2-3 days.

> Sterilize a wine-straining bag (this could be two pieces of muslin but it is a lot fiddlier), funnel, another bucket and demijohns. Add the remaining sugar to the bucket and put the bag into the funnel. Strain the wine into the bucket. Discard the fruit. Stir through to dissolve the sugar. Now pour the wine through the funnel into the sterilized demijohns. Fit the bungs with fermentation traps and fix onto the demijohns. If necessary top up to within 2.5cm (1in) of the top with cold, boiled water. Move the wine to a cooler place (15-16°C/59-61°F) until it clears. This will take a few months.

> Once the wine clears, you can siphon it off into clean demijohns or bottles, leaving behind the sediment. Top the bottles up if necessary to within 2.5cm (1in) of the top with cooled, boiled water. You can sample your wine after 6 months, but it will be better after a year.

RASPBERRY WINE

Wow, I am pleased with this. We love this dry wine full of fruit and flavour, not to mention the glowing colour gleaming through the glass. What a lovely summery flavour to enjoy in the middle of winter. Either serve very chilled on its own or mix with sparkling white wine and serve as an aperitif or to have with dessert. Frozen raspberries are fine to use as they release more juice after being frozen. This means you can pick and freeze your own raspberries or those from a farm, or take advantage of offers in the supermarket, until you have enough to turn into wine.

MAKES 5 LITRES (9 PINTS)

- 1.6kg (3lb 8oz) raspberries
- 1 Campden tablet (optional)
- 1.2kg (2lb 10oz) caster or granulated sugar
- 4.5 litres (7¾ pints) boiling water
- pectic enzyme (pectolase) – refer to the manufacturer's instructions for quantity needed
- an all-purpose wine yeast or white wine yeast such as Lalvin 71B-1122 – refer to the manufacturer's instructions for quantity needed
- yeast nutrient – refer to the manufacturer's instructions for quantity needed

> Follow the instructions for Doctor Maslin's Damson Wine (see left), substituting the damsons for raspberries.

RHUBARB AND GINGER WINE BY DEBI KING

This is a pale pink, dry wine that has a delicate but clear flavour of rhubarb with a background kick of heat from the ginger. I love it as an aperitif or served in a shot glass as part of a dessert made with rhubarb. Debi uses the method invented by Mrs Suzanne Tritton in C J J Berry's book First Steps in Winemaking, adding rhubarb for body in the wine – the taste is not strong, but she feels it makes a better ginger wine for its presence. She adds lots of sugar because she likes it quite sweet, potent and fiery, but you could reduce the sugar by 250g (9oz) if you wish, although the wine will be less strong. Debi told me it is best to use the rhubarb at the beginning of the year and not to get it too hot, or you can have problems with it turning to jelly.

MAKES 4.5 LITRES (7¾ PINTS)

- 300g (10½oz) fresh ginger
- 1.25kg (2lb 10oz) rhubarb
- 1.25kg (2lb 10oz) golden caster or granulated sugar
- 1 Campden tablet (optional)
- cooled, boiled water
- dessert wine/high alcohol yeast – refer to the manufacturer's instructions for quantity needed
- yeast nutrient – refer to the manufacturer's instructions for quantity needed

> To get a good ginger flavour, you need to work at it. Peel the ginger and chop finely or blitz in a food processor. Wipe the rhubarb with a damp cloth, but don't peel it. Chop the rhubarb finely with a knife or in a food processor.
> Put the rhubarb and ginger into a fermenting bucket and stir in the sugar. Add the Campden tablet (if using). Put on the lid and set aside at room temperature for at least 24 hours (up to 2 days) to allow the sugar to draw out the juices from the fruit.
> Strain off the sugary juices into a sterile jug, cover and set aside. Return the fruit pulp to the bucket and pour in 2 litres

(3½ pints) of cooled, boiled water. Stir well with a sterilized spoon and strain again to collect all the sugary juice, discarding the fruit. Place all the juice back in the fermentation bucket and make up to 4.5 litres (7¾ pints) with cooled, boiled water.

> Prepare the yeast and yeast nutrient by stirring them into a little cooled, boiled water (or refer to the manufacturer's instructions). Add the yeast mixture to the bucket with the juice and set aside at room temperature (20–25°C/68–77°F) until fermentation slows right down (i.e. the bubbles drop to fewer than one per minute, which you can see happen through the fermentation trap).

> Place a sterilized funnel in your demijohn and pour in the wine. Fit the bungs with fermentation traps and move to a cool room (16°C/61°F) until the wine clears. This will take approx. 4 months. Rack and bottle when finished (see page 195)

SPARKLING ELDERFLOWER WINE BY LUTHER DAVIES

This is an old family recipe that our friend Hannah's grandfather used to make. It is best to pick the flowers early in the morning and when they are still young. If the petals shake off easily, they are past their best. Dip any leftover flowers in a light batter and fry. Serve drizzled in honey with a little grating of lime zest.

MAKES APPROX. 5 LITRES (9 PINTS)

- 40 fully ripe elderflower heads, ideally picked when dry
- 1.5kg (3lb 5oz) granulated sugar
- 4.5 litres (7¾ pints) boiling water
- 1 teaspoon Champagne yeast
- juice of 2 lemons
- sugar cubes

> Shake off any insects from the elderflowers but do not wash them. Dissolve the granulated sugar in the boiling water in a large saucepan over a low heat. When all the crystals have dissolved, add the elderflowers immediately. Remove from the heat and leave to cool. Cover the pan with a lid and set aside at room temperature (20–25°C/68–77°F) for 2 days. Place a muslin in a sieve and pour through some boiling water from a kettle to sterilize it. Strain the elderflower juice through the muslin into a fermenting bucket. Stir in the yeast and lemon juice. Put on the lid and set aside in a warm place (16°C/61°F) for 14 days until the vivacious bubbling stops.

> Strain the wine through a muslin again, and then bottle in used (and washed!) Champagne or sparkling wine bottles. Add 1 granulated sugar lump to each bottle. If using corks, these will need to be wired down. Alternatively, use swing-top bottles. Store the bottles vertically in a cool place for 6 months. Luther warns of unlikely explosions from the continuing fermentation in the bottle due to the build-up of gas – so do make sure you store the bottles away from people! We kept ours in the garage and uncorked it for the New Year without any explosions!

APPLE CIDER

This is a wonderfully easy recipe based on one from Darina Allen's book Forgotten Skills of Cooking. We pick Bramley apples from our local pick-your-own farm (Home Cottage Farm in Iver, Bucks). They are enormous apples and have a wonderful crisp flavour. Not enough people use these farms, and rely instead on supermarkets, so I am on a mission to get more people to have a great, inexpensive day out. It has nothing to do with queuing, junk food or expense and we come away with fresh fruit and plenty of things to do with them.

MAKES APPROX. 7.5 LITRES (13½ PINTS)

- 3kg (6lb 8oz) cooking apples
- 7.5 litres (13½ pints) cold water
- 900g (2lb) granulated sugar
- 50g (1¾oz) fresh ginger, chopped
- 3 cinnamon sticks

> Grate the apples in a food processor – skin, cores and all. Put them into a fermentation bin and cover with the cold water. Stir with a sterilized spoon, leaving it in the bin. Cover and stir every day with the spoon for a week. Strain through a sieve and return to the bucket.
> Stir the sugar into the juice, add the spices and set aside to macerate for a day. Strain through clean muslin. Pour into sterilized bottles and seal with screw-top lids. Store in a cold, dry place for up to 6 months. Wait 3 months before sampling.

ROSEHIP MEAD

We collected the rosehips for this as soon as they were ripe, placing them in a bag in the freezer until we had enough. This recipe is based on C J J Berry's recipe in his book First Steps in Winemaking. Although we have called this rosehip mead, the correct term is rhodomel, because mead is traditionally made with berries. Rosehips are rich in vitamins C, D and E and are a good source of antioxidants. During World War II, British children were paid to collect rosehips to make into syrup. This was drunk to obtain vitamin C in the fight against scurvy.

MAKES APPROX. 8 LITRES (14 PINTS)

- 2kg (4lb 8oz) rosehips
- 4 litres (7 pints) hot water
- 2kg (4lb 8oz) unpasteurized, organic honey
- 8 litres (14 pints) cold water
- 15g (½oz) citric acid
- yeast nutrient – refer to the manufacturer's instructions for quantity needed
- high alcohol yeast – refer to the manufacturer's instructions for quantity needed

> Wash the rosehips, discarding any large stems. Put them into a large saucepan with the hot water and bring to the boil. Cook until tender, approx. 15–20 minutes. Mash with a potato masher to break up the hips so that they release their juices. Line a sieve with muslin and pour through a kettleful of boiling water to sterilize it. Strain the rosehip mixture through the muslin in the sieve into a fermenting bucket with a lid. Bring up the sides of the muslin to squeeze the hips so you extract as much of the juice as possible.
> Add the honey, cold water, citric acid and yeast nutrient and stir thoroughly to dissolve the honey. Allow the mixture to cool slightly, until it is lukewarm, and then stir in the yeast. Cover the bucket with a lid and set aside to ferment at room temperature (20–25°C/68–77°F) until the vivacious bubbling stops. Strain into demijohns and set aside in a cooler place (16°C) until fermentation ceases; this will take a few months. Rack and bottle as for Doctor Maslin's Damson Wine on pages 196–7.

Kombucha is a fermentation of sweetened tea made with a starter culture. It has been drunk in Russia, where it is called kvass, China and Japan for centuries. During fermentation, beneficial bacteria and yeasts present in the culture metabolize the sugar and turn it into acetic acid. When properly cared for and regularly cultured, they produce a wonderful probiotic-rich beverage and will continue to grow and reproduce indefinitely.

Like kefir (see pages 174–6), kombucha is a refreshing and energizing drink that is thought to have health-giving properties. I prefer to drink kombucha while it is still young, when it is fresh and light (after fermenting for approx. 4 days), but you could mature it for longer if you wish for a stronger flavour.

To make your own kombucha at home, you will need a starter culture bought from an internet supplier (see suppliers page 243). This is sometimes called a SCOBY – an acronym for Symbiotic Culture Of Bacteria and Yeast. For best results, follow the instructions from your supplier because quantities vary depending on the size of your SCOBY. Do not use metal utensils when making kombucha.

> METHOD Brew some sweetened tea and let it cool. Transfer to a glass jar and float the culture on top. Cover with a tea towel and set aside at room temperature for 3–4 days before tasting.
> When you are happy with the flavour, drain off the tea and store in the refrigerator to enjoy chilled. You can then make another batch, reusing the mother, which will continue to grow. Eventually you will be able to give part of that mother to a friend to make their own kombucha.

You can vary the taste by trying different teas – our favourite kombucha consists of two-thirds black tea to one-third redbush. Alternatively, flavour your tea by infusing it with fresh herbs or by adding lemon or ginger.

HEAT

In the early 19th century Nicolas Appert, a French confectioner and brewer, discovered that if he sealed food in a glass container, then heated it in boiling water, the food inside would stay edible for months afterwards. It was said that he made 'the seasons stand still' and his invention won him a 12,000-franc prize offered by Napoleon in 1809 to find a method of preserving food so that he could efficiently feed his troops. Keeping food from the air and heating it to a high enough temperature to kill micro-organisms preserves it from spoilage. Appert perhaps didn't fully understand how his idea worked, but his discovery marked the beginning of canning. His ideas spread and the Englishman Peter Durand began experimenting with heating food in metal containers and then sealing them. In 1810 King George III gave him a patent for his technique. The term 'canning' came from the tin-coated iron canisters he used, which were similar to those used to store tea.

We often have the misconception that preserved food is inferior to fresh. However, the key to successful preserving is to bottle ingredients when they are in season – not only will they be at their best at this time but they will also be less expensive. Canning, as it is known in the US (even though glass jars are used not tin cans), opens up a whole realm of possibilities too good to miss out on in this book. With the right equipment we really can make our own ready meals, sauces, stews and soups and store them out of the refrigerator and in the cupboard ready to pull out, reheat and enjoy. Putting food in jars, often called 'putting up', gives you more freezer space and it doesn't cost energy for storage. We generally keep bottled goods in our garage, but you could use a shed, a dark larder, utility room, spare room where the heating is off, cellar or *cantina* – just make sure the temperature doesn't drop below freezing or the glass could shatter.

THE EFFECT OF HEAT

In this chapter, we look at the preserving effect heat has on food after it has been bottled or 'canned'. There are two methods of heat-processing depending on whether your food is high in acid or low in acid (see right):

WATERBATHING is safe for high-acid foods and involves heating your jars in a waterbath to 100°C (212°F) for a controlled period of time (see pages 206-7 for instructions). It will work for high- and low-sugar products so it ideal for low-sugar jams, cordials and fruits with or without syrup.

PRESSURE CANNING is essential for low-acid foods (see right). This method involves heating the jars in a pressure canner (not to be confused with a pressure cooker) to 115°C (239°F) for a controlled period of time (see pages 213-14 for instructions). The amount of time the jars should be processed for and the pressure needed is difficult to calculate at home, so it is better to follow the recipes here or from a reputable source.

There are two main recognized authorities on pressure canning, both US based as it is widely practised there. The US Department of Agriculture (USDA) gives clear advice on safe practice. For more information, see their book *Complete Guide to Home Canning and Preserving* or refer to their website. Another very good book is the *Blue Book Guide to Preserving*, which gives explanations of water canners and pressure canning. I recommend getting hold of both if you want to invest in a pressure canner and start canning.

NOTE: People used to heat-process in the oven, but this method is no longer recommended because it is unreliable and temperatures are difficult to maintain inside the jars over a long period.

BOTULISM

The reason you need to process low-acid foods at a higher temperature than acid foods is due to the greater risk of botulism – a deadly form of food poisoning caused by the bacterium *Clostridium botulinum*, which can survive in low-acid conditions even after boiling at 100°C (212°F). *Clostridium botulinum* is very resilient and can survive harmlessly in soil for many years, but if it is given the right conditions to multiply it can produce a deadly toxin. The reason we recommend pressure canning, rather than waterbathing, for low-acid foods is because the temperature inside a pressure canner is pressurized and therefore high enough to destroy *Clostridium botulinum* bacteria. Note that acid foods contain enough acid to block the growth of bacteria after waterbathing at 100°C (212°F).

ACIDITY AND PH

The first step with heat-processing is to discover if your food is high in acid or low in acid. Then you can determine which method of heat-processing is required: waterbathing (high acid) or pressure canning (low acid). The safest method to determine the pH value is using pH strips, which are available online. Alternatively, you can refer to the list, right. Low-acid foods have pH values higher than 4.6; this group includes most vegetables, meats, sauces, stews, poultry and seafood. Combinations of low- and high-acid foods should be treated as low acid and processed by pressure canning.

Note that the acidity levels of low-acid foods can be increased by adding lemon juice, citric acid or vinegar.

HIGH- AND LOW-ACID FOODS

HIGH-ACID FOODS

These foods are naturally acidic with a pH of 4.6 or lower. All are suitable for heat-processing by waterbathing – see pages 206–7 for instructions and refer to the individual recipes for timings. Don't get confused, however, as some of these fruits, such as apricots and peaches, appear as low-acid in the Sugar chapter. That is because their acidity is not high enough for setting jam but is high enough for waterbathing. The exception is figs, which need additional lemon juice to bump up their acidity.

FRUIT
apples
apricots
blackberries
cherries
gooseberries
lemons
limes
peaches
pears
plums
redcurrants
tomatoes

OTHER FOODS
fruit coulis and compotes
high-acid fruits in syrup
low-sugar jams
pickles
sauerkraut

LOW-ACID FOODS

These foods should all be heat-processed in a pressure canner – see pages 213–14 for instructions and refer to individual recipes for timings.

VEGETABLES
asparagus
beetroot
carrots
green beans
mushrooms
okra
peppers
peas
pulses
spinach
sweetcorn
turnips

OTHER FOODS
figs
meat sauces
poultry
seafood
stews, meatballs and *ragùs*

A NOTE ON TOMATOES

Although tomatoes are generally considered to be an acid food, it is worth noting that some varieties can have pH values slightly above 4.6. For this reason, the USDA suggests that further acid in the form of lemon juice, citric acid or vinegar is added to processed tomatoes to guarantee acidity levels. We have followed this advice in our recipes for passata and salsa (see pages 209–10), however I know Giancarlo's family and others in Italy have been canning jars of passata for years without any ill effects and wouldn't dream of adding lemon juice to their jars. This may be because over the years tomatoes have been selectively grown for sweetness and some acidity has been lost. Note that if you combine tomatoes with meat (a low-acid food), the resulting *ragù* should be treated as low-acid and processed by pressure canning (see pages 213–14).

A NOTE ON JAMS

Foods that contain over 60 per cent sugar do not need to be heat-processed, as explained on page 43. However, if the figure drops below 60 per cent – for example, for low-sugar jams and spreads – the jars should be heat-processed after bottling for the time that we have indicated in the recipe.

FAT, OIL AND CANNING

Fats and oils should be avoided or used in minimal quantities in recipes or poured away prior to canning. This is because they can coat the food and provide an anaerobic environment where the bacteria that cause botulism can breed. If you want to can gravy or stock it is better to remove the fat after it cools before canning. The same goes for *ragù* – simply pour off the excess oil before bottling.

PRESSURE CANNERS AND PRESSURE COOKERS

Pressure cookers are not suitable for pressure canning because the temperature is not great enough to kill the spores of the bacterium *Clostridium botulinum*. Pressure canners are larger than pressure cookers and therefore they can process food at higher temperatures. Pressure canners take longer to reach pressure and longer to cool down than pressure cookers.

Pressure cookers are useful for speeding up the cooking time of jams and stews, etc. because they heat to a higher temperature than boiling point, making them more efficient and energy saving than a normal saucepan on the hob. However, they do not reach the same temperature as pressure canners, so don't confuse the two. We sometimes use a pressure canner for waterbathing high-acid foods (see page 209 for instructions).

* GENERAL ADVICE FOR HEAT-PROCESSING

JARS, BOTTLES AND LIDS

You cannot use ordinary glass jam jars for heat-processing because they don't have thick enough glass to withstand the heat. The best jars to buy are Kilner or Le Parfait jars, which come with rubber seals and clips to allow the steam to escape. Alternatively, you can buy Balls or Mason glass jars with two-part lids, which consist of a flat disc held in place by a screw band; these are ideal because the disc part forms a vacuum when it is secured correctly, meaning you can check the seal before you tighten the screw band. Check the rubber seals are not damaged in any way before using. New metal discs for Mason jars should be used each time.

Specialist jars are available from some cook shops or online. You can reuse the jars so it is worth investing in, say, twelve of three different sizes. I would recommend the 250ml (9fl oz) size for apple butter and jam, 500ml (18fl oz) jars for vegetable dishes and 1 litre (1¾ pints) jars for *ragù* or bean soup. The lids are not reusable but the screw bands are.

All jars should be examined before use to make sure there are no chips or cracks in the glass. Also ensure that the new lids are not damaged in any way.

PREPARATION FOR HEAT-PROCESSING

Clean the jars and lids in hot soapy water and rinse thoroughly or put them through a dishwasher cycle. Heat the rubber seals, jars and lids in simmering water to 82°C (180°F) or just above; do not allow the lids to boil or the rubber or plastic will perish. Alternatively, put the jars in the oven at 85°C/185°F/gas mark ¼. If using the hot-pack method, store the jars in the water, dishwasher (with the door closed) or oven until you are ready to fill them as they should be hot for processing.

NOTE: This method does not sterilize but simply prepares jars for processing as long as the processing time is longer than 10 minutes. If it is less than that, say for a small jar of pickles, the jars and lids should be sterilized, you can see how to do this in the general instructions on page 10.

FILLING THE JARS

Fill the jars with food allowing 7mm (⅜in) headroom for jams and jellies, 1.5cm (⅝in) for fruits and tomatoes and 2.5cm (1in) for low-acid foods to allow for expansion. Don't overfill the jars or the contents will bubble up inside the jar and overflow, ruining the seal. Remove any air bubbles that are trapped inside the jar by poking them with a sterilized skewer or narrow spatula. It is not necessary to do this for liquid foods and drinks. Clean the rim of the jars with water or a little vinegar on kitchen paper to ensure a good seal.

FASTENING THE LIDS

Lift the lids out of the hot water with a magnetic prong or tongs and shake off the water. For Kilner-style jars, put the lids on, with rubber seals in place, and secure them with the spring clip. For two-part lids, put on the flat disc but don't fully tighten the screw band at this stage – a good technique, which I use, is to tighten the screw band fully first and then untighten it by just 2cm (¾in). This is called finger tight (as opposed to using your full hand strength to tighten the lid). This will allow for expansion. If this is not done properly the food will leak out and water will seep in; alternatively, the lids will bulge and bend under the pressure because the air cannot escape.

TESTING FOR A SEAL

After heat-processing, allow the jars to stand in the water for 5 minutes to let the contents settle before removing them with tongs. Keep them upright at all times and leave them to cool completely for 24 hours before checking the seals to see if a vacuum has formed. NOTE: You can't check the seals with Kilner or Le Parfait jars.

> METHOD For Mason-style lids, remove the screw bands and try to lift the lids, they should feel stuck to the jars. If this is the case the jars are suitable for long-term storage. If you can lift the lids off the jars at this stage, they haven't sealed completely and won't be suitable for long-term storage; transfer them to the refrigerator and eat within a couple of days. Providing a vacuum has formed, I tend to remove the screw bands from Mason or Balls-style jars before storing as I find they sometimes corrode and rust – although I do replace them for transport if I am giving the product away.

> NOTE: If your jars haven't sealed correctly, you can repeat the heat-process again for things like jam or bottled fruit and vegetables (but not meat or fish). However, in my experience, the produce usually ends up too soft and overcooked after heat-processing a second time.

STORAGE OF JARS AND HOW LONG WILL THE FOOD LAST?

Clean the jars if they are sticky. Label with the food type and date you processed them. Jars of food that are properly waterbathed or pressure canned will last up to a year if stored in a cool, dark place, preferably between 10–20°C (50–68°F).

HEAT-PROCESSING EQUIPMENT: WHAT TO BUY

To avoid unnecessary buying and storage of bulky pots and pans it is a good idea to decide what exactly you want to can. If you plan to process low-acid foods (see page 203) you will have to buy a pressure canner, which is purposely designed for the job (see pages 213–14). If you are only bottling on an occasional basis and don't want to process low-acid foods, you can use a large, heavy-based stockpot, pressure cooker or a purpose-built boiling water canner as a waterbath (see below). Of course, you can waterbath in a pressure canner, and this will speed up the process because pressure canners heat up more quickly, but this isn't an essential piece of kit. If you have bought a boiling-water canner, follow the manufacturer's instructions.

ADDITIONAL EQUIPMENT

- jam lifters/tongs for lifting the jars out of the boiling water
- funnel for filling jars
- magnetic prong for lifting the lids
- digital thermometer for accurately measuring the temperature of the water

* HIGH-ACID RECIPES

The following recipes are all suitable for waterbathing because they are all high in acid. However, if you decide to alter the recipes we cannot guarantee that they will suitable for long-term storage.

WATERBATHING

You can use any large, heavy-based saucepan such as a stock pan for waterbathing provided it has a tight-fitting lid and it is deep enough to accommodate your jar(s). Make sure that you fit a wire or wooden rack in the bottom to stop the jars from coming into direct contact with the base of the saucepan or they could crack. If you don't have a rack, simply cut out a circle of cardboard and place it in the bottom of the pan or sit the jars on a folded tea towel. Boiling-water canners have specially fitted racks inside.

Of the two methods of waterbathing, also known as heat-processing, hot-packing is generally thought to be better because more air is expelled from the food. This helps maintain flavour and colour over time and the food is less likely to float.

Follow the raw-pack method if your food is cold or the hot-pack method if your food is hot.

RAW-PACK METHOD WATERBATHING (HIGH-ACID FOODS ONLY)

This method is suitable for raw or blanched, high-acid fruits bottled in brine, water or sugar syrup. This includes Bottled Whole Tomatoes (see right) and raw fruit in light syrup or water (see pages 208–9).

Make sure you use specialist jars for waterbathing and lids in perfect condition (see page 204). Fill the cold, sterilized jars with your cold fruit and top up with hot liquid (brine or sugar syrup), leaving 1.5cm (⅝in) headroom to allow for expansion. Remove any air bubbles in the jar by poking them with a sterilized skewer or similar. Wipe off any splashes around the rim with kitchen paper to ensure a good seal. Put on the lids (see page 205); note that screw bands should not be fully tightened at this stage.

Place the filled jars upright on the rack inside the pan. Wind a tea towel around the jars to stop them clattering about; this isn't necessary if you have a specialist rack designed to keep the jars apart. For best results, they should be at least 1cm (½in) apart to allow the water to circulate.

Fill the pan with cold water so that it covers the tops of the jars by at least 5cm (2in). Put the lid on the pan and place it over a medium heat. Increase the temperature and bring the water to a rolling boil (100°C/212°F) and then set your timer. Process for the time indicated in the recipe. The water should be visibly boiling throughout the whole process, although you might have to turn the heat down to stop it spurting over your oven.

After processing, remove the pan from the heat and allow the jars to stand for 5 minutes before attempting to remove them. Remove the jars, one at a time, from the boiling water using tongs or a heatproof rubber glove, keeping them upright at all times. Leave to stand on a heatproof surface and test the seals after 24 hours (see page 205).

BOTTLED WHOLE TOMATOES

If you are lucky enough to be able to grow or buy fragrant, strong-tasting tomatoes, then do bottle them up when they are at their peak and enjoy well after summer has gone. Giancarlo's family gathered together every year to do this and jars of these bright red fruits lined the walls of their *cantina*. Over winter they would gradually be used up until the room was bare – just in time for the new crop to emerge the following summer. Bottled whole tomatoes are wonderful for tomato sauce, ketchup, casseroles and *ragù*.

- 500ml (18fl oz) or 1 litre (1¾ pints) Kilner or Mason-style jars
- flavourful, perfect tomatoes
- lemon juice or citric acid
- salt

> Make a cross in a non-stalk end of each tomato. Wash the tomatoes in cold water and drain. Plunge them into boiling water for a minute or until the skins start to split. The easiest way to do this is in a wire basket or sieve that will fit into a large saucepan of boiling water. Drain and plunge into very cold water to stop them cooking. Peel off the skins with your fingers and a knife. Either leave them whole or cut into halves or quarters. Cut away the cores.

> To ensure enough acidity in the tomatoes add ¼ teaspoon of citric acid or 1 tablespoon of lemon juice to each 500ml (18fl oz) jar and ½ teaspoon of citric acid or 2 tablespoons of lemon juice to each 1 litre (1¾ pints) jar. Raw pack the tomatoes into 500ml (18fl oz) or 1kg (2lb 4oz) jars, following the instructions left. Pour over boiling water leaving 1.5cm (⅝in) headroom. Add ½ teaspoon of salt to each 500ml (18fl oz) jar and 1 teaspoon of salt to each 1 litre (1¾ pints) jar. Release any air bubbles and wipe the rims. Seal according to the instructions on page 205. Process in a waterbath for 40 minutes for 500ml (18fl oz) jars and 45 minutes for 1 litre (1¾ pints) jars.

VARIATION

TOMATOES IN THEIR OWN JUICE

To process tomatoes in their own juices, raw pack as above but put more tomatoes into the jars and squash them down so that their juices come out and cover the tomatoes instead of the boiling water. Waterbath 500ml (18fl oz) and 1 litre (1¾ pints) jars for 1 hour 25 minutes. After processing, carefully remove the jars from the water and allow to cool. Test the seals after 24 hours. Remove the screw bands if they have been used and store jars in a cool, dark place for up to a year.

RAW-PACKING FRUIT

We only eat fruit in a very light sugar syrup, such as 25g (1oz) caster sugar to 75ml (2½fl oz) water for 1 litre (1¾ pints) of sugar syrup. The sugar helps the fruit to keep its shape, colour and flavour but it is not needed for preserving in the case of waterbathing. The heat and vacuum does the job instead. Therefore you can cover the raw or hot-packed fruit in boiling water instead for a healthy option. Try adding cinnamon, vanilla and ginger.

> Prepare the sugar syrup by dissolving the sugar in the water or fruit juice.
> Wash the fruit in cold water. Peel, stone and cut the fruit into halves or quarters as necessary. As you prepare the fruit drop it into acidulated water to stop it discolouring – 1 litre (1¾ pints) water to 90ml (6 tablespoons) lemon juice is fine. Drain and raw-pack into jars following the instructions opposite. For the processing times follow the guide below.

RAW-PACK FRUIT TIMINGS

Sliced apple, rhubarb, berries and pineapple need 15 minutes for 500ml (18fl oz) jars and 20 minutes for 1 litre (1¾ pints) jars.
Apricots and plums need 20 minutes for 500ml (18fl oz) jars and 25 minutes for 1 litre (1¾ pints) jars.
Cherries need 25 minutes for either 500ml (18fl oz) or 1 litre (1¾ pints) jars.

HOT-PACK METHOD WATERBATHING (HIGH-ACID FOODS ONLY)

This method is suitable for hot, high-acid foods such as Antonio's Tomato Sauce (page 210), Giorgio's Salsa (page 209) and cordials, coulis and elixirs (see pages 60–2).

> Make sure you use specialist jars for waterbathing and lids and seals in perfect condition (see page 204). Fill the hot, sterilized jars with your hot fruit or vegetables and top up with hot liquid (brine or sugar syrup) if necessary, allowing 1.5cm (⅝in) headroom. For best results, sugar syrup should be heated to 60°C (140°F) before bottling. Remove any air bubbles in the jar by poking them with a sterilized skewer or similar. Put on the lids (see page 205); note that screw bands should not be fully tightened at this stage. Wipe off any splashes around the lid with kitchen paper.
> Place the filled jars upright on the rack inside the pan. Wind a tea towel around the jars to stop them clattering about; this isn't necessary if you have a specialist rack designed to keep the jars apart. For best results, they should be at least 1cm (½in) apart to allow the water to circulate.
> Fill the pan with warm water (38°C/100°F) so that it covers the tops of the jars by at least 5cm (2in). Put the lid on the pan and place it over a low to medium heat. Bring slowly to 88°C (190°F) – depending on the size of your pan, the water should take approx. 30 minutes to heat. Increase the heat and bring the water to a rolling boil (100°C/21°2F) before setting your timer. Process for the time allocated in the recipe. The water should be visibly boiling throughout the whole process, although you might have to reduce the heat to stop it spurting over your oven.
> After processing, switch off the heat and allow the jars to stand for 5 minutes before attempting to remove them. Remove the jars, one at a time, from the boiling water using tongs or a heatproof rubber glove, keeping them upright at all times. Leave to stand on a heatproof surface and test the seals after 24 hours (see page 205).

HOT-PACK FRUIT TIMINGS

Cherries and berries need 15 minutes for 500ml (18fl oz) jars or 20 minutes for 1 litre (1¾ pints) jars. Apricots, peaches, pears and plums need 20 minutes for 500ml (18fl oz) jars and 25 minutes for 1 litre (1¾ pints) jars.

USING A PRESSURE CANNER FOR WATERBATHING

WATERBATHING METHOD (HIGH-ACID FOODS ONLY)

Depending on the size of your pressure canner you can use the larger models to waterbath high-acid foods as long as the jars will fit on the rack and you can cover them with 5cm (2in) of water. Follow manufacturers' instructions (see suppliers on page 243).

GIORGIO'S SALSA FOR FAJITAS

This is a spicy, hot salsa for eating with fajitas. It is a great recipe for using up summer gluts of tomatoes and peppers. We developed it after much trial and error with our son Giorgio so as to avoid having to buy packets and jars of ready-made salsa for our Mexican suppers.

MAKES APPROX. 2KG (4LB 8OZ)
USE 500ML (18FL OZ) JARS

- 1.2kg (2lb 10oz) flavourful, firm but ripe tomatoes
- 4 tablespoons extra virgin olive oil
- 3 red onions, finely chopped
- 3 garlic cloves, finely chopped
- 3 fresh red chillies, finely chopped
- 1 red pepper, diced into 1cm (½in) cubes
- 1 green pepper, diced into 1cm (½in) cubes
- 3 tablespoons lime or lemon juice
- 3 teaspoons ground coriander
- 3 teaspoons ground cumin
- 1 teaspoon dried oregano
- 4 tablespoons red wine vinegar
- 2–4 teaspoons golden caster sugar, to taste
- 2 teaspoons fine sea salt
- 2 tablespoons tomato purée

> Make a cross in the non-stalk end of each tomato and plunge them into boiling water for a couple of minutes or until the skins split. Remove from the water and drench in cold water to stop them cooking. Peel off the skins and cut into 1.5cm (⅝in) dice, discarding the seeds.
> Heat the oil in a large saucepan and gently fry the onions until soft. Add a little water to them if they start to stick. Add the garlic and chilli and fry gently for a couple of minutes. Add the remaining ingredients, except for the tomatoes, and stir through until hot. Add the tomatoes and taste for seasoning. Bring to the boil and simmer for 10 minutes. Bottle into warm, sterilized 500ml (18fl oz) jars, leaving 2.5cm (1in) headroom, and put on the lids (see page 205). Process in a waterbath using the hot-pack method for 15 minutes (see opposite).

ANTONIO'S PASSATA

Antonio Sanzone, Head Chef, is from Puglia. As a child, his family used to buy tomatoes when they were still slightly green for making into *passata* because they were cheaper like that, and then they would spread them out on trays to ripen in the sun at home. I have often seen tomatoes for sale in Italy marked *per passata*, for sieved tomato sauce. They give the best flavour this way and make a very versatile *passata*. Or you can take the recipe one stage further and make it into a tomato sauce before bottling.

**MAKES 3.5 LITRES (5½ PINTS)
(7 X 500ML/ 18FL OZ JARS)**

- 8 litres (14 pints) water
- 160g (5¾oz) salt
- 3kg (6lb 8oz) San Marzano tomatoes
- 7 sprigs of basil
- 7 garlic cloves, peeled and green centres removed
- 7 small fresh bay leaves, crushed
- 2 teaspoons caster sugar
- citric acid or lemon juice

> Put the water in a large saucepan over a medium heat and add the salt. Stir to dissolve. Meanwhile, wash the tomatoes. Once the water comes to the boil, drop in the tomatoes and simmer for 10–15 minutes until the skins split and the tomatoes start to soften. Use a sieve to remove the tomatoes from the pan and transfer them to a large bowl.
> Place a sprig of basil into each cold, sterilized jar, along with a garlic clove, a bay leaf, ½ teaspoon of sugar and ¼ teaspoon of citric acid or 1 tablespoon of lemon juice.
> Put the tomatoes through a *passatutto* or food mill to get rid of the skins and pips. Pour the strained tomatoes into the jars with the flavourings, leaving 1.5cm (⅝in) headroom and stir through. Fasten the lids, put the jars into a waterbath and process for approx. 45 minutes using the raw-pack method (see page 208). Leave to cool in the water. Store for up to a year in a cool, dark place.

VARIATION

ANTONIO'S TOMATO SAUCE
This tomato sauce can bottled and waterbathed to extend its shelf-life using the hot-packing method described on page 208.

**MAKES 1 LITRE (1¾ PINTS)
(2 X 500ML/ 18FL OZ JARS)**

- 2 tablespoons olive oil
- 1 red onion, finely chopped
- 1 carrot, finely chopped
- 1 celery stick, finely chopped
- 1.5 litres (1⅓ pints) tomato *passata* (see left)

> Heat the oil in a saucepan and fry the onion, carrot and celery until soft, approx. 5–10 minutes. Add the passata and bring to the boil. Reduce the heat to a simmer and cook for 30 minutes. Pour into warm, sterilized jars, leaving 2.5cm (1in) headroom and waterbath using the hot-pack method on page 208.
> To serve, heat the sauce in a pan and add salt to taste. Pour drained, cooked pasta into the sauce and toss to combine.
> For an *Arrabiata* sauce add 1 teaspoon of chilli flakes with the onion.

* BOTTLED FRUITS

Homemade bottled fruits are a marvellous shortcut for a quick dessert. Imagine Caramelized Oranges in Brandy (see pages 167–8) served with luscious whipped cream, mulled pears with cinnamon ice cream or peaches in brandy syrup. Or for breakfast or a snack, cooked apples or rhubarb is a treat with yogurt and granola.

FRUIT BOTTLING TIPS
- Always choose fruit in perfect condition.
- Take care when handling fruit not to bruise it.
- Use a sterilized chopstick to push the fruit down in the jar so it is totally submerged in the sugar syrup.
- After heat-processing, allow the jars to cool for 5 minutes in the waterbath before lifting them out carefully with

jar lifters; make sure you keep the jars upright and handle with care.

- Store in a cool, dry, dark place.
- If you have any fruit syrup left over after bottling your fruits, you can always bottle it separately in sterilized jars and waterbath as before or keep it in the refrigerator for up to 2 weeks. We like to thicken the syrup slightly first by boiling rapidly for 5 minutes or until it thickens to our liking. Use it for sweetening cocktails or fruit salad.

PEARS IN SPICED RED WINE SYRUP

For a sumptuous pudding in a hurry, open a jar of these and serve with whipped cream sweetened with caster sugar and a dash of amaretto liqueur.

MAKES 3 X 1 LITRE (1¾ PINTS) JARS

- 1 litre (1¾ pints) red wine
- 2 tablespoons mild honey
- 300g (10½oz) light soft brown sugar
- 12–16 pears, peeled, quartered and cored
- 3 x 5cm (2in) cinnamon sticks
- 9 cloves
- 3 star anise (optional)
- 3 strips of orange zest

> Put the wine, honey and sugar in a medium saucepan and bring to the boil to dissolve the sugar. Divide and hot-pack the pears and spices between three warm, sterilized jars. Pour over the hot syrup, leaving 1.5cm (⅝in) headroom, wipe the rims and put on the lids. Remove any air bubbles. Process in a waterbath using the hot-pack method for 25 minutes (see page 208). Allow to stand for 5 minutes in the water before removing the jars with jar lifters. Store in a cool, dark place for up to a year. Once opened keep in the refrigerator and consume within 5 days.

VARIATIONS

PEARS IN CINNAMON AND VANILLA SYRUP

Follow the recipe for Pears in Spiced Red Wine Syrup (see left), replacing the wine, honey and sugar with 500ml (18fl oz) water and 200g (7oz) golden granulated or caster sugar. Flavour each jar of pears with a split vanilla pod, 2 strips of lemon zest and a cinnamon stick. Process as before.

PEACHES IN BRANDY SYRUP

Follow the recipe for Pears in Spiced Red Wine Syrup (see left), replacing the wine, honey and sugar with 600ml (20fl oz) water, 500g (1lb 2oz) golden caster sugar and 400ml (14fl oz) brandy or amaretto. Blanch the peaches in boiling water and slip off the skins. Cut them in half and remove the stones. Divide the peaches between the jars, omitting the flavourings and top up with the amaretto sugar syrup. Process in a waterbath using the hot-pack method for 10 minutes (see page 208).

COOKED APPLE SLICES

Follow the recipe on page 236 but instead of freezing pour hot into warm, clean 500ml (18fl oz) or 1 litre (1¾ pints) jars, leaving 1.5cm (⅝in) headroom. Wipe the jar rims to ensure a good seal. Remove any air bubbles and put on the lids. Process in a waterbath using the hot-pack method for 20 minutes for both jar sizes (see page 208). Allow to stand for 5 minutes in the water before removing the jars with jar lifters. Store in a cool, dark place for up to a year. Once opened, keep in the refrigerator and consume within 5 days.

FRUIT PURÉES

Any high-acid fruit purée can be sweetened or left natural and hot-packed for 15 minutes for both 500ml (18fl oz) and 1 litre (1¾ pints) jars, leaving 1cm (½in) headroom.

COOKED RHUBARB

I like to add only a little sugar to this and use the natural sweet flavour of vanilla to counter the acidity of the rhubarb. I eat it cold with yogurt or dress it with crumble (see page 236) and bake it until bubbling hot.

MAKES APPROX. 1 LITRE (1¾ PINTS) JAR OR 2 X 500ML (18FL OZ) JARS

- 1kg (2lb 4oz) rhubarb
- 1 vanilla pod, split or a few drops of vanilla extract
- up to 250g (9oz) granulated caster sugar, to taste

> Wash and chop the rhubarb into bite-sized pieces. Put into a saucepan with the vanilla and a little sugar over a low heat.

> Stir frequently until the water comes out of the rhubarb. Bring to the boil and taste, adjusting the sugar as necessary. Remove the vanilla pod and bottle straight away into hot, clean 500ml (18fl oz) or 1 litre (1¾ pints) jars, leaving 1.5cm (⅝in) headroom and removing any air bubbles. Wipe the jars to ensure a good seal and put on the lids.

> Process in a waterbath using the hot-pack method for 15 minutes for 500ml (18fl oz) and 1 litre (1¾ pints) jars (see page 208). Allow to stand for 5 minutes in the water before removing the jars with jar lifters. Store in a cool, dark place for up to a year. Once opened keep in the refrigerator and consume within 5 days.

VARIATION

Add a little grated fresh or stem ginger or a length of orange peel to the rhubarb in place of the vanilla.

CORDIALS

Follow the steps below to extend the shelf-life of the cordial recipes in the Sugar chapter (see pages 61–2). These instructions are based on Pam Corbin's advice in her wonderful book *Preserves*.

Sterilize the corks, swing-top lids, screw tops and all bottles by putting them into your waterbath and bringing them to the boil. Store them in the waterbath until you are ready to use them.

Fill the bottles with cordial. Allow 2.5cm (1in) headroom for screw-top and swing-top bottles or 3cm (1¼in) for cork tops.

Seal the lids: avoid tightening the lids completely on screw-top bottles to allow steam to escape; swing tops are fitted with a rubber seal that allows steam to escape so these can be closed; corks should be sealed onto the bottles with insulation tape or wires to stop them popping off during heat-processing.

Stand the bottles upright in the waterbath, placing them on a folded tea towel or a piece of cardboard so that they do not come into direct contact with the base of the pan. If necessary, wrap a tea towel in between the jars to stop them clattering around, but make sure that the water can travel easily between them.

Fill the pan with water to within 2.5cm (1in) from the top of the bottles. Bring to a simmer (88°C/190°F) and keep at that temperature for 20 minutes.

Remove from the heat and allow the bottles to stand for 5 minutes before carefully removing them from the water, keeping them upright. Place them on a heatproof surface to cool completely.

Fasten the lids tightly before storing. Corks should be sealed afterwards by dipping them into melted paraffin or beeswax.

Store in a cool, dark place for up to a year. Once opened, keep in the refrigerator and consume within 3 weeks.

For fruit sauces such as Cranberry Sauce (page 54), process as for the Fruit Purées (see left).

* LOW-ACID RECIPES

The recipes that follow must be heat-processed in a pressure canner for long-term storage (see page 205). This is because they are low-acid recipes. Follow the instructions carefully regarding processing times. Note that if you decide to alter the recipes we cannot guarantee that they will be suitable for long-term storage.

PRESSURE CANNING

We recommend that you buy a pressure canner fitted with a weighted dial, otherwise it has to be checked every year. You can buy a tester in the US and do this yourself, see suppliers on page 243. Ours is a 23-quart pressure canner made by Presto, it has a weighted gauge and dial gauge so it does not need the annual check-up (refer to the USDA website for how to care for your pressure canner). The weighted gauge may mean you end up processing over the recommended pressure of 10–11 psi, however it is better to err on the side of caution.

Pressure canners can be bought online; they are usually imported from the US. We have given basic instructions for pressure canning, however always refer to the manufacturer's instructions as different brands vary slightly.

PRESSURE CANNING METHOD (LOW-ACID FOODS)

This method is suitable for processing low-acid foods (see page 203), which must be heated to 115°C (239°F) to kill botulism spores. Note that no other heat-processing method will achieve this temperature.

For hot food, use hot water in your pressure canner and warm, clean jars. For cold food, use cold water in your pressure canner and cold, clean jars.

Make sure you use specialist jars for pressure canning with two-part lids (see page 204). The disc-shaped lids should be brand new; screw bands can be reused as long as they are in perfect condition. Always follow the recipe carefully regarding jar size because different sized jars will require different processing times.

Put the rack into the pressure canner and fill with approx. 8cm (3¼in) cold or hot water, depending on whether you are processing cold or hot food. This is the correct amount for up to 40 minutes processing; add more water if processing for longer.

Fill the sterilized jars with food almost to the top, leaving 2.5–3cm (1–1¼in) headroom, depending on how much the food will expand, and remove any air bubbles with a sterilized chopstick (see page 205). Put on the lids (see page 205); note that screw bands should not be fully tightened at this stage. Wipe off any splashes around the lid with kitchen paper.

Lower the filled jars into the canner, keeping them upright at all times. Wind a tea towel around the jars to stop them clattering about; this isn't necessary if you have a specialist rack designed to keep the jars apart. For best results, jars should be at least 2cm (¾in) apart to allow the water to circulate around them.

Put the lid on the canner, leaving the weight off the petlock or vent port. Place the canner over a high heat and allow the steam to vent vigorously for 10 minutes at full strength before putting on the weight. The pressure will rise, as seen on the dial gauge, and the weighted gauge will begin to jiggle. When the pressure specified in the recipe is reached, normally this is 10 pounds, start your timer. Process for the time indicated in the recipe. If necessary, adjust the heat to maintain the correct pressure for the full time. Note that if the pressure drops below the specified amount during processing you will have to start the whole process again from the beginning – as before, wait until the correct pressure is achieved before starting your timer.

Once the time is up, switch off the heat and allow the canner to depressurize and cool. Don't attempt to remove the weight and lid until the dial gauge reads zero. Remove the weight first. If there is no more hissing, you can carefully open the lid – standing at arm's length to avoid any hot steam. Remove the jars from the canner with tongs, keeping them upright. Put them on a heat-resistant surface and allow them to cool completely. Check the seals after 24 hours (see page 205).

VEGETABLE CANNING TIPS

- Always choose young, tender vegetables in perfect condition.
- Can vegetables as soon as possible after picking and avoid bruising.
- Vegetables can be raw-packed as in the Peas in Sweet Brine or hot-packed as in the Bottled Asparagus.
- If using salt, only use pure sea salt without anti-caking agents and iodine.
- Use a sterilized chopstick to push the vegetables down in the jar so they are totally submerged in the brine.

- After heat-processing, allow the jars to cool for 5 minutes in the pressure canner before lifting them out carefully with jar lifters; make sure you keep the jars upright and handle with care.
- Store in a cool, dry, dark place.

PEAS IN SWEET BRINE

I have a guilty secret of really liking canned peas. These bottled peas make a great standby vegetable to serve with steak or to put into an egg frittata.

> Wash the peas in plenty of cold water. Raw-pack into cold sterilized jars, leaving 4cm (1½in) headroom. Add ½ teaspoon of salt and ½ teaspoon of caster sugar to each 500ml (18fl oz) jar. Pour boiling water over them, leaving 2.5cm (1in) headroom. Remove the air bubbles with a sterilized chopstick and fasten on the lids (see page 205). Process 500ml (18fl oz) jars at 10 pounds pressure for 40 minutes in a pressure canner (see left). Keep in a cool, dark place for up to a year.

BOTTLED GREEN BEANS

We grow runner and long beans in our garden, both are ideal for bottling. Although I must admit I prefer to freeze them or make them into a curry, see page 219, bottling beans keeps the space at maximum in my freezer.

> Raw-pack following the instructions for Peas in Sweet Brine (see above), omitting the sugar and leaving 2.5cm (1in) headroom. Process 500ml (18fl oz) jars in a pressure canner for 20 minutes and 1 litre (1¾ pints) jars for 25 minutes at 10 pounds pressure. Keep in a cool, dark place for up to a year.

BOTTLED ASPARAGUS

Canning is the perfect way to make the most of the asparagus season. By preserving them in lightly salted water their taste is not altered in any way. To serve, simply heat and dress with lemon and butter or toss cold into a salad.

- fresh asparagus
- fine salt (optional)

> Wash and trim the asparagus, removing the tough woody ends. Wash again in cold water. Either leave whole or cut into pieces. Plunge the asparagus into boiling water for 3 minutes then, using tongs, pack into clean, hot Mason or Balls jars leaving 2.5cm (1in) headroom. Discard the cooking water and boil fresh water to pour over them as it can be bitter. The spears should stand tall but not be too tightly packed so that the water can circulate around them. Pour over boiling water leaving 2.5cm (1in) headroom. Add ½ teaspoon of salt to 500ml (18fl oz) jars and 1 teaspoon to 1 litre (1¾ pints) jars if you wish. Wipe the seals and fasten the lids, finger tight. Process for 30 minutes for 500ml (18fl oz) jars and 40 minutes for litre jars at 10 pounds pressure in a pressure canner. Keep in a cool, dark place for up to a year.

GARDEN IN A JAR

I love this versatile mixture of vegetables. I try to use as much homegrown produce as possible, picking and canning in the same day. The jars make a great standby vegetable to serve I serve them heated straight from the jar with grilled meats and hot chicken or stir them into fried onion adding some Bottled Whole Tomatoes (page 207), a dash of red wine, a sprig of thyme and a little tomato purée for a quick ratatouille.

- Use a mixture of carrots, courgettes, peppers, butter beans, peas, onions, and tomatoes. (Even if you add tomatoes to this mixture, process in a pressure canner as you cannot be sure the amount will have enough acid to waterbath.)

> Hot-pack the vegetables into 500ml (18fl oz) or 1 litre (1¾ pints) jars, top up with boiling water, leaving 2.5cm (1in) headroom. Add ½ teaspoon of salt for 500ml (18fl oz) jars and 1 teaspoon for litre jars. Remove the air bubbles with a sterilized chopstick and fasten on the lids (see page 205). Process 500ml (18fl oz) jars at 10 pounds pressure for 1½ hours and 1 litre (1¾ pints) jars for 1½ hours in a pressure canner (see pages 213–14). Keep in a cool, dark place for up to a year.

TUSCAN RAGÙ

This is Giancarlo's staple *ragù* recipe, which we always have in the house. It is perfect for lasagne or simply eaten with hot pasta. Any leftover pasta already mixed with the sauce can be heated up the next day in the oven with cream and grated cheese for *pasta al forno*. Giancarlo's father made this *ragù* every ten days for himself until he was 84 years old. He kept his in jars in the refrigerator, eating a jar every lunchtime at noon with hot pasta. When he ran out, it was time to make some more. Now we are into pressure canning, Giancarlo makes a big batch every few months and stores the jars in our garage.

MAKES 4 X 1 LITRE (1¾ PINTS) JARS – EACH ONE SERVES 10

- 6 tablespoons olive oil
- 800g (1lb 12oz) *soffritto* (see pages 231–3)
- 2 garlic cloves, peeled but left whole

>>>

- 1 sprig of rosemary
- 1kg (2lb 4oz) minced pork
- 1kg (2lb 4oz) minced beef
- 400ml (14fl oz) red wine
- 1.5 litres (2⅓ pints) Antonio's *Passata* (see pages 209–10)
- salt and freshly ground black pepper

> Heat the olive oil in a large, non-stick frying pan, add the soffritto and cook over a medium heat for approx. 15 minutes. Add the garlic and rosemary.

> Increase the heat, add the pork and beef and cook until the liquid from the meat has evaporated. Keep stirring so that the mixture does not stick to the bottom of the pan. When it feels dry, add the red wine and stir well – notice how the smell changes once the alcohol has burned off after a few minutes then add the tomato passata, stirring well to combine. Bring to the boil, then reduce the heat and simmer, uncovered, for approx. 2 hours. Stir frequently to make sure it doesn't catch on the bottom of the pan and add a little hot water if it looks dry. Taste and adjust the seasoning if necessary. Scoop off any excess oil with a spoon and discard.

> Either use immediately or pour into warm, sterilized 500ml (18fl oz) or 1 litre (1¾ pints) jars, leaving 2.5cm (1in) headroom. Wipe the top of the jars with water or vinegar to ensure a good seal and fasten the lids, finger tight. Process immediately while still hot. Process both jar sizes for 25 minutes at 10 pounds pressure in a pressure canner (see pages 213–14). Store in a cool, dark place for up to a year. Once opened keep the jar in the refrigerator for up to 10 days.

> NOTE: Instead of pressure canning, the *ragù* can be frozen in sealed plastic containers; use within 3 months.

ALTITUDE

Water boils at different temperatures according to your altitude and the barometric pressure of your location – so the higher you are, the more time it takes to process your food. We have based our recipes on locations below 1,000 feet above sea level, as nearly all of the inhabited areas of the UK are below that, however if you live outside the UK please refer to the chart below and adjust the timings accordingly.

This chart is based on one in *Ball's Blue Book Guide to Preserving*, which is a great sourcebook for those wishing to preserve a lot of produce using the heat-processing method.

WATERBATHING

ALTITUDE IN FEET	INCREASE IN PROCESSING TIME
1,001–3,000	5 minutes
3,001–6,000	10 minutes
6,001–8,000	15 minutes
8,001–10,000	20 minutes

PRESSURE CANNING

ALTITUDE IN FEET	WEIGHTED GAUGE	DIAL GAUGE
0–1,000	10	11
1,001–2,000	15	11
2,001–4,000	15	12
4,001–6,000	15	13
6,001–8,000	1	5
148,001–10,000	15	15

ZUPPA DI FAGIOLI – BEAN SOUP

Bean soups are popular all over Italy, but particularly in Tuscany where the Tuscans are known as the *mangiafagioli*, the bean-eaters. Giancarlo grew up eating bean soup; his mother grew cannellini and borlotti beans in her garden and dried them every year so that they could provide the family with 'poor man's meat,' as they were known, to last throughout winter. I was even told when I was about to marry Giancarlo that I should learn to make bean soup – as every Tuscan expects it from his wife!

This is an easy soup to make with a good herby base flavour provided by the *soffritto* (see pages 231–3). Other beans can be used for this, such as small white haricots. For a thicker soup, blend one-third of the soup and add back to the rest. We often stir in cooked pasta at the end to make *pasta fagioli*. Alternatively, we add a couple of tablespoons of tomato purée to 1 litre (1¾ pints) of soup with some cooked sausages for a sausage casserole.

SERVES 12 (MAKES 3 X 500ML/ 18FL OZ JARS)

- 6 tablespoons extra virgin olive oil
- 600g (1lb 5oz) *soffritto* (see pages 231–3)
- 2 sprigs of rosemary
- 3 garlic cloves, peeled and lightly crushed with the flat of a knife
- 500g (1lb 2oz) borlotti or cannellini beans, soaked overnight and drained
- 2.5 litres (4 pints) Brown Chicken Stock (see pages 229–30) or vegetable stock
- 1 teaspoon bicarbonate of soda

> Heat the olive oil in a large, heavy-based saucepan and fry the soffritto with the rosemary and garlic for approx. 5 minutes. Add the beans and stir through, pour in the stock and bring to the boil. Simmer gently for 30 minutes. (If you plan to eat

some of the soup straight away, you will need to cook the beans for a further 1½ hours until tender.) Scoop off any excess oil with a spoon and discard.

> Add the bicarbonate of soda to soften the bean skins and stir well. Pour into warm, sterilized jars, leaving 3cm (1¼in) headroom, wipe the top of the jars with water or vinegar to ensure a good seal and fasten the lids, finger tight. Process for 1½ hours at 10 pounds pressure in a pressure canner (see pages 213–14). Store in a cool, dark place for up to a year. Once opened, keep in the refrigerator and use within 4 days.

CASSOULET

This recipe by Richard Bertinet is totally delicious. It makes a real meat feast that is great for a special occasion. We make some to eat straight away and then have fun bottling the rest to enjoy another day when we know all we need to do is open the jar and reheat until piping hot.

MAKES APPROX. 4 X 1 LITRE (1¾ PINTS) JARS

- 6 medium onions
- 3 cloves
- 1 large, thick piece of pork rind
- 500g (1lb 2oz) haricot blanc, soaked overnight and drained
- 4 carrots, cut into 5mm (¼in) dice
- 1 bay leaf
- 6 black peppercorns
- 8 garlic cloves
- 400g (14oz) *pancetta*, cut into lardons
- 175ml (6fl oz) dry white wine
- 800g (1lb 12oz) diced leg of mutton
- 1 portion of duck confit (see pages 155–6)
- 6 very ripe tomatoes or 4 tablespoons tomato purée
- 8 Toulouse sausages
- salt and freshly ground black pepper

>>>

TO SERVE

- 200g (7oz) stale bread
- a small bunch of curly parsley, roughly chopped
- 50g (1¾oz) butter

> Peel one of the onions and push the sharp pointed end of the cloves into it. Peel the other onions and dice.
> Take a large, heavy-based casserole and line the bottom with the pork rind, skin-side down. Scatter over the beans and add the diced carrot, diced onion and whole, studded onion. Add the bay leaf and peppercorns. Keeping the skins on, crush the garlic cloves with the flat side of a knife and add to the pan with the pancetta. Pour over the wine and top up the pan with cold water to cover. Put the pan over a medium heat and bring to the boil. Reduce the heat and simmer gently, stirring occasionally.
> Season the pieces of mutton. Add 4 tablespoons of the duck fat from the duck confit to a frying pan and put on a high heat. Add the mutton and fry until it is browned. Add the browned meat and the cooking juices, to the casserole pan and simmer gently, covered, for 1½ hours.
> Meanwhile, prepare the tomatoes (if using). Score each one with a cross, plunge into boiling water for 30 seconds and then into cold water. Peel off the skins, cut into quarters and scoop out the seeds and juice. Chop the flesh into small dice.
> Add the tomatoes (or tomato purée) to the casserole with the sausages, stir through and simmer for a further 30 minutes, covered. Finally, stir in the pieces of duck from the confit. Continue to cook for a further 30 minutes until the beans are tender and the meat is heated through and starting to disintegrate

slightly. Remove from the heat, put a lid on the pot and set aside to cool overnight. Scoop off any excess oil with a spoon and discard. Either eat straight away, keep in the refrigerator for up to a week or can it in a pressure canner. To do this, pick the meat from the bones and cut the sausages into thirds, add to the casserole and discard the bones. This is so that the sauce can pass easily between the smaller pieces of meat and the cassoulet can be thoroughly heated in the jars in the canner. Discard the pork rind and whole studded onion. Reheat the casserole so that the cassoulet is bubbling, adding a little hot water or stock to make sure there is enough liquid to cover the meat and beans, then hot-pack into hot 1 litre (1¾ pints) jars. Process in a pressure canner for 1½ hours at 10 pounds pressure.

> To serve, discard the pork rind and the whole studded onion (if the cassoulet wasn't canned) and decant your cassoulet into an ovenproof dish. Blitz the stale bread in a blender to make breadcrumbs, add the parsley, butter and 2 tablespoons of the fat from the duck confit. Scatter the breadcrumbs over the top of the cassoulet and bake in the oven at 180°C/350°F/gas 4 for approx. 45 minutes or until heated through.

GREEN BEAN CURRY

Manjula Samarasinghe, who I travelled around Sri Lanka with, gave me this recipe. Here the spice paste is enriched with coconut milk to form a creamy sauce that works well with a variety of vegetables, such as green beans, potatoes, mushrooms, lentils and okra.

MAKES 3 X 500ML (18FL OZ) JARS (EACH JAR SERVES 4)

- 1kg (2lb 4oz) green beans – French or runner
- 1 portion of Sri Lankan Spice Paste for Vegetable Curries (see pages 233–4)
- 2 x 400ml (14fl oz) cans coconut milk
- 200ml (7fl oz) water
- fine sea salt, to taste
- dried red chilli flakes, to taste

> This recipe couldn't be simpler. Top and tail the beans and cut into bite-sized lengths approx. 3cm (1¼in). Simply spoon the paste into a large, non-stick frying pan and add the beans, coconut milk and water. Cook over a medium heat for approx. 5 minutes. Taste and adjust the seasoning if necessary with salt and more chilli if you like it hot. Spoon the curry into warm, sterilized 500ml (18fl oz) or 1 litre (1¾ pints) jars, leaving 2.5cm (1in) headroom, fasten the lids and process for 30 minutes at 10 pounds pressure in a pressure canner (see pages 213–14). Store for up to a year in a dark, cool place. Once opened, consume within 3 days and store in the refrigerator.

BEETROOT CURRY

We grow beetroot every year but I had never thought of putting them into a delicious curry before our visit to Sri Lanka. Their earthy sweetness works brilliantly in spicy dishes such as this. I like to serve this with the Green Bean Curry (see left) and rice.

MAKES 4 X 500ML (18FL OZ) JARS (EACH JAR SERVES 4)

- 3 shallots or 1 onion, finely sliced
- 3 tablespoons coconut oil
- 2 portions of Sri Lankan Spice Paste for Vegetable Curries (see pages 233–4)
- ½ raw beetroot, peeled and cut into matchsticks
- 850ml (1½ pints) water or coconut milk or the two combined
- fine sea salt, to taste
- dried red chilli flakes, to taste

> In a large, non-stick frying pan, fry the shallots in the oil over a low heat until soft. Add the paste and cook for 3 minutes, stirring, until the paste darkens slightly. Add the beetroot and stir well to coat it in the spices. Cover with a lid and cook over a low heat for 5 minutes until soft. Add the water or coconut milk. Taste and adjust the seasoning if necessary with salt and a little more chilli if you like it hot. Scoop off any excess oil with a spoon and discard. Spoon into warm, sterilized 500ml (18fl oz) or 1 litre (1¾ pints) jars, leaving 2.5cm (1in) headroom. Wipe the rims, fasten the lids and process 500ml (18fl oz) jars for 35 minutes and 1 litre (1¾ pints) jars for 40 minutes at 10 pounds pressure in a pressure canner (see pages 213–14). Store for up to a year in a dark, cool place. Once opened, consume within 3 days and store in the refrigerator.

COLD

Chilling and freezing are among the earliest and least complicated methods of preserving. When you chill food you slow the growth of micro-organisms, which means that you delay spoiling and rotting. If you take the process further to freezing point this growth is halted completely, until the food is warmed again. Most foods are not changed by chilling or freezing, unlike other methods of preserving that transform them in some way. Colour, texture, vitamins and minerals are kept intact and if foods are frozen as soon as possible after picking they will actually have more nutritional value than fresh ones that have been travelling for days.

* CHILLING

Before refrigerators became commonplace in the 1950s, families had to use the coolest part of the house to store their produce – perhaps a larder, cellar or outside space. Our house was built in the 1960s and sadly a larder wasn't included in the original plan. However, I have learned to store all kinds of fruit, herbs and vegetables very happily in securely covered boxes in the cool air of our garage. They last much longer out there and don't take up room in my refrigerator. Potatoes are ideal for storing in a dark garage or shed, preferably in paper or hessian sacks with the neck slightly open to allow excess moisture to escape; moisture and light are the enemy, so don't store them in plastic bags! Empty your bags or sacks out every now and again to check none of the potatoes are going bad, and no pests or insects have got in.

In Italy many people still have a cantina. Similar to an American root cellar it is an area below ground or in a cool, insulated area of the house with a north-facing window and an earth or gravel floor to provide some humidity and help regulate the temperature throughout the year. The first time I saw Giancarlo's family cantina it was like finding an Aladdin's cave full of gleaming jars of *ragù*, tomato passata, peas in brine and jams, all with their handwritten labels. Our friend Nello, a Tuscan smallholder, keeps his legs of prosciutto in his cantina, hanging them above boxes of ripening tomatoes, drying onions and garlic, and dried corn and bread for the chickens. The produce to be kept cooler is close to the ground, whereas vinegars and wines, which need a small amount of warmth for fermentation, are kept higher up.

Our grandparents' generation wrapped apples individually in newspaper and kept them in crates or cardboard boxes in a cold place in the house; this is a great practice to revive. You just need to check your storage box regularly because if one fruit goes bad the ethylene it gives off will hasten the ripening of the others, hence the expression 'one bad apple spoils the barrel'. Some people swear by storing dried elderflowers in with their apples to help them keep better – and lend their floral-pineapple taste to the apples as a bonus. You can use the same cold storage method for quinces, Sharon fruit and unripe tomatoes, just bringing out a few before you need them to give them a chance to ripen.

STORING IN SAND

An alternative for root vegetables is to store them in a child's sandpit or in silver sand or sawdust in wooden or cardboard boxes, raised up from the ground so they don't become damp – this way, they will keep over winter. Separate each vegetable into its own box and label it, so you don't have to do a lucky dip each time you need a carrot or parsnip!

CHILLING IN THE GROUND

If you grow your own vegetables, one of the simplest ways to keep them cool is just to leave them in the ground, rather than pulling them up, provided you have well-drained soil. Parsnips and carrots, potatoes, Brussels sprouts, cabbages, Jerusalem artichokes, leeks and cauliflowers can all be treated in this way, but should be covered with fleece or straw to protect them from severe frost and snow. Some root vegetables such as carrots and parsnips actually become sweeter when left in the ground as the sugar content of the root increases in the cold.

CLAMPING

Clamping, or storing harvested root vegetables outside in mounds of earth, is an effective way to keep them cool and fresh during the winter months. My grandfather, Leonard Beresford, who was Town Clerk of Littlehampton in the 1930s and 1940s, used to advise people on how to grow and store vegetables in this way as one of his wartime duties. He and my late father dug up their neat little lawn, much to my grandmother's disapproval, and gave it over to rows of carrots, potatoes and parsnips, which, when harvested, could be buried in earth and straw for months. The store would be sealed up with hessian to keep the vegetables cold but above freezing point and also to keep out oxygen, frost, excess moisture and light, all of which could encourage them to decay. In Italy, Giancarlo remembers his family doing the same thing: one of his jobs was to go out and fetch the potatoes and carrots from their clamps throughout the winter.

If you want to try clamping, only use vegetables in perfect condition and remove stalks and leaves first, as these will rot. Never wash vegetables before storing them. Find an area of dry ground on which to mound up your vegetables and dig a shallow trench 15cm (6in) deep almost all around it so that rainwater is able to drain away easily. (The part that is left is where you will tread to get to your store.) Next put a layer of straw down on the ground followed by your vegetables. Cover the vegetables with a thick layer of straw and top with a layer of soil from the trench you have dug. Some people finish with a layer of plastic to protect against heavy rain, but this is a more modern addition. If you do use plastic, make sure it doesn't tightly surround the clamp, making it completely airtight, or condensation will set in.

* FREEZING

Freezing is an efficient form of preserving that doesn't change the flavour and texture of most foods. Big in the 1950s and 1960s, it has recently become more associated with bags of pre-chopped frozen vegetables, burgers and ready meals, rather than being appreciated for what it really is – that is, a brilliant way to preserve all kinds of food. Now, thankfully, creative freezing is becoming fashionable again. It is a perfect method of storing everything from nuts and leftover egg whites to your own sauces and bases for curries, etc.

Clarence Birdseye may have made the biggest impact on the consumer when he perfected the art of mass-freezing, packaging and selling frozen food to the public in 1930, however the first meat to be frozen, thanks to the force of nature, was probably that of mammoths, who have been discovered frozen intact after 15,000 years. According to the Inuits, who have been known to dip into their supply of frozen mammoth in hard times, the meat is still good enough to eat, if a little tough! The early Japanese and Koreans freeze-dried their fish, Indigenous peoples in Peru and Bolivia freeze-dried potatoes, while the Ancient Chinese, Greeks and Romans stored ice and mountain snow in cellars or icehouses to keep food cold.

Freezing has been practised all over the world throughout history as a way of preserving food. In 1574 Nicolás Monardes, the Spanish physician, wrote of ice being transported to Paris all the way from Flanders. This allowed a whole new form of food to be developed, from chilled jellies to frosted fruits and iced sherbets. In England, James I commissioned the first brick-lined, round 'ice houses' for Greenwich Park and Hampton Court Palace in the 17th century, and by the 19th century there were

3,000 ice houses in wealthy family homes throughout the UK; many of these igloo-like structures still exist today. In 1819 the architect John Buonarotti Papworth wrote: 'the icehouse forms an excellent larder for the preservation of every kind of food liable to be injured by heat in summer; thus fish, game, poultry, butter, etc. may be kept for a considerable time'.

In the late 18th century Alexander Dalrymple, a Scot who worked for the British East India Company, noted the way Chinese fishermen used ice to transport their fish. He brought the idea home and before long Scottish fishermen, with the help of MP George Dempster, started to use this method to transport their fish further afield for sale. Ice revolutionized fish sales in the UK and helped the Scottish fishermen to earn a fair wage. It wasn't long after this that blocks of ice were taken to sea on boats in order to freeze the fish as soon as it was caught – the first step towards state-of-the-art freezing of fish at sea.

In the 1920s and 1930s inventor Clarence Birdseye (who had worked as a fur trapper in Canada and seen the way fish froze quickly once caught, but tasted the same when thawed) battled against his own poverty and the public's fear of the new to develop the first method of fast freezing and packing food. His wife Eleanor had to put up with fish flipping around in her bathtub as Clarence continued his quest, but finally his determination paid off when he discovered a way of fast-freezing foods by sandwiching them between plates which were dipped into a brine of calcium chloride. In 1929 he received a $22 million pay-out for his invention and in 1930 the first quick-frozen produce was sold to the public.

OUR FAVOURITE FREEZER ITEMS:

SPICE CUBES (see page 227) to use as a shortcut for everyday cooking.

SLICED SOURDOUGH BREAD so we never run out of fresh bread.

SOFFRITTO (see pages 231–3) to use as a base for soups and ragùs.

SPICE PASTES (see pages 232–7) to use as shortcuts for dinner every week.

BEEF (see page 226), chicken thighs, sausages.

BISCUIT DOUGH (see page 225).

REDUCED STOCK (see pages 230–2) for gravies, risottos and soups.

PESTO CUBES for quick pasta suppers (see page 227).

FROZEN BANANAS, GRAPES, BERRIES AND PLUMS for smoothies (see pages 238-41).

NOTES ON HOME FREEZING

TEMPERATURE This should be kept between -12°C (10°F) and -9°C (16°F). If you are going to freeze a big batch of food, remember to switch the freezer onto 'fast freeze' a couple of hours beforehand so that your food can be frozen as quickly as possible. This keeps the ice crystals as small as possible and causes less damage to the cells of the food.

RESTOCKING YOUR FREEZER Don't cram as much fresh food as possible into your freezer in one go – it will raise the temperature of the freezer. Ideally you should freeze no more than 10 per cent of the total capacity in one go.

VACUUM BAGS These work really well. Not only do they reduce the chance of freezer burn (see right), but you also end up with flat bags that take up much less space in the freezer. To use, simply fill the pouches and then suck out the air using a pump. If you don't have a pump, you can use a straw to suck out the air from the bag before quickly sealing it.

FREEZER BURN This happens when water evaporates from the surface of the food in the freezer air. It leaves behind empty pockets that appear like white spots. Although freezer burn is not harmful it does affect flavour and texture. To prevent freezer burn, choose containers that provide a snug fit, to eliminate as much air as possible. Vacuum freezer bags also work well in this respect (see left).

LABELLING It sounds pedantic, but life is much easier if you label whatever you freeze – and in the case of sauces and stocks, remind yourself of what quantity is in each portion. For example, I freeze Thai green curry paste in labelled portions that are the right size for a curry for four.

KEEP A LIST If your freezer is big and stuffed with little pots of sauces, spice cubes or vegetables, it is a really good idea to keep a list of what is in there. An inventory helps you see what you have and shows you what needs using up sooner rather than later. Keep the list on a tablet computer or mobile phone and add and delete items as necessary.

SAFE DEFROSTING Meat, fish and poultry should ideally be defrosted slowly in the refrigerator. This way, they will never be in the 'danger zone' at which bacteria start to grow (5–57°C/41–135°F). For speedy defrosting, put the meat in a plastic bag in a sink of cold water; if the water becomes warm, change it to cold again. Microwaving is only recommended if used on the appropriate 'defrost' setting and only for small cuts that won't take too long to defrost (otherwise the meat will start to cook). Always cook food as soon as it has defrosted.

REFREEZING It is perfectly safe to freeze items that you have cooked from a previously frozen piece of meat. For example, it's fine to defrost raw chicken overnight in the refrigerator, cook it thoroughly the next day into a curry and re-freeze it when it is cold as a curry. What you mustn't do is defrost meat and poultry and re-freeze it again without cooking.

LIQUIDS I expect most of us have inadvertently frozen a bottle of wine we were trying to chill in a hurry. Either the bottle has cracked or the cork has come out. This is because liquid expands by 10 per cent when frozen. As a general rule, don't overfill containers. Make sure you leave at least 2cm (¾in) headroom to allow for expansion; this will prevent lids being forced off during freezing.

WHAT TO FREEZE AND HOW?

Most foods freeze well and as a rule of thumb can be frozen for up to 3 months without harm; after this time they may start to deteriorate. Some vegetables are held in suspended animation if frozen immediately after being picked – for example, peas are arguably better transported frozen rather than fresh. Other foods, such as strawberries, retain their flavour but may lose their texture (refer to 'What not to freeze' on page 226 or a guide on things to avoid).

• **FRUIT AND VEGETABLES**

RAW VEGETABLES Blanch in boiling water for 3 minutes before freezing; refresh under cold running water and drain really well. Blanching destroys most enzymes and bacteria and helps maintain colour, texture, flavour and vitamin C.

ELDERFLOWERS AND WILD BERRIES, SUCH AS ELDERBERRIES, SLOES AND ROSEHIPS Gather these as you find them and 'open freeze' on a tray in the freezer. Once frozen, pack into freezer bags and seal.

HERBS Either finely chop and 'dry freeze' on trays (see pages 226–8) or combine with olive oil and freeze in ice-cube trays .

EGG WHITES Keep a container in the freezer for raw egg whites and add to it whenever you separate eggs for baking. To turn your egg whites into meringues, simply defrost them and whisk in double their weight of sugar.

HARD CHEESE AND BUTTER Seal in vacuum bags or wrap tightly in foil. Defrost in the refrigerator overnight. Grated Parmesan also stores well.

• EVERYDAY BASICS

BREAD Cut whole loaves into slices first and pack into ziplock bags – this way, you can take out individual slices for toasting straight from the freezer (whereas whole loaves would take considerably longer to defrost and could dry out). Part-baked loaves are also ideal for freezing – just finish off in the oven.

BREADCRUMBS AND NUTS These are perfectly fine frozen. Pile them into freezer bags, taking care to expel as much air as possible, label and pop in the freezer.

CRUMBLE TOPPING This freezes well and is a great shortcut when you are cooking in a hurry. A basic recipe for six is: 250g (9oz) butter, 250g (9oz) plain flour, 250g (9oz) caster sugar and 300g (10½oz) ground almonds. Simply rub the butter into the flour to form breadcrumbs (I use a food processor for this) and stir in the sugar and almonds. Pack into a sealed container and freeze until needed.

BISCUIT DOUGH It is always worth doubling recipes for biscuit dough and keeping a batch in the freezer ready to go. A good shortcut is to shape the dough into three log shapes and freeze wrapped in sheets of baking parchment. Then all you have to do is cut out the shapes and bake them in the oven when you need them. To make 50-60 x 4cm (1½in) diameter almond biscuits: mix 125g (4½oz) salted butter or unsalted butter with a pinch of salt, 125g (4½oz) golden caster sugar, 125g (4½oz) plain or '00' flour, 125g (4½oz) ground almonds, 20ml (4 teaspoons) double cream, seeds from 1 vanilla pod and 1 teaspoon of baking powder. Roll into logs and freeze for up to 3 months. Remove from the freezer and leave for 10 minutes before cutting into circles 8mm (⅜in) thick. Cook for 10 minutes at 180°C/350°F/gas 4 for defrosted and frozen dough.

STOCK I always keep chicken stock, seafood stock and meat stock in my freezer (see pages 230–2), as well as bags of vegetable scraps and roast chicken carcasses to turn into stock another day when I have more time.

PASTA SHEETS To freeze pasta sheets, cook for 2 minutes in salted boiling water, put into iced water for 2 minutes, remove and dry on a clean tea towel. Stack interleaved with baking parchment and freeze. Fresh stuffed pasta also freezes well: simply 'open freeze' on trays dusted with semolina and bag up once frozen. Keep for 3 months.

PASTRY All varieties of raw pastry dough freeze well. However, choux pastry freezes well after cooking too. To crisp up profiterole buns after defrosting, pop them briefly into an oven for 5 minutes at 180°C/350°F/gas 4.

PIZZA BASES I usually make a big batch of pizza dough and bake a few bases for just 2 minutes to go in the freezer. This way the children have access to quick meals they can finish themselves. Try the sourdough recipe on pages 280–4; the dough has an amazing flavour.

• MEAT AND POULTRY

We often buy a beef box from our local estate. The beef is hung for 28 days, is organic and we know the farmer. We cut out the middleman so the price is good for the amazing flavour and quality. However, we couldn't benefit from this kind of project without a freezer because we have to buy a large quantity in one go.

While meat freezes well, meat that has been previously frozen can sometimes end up having a slightly hard, rubbery texture. Put simply, as meat freezes ice crystals burst through the cells and puncture them, and then as the meat defrosts fluids leak out of the cells, which dehydrates the meat further. When you subsequently cook the meat, it leaks more water again, which is what gives you that rubbery texture. Cooked meat is less affected by freezing, as some of the fluid has already come out, and so the cells are not affected in the same way.

Here are a few tips to minimize the damage done to fresh meat when you freeze it. First of all, freeze it as quickly as possible. Lay it, open to the cold, on trays with the freezer set to 'fast freeze'. As soon as the meat is frozen, wrap it up tightly in baking parchment or vacuum bags and label. Use it in a matter of weeks rather than months, as it will go on deteriorating due to the loss of fluid from the cells.

* WHAT NOT TO FREEZE?

FOODS WITH A HIGH WATER CONTENT, such as tomatoes, peppers, marrows, cucumbers, radishes, lettuce, watercress, melons, avocados, bananas and strawberries, all turn to mush when you defrost them. That doesn't mean you can't freeze these foods, it's just you are better off cooking them after defrosting rather than eating them raw. Bananas, melons, avocados and strawberries are fine to whizz into a smoothie from frozen (see pages 238–41). Or try dropping single frozen strawberries into a drink instead of ice cubes; by the time they defrost, you will have finished the drink and can eat the strawberry.

CUSTARDS, MAYONNAISE, EGG-BASED SAUCES AND MILKY SAUCES, SUCH AS BÉCHAMEL These can become watery and lumpy when defrosted.

STEWS THAT CONTAIN POTATOES Frozen potato becomes mushy when it defrosts, so freeze the stew without the potatoes.

GRAVY Most gravies contain fat, which separates on defrosting. It is better to freeze stock to add to meat juices after roasting (see pages 230–2).

PREPARING FOOD FOR THE FREEZER
HERBS
- Herbs keep well in damp kitchen paper in the refrigerator, however most can be frozen for up to 3 months.
- DRY FREEZING This method is suitable for soft herbs such as basil, dill, coriander, chives, tarragon and mint. The advantage of 'dry freezing' is the herbs freeze quickly, locking in flavour, although they often darken as they defrost – so don't expect to use them as a flash of bright green garnish.

METHOD Chop your herbs finely, spread them over a tray and put it in the freezer. Once frozen, gather them up and pack into freezer bags ready to use in cooking. Store for up to 3 months.

• HERB OIL AND BUTTER CUBES This method is suitable for any herbs and the advantage is the herbs keep their colour better. Think coriander in olive oil mixed into couscous, dill in butter in potato salad, tarragon in butter for hot chicken or basil in extra virgin olive oil in tomato soup or just melted onto hot crusty bread.

METHOD Finely chop your herbs and sprinkle into ice-cube trays until half full. Top up with extra virgin olive oil (don't use sunflower oil because it doesn't freeze!) and put into the freezer. For butter cubes mix the herbs and butter together first and pack into the ice-cube tray. Once frozen, pack into sealed bags and store for up to 3 months. To use, stir into hot cooked pasta, vegetables or couscous.

• PESTO CUBES Pesto is great frozen into cubes too – when melted it tastes as fresh as if it had just been prepared. Flavio, our son, loved pesto and pasta as a child and it makes a great quick supper. All you need to do is pull out a cube or two of pesto from the freezer, defrost briefly in the microwave or melt in a hot pan and stir it into the hot pasta once it is cooked.

METHOD To make pesto for six people, blitz 50g (1¾oz) fresh basil, 1 small peeled garlic clove with 50g (1¾oz) toasted pine nuts in a food processor. Gradually pour in 125ml (4fl oz) extra virgin olive oil and blitz to a coarse paste. Add 25g (1oz) Parmesan and blitz very briefly. Freeze in ice-cube trays. Once frozen, pack into sealed bags and store for up to 3 months.

ICE CUBES For fun, you can freeze whole mint leaves in ice cubes for adding to rum-based drinks or borage flowers for gin and tonic.

• SPICE CUBES One of my favourite ideas came from our son Giorgio, who loves steamed broccoli or spinach sautéed in extra virgin olive oil with finely chopped garlic and chilli. He thought that we could simply freeze the garlic and chilli, already chopped, in oil in our ice-cube trays. We tried it and have been doing it ever since. It has to be extra virgin olive oil; others don't freeze as well and won't have the finished flavour. While the broccoli steams, I melt a spice cube in a small frying pan and then toss in the drained broccoli as soon as it is cooked – delicious! With some chopped parsley added to the mix, these also make an instant pasta sauce. Put some pasta on to cook and melt the cubes in a frying pan. When the pasta is done, drain it and combine with the spicy oil in the frying pan.

A good shortcut for Indian dishes is to prepare the individual ingredients in advance and freeze them in ice-cube trays. Try individual portions of finely chopped ginger, chilli or garlic mixed with oil; they are a great time-saver.

STOCKS, GRAVY AND SAUCES

Like most people, I often have to cook in a hurry – but having a collection of reduced stocks in my freezer helps me make gravies and sauces quickly to accompany sausages, pork chops, steak, chicken, duck breasts, etc.

• STOCKS Freezing comes into its own twice over when it comes to stocks. My freezer is full of bags of scraps that might otherwise be thrown away: carcasses from roast chickens, ends of salami, fish bones, prawn shells, vegetable peelings and onion trimmings, parsley stalks, etc. – all perfect for the stockpot. Once I have enough to make a big batch of stock, I boil everything up and, once cold, pour it into freezer containers or ice-cube trays ready to go in the freezer. Then, when I roast a joint of meat, I will add a few cubes to the gravy, along with 1 tablespoon of Apple and Rosemary Jelly (see page 56). Together with chef friends Brian Turner and Jasper Aykroyd we agreed you need three essential stocks in your freezer: seafood, brown chicken and meat (see pages 230–2 for recipes).

NOTES ON STOCK-MAKING

Giancarlo and I have been making stocks for years, however we are still experimenting with ways to perfect them. Here are some tips:

INGREDIENTS What you put into your stock tends to be dictated by the seasons and what you have to hand (although freezing vegetable, fish and meat trimmings ready to go helps). Bear in mind that certain additions will have an influence on the finished flavour, such as mushrooms, fennel, butternut squash peelings, herbs, tops and tails of spring onions and peppers. Onions, leeks, carrots, celery are nearly always included for a base flavour. Never use cabbage or starchy vegetables such as potatoes or anything starting to go off.

VEAL is regarded as the king of stock. However it can be heavy, and many people prefer to use chicken as it is more adaptable. Pork trotters, ears, tail, skin, nose, etc. are always a welcome addition to any stock, for body.

For CHICKEN STOCK, either use a leftover roast chicken carcass or the raw carcass left over from boning a bird; if you have one available, a whole broiler (an old bird that doesn't lay any more) or a capon (a castrated male bird) also give very good flavour.

SALT This is much better left out of stock, especially if you are going to reduce it before or after freezing as the process of reduction concentrates the flavour.

TO BROWN OR NOT TO BROWN? This depends on how intense you want your stock. Most of the time you will want to brown your vegetables and bones/chicken wings first, either with a little olive oil in a roasting tray in a hot oven (200°C/400°F/gas 6) or in a heavy frying pan on the hob until an even chestnut colour all over but definitely not burnt. This caramelization gives the stock a rich colour and deepens the flavour. In darker stocks it is nice to add some halved tomatoes when roasting your bones and vegetables.

For a light colour and flavour (especially if using veal), you can opt out of the browning process. Simply put the meat into a stockpot and pour over some boiling water from the kettle to scald the meat and sterilize the surface. Pour away the water before adding the remaining ingredients and topping up with fresh water.

THE GOLDEN RULE Never let your stock boil too hard or it will become cloudy and bitter. Think slow, bubbling brook not white-water rapids!

REDUCING To concentrate the flavour of your stock for use in sauces, etc. we like to strain it first, then reduce the stock by letting it bubble away gently until it has reduced by a third of its original volume. It can then be cooled and frozen in the normal way; like this, it takes up less room in the freezer.

* STOCK RECIPES

The following stock recipes are designed to make big batches for the freezer, and require big pans, however you can make less if you prefer. We haven't included a recipe for vegetable stock because it only takes 30 minute to make from fresh. We freeze bags of vegetable peelings for this purpose – celery tops, parsley stalks, carrot peelings, onion skins, etc. – and boil them up when we need some vegetable stock.

ROASTED SEAFOOD STOCK

If you have ever eaten spaghetti with clams, risotto with seafood or fish soup in a restaurant at the water's edge on holiday in Italy or France and wanted to recreate that flavour, this is how to do it. To transform a recipe from the bland to the sublime, reduce the stock to one-third of its original volume, just a few spoons, and freeze in small amounts.

MAKES APPROX. 2 LITRES (3½ PINTS)

- 1kg (2lb 4oz) mixed shellfish shells, such as those from prawns, langoustines, lobster and crab
- 75ml (2½fl oz) olive oil
- 2 carrots, roughly chopped
- 1 large white onion, roughly chopped
- 2 celery sticks, roughly chopped
- a large handful of parsley stalks
- 100ml (3½fl oz) brandy
- 100g (3½oz) tomato purée
- 5 litres (9 pints) cold water

> Preheat the oven to 180°C/350°F/gas 4. Put the shellfish shells in a roasting tray and bake for 30 minutes or until they become crisp and dry.
> Heat the oil in a large saucepan or stockpot and add the carrots, onion and celery. Fry over a medium to high heat for approx. 15 minutes until lightly browned, allowing the vegetables to catch and caramelize on the bottom of the pan. Add the shells from the oven and the parsley stalks and stir through. Pour in the brandy and let the alcohol evaporate for a few minutes.
> Rinse out the tray in which you roasted the shellfish shells with a little water and add the liquid to the pan. Add the tomato purée to the pan, stir through and then add the cold water. Bring to the boil, turn down to a gentle simmer and bubble away gently for 1½–2 hours or until the stock thickens. Strain through a muslin to obtain a clear stock or through a fine metal sieve for a thicker stock. If you wish, return the stock to the pan and reduce by one-third for a concentrated flavour. Cool thoroughly before freezing in vacuum bags or ice-cube trays.

BROWN CHICKEN STOCK

This is our friend Brian Turner's recipe, which works every time. This stock makes an excellent vegetable soup or a great base for risotto. If you don't have two carcasses, freeze one until you have another one ready.

MAKES APPROX. 2 LITRES (3½ PINTS)

- 4 tablespoons olive oil
- carcasses and leftovers from 2 roast chickens
- 2 brown or white onions, roughly chopped
- 2 leeks, roughly chopped
- 2 celery sticks, roughly chopped
- 2 carrots, roughly chopped
- 6 tomatoes, roughly chopped
- 2 garlic cloves, finely chopped
- 6 parsley stalks
- 1 bay leaf
- 1 sprig of thyme
- 7 litres (12¼ pints) cold water

>>>

> Heat the oil in a large saucepan or stockpot. Pull the roast chicken bones into pieces and add to the pan along with the onions, leeks, celery and carrots. Stir over a medium to high heat for 15–20 minutes until everything is lightly browned. Add the tomatoes, garlic, parsley stalks, bay leaf and thyme and top up with the water. Bring to the boil and skim off any scum. Now reduce the heat to a gentle simmer and bubble away gently for 2–3 hours before straining. You can either pass the stock through a muslin to obtain a clear stock or through a fine metal sieve for a thicker stock. If you want to concentrate the flavour further, you may wish to reduce the stock at this stage by returning it to the pan and simmering it gently until it has reduced by one-third. Cool and freeze in vacuum bags or ice-cube trays.

JASPER AYKROYD'S MEAT STOCK

This is an essential ingredient in rich gravies and sauces, especially if you reduce it well at the end so it has a really intense flavour. Jasper says he 'tends' to his stock rather like a sleeping child, checking on it every now and again.

MAKES APPROX. 3 LITRES (5¼ PINTS)

- 1kg (2lb 4oz) pork, veal and beef bones, roughly chopped
- 2 large white or brown onions
- 50ml (2fl oz) extra virgin olive oil
- 2 celery sticks, roughly chopped
- 2 carrots, roughly chopped
- 2 garlic cloves, halved
- 1 sprig of rosemary
- 2 bay leaves
- a few parsley stalks
- 1 teaspoon black peppercorns
- 2 cloves

- 300ml (½ pint) red wine or brandy
- 6 litres (10½ pints) cold water

> Preheat the oven to 200°C/400°F/gas 6. Put the bones into a roasting tray and roast for 20 minutes. Meanwhile, peel the onions and cut each one into roughly ten pieces; set aside the ends along with the outer skins. Heat the oil in a very large stockpot and add the centre parts of the onion with the celery and carrots. Fry over a medium–high heat until golden brown, approx. 15–20 minutes.

> Remove the roasting tray from the oven and scatter over the reserved onion skins and ends. Return to the oven for a further 20 minutes or until the onion skins start to brown. Remove the tray from the oven, pour away most of the fat (you can use this for roast potatoes or Yorkshire pudding) and transfer the bones and onion skins to the stockpot. Add the garlic, herbs and spices.

> Place the roasting tray on the hob over a medium heat and pour in the red wine or brandy. Bring to the boil, stirring all the time, and allow the alcohol to reduce for 5 minutes. Pour the reduced liquor into the stockpot, top up with the water and bring to the boil. Immediately reduce the heat to a gentle simmer and skim off all the scum and fat that has risen to the surface – this will taint the stock and make it cloudy. Simmer away gently for 4–5 hours or until the stock has reduced by half its original volume. It will more-or-less take care of itself, but keep an eye on it as it will need skimming from time to time. Once the stock is ready, strain it through a colander to remove the bones and again through a sieve.

> If you wish, you can now reduce the stock by pouring it into a smaller saucepan or back into the stockpot and letting it

bubble away gently until it has reduced by one-third. I like to reduce mine a lot to give it a really intense flavour. Freeze in ice-cube trays or silicone containers to use in gravies and sauces.

* GRAVIES AND SAUCES

Frozen chicken and meat stock makes flavourful gravies and sauces. I wouldn't recommend freezing gravy because of its high fat content, which causes it to separate when you defrost it. Far better to make your gravy fresh using fresh meat juices from the Sunday roast flavoured with your homemade frozen stock.

MAKING GRAVY

Once your joint of meat is cooked, remove it from the roasting tray and set aside on a plate to rest, covered with foil and a cloth to keep in the heat. (For small amounts of meat or sausages, fry until done and keep them in the pan.) Pour away any fat from the roasting tray or frying pan, but keep the all-important cooking juices. Set the pan over a medium heat, add a good dash of wine – whichever colour you prefer – and deglaze the pan, i.e. scrape the caramelized brown areas from the bottom (don't use any burnt bits as they will spoil the stock). Let the wine bubble away for a few minutes, and then whisk in a little cornflour mixed with some cold water. Don't worry about lumps, if there are any, because you will sieve it later. Now add the stock. You can either use frozen cubes straight from the freezer if you are making a small amount of gravy, or defrost a large amount of stock fully beforehand and add it once it is

liquid again. Bring the gravy to the boil and whisk it well. Strain if necessary and season to taste with salt and pepper.

FLAVOURING YOUR GRAVY You can adapt the basic gravy recipe with different flavours. For a herby gravy to serve with chicken, add some chopped rosemary or thyme; for a sweeter gravy to serve with roast lamb, add 1 tablespoon of Redcurrant Jelly (see pages 56–7) or Apple and Rosemary Jelly (see page 56); for a rich onion gravy to serve with sausages or roast beef, add a spoonful of homemade Spiced Red Onion Marmalade (see page 32).

GIANCARLO'S SOFFRITTO

A good flavourful *soffritto* forms the base of all hearty Italian stews, soups and *ragùs*. We grow celery and carrots in our garden and make up batches of this *soffritto* when we have a glut of vegetables. The flavour is so much more intense made with our own homegrown celery and carrots, which are definitely sweeter than any vegetables from the supermarket.

MAKES APPROX. 200G (7OZ) (ENOUGH FOR 1 RAGÙ OR CHICKEN CASSEROLES FOR 6 PEOPLE)

- 150ml (¼ pint) extra virgin olive oil
- 1½ red or white onions, very finely chopped
- 2 celery sticks, very finely chopped
- 1 carrot, very finely chopped
- 1 teaspoon salt and plenty of freshly ground black pepper
- 2 sprigs of fresh rosemary
- 3 bay leaves
- 2 garlic cloves, left whole and crushed with the flat side of a knife

> Heat the olive oil in a pan and add the onion, celery, carrot and seasoning. Add

the rosemary, bay leaves and garlic and cook over a low heat for 15 minutes, stirring often, until the onion is soft and sweet. Remove the rosemary and bay leaves, cool and freeze in vacuum bags or small plastic containers.

> Use in the Tuscan *Ragù* recipe on pages 215–16.

* SPICE PASTES

Now we have started making and either chilling or freezing these little pots of spice paste I wonder how we coped without them. The following recipes are for Thai, Sri Lankan and Indian curry bases. They can be made in big batches and used straight away or chilled in the refrigerator, or frozen in ice-cube trays or bags.

KAY PLUNKETT-HOGGE'S GREEN CURRY PASTE

Kay was born and brought up in Thailand and speaks the language fluently. She is a cookbook writer and runs classes demonstrating Thai cooking. We persuaded her to part with her recipe for this classic Thai paste. I went shopping with Kay for the ingredients and she reminded me that fresh ingredients make the best paste. For vegetarians and those that don't like the strong fish flavour, leave out the shrimp paste. The paste also makes a great soup if combined with lightly fried courgettes, peas, green beans and coconut milk.

MAKES ENOUGH PASTE FOR 4 CURRIES FOR 4 PEOPLE

- 2–4 tablespoons roughly chopped green bird's eye chillies (depending on how hot you like your curry)
- 4 tablespoons chopped galangal or ginger
- 4 lemongrass stalks, chopped
- 8 Thai shallots, chopped
- 4 teaspoons grated makrut lime zest
- 1 large bunch of fresh coriander (stems, roots and leaves), chopped
- 2 teaspoons coriander seeds
- 4 teaspoons white peppercorns
- 2 teaspoons ground cumin
- 4 flat teaspoons Thai shrimp paste (optional)
- good pinch of salt

> Pound the hardest ingredients first to a fine powder in a pestle and mortar, then add the remaining ingredients. Grind to a smooth paste. Divide into four portions. Use straight away, or store in a sealed container in the refrigerator up to 3 days; alternatively, freeze in small vacuum bags or sealed plastic containers for up to 3 months.

KAY PLUNKETT-HOGGE'S GREEN CURRY WITH CHICKEN AND BAMBOO SHOOTS

This is Kay's recipe for a gorgeously creamy, spicy Thai green curry. We love the sweetness and, as Kay says, it sings with colour and flavour. She prefers to use whole bone-in chicken thighs; she skins most of them but leaves a couple with the skins on for added oil and flavour. The meat can also be diced, which reduces the cooking time. Kay uses bamboo shoots that have been vacuum-packed in water rather than canned ones. These are available from most Thai stores in easy-to-use chunks. If you can't find them the canned sliced ones are fine as well. You can substitute the chicken for pork, beef or prawns.

SERVES 4

- 1 tablespoon oil
- 1 portion of Kay Plunkett-Hogge's Green Curry Paste (see page 232)
  400ml (14fl oz) can coconut milk
- 100–200ml (3½–7fl oz) water (amount depends on the thickness of your coconut milk)
- 700g (1lb 9oz) chicken thighs
- 2 tablespoons Thai fish sauce (*nam pla*)
- 1 tablespoon sugar
- 200g (7oz) bamboo shoots, chopped
- 2 Thai aubergines, quartered
- 100g (3½oz) pea aubergines (if you can't find these add an extra 100g/3½oz Thai aubergines)
- a handful of Thai sweet basil (or Italian basil if you can't find Thai basil), shredded

> Heat the oil in a wok or large, heavy-based frying pan and fry the paste until it releases its fragrance – approx. 1 minute. Add 200ml (7fl oz) of the coconut milk and bring to the boil slowly, stirring to dissolve the paste. Once the paste has dissolved, add the water and chicken. Bring to the boil, and then add the rest of the coconut milk. Bring back to the boil, and then simmer for up to 45 minutes or until the chicken is cooked through. Add the fish sauce and the sugar, taste and adjust the seasoning if necessary. Stir in the bamboo shoots and aubergines and boil for a further 3 minutes. Throw in the basil and serve accompanied with rice.

MANJULA SAMARASINGHE'S SRI LANKAN SPICE PASTE FOR VEGETABLE CURRIES

Manjula and I share a love of food. When travelling with her in Sri Lanka she introduced me to her country's cooking and we were amazed to see the variety of vegetarian curries made from mango, jackfruit, beetroot, green beans, mushrooms, lentils, okra and potatoes. Now we eat Sri Lankan curry and rice twice a week at home using Manjula's spice pastes. Sri Lankan curry paste is normally very hot, but we have made this version medium–hot. However, feel free to adjust the number of chillies to your personal taste.

MAKES ENOUGH PASTE FOR 4 VEGETABLE CURRIES FOR 4 PEOPLE

- 30g (1oz) coriander seeds
- 2 teaspoons fennel seeds
- 1½ teaspoon black mustard seeds
- 2 teaspoons cumin seeds
- 6cm (2½in) cinnamon stick
- 1 teaspoon ground turmeric
- 4 cardamom pods, husks discarded
- 10 curry leaves
- 10–15 fenugreek seeds
- 1 onion, roughly chopped, depending on strength
- 5 green chillies, finely chopped
- 4 teaspoons fine sea salt
- 150ml (¼ pint) coconut oil

> Toast the spices in a dry frying pan for a minute or two until they release their aroma; cool and grind to a fine powder in a spice grinder or pestle and mortar. Combine the spices with the onion, chillies, salt and oil. Divide the paste into four portions. Either use straight away or store in a sealed container in the refrigerator for up to a month; alternatively, freeze in small vacuum bags or sealed plastic containers for up to 3 months.

MANJULA'S SRI LANKAN SPICE PASTE FOR MEAT AND CHICKEN CURRIES

This paste is devised for chicken or meat curries. We make it with chicken, but you could use goat, beef or lamb instead.

MAKES ENOUGH PASTE FOR 4 CURRIES FOR 4 PEOPLE

- 50g (1¾oz) coriander seeds
- 2 teaspoons cumin seeds
- 2 teaspoons fennel seeds
- 10–15 fenugreek seeds
- 1 teaspoon black mustard seeds
- 2 teaspoons black peppercorns
- 8 curry leaves
- 25g (1oz) garlic, finely chopped
- 4 teaspoons salt
- 25g (1oz) fresh ginger, finely chopped
- 2 onions, finely chopped
- 100ml (3½fl oz) coconut oil

> Toast all the spices in a dry frying pan over a low heat until they just start to brown, approx. 5 minutes; cool on a plate (or a piece of paper, so you can put the spices straight into the grinder). Grind to a powder in a spice grinder or pestle and mortar.
> Put the garlic, salt, ginger and onion in a bowl. Pour in the oil and stir in the ground spices to form a paste. Divide the mixture into four portions. Either use straight away or store in a sealed container in the refrigerator for up to a month; alternatively, freeze in small vacuum bags or sealed plastic containers for up to 3 months.

MANJULA'S CHICKEN CURRY

This recipe is for a 'wet' chicken curry to serve with rice or hoppers (see page 185). Manjula often adds chopped raw potatoes with the chicken to bulk out the curry. Manjula prefers to use a whole jointed chicken rather than chicken breasts because she finds it gives the sauce a better flavour, but for speed you can always use skinless chicken breasts. This recipe works equally well with raw king prawns, which require just a few minutes cooking time; if using prawns, leave out the potatoes and use parsley at the end instead of curry leaves.

SERVES 4

- 2 tablespoons coconut oil
- 1 portion of Manjula's Sri Lankan Spice Paste for Meat and Chicken Curries (see left)
- 3 skinless chicken breasts, cut into bite-sized pieces
- 150ml (¼ pint) water, canned tomatoes or coconut milk
- sea salt and freshly ground black pepper
- a few fresh or dried curry leaves or fresh coriander leaves, to garnish

> Heat the oil and spice paste in a medium saucepan, stirring over a medium heat for a few minutes until the paste darkens slightly. Add the chicken and stir through, letting it fry in the paste for 5 minutes until seared all over. Pour in the water, tomatoes or coconut milk and simmer gently until the chicken is cooked through, approx. 15 minutes. Taste and adjust the seasoning with salt and black pepper if necessary. Serve with rice and garnish with curry leaves or coriander.

TIKKA MASALA CURRY PASTE

This is our version of the base for this much-loved Anglo-Indian dish. The recipe is loosely based on Rupa Goolati's where the paste is mixed with yogurt and used to marinate and tenderize the chicken. I freeze our paste in four portions in vacuum bags and flatten them so that they take up little space in the freezer. The paste defrosts quickly and so makes a great midweek supper.

MAKES ENOUGH PASTE FOR 4 CURRIES FOR 4 PEOPLE

- 1 heaped tablespoon coriander seeds
- 1 teaspoon cardamom seeds, husks discarded
- 6 teaspoons cumin seeds
- 10 black peppercorns
- 4 cloves
- ½ teaspoon finely grated nutmeg
- 6 tablespoons lemon juice
- 4 red onions, roughly chopped
- 3–4 red chillies, seeds discarded, roughly chopped
- 10–12 black peppercorns
- 16 garlic cloves, peeled
- 5cm (2in) piece of fresh ginger, peeled and roughly chopped

> Grind the spices to a smooth, fine powder using a pestle and mortar or a spice grinder. Blend with the remaining ingredients in a food processor to form a paste. Divide into four portions. Use straight away or keep in the refrigerator, covered, for a week or freeze in small vacuum bags or plastic containers with a lid for up to 3 months.

CALDESI CHICKEN TIKKA MASALA

Although chicken is the standard way to enjoy this recipe, it works really well with salmon or king prawns. We like to use chicken thighs with the bone in for flavour, but they do take longer to cook. To cut down the cooking time, take the bone out or use breast meat. If we are barbecuing, threading the chicken breast onto skewers is a great option. For a healthy alternative, stop after grilling the chicken or fish and serve with a salad, omitting the sauce.

SERVES 4

- 1 portion of Tikka Masala Curry Paste (enough for 4 people, see left)
- 50ml (2fl oz) Greek yogurt
- 800g (1lb 12oz) skinless chicken thighs and/or breasts, cut into 4cm (1½in) cubes
- 1 tablespoon ghee or salted butter
- 2 heaped tablespoons tomato purée
- 3 tablespoons double cream (omit this if you are using coconut milk)
- 200ml (7fl oz) water or coconut milk
- juice of ½ lemon
- fine sea salt
- 2–3 teaspoons sugar
- coriander or curry leaves, to garnish

> Mix one-third of the tikka masala curry paste together with the yogurt in a bowl and add the chicken. Set aside the remaining paste in the refrigerator for later. Toss to combine, cover and leave to marinate in the refrigerator for at least 30 minutes and up to a day. The longer the marinating time, the better the flavour.

> Preheat the grill to medium. When ready to cook the chicken, lay the pieces onto a grill and pour over any remaining yogurt. Collect the juices in a tray underneath. Cook the chicken for 15–30 minutes, turning halfway through cooking, until it

>>>

is cooked through and tinged dark brown around the edges. The cooking time will vary depending on the size of the pieces. They can be threaded onto a skewer to make them easier to turn.

> Meanwhile, heat the ghee or butter in a large frying pan. When melted, add the remaining tikka masala paste and stir through. Fry for 5 minutes over a medium heat. Add the tomato purée, cream (if using), water or coconut milk. Heat through and then add the lemon juice, salt and sugar to taste. Add the chicken to the pan with the juices from the grill pan. Stir through to combine, season to taste adding more salt or chilli, if you like, and serve scattered with torn coriander or curry leaves. Serve with rice, Mango Chutney (see page 29) and Cyrus Todiwala's Lime Pickle (see pages 151–2).

* FRUIT

As well as freezing raw fruit such as blackberries or raspberries, we like to keep a stock of homemade fruit purées in our freezer ready for turning into crumbles and pies, or serving alongside roast meats.

COOKED APPLE

Cooked apple can be turned into a filling for an apple crumble or pie, eaten as it is with yogurt and granola, served as apple sauce for roast pork or reduced to make apple butter or cheese. I can't bear to see wonderful English apples fall to the ground around the country while we buy ones from afar. All we need to do it learn how to preserve our own varieties to enjoy them all year round. I like to use a couple of handfuls of blackberries in crumbles when I have them. Quince and pears are great mixed with apple too.

MAKES ENOUGH FOR 4 CRUMBLES FOR 6 PEOPLE

- 4kg (9lb) cooking apples, peeled, cored and sliced
- 2 x 6cm (2½in) cinnamon sticks
- 100g (3½oz) raisins (optional)
- 200g (7oz) soft brown sugar
- 1 litre (1¾ pints) cold water

> Put the apple, cinnamon sticks, raisins and sugar in a large saucepan, cover with the cold water and bring to the boil, partially covered with a lid. Reduce the heat and simmer gently for 10–15 minutes, or until just soft, stirring occasionally to make sure the sauce cooks evenly. Once the apples are just soft, remove the pan from the heat and set aside to cool. Divide into four portions and freeze in small vacuum bags or sealed plastic containers for up to 3 months. Cooked apple could also be waterbathed in jars, see pages 206–7.

APPLE CRUMBLE

To make up a crumble use one portion of Cooked Apple. The crumble topping can be made up in advance and will keep very well in the freezer. Open freeze on a tray and gather up into bags once frozen. Keep for 3 months in the freezer. For a variation, add a handful of oats or chopped almonds to the crumble.

SERVES 6–8

- 125g (4½oz) butter
- 125g (4½oz) plain flour
- 125g (4½oz) caster sugar
- 125g (4½oz) ground almonds
- 1 portion of Cooked Apple (see left)

> Preheat the oven to 180°C/350°F/gas 4. Rub the butter, flour, sugar and ground almonds together by hand to make

the crumble mixture. Put the cooked apples in a baking dish and scatter the crumble on top. Bake for 30–40 minutes or until golden. Serve with homemade Crème Fraîche (see page 180).

QUINCE AND APPLE

This makes a really fruity and zingy filling for crumbles or pies, and it also doubles as a sauce to complement salty roast pork. Make as much as you can when quinces are around and freeze in portions.

MAKES ENOUGH FOR 1 CRUMBLE FOR 4 PEOPLE (OR 16 SERVINGS WITH ROAST PORK)

- 2 quinces
- juice of 1 lemon
- 1 vanilla pod, split into two
- 200ml (7fl oz) cold water
- 2 cooking apples
- 100g (3½oz) caster sugar

> Peel and core the quinces and cut into thin slices. Put these into a saucepan with the lemon juice, vanilla pod and cover with the water. Bring to the boil and cook until just soft, approx. 20 minutes. Meanwhile, peel and core the apples and cut them into thin slices. Once the quinces are just soft, stir in the apples and sugar. Cook for a further 5 minutes. Eat straight away as a sauce or cool and freeze in small vacuum bags or sealed plastic containers for up to 3 months. To make into a crumble follow the recipe on pages 236–7.

FROZEN COCONUT SAMBAL

In Sri Lanka coconuts are grated using a machine that clamps onto a table and is turned by a handle. The sharp end is shaped like half a lemon with a series of serrated blades that grind the two halves of the coconut down from the inside. Grated coconut is primarily used to make coconut milk and oil. Coconut graters are available from some international grocers, however a simple grater would work too: break the coconut into pieces and grate the white part only.

Coconut sambal is delightful served with the hoppers on page 185, or as an accompaniment to the Sri Lankan curry on page 234.

MAKES 250G (9OZ) – ENOUGH FOR 8 PORTIONS

- 1 coconut
- ½ onion or 1 small banana shallot, finely chopped
- 1 garlic clove, finely chopped or grated
- 1–2 teaspoons fine salt, to taste
- generous pinch of freshly ground black pepper
- a few curry leaves (optional)
- 1 flat teaspoon chilli powder
- 2–4 teaspoons lemon juice, to taste

> Crack open the coconut with a hammer and grate the flesh on a fine grater. If possible, try to include some of the brown skin, which contains some of the oil and flavour. Combine the onion, garlic, salt, black pepper and curry leaves (if using) in a pestle and mortar and pound to a smooth paste. Add the chilli powder, followed by the grated coconut. Pound again with the pestle for a couple of minutes until well blended, and then spoon the contents into a bowl. Stir in the lemon juice to taste and season with more salt or pepper if necessary. Either eat straight away or divide into small containers and store in the refrigerator for up to 5 days or in the freezer for 3 months.

FREEZER PICKLED CUCUMBERS

I remember playing the word game hangman with my children once and getting down to '_u_umber'; the unfortunate man was nearly hung and they just couldn't guess the missing letter – even though cucumber was one of their favourite foods! I worried about their future but we laugh to this day about it and often refer to the long, green vegetables as '_u_umbers'.

This recipe is a great way to use up small amounts of leftover spiced vinegar or gluts of cucumbers from your vegetable patch. This version is based on Lynda Brown's recipe from her Preserving Book. I like to make it in small batches as it is quick to make and I don't want to take up too much room in the freezer. For best results, defrost the cucumbers the day before you need them and use in homemade burgers, with sausages and sauerkraut or in a sandwich with Cheddar cheese.

MAKES APPROX. 650G (1¾LB 7OZ) (ENOUGH FOR 3 PORTIONS EACH SERVING 4 PEOPLE)

- approx. 500g (1lb 2oz) cucumber
- 2 shallots, very thinly sliced
- 1–2 teaspoons salt
- 50g (1¾oz) golden caster sugar
- 1 teaspoon mustard seeds
- a small handful of dill leaves
- 120ml (4fl oz) white wine vinegar or Quick Spiced Vinegar (see page 15)

> Thoroughly wash the cucumbers and cut into approx. 3mm (⅛in) slices. Layer up the cucumber slices with the shallots in a glass or plastic bowl, sprinkling each layer with salt. Cover and set aside in a cool place for 2 hours; this process will draw out the moisture from the cucumbers and help to keep them crisp. Tip into a colander and rinse under very cold water.

Drain well, pressing out any surplus liquid with a small saucer.
> Transfer the slices to a clean bowl and layer them up with the sugar, mustard seeds and dill leaves. Pour over the vinegar and weigh down the cucumbers with a small saucer. Cover and set aside in the refrigerator overnight.
> The following day, divide the mixture into small containers, cover and freeze. Do not overfill your containers as the liquid will expand in the cold. To use, thaw overnight in the refrigerator. Once defrosted, store in the refrigerator and consume within a week.

* SIMPLE SMOOTHIES AND FROZEN DESSERTS

I remember watching an Eddie Izzard sketch about fruit bowls being a place where we watch fruit rot, and how we actually end up throwing all of it away apart from the oranges. However, since learning this trick I never throw out fruit any more. No more soft, black bananas and wrinkled apples in our house, thank you! We used to make smoothies with ice cubes and fresh fruit, which does water the taste down, however this version uses just pure, cold fruit, so it has a great flavour.

FREEZING FRUIT FOR SMOOTHIES

You can use all sorts of fresh fruit for smoothies. For larger fruit, such as apples, oranges, mangoes, clementines, plums, kiwis or bananas, I chop the fruit into 3cm (1¼in) cubes and freeze it on trays in the freezer. I leave the skins on for apples, but peel the rest. For grapes, raspberries, blueberries and strawberries, freeze whole on open trays to stop them sticking together. Once your fruit has frozen solid, bag it up into freezer bags or boxes. I always use separate bags or boxes for individual fruits so that I can offer choices to fussy children – mentioning no names.

When you want to make a smoothie, chose the fruits you like and put them into a food processor (still frozen). You can either blitz them on their own or combine them with other fresh fruit, fruit juice, milk, yogurt or a dash of honey and whizz until smooth. I like to add vanilla seeds and/or cinnamon to yogurt-based smoothies. A little lump of fresh or frozen ginger works well with either fruit or dairy smoothies. Avocados and carrots work well too.

FROZEN DESSERTS

FROZEN YOGURT

Frozen fruit is great to whizz into yogurt for a healthy frozen dessert. I wouldn't recommend freezing bananas or strawberries for desserts in general, because their texture suffers, however it is fine to freeze them to combine with yogurt. Just take a handful of frozen fruit and mix with 150ml (¼ pint) of yogurt per person. Sweeten to taste with honey or drizzle some over the top. Serve straight away.

MAKING ICE CREAM AND SORBET IN THE FREEZER WITH NO ICE-CREAM MACHINE

Thanks to the ingenious trick of a chef friend of ours, Stuart Green, we can now make wonderfully smooth ice creams and sorbets without an ice-cream machine. All you need to do is freeze your mixture in ice-cube trays or small yogurt pots and then whizz it in a blender once it has frozen to form a smooth, soft fluff I find flexible silicone muffin moulds work well too because they are easy to turn out and make a small enough quantity to be ground easily by the blades of the food processor.

NO-CHURN SEVILLE ORANGE SORBET

This makes a great last-minute dessert. Serve in chilled glasses.

SERVES 6–8

- 6 Seville oranges, washed
- 200g (7oz) caster sugar
- 400ml (14fl oz) cold water

> Grate the zest of two of the oranges into a saucepan. Add the sugar and water and dissolve the sugar over a medium heat. Remove from the heat and allow to cool. Cut all six oranges in half and squeeze out the juice. Stir the juice into the sugar syrup and strain into a jug. Pour into flexible ice-cube trays or silicone muffin moulds and transfer to the freezer.

> Once the sorbet has frozen solid, remove from the freezer and turn out the moulds into a food processor. Blitz to give the texture of a soft but firm sorbet. Either serve straight away in chilled dishes or re-freeze in a sealed container and store for up to 3 months.

NO-CHURN STRAWBERRY ICE CREAM

This is a quick ice cream recipe that doesn't require a custard base. Feel free to substitute the strawberries for the same weight of raspberries, mango, blackcurrants or cherries.

SERVES 10–12

- 1kg (2lb 4oz) strawberries
- 275g (9¾oz) caster sugar
- 500ml (18fl oz) double cream
- 125ml (4fl oz) milk

> Remove the green stalks from the strawberries and cut each one in half.

Put them into a saucepan with the sugar and bring slowly to the boil, stirring to dissolve the sugar. Reduce the heat and simmer for 10–15 minutes until the strawberries soften.

> Pass the strawberries through a fine sieve into a bowl; you should end up with approx. 500ml (18fl oz) fruit purée, depending on how juicy your fruit is. (If you have more than this amount, reserve some to serve as a sauce.) Add the cream and milk to the purée, stir well and set aside to cool.

> Pour the mixture into small silicone moulds or ice-cube trays and place in the freezer. Once frozen, you can bag up the frozen cubes into containers and store them for up to 3 months or use them straight away. To serve, put the cubes or moulds into a food processor and whizz until soft. (A dash of milk can help to get the cubes going through the blades.) Serve straight away in chilled dishes or shot glasses.

SMOOTHIES

These are some of our favourite smoothie combinations.

KATIE'S BREAKFAST IN A GLASS

banana, avocado, ginger, orange, oats, kefir, cinnamon.

GIANCARLO'S MEMORIES OF TUSCANY

melon, pear, peach, honey, milk

GIORGIO'S RED SKY IN THE MORNING

plum, blood orange, apple, ginger, apple juice

FLAVIO'S EXTRAVAGANZA

strawberry, raspberry, banana, vanilla ice cream, strawberry ice cream, apple, ginger, orange juice, yogurt, vanilla extract!

AND NOW FOR SOMETHING COMPLETELY DIFFERENT

COLD LEMONS FOR THE ULTIMATE HOT BATH FULL OF ESSENTIAL OILS

When you have lemon halves left over after you have juiced them, don't throw them away: freeze them! Then at the end of a fulfilling day's preserving, throw a handful of them into a hot bath. The temperature will drop slightly – so allow for that – but the essential oils in the skins of the fruit will be released, the smell will be amazing, and you will feel wonderful afterwards.

SUPPLIERS & BIBLIOGRAPHY

SUPPLIERS

COOKING EQUIPMENT

Jam Jar Shop: www.jamjarshop.com
Kilner Jars: www.kilnerjar.co.uk
Lakeland: www.lakeland.co.uk
Le Parfait: www.leparfait.co.uk

COOKING COURSES

www.caldesi.com
See our website for a full range of preserving and cooking courses.

SAUSAGE-MAKING SUPPLIES

Weschenfelder: www.weschenfelder.co.uk

DEHYDRATORS

Excalibur Dehydrator:
www.excaliburdehydrator.com

SMOKING EQUIPMENT AND WOOD CHIPS, DUST ETC.

Big Green Egg: www.biggreenegg.co.uk
A US-made versatile egg-shaped barbecue that grills, makes excellent pizza as well as hot smokes meat, fish and vegetables. Try the maple-roast chicken, salmon on a cedar plank and alder wood chips for cooking pizza.

Bradley Smoker: www.bradleysmoker.co.uk
Still the only hot and cold smoker on the market. It makes life easy and takes the uncertainty out of smoking.

Hot Smoked: www.hotsmoked.co.uk
Everything you need for hot and cold smoking. Alyson Murray is lovely and a font of knowledge.

Weber: www.weber.com
These familiar dome-shaped barbecues will also act as smokers, working to infuse flavour throughout your meat with varying strengths, depending on the wood type or herb. If using the charcoal indirect method of smoking, keep the vents open and position the top vent on the opposite side to the wood, this will draw the smoke over the meat. We enjoyed succulent ribs that cooked long and slow over 9 hours. They also run courses at the Grill Academy in barbecuing and smoking.

BBQ Guru: www.bbqguru.com
A US-based company that is great for gadgets such as the DigiQ DX2 and CyberQ Wifi, which is the ultimate in temperature control information supplied to your phone.

CHEESE-MAKING SUPPLIERS

Moorlands Cheesemakers Ltd:
www.cheesemaking.co.uk

WATER AND MILK KEFIR GRAINS AND KOMBUCHA MOTHERS

Happy Kombucha:
www.happykombucha.co.uk
Michelle and Marcus Holborn. Great advice and a good range of these sought-after products.

PRESSURE CANNERS AND INFORMATION

National Presto Industries, Inc.:
www.gopresto.com
Pressure canners, lots of helpful advice and pressure canner testers.

BIBLIOGRAPHY

USEFUL BOOKS

Agricultural and Food Research Council
Home Preservation of Fruit and Vegetables
Stationery Office Books, 1989

Darina Allen
Forgotten Skills of Cooking
Kyle Books, 2009

C.J.J. Berry
First Steps in Winemaking
Nexus Special Interests, 1997

Margaret Briggs
Practical Household Uses of Salt
Abbey Press, 2012

Sherri Brooks Vinton
Put 'em up!
Storey Publishing, 2010

Lynda Brown
The Preserving Book
Dorling Kindersley, 2010

Pam Corbin
Preserves: River Cottage Handbook No. 2
Bloomsbury, 2008

The Culinary Institute of America and John Kowalski
The Art of Charcuterie
John Wiley & Sons, 2011

Maynard Davies
Secrets of a Bacon Curer
Merlin Unwin Books, 2007

Keith Erlandson
Home Smoking and Curing
Hutchinson 1977

Excalibur Products
Preserve it Naturally: The Complete Guide to Food Dehydration
Prentice Hall Trade, 2010

Marc Frederic
Le Charcutier Anglais
Moorish Foods, 2011

The Good Cook
Preserving
Time Life Books, 1981

Janet Greene, Ruth Hertzberg and Beatrice Vaughan
Putting Food By
Penguin, 2010

Jane Grigson
Charcuterie and French Pork Cookery
Penguin, 1970

Andy Hamilton
Booze for Free
Eden Project Books, 2011

Wardeh Harmon
The Complete Idiot's Guide to Fermenting Foods
Alpha, 2012

Anissa Helou
Lebanese Cuisine
Grub Street, 2003

Ikuko Hisamatsu
Tsukemono: Japanese Pickling Recipes
Japan Publications Trading Company, 2010

Ghillie James
Jam, Jelly and Relish
Kyle Books, 2010

Sandor Ellix Katz
The Art of Fermentation
Chelsea Green Publishing Company, 2012

Wild Fermentation
Chelsea Green Publishing Company, 2003

Alex Lewin
Real Food Fermentation
Quarry Books, 2012

Vivien Lloyd
First Preserves
Citrus Press, 2011

Deborah Madison, Eliot Coleman and Centre Terre Vivante
Preserving Food Without Freezing or Canning
Chelsea Green Publishing Company, 2007

Marisa McClellan
Food in Jars
Running Press, 2011

Harold McGee
McGee on Food and Cooking: An Encyclopedia of Kitchen Science, History and Culture
Hodder & Stoughton, 2004

Paul Peacock
The Smoking and Curing Book
The Good Life Press, 2009

Michael Ruhlman and Brian Polycn
Charcuterie
W. W. Norton, 2005

Ed. Helen Sabieri
Cured, Fermented and Smoked Foods: Proceedings of the Oxford Symposium on Food and Cookery 2010
Prospect Books, 2010

Nick Sandler and Johnny Acton
Preserved
Kyle Cathie, 2009

Oded Schwartz
Preserving Through the Year
Dorling Kindersley, 2012

Sue Shephard
Pickled, Potted and Canned
Simon & Schuster, 2000

Dick and James Strawbridge
Made at Home: Curing & Smoking
Mitchell Beazley, 2012

Kate Walker
Practical Food Smoking
Angels' Share, 2012

Lindy Wildsmith
Cured
Jacqui Small, 2010

Beryl Wood
Let's Preserve It
Vintage, 2010
US Department of Agriculture
Complete Guide to Home Canning and Preserving
Dover Publications, 1999

USEFUL BLOGS AND SITES

Bradley Smoker
http://forum.bradleysmoker.com
Smoking recipes shared and queries answered by other enthusiasts, mainly in the US.

A Gardener's Table
www.agardenerstable.com
This is a fascinating read from Linda Ziedrich. She answers so many queries with her in-depth well-researched writing.

Hunter Angler Gardener Cook
www.honest-food.net
Good recipes and advice on wild game and charcuterie.

Nourishing Days
www.nourishingdays.com
Shannon writes from her homestead in Texas about self-sufficiency. I love the recipes and her journey in fermentation.

Wild Fermentation
www.wildfermentation.com
A great site for ideas, news, recipes and problem solving for fermented foods.

ACKNOWLEDGEMENTS

The experts we learned from and the courses that got us started... Jasper Aykroyd, aka The Bacon Wizard. What can I say, you are talented, clever, fun and your cured meats are the best. I don't think anyone has ever shown me the patience you did over the Salt and Air chapters. For bacon and all forms of curing solutions as well as curing courses, Jasper Ackroyd is a fantastic consultant, contact him at: jasper@baconwizard.co.uk.

Marc Frederic, The English Charcutier, for his enthusiasm, passion and knowledge. And a good laugh too.

Christine Ashby – cheese-maker extraordinaire – she simply makes people want to make yogurt and cheese. For more information see www.abcheesemaking.co.uk.

Katy Rodgers, for showing us her award-winning dairy produce and helping us produce amazing yogurt and crème fraîche – www.knockraich.com.

Sally Morgan and Marc Frederic for getting us started in sausages and smoking at Empire Farm – www.empirefarm.co.uk.

For Foraging walks in London contact www.foragelondon.co.uk.

Debi King, for her knowledge and patience in helping make country wines.

Vivien and Nigel Lloyd, what a pleasure to have got to know you this last year. Your knowledge is phenomenal, thank you for sharing it and your years of experience with us.

Sukie and Bill Barber taught us how to smoke and have answered questions and queries ever since. Their fascinating courses and demonstrations cover many food related topics from rearing their own livestock, growing fruit and vegetables, to bread making, preserving and smoking – billandsukie@gmail.com.

Reiko Hara, teacher of Oriental Cookery for her help on Japanese foods.

Iain Spink makes fantastic Arbroath Smokies in the traditional way – available by mail order at www.arbroathsmokies.net.

Jane Milton and Maxine Clark, for their advice on our Scottish tour of smokers.

Brian McLeod, for helping with research, planning our Scottish trip and generally making us laugh a lot.

A huge, heartfelt thank you from us both to... Kyle Cathie, when you took me out to lunch and quietly mentioned writing a book about preserving I had no idea of the enormity of the journey we were about to embark upon. It has been a fascinating if hair-raising ride, we have loved it and wouldn't have missed the opportunity for a moment. It really has changed our lives for the better.

Sheila Abelman, thank you for introducing me to Kyle all those years ago and getting this book started.

Vicky Orchard, we've discussed, laughed, disagreed, fussed, tweaked and above all cared for and loved this book – may it live long and give years of pleasure to all those that read it. Thank you to you and your assistant Laura Foster.

Copy editor Catherine Ward, thank you so much for painstakingly reading the text and correcting my awful grammar without patronising me once.

Sheila Keating, you are an amazing and talented lady. Thank you for making this so much easier.

Manjula Samarasinghe, I couldn't have had a better assistant to help me on this journey. You have endlessly cooked, tasted, learned, washed up, eaten yogurt with jam, too much sourdough, drank tea and discussed fermentation with me!

Jim Davies, for taking over my work without moaning even once while I wrote the book.

My brother, Philip, for building our meat boxes, getting smoked out and chopping logs with a blunt axe in -3°C. True dedication and brotherly love.

Gemma Harris, for giving up your day to us to teach us about fermenting, drying and making amazing cordials.

John Watkins from Bradley Smokers for your advice and support.

Pernilla Daniels for her Swedish recipes and translation.

Ian Bethwaite and Carrie Darby for all your knowledge, research and support. From supplying the 'gherkin advice line' to answering 'what is a bean weevil?' you were always there for me.

Sian and Steve Adams, for introducing me to the Big Green Egg and letting me smoke cauliflowers, pulled pork and peppers on theirs.

Livia and Nello Ceccuzzi whose lifestyle on their smallholding in Tuscany is an inspiration to us.

Andrew Fairlie at Gleneagles who let us into his kitchen and shared his recipes with us.

To our chefs, Gregorio Piazza, Antonio Sanzone and Stefano Borella for helping us research and test the recipes over and over again!

INDEX